DOGMATI(

Volume I

The True Religion

by Monsignor G. Van Noort, S.T.D.

From the Fifth Edition Edited by
REV. J. P. VERHAAR, S.T.D.

Translated and Revised by
JOHN J. CASTELOT, S.S., S.T.D., S.S.L.,
WILLIAM R. MURPHY, S.S., S.T.D.

THE NEWMAN PRESS
Westminster, Maryland
1961

First published 1955

Second printing 1959

Third printing 1961

The present volume is a translation of the 5th edition of Msgr. van Noort's *Tractatus de Vera Religione*, edited by J. P. Verhaar. Because of the extensive revision made by the translators the English translation may be called the 6th edition of Msgr. van Noort's dogmatic treatise.

Library of Congress Catalog Card Number: 55-10552

Preface

People occasionally complain that it is difficult to find a complete, up-to-date, scientific course of dogmatic theology in English. It is our sincere hope that the present translation of Monsignor Van Noort's series of dogmatic textbooks will meet the need implicit in that complaint.

All priests know of many excellent manuals of theology in Latin. Many, however, confess that their long years in the ministry have seen them lose their mastery of that language and, as a consequence, the urge to pick up their seminary textbooks is not too strong. Our own teaching experience forces us to admit that many seminarians whose knowledge of Latin is insufficient fail to derive all that they should from their course in theology. Then, too, with the recent growth of interest in theology, a considerable number of nuns, brothers, and educated laymen who wish to study theology scientifically find the door barred to them because they do not know Latin. We sincerely hope that this work will make available to all interested students a full course of dogmatic theology in English.

In our translation we have tried to render the text into modern English and at the same time preserve the meaning of the original. In those instances where we have found consecrated phrases very difficult to translate, we have put into parentheses, alongside the English expedient, the familiar Latin formula.

Although many excellent Latin manuals are available, we have selected Van Noort's for these two reasons: 1. the work is most faithful to the theology of St. Thomas; 2. the author, a teacher of long experience, shows extraordinary clarity, open-mindedness, and sound judgment in his presentation of theological problems. Van Noort has a peculiar ability to expose the heart of a problem succinctly and to define it in sharp outlines. He never avoids deep problems; yet in his treatment he omits useless subtleties which might be of interest to specialists, but which would only bewilder novices. He is equally proficient in speculative and positive theology and combines both harmoniously. It is this over-all sense of proportion, of clarity, and of balance that makes his text one of the finest manuals available.

In our revision of the work, we have maintained the substance of the original. Revisions have been made only when called for by more recent pronouncements of the Church, or by the growth due to recent scholarship in Scripture and the other branches of positive theology. Most of these revisions will be found in the notes. The original bibliography upon which the work was built has been retained, but we have made additions in various places.

The original marginal numbers of Van Noort and the additions made by Verhaar have been retained. We have thought it wise to add a detailed outline at the beginning of each article for pedagogical purposes. A completely new index has been made.

In the present volume the most notable changes will be found in the "Introduction to the Entire Field of Theology" and in "Religion in General." In these sections recent scholarship has enabled us to amplify and certify some points which Van Noort omitted or advanced in tentative fashion only. In the second appendix we have added a few remarks to clarify his treatment of the involved question of the Parousia.

Since some complain that dogmatic theologians and scriptural scholars are uncooperative, we thought it wise to have a professor of Scripture and a professor of dogmatic theology join forces in bringing Van Noorts work to the English-speaking world. As an exegetical discussion of all the scriptural texts involved would have rendered this volume exceedingly cumbersome, we have been content to incorporate the conclusions of such discussion. For a full treatment of scriptural questions we refer the reader to A Catholic Commentary on Holy Scripture (London: Thomas Nelson and Sons, Ltd., 1953). Scriptural quotations in the present work are taken from the Douay version of the Old Testament, except for Genesis to Ruth and Psalms, where we have used the new Confraternity Translation, and for Isaias, where we used that of Monsignor Kissane. All New Testament citations are from the Confraternity Translation.

All footnotes, whether German, French, Latin, or Dutch, have been translated. Such translations are original save in those places where credit is given others.

We warn any non-professional reader that he will find the opening chapter on the nature and history of theology technical

Acknowledgments

We wish to thank the following publishers for permission to quote from their publications:

THE AMERICA PRESS, New York
The Church and Modern Science, 1951.

BROWNE & NOLAN, LTD, Dublin
The Book of Isaiah, translated from a critically revised Hebrew text with a commentary and critical notes, by Msgr. Edward J. Kissane. Volume I, 1941; Volume 2, 1944.

THE BRUCE PUBLISHING COMPANY, Milwaukee
Outlines of Moral Theology by Francis J. Connell, C.Ss.R., 1953.

THE CATHOLIC TRUTH SOCIETY, London
Studies in Comparative Religion, edited by Ernest C. Messenger. Volume I, 1934.

DESCLEE ET CIE, Paris
Manual of Patrology by F. Cayre, A.A., translated by H. Howitt, A.A. Volume I, 1936.

DODD, MEAD & COMPANY, New York
Orthodoxy by G. K. Chesterton, 1909.

THE GRAIL, St. Meinrad
Rome and the Study of Sacred Scripture.

B. HERDER BOOK COMPANY, St. Louis
The Mysteries of Christianity by Matthias Joseph Scheeben, translated by Cyril Vollert, S.J., 1946.

NATIONAL CATHOLIC WELFARE CONFERENCE, Washington
Translation of Pope Pius XII's encyclical, *Humani Generis*, 1951.

THOMAS NELSON & SONS, Edinburgh
A Catholic Commentary on Holy Scripture, 1951.

THE NEW AMERICAN LIBRARY OF WORLD LITERATURE, INC., New York
Man Makes Himself by Gordon Child, Mentor Edition, 1951; *The Meaning of Evolution* by George Gaylord Simpson, Mentor edition, 1951;

ACKNOWLEDGMENTS

Science and the Modern World by Alfred North Whitehead, Mentor edition, 1951.

THE PAULIST PRESS, New York
The Question Box by Bertrand Conway, C.S.P., 1929.

SHEED & WARD, INC., New York
Primitive Man and His World Picture by Wilhelm Koppers, translated by Edith Raybould, 1951;
Social Origins by Eva J. Ross, 1936.

XAVIER UNIVERSITY PRESS, Cincinnati
Christian Origins by Arthur P. Madgett, S.J. Volume I, 1948.

List of Abbreviations

AAS . . . . Acta Apostolicae Sedis

ACW . . . . Ancient Christian Writers

ASS . . . . Acta Sanctae Sedis

AtAb . . . . Alttestamentliche Abhandlungen

Bibl . . . . Biblica

Bibl Zf . . . . Biblische Zeitfragen

BiZ . . . . Biblische Zeitschrift

CCHS . . . . A Catholic Commentary on Holy Scripture

DAFC . . . . Dictionnaire apológetique de la foi catholique

DB . . . . Denziger-Bannwart-Umberg,
                Enchiridion Symbolorum

DTC . . . . Dictionnaire de theologie catholique

ETL . . . . Ephemerides Theologicae Lovanienses

Greg . . . . Gregorianum

HE . . . . Historia Ecclesiastica (Eusebius)

MG . . . . Migne, Patrologia Graeca

ML . . . . Migne, Patrologia Latina

NRTh . . . . Novelle revue theologique

NtAb . . . . Neutestamentliche Abhandlungen

PhJ . . . . Philosophisches Jahrbuch des ¨Gorresgesell-
                schaft

RAp . . . . Revue apologétique

RBibl . . . . Revue biblique

RCF . . . . Revue du clérge Français

Rev. de philosoph . . Revue de philosophie

RJ . . . . Röuet de Journel, Enchiridion Patristicum

RPA . . . . Revue pratique d'apologétique

RSPT . . . . *Revue des sciences philosophiques et theo-*
                        logiques

RSR . . . . *Recherches de science religieuse*

RSS . . . . *Rome and the Study of Sacred Scripture*

S.C.G. . . . . St. Thomas, *Summa Contra Gentiles*

S.Th. . . . . St. Thomas, *Summa Theologiae*

STS . . . . *Strassburg Theologische Studien*

ThGl . . . . *Theologie und Glaube*

ThLZ . . . . *Theologische Literaturzeitung*

ZkTh . . . . *Zeitschrift fur katholische Theologie*

Contents

		Page
Preface	.	v
Acknowledgments	.	ix
Introduction to the Entire Field of Theology	..	xv
Introduction to Fundamental Theology	..	xlvii

SECTION I

A Scientific Analysis of Religion in the Abstract

I. On Religion in General 1

    Article I. The Objective Foundation of Religion and the Obligation to Practice It 11

    Article II. The Unity of the True Religion . . . 23

II. Revealed Religion 33

    Article I. Revelation Is Possible 34

    Article II. The Necessity of Revelation 48

    Article III. The Recognizability of Revelation . . . 57

SECTION II

The Truth of the Christian-Catholic Religion

I. The Sublimity of the Christian-Catholic Religion 111

II. Christ Had a Divine Mission 127

    Article I. Christ's Extraordinary Holiness Proves His Divine Mission 137

    Article II. Christ's Prophecies Prove His Divine Mission 147

CONTENTS

Page

Article III. Christ's Miracles Prove His Divine Mission   154
Article IV. Christ's Resurrection Proves His Divine Mission 165

III. THE DIVINE ORIGIN OF CHRIST'S WORK OR OF THE CHRISTIAN-CATHOLIC RELIGION 189

  Article I. The Divine Origin of the Christian-Catholic Religion Is Proved by Physical Miracles 191

  Article II. The Divine Origin of the Christian-Catholic Religion Is Proved by Its Marvelous Spread and Conservation 200

  Article III. The Divine Origin of the Christian-Catholic Religion Is Proved by Its Perennial Fruitfulness in the Field of Holiness 220

  Article IV. The Miraculous Steadfastness of the Martyrs Proves the Divine Origin of the Christian-Catholic Religion 229

IV. GOD FORETOLD CHRIST AND HIS WORK 241

  Article I. The Existence of Messianic Prophecies . . 243

  Article II. A Summary Exposition of Messianic Prophecies 252

CONCLUSION TO THE ENTIRE TREATISE 272

APPENDIX I. REVEALED RELIGION BEFORE CHRIST 279

APPENDIX II. CHRIST'S TEACHING ON THE PAROUSIA . . . 285

SCRIPTURAL INDEX 303

INDEX OF AUTHORS 309

GENERAL INDEX 317

Introduction to the Entire Field of Theology

I. THE CONCEPT OF THEOLOGY:

Etymological meaning and real definition:

1. a science;
2. a supernatural science;
3. treating of both God and creatures.

II. CONNECTIONS BETWEEN DOGMATIC AND FUNDAMENTAL THEOLOGY AND FAITH:

1. dogmatic theology differs from fundamental;
2. dogmatic theology differs from faith, but is closely bound to it.

III. DIVISION OF THEOLOGY:

1. by subject-matter;
2. by method.

IV. A BRIEF HISTORY OF SYSTEMATIC THEOLOGY:

1. patristic era;
2. scholastic era;
3. modern era.

V. MODERN AUTHORS OF THEOLOGY:

a selected bibliography.

Introduction to the Entire Field of Theology

Preliminary Remarks

If you were to tell the average American that theology is a science, he would probably be startled. In his vocabulary, science means physics, chemistry, biology, medicine and other branches of learning whose methods are mainly empirical. Theology, in his vocabulary, is a nebulous word standing for anything from mythology to mysticism.*

This failure to realize that theology is a highly specialized field accounts for much of the popular irritation that rises when a theologian innocently employs such terms as circumincession, hypostatic union, or *ex opere operato*. A lawyer may remark that he is holding a deed in escrow, or a doctor that he has just performed a pre-frontal lobotomy, and each will be listened to respectfully by the layman. Should a theologian lapse into such technical terms, a layman may be irritated. The real cause of the irritation is a failure to grasp that theology is a special science having a perfect right to its own technical jargon.†

That is why it seemed useful to open this entire dogmatic series with a technical discussion of the nature, methods, resources, and divisions of the science of theology. The beginner in theology is then in a position to understand what distinguishes this science from all other sciences, what its own special methods of demonstration are, and, finally, how to appreciate the validity of its conclusions.

I. The Concept of Theology ‡

The term "theology" is derived from two Greek words: *theos,* which means God, and *logos,* which means word, discourse, or study. Even in its etymological sense, theology means the science of

---

* Many people, for example, mistake a purely rational treatise on the existence of God, or the immortality of the soul, as "theology." Others think that any scientific study of the Bible, or any excursion into the field of comparative religion is "theology."

† Undoubtedly the Protestant Reformation, with its contempt for scholastic terminology and its naive insistence that any man could read the Bible and

God, knowledge about God. One can acquire knowledge about God and things related to Him either by the light of reason alone, or by the aid of divine revelation; each type of knowledge can be either popular or scientific in nature. In professional usage, sanctioned since at least the thirteenth century, theology in the strict sense of the term, or *dogmatic* theology, means scientific knowledge about God and matters related to Him that has been derived from revelation. Theology, therefore, may be defined as a *supernatural science which treats of God and of creatures in their relationship to God.*

1. Theology is a science. Dogmatic theology has the following functions: 1. from the sources of revelation it demonstrates the existence of various truths about God; 2. it explains and illustrates those revealed truths insofar as it is possible to do so; 3. it defends those truths against the attacks of opponents; 4. it deduces conclusions from those revealed truths; and 5. it assembles those truths, together with the conclusions drawn from them, into one harmonious system. Such activities are clearly scientific in character; and the systematic arrangement of truths which results from them definitely deserves the name of science.[1]

2. A supernatural science. All other sciences use as their *objective* principles of demonstration (the principles *from* which knowledge is deduced) either intrinsic evidence, or experimentation, or human authority. They use as their *subjective* principle (the principle *by* which the knowledge is deduced) exclusively the light of human reason. Since all these principles are natural, the sciences resting upon them are properly described as natural sciences.

Dogmatic theology, on the other hand, uses as its objective principle of demonstration, God's revelation. (The revelation is contained in Sacred Scripture and Tradition and is proposed to us by the Church.) It uses as its subjective principle, reason enlightened by the gift of faith. Both these principles are obviously beyond the domain of mere nature. Consequently the science which rests upon them is called a supernatural science.

---

find it lucidly clear, played a large role in building up a hostile mentality to the science of theology in Anglo-Saxon countries.

‡ A great deal has been written about the nature, development, and extent of the science of theology during the last thirty-five years. One topic for debate, for example, is the definibility of "theological conclusions." For modern works concerning theology as a science see the special bibliography on pp. li-lii.

That is why theology, in the strict sense of the term, differs vastly from theodicy.[2] Theodicy is simply a branch of philosophy. It treats of God not insofar as He is knowable by revelation and faith, but merely insofar as He is knowable from the created universe by the unaided light of human reason. Even though theology and theodicy touch partially upon the same problems (for example, God's foreknowledge and the problem of evil) they are radically distinct sciences because: "a diverse aspect of knowability (diversity of formal object) produces diverse sciences." (St. Thomas, *S.Th.*, Ia, 1, 1 ad 2.)

3. Theology treats of God and of creatures. Here we consider the subject matter, technically called the *material* object,[*] of theology. This material object is twofold: primary and secondary. The primary material object is God Himself and His mysteries; the secondary material object [**] is creatures in their relationship

---

[*] The material object of any science is simply the thing or subject studied; the formal object is the special aspect under which the material object is viewed and studied by a particular science; it is that aspect of the subject with which the science is primarily concerned and to which it refers all else that it may have to study merely as background material. Thus the formal object of mathematics is quantity; of medicine, health. Each science has its own distinctive principles by which it reaches and scrutinizes its formal object: the light cast on the formal object by these distinctive principles is called technically that science's special medium or special light (*lumen sub quo, objective formale quo*). Note that the same material object may be the formal object of different sciences. For example, man can be studied by such sciences as medicine, anthropology, psychology, moral theology, etc. Each studies man (the same material object) under diverse aspects (formal object) and, employing distinctive scientific principles, apprehends man in a special medium or light. See J. Maritain, *An Introduction to Philosophy* (New York: Sheed and Ward, Inc., 1947), pp. 102–03; 106–07.

[**] G. Thils has written a provocative article on the secondary material object in ETL (April–September, 1953): "Le'objet matériel secondaire de la théologie," pp. 398–418. He objects that theologians overly restrict, at least in theory, the field of the secondary object by confining it to a consideration of efficient and final causality, or things as they come *from God* and tend *toward God*. They seem to neglect the aspect of exemplary causality. He tentatively suggests a broader definition of the field of the secondary object: "all creatures in all the relations which they have with and in the entire supernatural world." We feel that this broader definition is unnecessary and confusing on at least two counts: first, the standard theological description which views all creation as proceeding from God (efficient causality) and returning to God (final causality) implicitly and necessarily includes the aspect of exemplary causality; secondly, and more importantly, the definition tentatively proposed would make the field of theology *literally limitless*. Only God Himself can know the billion-fold relationships intertwining all created reality with "the entire supernatural world." This definition seems to confuse God's *knowledge* with God's *testimony*. Theology is not concerned with all

to God. Theology studies both God Himself and His creatures, but it studies creatures primarily in their relationship to God. Since

> all matters treated in sacred doctrine are viewed under the aspect of deity, either because they are God Himself, or because they have a relationship to God as their beginning or goal, it follows that God is in very truth the subject-matter of this science (St. Thomas, *op. cit.*, q. 1, a. 7).

The phrase, *under the aspect of deity,*[3] shows us the formal object, or the special aspect of the subject matter which exclusively belongs to the science of theology. God as known from creatures and studied by the light of reason is the formal object of theodicy; God as known to Himself alone and as manifested to creatures by revelation is the formal object, the special study, of theology alone:

> Sacred doctrine *essentially* treats God viewed as the highest cause; for it does not treat of Him only with reference to what is knowable about Him through creation—the way the philosophers know him . . . ; but it also treats of Him with reference to what *He alone knows about Himself* and communicates to others by revelation (St. Thomas, *op. cit.*, q. 1, a. 6).

II. Connections Between Dogmatic Theology, Fundamental Theology, and Divine Faith

From what has been discussed thus far it is evident: 1. that dogmatic theology differs from fundamental theology, and 2. that dogmatic theology differs from divine faith, though closely connected to it.

1. **Dogmatic theology differs from fundamental theology.** Dogmatic theology, since it uses as its objective principle God's revelation, presupposes the actual existence of that revelation as something already known. It presumes as proved that God has actually spoken and that the truths He has revealed are infallibly preserved in the Catholic Church. These facts, therefore, must be

---

that God knows about the relationships obtaining between created reality and the entire supernatural world; it seeks   discover what God has deliberately chosen to make known by His revelation.

already established before dogmatic theology begins. Establishing them is the task of fundamental theology.

Fundamental theology, then, derives its name from the fact that it demonstrates the principle, the foundation on which all theology rests, namely, the divine communication of truth.[4] Thus, fundamental theology acts as an introduction to dogmatic. Since it is customary to speak of the introduction of any science as part of that science, just as the foundation of a house is part of the house, so fundamental theology can rightly be called a part of theology, even though it differs from dogmatic theology in many ways.

For example, it is different from dogmatic theology in a. its *material* object (the thing or object *which* it investigates). In dogmatic theology the material object is God and creatures insofar as they are related to God; in fundamental theology the material object is the divine revelation itself and the faithful preservation of that revelation by the Church.[5] b. It differs also in its *formal* object (the object *by which,* or the *special aspect under which,* the material object is viewed). The formal object of dogmatic theology is divine revelation, insofar as the revelation itself furnishes proof of dogmas and offers an understanding of theological conclusions. In fundamental theology, on the other hand, the formal object is twofold.

It is twofold in the sense that it includes two facts: the actual existence of a divine message, and the preservation of that message by the Church. Now, the divine message is an historical fact. As such, it can be demonstrated from history and by the principles of reason. The infallible preservation of this divine message, on the other hand, is a fact which can be known *either by revelation or by reason.* It can be known by *revelation,* because Christ Himself has revealed to us both the way in which it was to be preserved (namely, by an infallible Church) and the characteristics by which that Church can be recognized. The preservation of that divine message may also be known by *reason:* reason can demonstate, on historical grounds, that the Church has always and clearly proclaimed herself the guardian of a divine revelation, and reason can also demonstrate, on historical grounds (by means of miracles and other arguments of credibility), that the Church's assertion is true.

It follows, then, that the formal object of fundamental theology, when it is proving the existence of revelation, is the natural knowability or the historico-philosophical knowability [6] of that revelation. When it is demonstrating the infallible preservation of the revelation by the Church, its formal object may be either the revelation itself (a supernatural knowability), or natural reason (an historico-philosophical knowability).[7]

Finally, if one but consider that a more complete knowledge of divine realities stirs a man voluntarily to love God more fervently, he will realize that St. Albert the Great has practically summed up the whole grandeur of theology in this axiom: "Theology is taught by God, teaches God, and leads to God." [8]

2. Theology differs from divine faith; yet it is most closely bound up with faith. *Theology differs from faith:* it differs a. from the point of view of its *material* object. Faith contains only revealed truths, whereas theology contains many additional truths connected with revelation. b. From the point of view of its *formal* object. The formal object of faith is the divine revelation as moving the intelligence to give firm assent to the authority of God revealing. In theology the formal object is that same revelation insofar as it demonstrates the existence of various revealed truths and offers an understanding of the conclusions that flow from them. Faith simply embraces the revealed truths with a firm assent, but does not make use of argumentation or discursive reasoning; neither does it draw up an orderly presentation of these truths, or seek to defend their truthfulness—in a word, it *does not proceed in a scientific fashion.* That is why St. Augustine says:

> A great many of the faithful are not equipped with that science even though they are richly equipped with faith itself. For it is one thing simply to know what truths a man ought to believe in order to gain heaven, but it is quite another matter to know how to feed the faithful those same truths and how to defend them against infidels (*De Trinitate*, bk. 14, 1, no. 3).

c. Theology differs from faith in its *certitude.* The certitude given by faith is the highest possible type, because it rests on God's own authority; the certitude of theology, because it blends reasoning with revelation, is much inferior.

Theology and faith are closely bound together. a. Theology presupposes faith and builds upon it. The revealed truths, with which theology is mainly concerned and from which it scientifically draws its conclusions, simply would not hold up unless accepted by faith. Consequently, were one to remove faith, there would remain in theological subject matter no sure knowledge of truth, and hence no science of theology, no theology at all.[9] This finds expression in the well-known scholastic axiom of St. Anselm: "I believe in order to understand." [10]

b. *Theology renders great assistance to faith.* By theology, as St. Augustine bears witness, "saving faith which leads to true happiness is born, nourished, defended, and strengthened" (*De Trinitate,* loc. cit.).

III. The Divisions of Theology

Even though theology is strictly one science because of the unity of its formal object,[11] one can make various divisions of it from the point of view either of the *matter* studied, or of the particular *method* of procedure used in its study.

1. **From the point of view of the matter studied.** It has already been said that fundamental and dogmatic theology do not blend together into one complete theological course, or into one and the same theological book as though they were simply two equal halves of one homogeneous whole. Rather, they are two distinct disciplines, one of which is essentially preparatory to the other. It is only with this restriction that theology (taken in a wide sense) is said to be divided into fundamental and dogmatic theology.

Fundamental theology deals with the very foundations on which all theology and even religion itself rest: namely, the actual existence of revelation, the channels through which the revealed truth comes to man, and the means by which he receives it.[12]

Dogmatic theology, on the other hand, deals separately with each of the revealed truths proposed and explained by the Church. It takes its name from the word "dogma." This term, taken in itself, may describe either practical norms for action or truths primarily of the intellectual order (speculative truths).* More modern usage reserves the term "dogma" exclusively to revealed truths of the intellectual order.

Dogmatic theology is subdivided into *theoretical* and *practical,* or *moral.* Theoretical theology deals with those truths which are not directly concerned with setting up a code of morals, but are primarily intellectual in character. Practical, or moral, theology deals with normative truths, those truths which a man is to accept

---

* The phrase "truths of the intellectual order" is used here deliberately to alert the reader to the fact that "speculative truths" does not mean guesswork, a connotation frequently carried by the English term.

(xxiii)

not merely intellectually, but that he is to put into practice in his daily life.* The following special sciences belong to practical theology: a. *moral* theology strictly so called, which deals with the Commandments, with what is right or wrong; b. *ascetical* theology, which treats of the perfection of the Christian life, the evangelical counsels, and all the ordinary means which lead one to Christian perfection; c. *mystical* theology, which treats especially of both the theory and the practice of the contemplative life; [13] d. *pastoral* theology, which looks to the guidance and governance of souls; and, finally, e. *canon law,* which deals with the laws laid down by the Church.

The foregoing division from the point of view of the matter studied is summarized in the following two schemas:

I. *Theology* (in a *wide* sense)	1. *Fundamental:*	a. Demonstration of Christian-Catholic Religion. b. The Church of Christ. c. The sources of Revelation. d. Divine Faith
	2. *Dogmatic:* (various individual truths contained in Revelation)	a. *Theoretical:* truths primarily of the intellectual order. b. *Practical:* truths directly looking to a code of conduct.
II. *Dogmatic Theology*	1. *Theoretical:* God: Unity and Trinity, Creation, Original Sin, Incarnation, Redemption, Mariology, Grace and Sacraments, Eschatology.	
	2. *Practical* (Various special sciences)	a. *Moral* (strictly so-called): Right and wrong. b. *Ascetical:* Christian Perfection. c. *Mystical:* Contemplative life. d. *Pastoral:* Care and government of souls. e. *Canon Law:* Laws of the Church.

* Practical (moral) theology is related to dogmatic theology as a part to the whole. That is why the scholastics and St. Thomas treated all revealed truths, both speculative and practical, in the same theological "summa." If, therefore, modern authors frequently juxtapose practical (moral) theology to dogmatic theology, this manner of speaking is by no means meant to signify that moral theology is not an intrinsic part of dogmatic theology. It follows that practical theology should be treated in such a way that its connection with the rest of dogmatic doctrine, and its dependence upon it, can be clearly noted. See Van Laak, *De theologia generatim,* p. 21.

2. From the point of view of method.[14] According to the manner in which the subject matter is handled, theology may be divided into *positive* and *speculative.*

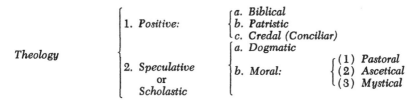

Positive theology accurately demonstrates the existence of the various truths of the faith by collecting and organizing the various statements of Sacred Scripture and the documents of Tradition. Its task is to show that such and such a truth really is contained in revelation. Positive theology, then, takes its name from the fact that its very method leads it to be almost exclusively concerned with the valid demonstration (Latin: *ponere*) of the actual existence of such or such a revealed truth.[15]

Positive theology is subdivided in accord with the emphasis it places on one or another source of revelation. It is called *Biblical* theology if it bases its arguments almost exclusively on Sacred Scripture. If it draws its arguments mainly from the Fathers of the Church, it is called *patristic* theology. If, finally, it draws mainly on the creeds and other official documents of the Church, it is called *credal* or *conciliar* theology. Akin to positive theology is *polemical* theology, whose purpose it is to defend individual revealed truths against the attacks of non-Catholics.[16]

Speculative or *scholastic* theology makes use of philosophy for the following purposes: 1. to offer a deeper and fuller understanding of the meaning of religious dogmas; 2. to harmonize dogmas with the principles of natural reason; 3. to illustrate dogmas by

---

F. J. Connell, C.Ss.R., an eminent American moral theologian, is careful to note the same point. "The earlier theologians usually treated both dogmatic and moral theology as two aspects of the one science of theology. Since the seventeenth century there has been a tendency to discuss them separately, so that the impression is given that they are two distinct sciences. This is incorrect; for theology, whether speculative or practical, is one science insofar as its formal object or motive is the same. However, because their material objects are very different (what we should believe, what we should do), we treat them in different courses in our seminaries and universities." *Outlines of Moral Theology* (Milwaukee: The Bruce Publishing Company, 1953), p. 4.

analogies drawn from the world around us; 4. to make clear the bonds of union existing between the various dogmas and between the dogmas themselves and natural truths; 5. to deduce various conclusions from the dogmas—some of which conclusions are not readily apparent from the first examination of the dogmas. Finally, speculative theology seeks to organize all sacred doctrine into one harmonious system. To sum up, it seeks to draw out some understanding of God's revealed truth, by investigating, as far as the frailty of human intelligence permits, precisely what a given thing is and why it is so.

St. Thomas describes the purpose of both methods, namely, positive and scholastic, as follows:

> A [theological] discussion may be conducted with either of two aims in view. One type of discussion aims at removing doubts as to *whether* a thing be true or not. In this type of discussion, one should have recourse above all to authorities, who are acknowledged by those taking part in the discussion. But there is another type of discussion used by teachers in the schools. It aims not so much at removing error, as at instructing the listeners in such a way that they will be led to *an understanding* of the truth that [the teacher] is trying to get across. In this type of instruction one must adduce reasons which analyze the core of the truth and which make known *how* the thing under discussion is true. Otherwise, if a teacher solves a problem by a naked appeal to authority, his audience will be assured *that* the thing is so, but they will gain no scientific knowledge or insight into it and will depart empty-handed (*Quodlibetales,* IV, q. 9, a. 18).

The very character of speculative theology gives it its name, for it reasons about revealed truths in a philosophical fashion (Latin: *speculari*). Because the scholastics, or learned men of the Middle Ages, laid special emphasis on speculative theology, it also goes by the name of scholastic theology.[17]

It should be clear, then, that speculative and positive theology are not two parts of theology, but only two different methods of approach to the same subject matter. In fact, the two cannot be altogether separated. Speculative theology presupposes the work of positive theology and rests upon it: it begins where that leaves off.[18] And positive theology, if it were to be completely separated from speculative theology, would not deserve the name of science.

But one or the other method of approach can predominate. That is why in the Middle Ages, when men enjoyed the peaceful possession of Catholic truth, they paid so much attention to speculative theology. But from the time of the Council of Trent (1545–1563) the very necessity of defending Catholic dogmas against the attacks of the early Protestants forced theologians to study positive theology with greater diligence. Things grew even worse in the eighteenth and in the first half of the nineteenth century. Quite a few people bitterly criticized scholastic theology as if it consisted of nothing but a mountain of useless problems and idle quibbling. Some even accused it of building a smooth highway leading straight to rationalism. Such people, confusing the science itself and a rational, moderate use of its method with the unfortunate excesses of some of the later scholastics, quite frequently caricatured a science of which they were really ignorant.

But the Church has always defended scholastic theology; in fact, she has paid tribute to it with the highest praise.[19] As St. Pius X had to defend speculative theology against the attacks of the Modernists, so too, in our own day, Pius XII has had to insist once more on its great value against the danger of "dogmatic relativism." He writes:

Hence to neglect, or to reject, or to devalue so many and such great resources which have been conceived, expressed and perfected so often by the age-old work of men endowed with no common talent and holiness, working under the vigilant supervision of the holy magisterium and with the light and leadership of the Holy Ghost in order to state the truths of the Faith ever more accurately, to do this so that these things may be replaced by conjectural notions and by some formless and unstable tenets of a new philosophy, tenets which, like the flowers of the field, are in existence today and die tomorrow; this is supreme imprudence and something that would make dogma itself a reed shaken by the wind. The contempt for terms and notions habitually used by scholastic theologians leads of itself to the weakening of what they call Speculative Theology, a discipline which these men consider devoid of true certitude because it is based upon theological reasoning.

Unfortunately these advocates of novelty easily pass from despising Scholastic Theology to the neglect of and even contempt for the Teaching Authority of the Church itself, which gives such authoritative approval to Scholastic Theology

(*Humani Generis*, NCWC Translation, 1950, pp. 8–9, sections 23–24).

Modern authors are careful to blend together harmoniously both positive and scholastic theology. This is definitely the best procedure, advocated by the Church herself:

Certainly, more attention must be paid to positive theology than in the past, but this should be done without any detriment to scholastic theology, and they should be disapproved of as showing modernist tendencies who exalt positive theology in such a way as to seem to despise scholastic theology (Pius X, *Pascendi Dominici Gregis*).

IV. A Brief Historical Outline of Systematic Theology *

The history of theology is usually divided into three major eras:
1. the *patristic* era: (1st–8th centuries)[20]
   up to St. John Damascene (d. 749);
2. the *scholastic* era: (12th–16th centuries)
   from St. Anselm (d. 1109) to the Council of Trent (1545–1563);
3. the *modern* era: (16th–20th centuries)
   from the Council of Trent to the present day.

In between the end of the patristic era and the beginning of the scholastic age there is a transitional period, today commonly labeled pre-scholastic (8th–12th centuries). But, inasmuch as theology, prior to the 12th century, was not yet synthesized into one organic unit, the patristic era and the pre-scholastic period will be described only briefly.

1. The Patristic Era. Patristic theology is characterized by the production of excellent monographs on individual points of doctrine. The Fathers did not write these monographs merely out of an academic desire to present Christian doctrine in an orderly fashion: they wrote them to defend Christian truths against the violent attacks of heretics.[21]

Monographs written in defense of the doctrine of the Trinity are:

St. Augustine's *De Trinitate* in twelve books;

* See the bibliography, pp. l–li.

St. Athanasius' *Contra Arianos orationes 1–3;*

St. Basil's *Adversus Eunomium* in three books and *De Spiritu Sancto;* and

St. Hilary's *De Trinitate* in twelve books.

Monographs written in defense of the doctrine of the Incarnation are:

St. Ambrose's *De incarnationis dominicae sacramento;*

St. Gregory's (Nyssa) *Adversus Apollinarem;*

St. Leo the Great's *Epistola dogmatica ad Flavianum;*

Pope Gelasius I's *De duabus naturis in Christo.*

These works were directed against the heresies of the Arians, the Apollinarists, the Nestorians, the Monophysites, and the Monothelites.

In addition, St. Augustine wrote numerous works against the Pelagians in defense of the doctrines on grace and original sin.[22]

For the rest, the Fathers of the Church taught the contents of Christian doctrine to their catechumens without scientific apparatus, or explained it to the faithful in sermons. Thus we may say that they prepared the way for, rather than produced, a systematic presentation of the whole field of theology.

Even in the patristic era, however, a few Fathers did attempt such a systematic presentation. These Fathers were of the Alexandrian school and produced a synthetic exposition of Christian doctrine as an antidote to offset heretical Gnosticism.[23]

In constructing a kind of Christian gnosis the following Fathers gave a rather systematic presentation of theology: Clement of Alexandria (d. 211–216) in his trilogy: 1st part, *Protrepticus* (a refutation of pagan errors and a demonstration of Christian truth); 2nd part, *Paedagogus* (moral regulations for Christians); 3rd part, *Stromata* (a theoretical exposition of the Chrisian Faith). Origen (185–253) also composed a large systematic work as a kind of Christian gnosis entitled *Peri árchon* (a treatise on fundamental doctrines, translated into Latin by Rufinus under the title *De principiis*). This work was composed of four books: 1. On God, His attributes, the Trinity, and on the angels; 2. the creation of matter, Divine Providence, man and freedom, sin, redemption, final consummation; 3. the moral life; 4. the inspiration and interpretation of Sacred Scripture. It should be noted that Origen and some other theologians of the Alexandrian school, in their eagerness to reach a deep understanding of Christian revelation, went astray on some points of Catholic

Faith (Diekamp, *Theologiae dogmaticae manuale,* 3rd edition, 1949, I, 93).

Several centuries later, and with far better success than the theologians of the Alexandrian school, St. John Damascene (c. 675–749) [24] wrote a large systematic work of theology entitled *De fide orthodoxa (An Exposition of the Orthodox Faith).* Damascene produced in this work not his own personal views, but an orderly summary of the traditional theology of the Greek Fathers.[25]

> *An Exposition of the Orthodox Faith [De fide orthodoxa]* comprises 100 chapters that have been divided into four books by the Latins, corresponding to the four books of Peter Lombard's *Sentences. Book I* (ch. 1–14) is a treatise "De Deo Uno et Trino." *Book II* (ch. 15–44) treats of the works of God (creation, angels, world, man) and of Providence. Philosophy and natural sciences also find a fairly large place here. *Book III* (ch. 45–73) explains the doctrine of the Incarnation by comparing it with heretical aberrations. Lastly, *Book IV* (ch. 74–100) deals with subjects that had found no place in the first three books (faith, sacraments, mariology, Scripture, veneration of the saints, and images), sometimes touches on matters already treated and comes to an end with a consideration of the Last Things (Cayré, *Manual of Patrology* [Tournai: Desclée & Cie, 1940] II, 332).

Of all the Fathers of the Church, none was better equipped by way of native genius and of theological knowledge to produce a complete, systematic treatment of theology than St. Augustine (d. 430). Yet he did not do so: he presented an outline rather than an actual elaboration in two of his works: *De Doctrina Christiana,* and the *Enchiridion.* In the first he presents a brief summary of dogmatic theology in this order: the Trinity and the divine nature, the Incarnation of the Son, the Redemption, the sanctification and consummation of man. In the second he makes a division according to the three theological virtues, faith, hope and charity, and under each of these headings he inserts major Christian truths. Even though Augustine did not produce a work analogous to the *Summa* of St. Thomas, he rightly holds first place among all the Fathers; for, by his many writings, he touched on almost all points of doctrine and illuminated them by his genius, laying a vast foundation for all future theological development.

(xxx)

Transitional Period (pre-scholastic):

Between the death of the last Father of the Church, St. John Damascene (d. 749), and the writings of St. Anselm (d. 1109) there stands a transitional period, now commonly labeled *pre-scholastic*.[26] During this period there was no formal study of theology such as it is known in medieval or modern times:

> When one speaks of the theological instruction furnished by the Carolingian schools, it would be a great delusion to conjure up a program of studies or a method of instruction such as were offered by the universities of the 13th century or the seminaries of the 17th century. There is scarcely any evidence that would allow us to assign to the theological teaching of this epoch any other scope than explanatory reading of the Bible, a few works of some Fathers, and the explanation of liturgical rites and prayers (J. de Ghellinck, *Le Mouvement Théologique du XIIe Siècle*, 2nd edition, 1948, p. 10).

The same state of affairs continued during the next century, "the century of iron," and in fact became even worse. The instruction of the clergy was extremely elemental and geared almost entirely to an immediate preparation for saying Mass, administering the sacraments, and other practical duties of their ministry.[27]

One important contribution of this whole period was the collecting and organizing of manuscripts by the monks. The monastic copyists performed an immense service, both for theology and for learning in general, by preserving for posterity both the works of the Fathers and classic Latin literature.[28]

Yet even during this transition period there were a number of men like Alcuin, Hincmar of Rheims, John the Scot, Paschasius Radbert, Lanfranc, Guitmond, and others, who did excellent work in defending and explaining particular points of doctrine.

> Thus, for example, Alcuin (d. 804) wrote a treatise of three books entitled *De fide sanctae et individuae Trinitatis* in which he discussed the Trinity, creation, the Incarnation, and eschatology. Even more noteworthy are the works of Paschasius of Radbert, abbot of Corbie (d. 860), and of Ratram, a monk of Corbie (d. after 868); both works were entitled *De corpore et sanguine Domini*. Inasmuch as the Fathers of the Church had not left any monographic productions on the doctrine of the Eucharist, and inasmuch as these men did not possess the

(xxxi)

highly technical theological vocabulary of later theologians, their attempt to treat the subject of the Eucharist is quite remarkable.[29]

Again, John the Scot, who was "the most brilliant of the ninth century scholars, and surely the best educated, knowing Greek as well as Latin," [30] produced a number of theological works, like *De Divina Praedestinatione* and *De divisione naturae*. Some of his ideas were, however, unorthodox.[31]

Finally, it should be noted that these men are called pre-scholastics because they prepared the way for the mature scholasticism of succeeding centuries by their application of what they learned from the seven liberal arts (as covered in the trivium and quadrivium) to the study of the Bible,[32] and by their growing interest in dialectics.[33]

2. The Scholastic Era. The characteristic note of this era is the production of *summae* of theology, which, unlike monographic productions, aimed at presenting a synthesis of the entire field of theology. The method followed was scholastic, which meant that the theologians of this era deliberately employed the tools of Aristotelian logic and metaphysics to order, analyze, and defend the entire body of revealed truth. They sought to penetrate the meaning of mysteries as far as human intelligence could.

One point that should also be noted is that these scientific presentations of revealed doctrine were born not from any need to ward off heretical attacks, but from a love for speculation. Aristotelian philosophy, which had but recently penetrated medieval Europe,[34] was as exciting a subject in that day as nuclear physics is to the twentieth century student. Medieval students took this new tool of learning and applied it to the field of knowledge they esteemed above all others: the revealed knowledge given by God —in order to comprehend more deeply and to defend more ably the gift of revelation.

a. *Beginnings of Scholastic Theology:*

In the 11th century St. Anselm of Canterbury (d. 1109), with his motto, "faith seeking understanding," inaugurated scholastic theology. Walking in the footsteps of St. Augustine, he expounded major theological themes in the following works:

the *Monologium* and *Proslogium*, which both deal with God Himself (the second contains his famous ontological argument for the existence of God);

the *Cur Deus Homo,* in which he answers the question, "Why did God become man?" by developing the theme of Christ's vicarious satisfaction;

the *De conceptu virginali et originali peccato,* in which he gives what was to become the classic definition of original sin, namely "the privation of original justice";

the *De concordia praedestinationis et gratiae cum libero arbitrio.*

Although St. Anselm is usually rated the "Father of Scholastic Theology," more attention is being paid recently to the large role played by Peter Abelard (d. 1142) in the formation of scholasticism.[35] Abelard it was who first introduced the term "theology" to the study of sacred doctrine, which up to that time had been called simply *"sacra pagina."* [36] Although Abelard went astray badly on a number of points of doctrine, such as the Redemption and original sin,[37] and was condemned for his errors, he actually was not a "rationalist," as many for a long time erroneously considered him.[38]

His spur to scholastic theology lies, however, not so much in his theological synthesis, as in his *formulation of method.* To Abelard goes credit for introducing, in all probability, the first *summa* of theology, his *De unitate et Trinitate divina* (c. 1118),[39] which he would later expand into his larger work, *Theologia Christiana.* In his *Sic et non,* which was an arsenal of conflicting patristic views, designed as a workbook for reconciling [40] these divergent opinions, and in his *Theologia Christiana* he developed his dialectical method by introducing into theology the *quaestio,* which would eventually become a standard part of the scholastic method of treating theological questions.[41]

Although Abelard introduced the first *summa* of medieval theology, it was Hugh of St. Victor (d. 1141) [42] who saved the new method by his own moderation and balance. In his *Didascalion* he had proposed drawing up some such summary manual of theology for beginners, to keep them from getting lost in a welter of opinions, such as were found in current patristic anthologies. He carried out this design in his great work, *De sacramentis.* Hugh was, however, more a mystical than a dogmatic theologian. In fact, he is often looked on as the Father of Medieval Mystical Theology.

Following Hugh of St. Victor came a number of scholastic theologians who gathered the teachings of the Fathers and organized them systematically into *Collections of Opinions (Summae sententiarum)* for the use of students. Notable among them were the following: Robert Pulleyn (d. 1153), Robert of Melun

(d. 1167), Roland (Pope Alexander III, d. 1181), Peter of Poitiers (d. 1205), and William of Auxerre (d. 1230).

Far surpassing any of the above mentioned authors of *summae* for his immense medieval influence was Peter the Lombard (d. 1164), called the "Master of the Sentences." His work, *The Four Books of the Sentences (Libri quattuor sententiarum)* achieved a fame in medieval days that is difficult to understand if the work is examined solely in the light of its intrinsic merits, without reference to the theological era in which it appeared.

> *The Four Books of the Sentences* has come down to us "with an escort of more than 500 commentators." St. Thomas himself wrote and published a commentary on the Lombard s work before he had himself become a *magister* in theology. The Lombard's work was used as the standard theological textbook in all the medieval universities and was not supplanted by the *Summa theologica* of St. Thomas until as late as the end of fifteenth century (J. de Ghellinck, *L'essor de la litterature Latine*, I, 76).

The immense vogue enjoyed by the *Libri quattuor sententiarum* was due neither to its depth, nor to its originality, but rather to its lack of these qualities. Peter the Lombard was very dispassionate, very impersonal in his approach to theology. He considered all the opinions of his contemporaries, borrowed from them selectively, and presented their divergent views with scientific precision. It was precisely this dispassionate approach, this calm sifting of many opinions, and their orderly presentation which made the work of Peter the Lombard such a fine pedagogical manual.

b. *The Golden Age of Medieval Scholasticism (13th century):*

The characteristic note of the scholastic period was the production of *summae* of theology in which the authors gave a synthetic exposition of the entire field of theology and deliberately employed the resources of logic and metaphysics to attain a deeper penetration and a more orderly exposition of revealed data.

The immediate causes [43] of the immense growth of scholastic theology in its golden age are assigned as three: 1. the recovery and translation of the complete works of Aristotle; 2. the Arabic and Jewish studies of Aristotle which touched on many religious questions and raised new problems which had to be solved by the scholastics; 3. the rise of the new religious orders from which came most of the great theological masters of the era. These men, penetrated by a deeply religious spirit, entered the rising universities and found one outlet for their own religious ardor in the field of theology.

Old Franciscan School:

In the 13th century, Alexander of Hales, an Englishman (d. 1245), who already held a chair in the University of Paris before entering the Franciscan Order, inaugurated the old Franciscan school of theology. Alexander, who was called the "Irrefutable Doctor," produced the first great theological *summa* of the era by his commentary on the work of Peter the Lombard. Even more important than Hales in the development of this school of theology was St. Bonaventure (d. 1274). St. Bonaventure, who was known as the "Seraphic Doctor," in addition to producing commentaries on the Lombard and many philosophical and exegetical works, wrote his *Breviloquium theologicae veritatis,* in which he gave a truly beautiful exposition of mystical theology. This school is characterized by an *affective* approach to theology.

Dominican School:

In the same 13th century, St. Albert the Great (d. 1280) and St. Thomas Aquinas (d. 1274) founded the Dominican school of theology. This school is characterized by its predominantly *intellectual* approach to theology. St. Albert, who was known as the "Universal Doctor" because of his enormous erudition, rescued Aristotelian philosophy from the corruption of its Arab commentators and used it as the faithful servant of Christian revelation.

St. Thomas, as Pope John XXII testified, "contributed more to the illumination of the Church than all the other doctors put together." His chief theological works are the following: [44]

   a. *The Commentary on the Four Books of the Sentences;*
   b. *Summa Theologiae;*
   c. *Summa Contra Gentiles;*
   d. *Quaestiones Disputatae;*
   e. *Opuscula.*

   a. St. Thomas' *Commentary on the Four Books of Sentences* is divided in this manner: the commentary on each distinction in the *Sentences* includes several questions, and the questions in turn are subdivided into articles.

   b. The *Summa Theologiae,* written at the height of St. Thomas' powers, is unquestionably his greatest work. It embraces three parts. The *First Part* considers "God and the origin of creatures from God"; the *Second Part* deals with "the movement of the rational creature towards God," that is, the goal of man and the means whereby he may attain that goal; the *Third Part* envisions "Christ, who, insofar as He is a man, is the way for us in our journey towards God." The *Second Part* includes two treatises, called the *First Part* of the *Second Part* and the *Second Part* of the *Second Part*. In the former St. Thomas considers our goal and the means to acquire it in a general way; in the latter treatment is given of that goal and means in particular.[45] There is also a *Supplement* to the *Third Part*, not completed by St. Thomas himself (death prevented that task), but by Reginald of Piperno,[46] who drew his material from St. Thomas' Commentaries on the *Four Books of Sentences*.

c. The *Summa Contra Gentiles* is properly translated as *A Defense of the Catholic Faith against the Pagans* ("pagans" including Aristotelian Arabs, learned Mohammedans, and Talmudic Jews). This work is divided into four books and each book is divided into several chapters. The scope of the work is as follows: in the first three books St. Thomas demonstrates by philosophic arguments the validity of the religious truths which fall within the grasp of unaided human reason; in the fourth book he demonstrates that revealed mysteries are not contradictory to reason.

d. The *Quaestiones disputatae* is a collection of many smaller works. Among these the major ones are *De potentia, De malo*, and *De veritate*.

e. Finally, there are St. Thomas' *Opuscula*: the *Compendium theologiae* (incomplete); *Expositio in Boetium de Ss. Trinitate; De articulis fidei et Ecclesiae sacramentis*. The second part of the last-named work was incorporated almost bodily by Pope Eugene IV into his *Decree for the Armenians*.

New School of Franciscan Theology:

In the same century one finds the new school of Franciscan theology, inaugurated by John Duns Scotus (d. 1308). Duns Scotus was known as the "Subtle Doctor." With extraordinary acuteness he subjected the work of his predecessors, and of St. Thomas in particular, to critical evaluation and parted company with both Aquinas and St. Bonaventure on numerous points. The characteristic note of Scotistic theology is the *primacy it gives to the will* over the intellect.

The Christian knows that love is the goal of all things, that God Himself only knows Himself in order to love Himself, and that our theology, whether it be that section which has as its object the necessary mysteries of God, or that which has as its object the things willed contingently by God, is a practical science (DTC 15.1, Col. 403).

Scotus held that theology did not fulfill the Aristotelian notion of a science in the full sense of the word. His school differs from the old Franciscan school in that it eliminates its affective approach and considers theological matters in an even more formalistic and dialectical fashion than that of St. Thomas.

Scotus' main works are two commentaries on the Lombard. The one is quite lengthy, the *Opus Oxoniense* (1300–1304), and the other more limited in scope, the *Reportata Parisiensia* (1306–1308). To the Scotistic school of this period belong: Francis Mayron (d. 1327), Anthony Andreas (d. 1320), Peter of Aquila (d. 1361).[47]

c. *Period of Decline of Medieval Scholasticism*
   (14th–15th centuries):
During the 14th century scholastic theology underwent a trying period. Scientific analysis deteriorated into mere quibbling and subtleties. This was due mainly to the school of nominalism inaugurated by William of Ockham (d. 1349), who attacked the theology of both Thomas and Scotus. The nominalists were so called because they denied the validity of universal ideas and held that they were merely names (Latin: *nomen*). The nominalists, furthermore, took the Scotistic principle of the primacy of the will, but so exaggerated it that they conceived of God's Will as being totally arbitrary. Because the nominalists denied the validity of universal ideas, they concluded that theological reasoning was useless and that Scripture is the only source of knowledge about God and His will. This doctrine, which underestimated human reason and claimed Scripture as the sole authority, really laid the foundation for Lutheranism.[48] The major names in the nominalist school, in addition to Ockham, are Peter of Alliaco (d. 1420) and Gabriel Biel (d. 1495).

d. *Period of Resurgence of Scholastic Theology*
   (15th–16th centuries):
Although no gigantic strides were made in the field of theology

during the period from the 14th century to the Council of Trent, still there were quite a number of theologians, who, by returning to the doctrine of St. Thomas, resumed the interrupted scholastic tradition of the golden age. These theologians returned to the medieval scholastic treatment of theology not only as regards its scholastic principles, but even as regards the choice of theological problems.[49]

Among these men we find the following: Aegidius Romanus (d. 1316), the master-general and most famous theologian of the Augustinian school; John Capreolus (d. 1414), whose *Defensiones* earned him the title of "Prince of the Thomists"—he defended the doctrine of St. Thomas against nominalists and Scotists;[50] Francis Sylvester of Ferrara (d. 1528), noteworthy for his commentary on the *Summa contra gentiles;* Cardinal Cajetan (Thomas de Vio, d. 1534), the greatest commentator on the *Summa theologiae* (his commentary is included in the Leonine edition of that masterpiece)—noted especially as the great defender of the distinction between essence and existence;[51] Nicholas of Cusa (d. 1464); Dionysius the Carthusian (d. 1471).[52]

During this whole period the theologians, in their treatises, put almost all their efforts into speculative theology. Positive theology was not, however, completely neglected,* for the outstanding theologians did a great deal of work on the interpretation of Scripture. With regard to patristic theology, they were usually content with simply using existing anthologies of the Fathers, which were not critical editions. This failure to utilize patristic theology is suffi-

---

* In the DTC 15.1, col. 412, no. 2, is the following interesting remark: Certainly the texts, both of the Bible and of the Fathers, were far from being ignored by scholasticism; in fact, it has been remarked that the humanists, often enough, did no more than put into print the manuscripts of the Middle Ages. But in this return to texts and recourse to authors the generation of 1500 did bring a *new point of view.* That generation inaugurated a study of texts not from a timeless and abstractive viewpoint, but from an *historical* one, from a viewpoint which was no longer that of an acquired tradition, but critical and heuristic. And first of all it was necessary to be sure of the purity of the text and the authenticity of its author. From such a viewpoint flowed a whole labor of textual and literary criticism, of editions, and of critical interpretations by recourse to historical context, philology, etc. This is what makes the difference, in the craftsmanship of approaching the Biblical text itself, between a Nicholas of Lyra, who was exclusively anxious about the theological sense, and a Laurent Valla or J. Colet or Erasmus. Erasmus rose up in protest particularly against theologians who lifted passages out of Scripture and accommodated them to their doctrine, without bothering about the context of these passages and their meaning within that context.

ciently explained by considering that there was great difficulty in finding the works of the Fathers and that there was little necessity at the time for a defense of the theology of the Fathers.

Appreciation of Medieval Scholastic Theology:

The value of scholastic theology has been so authoritatively and repeatedly stressed by the Church herself that one need here make but a few salient points. Scholastic theology, in the hands of its great medieval doctors, is especially noteworthy for its organic and synthetic approach to God's revelation. The intrinsic harmony existing between the various dogmas of the Catholic Faith, the harmonious inter-working of faith and reason, and above all the panoramic view of the continuity of God's work in both the natural and supernatural orders, such as it is exhibited in the works of the great medieval doctors, has never been equalled. In the hands of men equipped with both tremendous faith and native genius, the scholastic approach to the data of revelation—"faith seeking understanding"—produced a harvest of theological learning which has not been fully absorbed to this day.

Still, there lay inherent in the method of scholastic theology some seeds of danger which, in the hands of less able men, could sprout into weeds that would slowly throttle the science of theology. These seeds of danger may be listed as three: 1. the excessive preponderance of a method too exclusively rational and dialectical; 2. the danger of useless subtleties; 3. the tendency towards a crystallization of theology into petrified systems.[53]

These deficiencies in method needed correction by a correlative growth in positive theology. Such a development of positive theology was to take place, it will be noted, after the Council of Trent. It is this counterbalancing of speculative method with positive historical research that is characteristic of the golden era of modern theology.

3. The Modern Era (16th–20th centuries). A number of famous controversialists who defended the Catholic Faith against the attacks of heretics during the sixteenth century are worthy of note. These are: John Eck (d. 1543); Albert Pighius of Campia (d. 1542); Ruard Tapper (d. 1559); St. Peter Canisius (d. 1597); Thomas Stapleton (d. 1598); St. Robert Bellarmine (d. 1621); Cardinal Duperron (d. 1618); Jacob Gretser (d. 1625); and the Van Walenburg Brothers, Peter (d. 1675) and Adrian (d. 1669), of Rotterdam.

(xxxix)

It would be well to point out some of the differences that marked pre- and post-Tridentine theology. Systematic theology after the Council of Trent differs from earlier theology in the following three ways. a. The attacks of heretics forced theologians to give more attention to positive theology and unite the findings of that study to scholastic speculations. b. The *Summa Theologiae* of St. Thomas gradually replaced Peter the Lombard's *Libri quattuor sententiarum* as the source-book for theological lectures. This action resulted in a purer and deeper system of doctrine and a clearer method of presentation. c. Practical conclusions and applications of doctrine, previously presented in the same works along with theoretical questions, began to be treated separately and thereby wrought the division of theology into dogmatic and moral. The theologians who treated moral theology exclusively, or almost so, are omitted from the list of theologians which follows.

The first period after the Council of Trent (1550–1660) was the *golden age* of modern scholastic theology. During it appear the following famous theologians:

In the *Dominican* school: Francis of Vittoria (d. 1546); Dominic Soto (d. 1560); Melchior Cano (d. 1560); Dominic Bañez (d. 1604), who, the Molinists declare, is the "inventor of Thomism" and of physical premotion; Peter of Ledesma (d. 1616); Diego Alvarez (d. 1635); John of St. Thomas (d. 1644); Vincent Contenson (d. 1674), whose work, *Theologia mentis et cordis,* was a harmonious treatment of ascetical and mystical theology; John Gonet (d. 1681). Ranked as members of the Thomistic school are also William Estius (d. 1613); Francis Silvius (d. 1649), whose commentary on the *Summa* deserves consultation even today; and the Salmanticenses, of the Order of Carmel, whose *Cursus in Summam theologiae* has been called the most definitive work of all Thomists (1679).

In the *Jesuit* school: Cardinal Francisco Toledo (d. 1596); Louis Molina (d. 1600), the foremost defender and advocate of the *scientia media;* Gregory of Valencia (d. 1603); Gabriel Vasquez (d. 1604); Francis Suarez (d. 1617), rated above all others as "the outstanding doctor"; Leonard Lessius (d. 1623); Martin Becanus (d. 1624); John Martin de Ripalda (d. 1648); Cardinal John de Lugo (d. 1660), who specialized, however, in moral theology.

In the *Scotistic* school: Theodore Smising (d. 1626), and John Bosco (d. 1684).

During this period of theological history, the following did excellent work in the field of *positive* theology: Denis Petavius,

S.J. (d. 1652); John Morin (d. 1659); and Louis Thomassin (d. 1695). The latter two were members of the Oratorian Order.

The following century (1660–1760) might be called the *Age of the Epigoni*. Even though this period is lacking in great genius, it nonetheless gave rise to a number of theologians whose works are commendable for their solidity and clarity of doctrine and for their relative brevity. Among them we may mention the following:

Dominican school: Cardinal Vincent Gotti (d. 1742); Rene Billuart (d. 1757); Bernard Maria de Rubeis (d. 1775).

Jesuit school: James Platel (d. 1681); Paul Antoine (d. 1743); John Baptist Gener (d. 1781); the authors of the *Theologia Wirceburgensis* (Holtzclau, d. 1783; Kilber, d. 1782; Neubauer, d. 1795).

Franciscan school: Claude Frassen (d. 1711), whose *Scotus academicus* is rated the best and most lucid work of the Scotist school; Thomas of Charmes (a Capuchin, d. 1765).

Augustinian school: Laurence Berti (d. 1766).

Oratorian school: Casper Juénin, (d. 1713), whose writing is tinged with Jansenism.

Sorbonne scholars: Charles Witasse (d. 1716, who was also a Jansenist), and Honoré Tournely (d. 1729).

There follows the *Period of Decadence* (1760–1840). During this period both philosophy and scholastic theology hit an all time low. Positive theology brought forth practically no fruit, and even the Catholic mentality grew sick and feeble. Some of the men of this period, who were ignorant of ancient scholastic teaching and imbued with a false philosophy, yearned to produce a deeper exposition of theology. Thus Baader, Hermes, and Gunther became teachers of error, because they had never learned the truth.

But better times were in the making. Men who did the spadework for the rise that was to come were the following: Bruno Liebermann (d. 1844); Henry Klee (d. 1840); Francis Staudenmaier (d. 1856); Henry Denzinger (d. 1883); and, more than any other, John Perrone (d. 1886) and Joseph Kleutgen (d. 1883), both of the Society of Jesus.

From the time of the Vatican Council there began a happy rebirth of scholastic theology.

V. Modern Authors of Theology

It may be useful to give a list, even though very incomplete, of authors who in our own time (that is, from the time of the

Vatican Council to the present) have produced works of systematic theology. Those theologians who have written only on specialized questions or particular tracts of theology will not be mentioned here.

The following authors have written on both fundamental and dogmatic theology:

L. Billot, S.J.: *De Ecclesia Christi:* vol. I, *De credibilitate Ecclesiae et intima ejus constitutione,* 5th ed., 1927; vol. II, *De habitudine Ecclesiae ad civilem societatem,* 2nd ed., 1922; *De inspiratione Sacrae Scripturae,* 4th ed., 1928; *De immutabilitate Traditionis,* 3rd ed., 1922; *De Deo Uno et Trino,* 7th ed., 1926; *De Verbo Incarnato,* 9th ed., 1949; *De Ecclesiae Sacramentis,* vol. I, 7th ed., 1931; vol. II, 8th ed., 1947; *De personali et originali peccato,* 5th ed., 1924; *De virtutibus infusis,* 4th ed., 1928; *De gratia Christi,* 4th ed., 1928; *Quaestiones de novissimis,* 8th ed., 1946.

F. Egger: *Enchiridion theologiae dogmaticae generalis,* 5th ed., 1913; *Enchiridion theologiae dogmaticae specialis,* 9th ed., (revised by A. Mayer) 1928.

J. B. Heinrich: *Dogmatica theologia,* 10 vols., 1881–1904. (The work from volume seven on was completed by C. Gutberlet.)

H. Hurter, S.J.: *Theologiae dogmaticae compendium,* 3 vols., 11th ed., 1903.

L. Lercher, S.J.: *Institutiones theologiae dogmaticae,* 4 vols., 3rd ed., 1939 ff.

J. Lottini, O.P.: *Introductio ad sacram theologiam,* 1 vol.; *Institutiones Theologiae dogmaticae specialis,* 3 vols., 2nd ed., 1911ff.

P. Mannens: *Theologiae dogmaticae institutiones,* 3 vols., 2nd ed., 1910–1915.

C. Manzoni: *Compendium theologiae dogmaticae,* 3rd ed., 1920–1922.

H. Mazzella: *Praelectiones scholastico-dogmaticae breviori cursui accomodatae,* 4 vols., 5th ed., 1919.

P. Minges, O.F.M.: *Compendium theologiae dogmaticae generalis,* 2nd ed., 1923; *Compendium theologiae dogmaticae specialis,* 2nd ed., 1922.

D. Palmieri, S.J.: *De Romano Pontifice cum praeleg. de Ecclesia; De Deo creante et elevante; De peccato originali et immaculata conceptione; De gratia actuali; De poenitentia; De matrimonio.*

Chr. Pesch, S.J.: *Praelectiones dogmaticae*, 9 vols., 5th–6th ed., 1925 ff.; *Compendium theologiae dogmaticae*, 4 vols., 6th ed., 1941–42.

M. J. Scheeben: *Handbuch der katholischen Dogmatik*, 4 vols., Neudruck 1925 (vol. 4 written by L. Atzberger).

Th. Specht: *Lehrbuch der Apologetik oder Fundamentalthe-ologie*, 2nd ed. (revised by G. Bauer), 1924; *Lehrbuch der Dogmatik* (revised by G. Bauer), 2 vols., 3rd ed., 1925.

Adolph Tanquerey, S.S.: *Synopsis theologiae dogmaticae*, 3 vols., 26th ed., 1949 (vol. I revised by J. B. Bord; vols. II & III by R. de Geoffre).

G. B. Tepe, S.J.: *Institutiones theologiae*, 4 vols., 1894.

Tromp, S., *De Revelatione Christiana*, 6th ed., 1950.

Tromp, S., *De Sacrae Scripturae Inspiratione*, 5th ed., 1953.

Zapelena, T., *De Ecclesia Christi* (Pars Apologetica), 5th ed., 1950.

Zapelena, T., *De Ecclesia Christi* (Pars Dogmatica), 2nd ed., 1954.

G. Zaccherini: *Theologiae dogmaticae speculativae cursus*, 1919.

The following authors produced works dealing exclusively with fundamental theology:

A. D'Alès, et al.: *Dictionnaire Apologétique de la Foi Catholique*, 4 vols., 4th ed., 1913–1928.

A. Bougaud: *Le Christianisme et les temps présents*,[54] 5 vols., 7th ed., 1901.

J. Brunsmann, S.V.D.: *Lehrbuch der Apologetik*, 1 vol., 1924.

G. Casanova, O.F.M.: *Theologia fundamentalis*, 1899.

Cotter, A.: *Theologia fundamentalis*, 1940.

Cardinal Dechamps: *Entretiens sur la démonstration cath-olique*, 1856.

A. Dorsch: *Institutiones theologiae fundamentalis*, 2 vols., 2nd ed., 1928.

Duilhé de Saint-Projet: *Apologie scientifique de la Foi chré-tienne*, revised edition (by Sanderens), 1921.

H. Feeder: *Apologetica sive theologia fundamentalis*, 2 vols., 1920.

J. V. de Groot, O.P.: *Summa apologetica de Ecclesia*, 3rd ed., 1906.

C. Gutberlet: *Lehrbuch der Apologetik*, 3 vols., 4th ed., 1922.

F. Hettinger: *Lehrbuch der Fundamental-Theologie*, 3rd ed.

(revised by S. Weber), 1913; *Apologie des Christentums*, 5 vols., 10th ed. (revised by Muller), 1915.

Ph. Kneib: *Handbuch der Apologetik*, 1912.

A. Michelitsch: *Elementa Apologeticae sive Theologiae fundamentalis*, 1925.

N. M. Neguerulea: *Lecciones de Apologetica,'* 2 vols., 2nd ed., 1927.

Norbertus A. Tux, O.F.M., Cap.: *Compendium theologiae fundamentalis ope scriptorum p. Alberti a Bulsano*, 2 vols., 1890.

J. Ottiger, S.J.: *Theologia fundamentalis*, 2 vols., 1897–1911.

G. Reinhold: *Praelectiones de theologia fundamentali*, 2 vols., 2nd ed., 1915.

P. Schanz: *Apologie des Christentums*, 3 vols., 4th ed., (revised by W. Koch), 1910.

A. Schill: *Theologische prinzipienlehre*, 4th ed. (revised by H. Straubinger), 1914.

A. Stokl: *Lehrbuch der Apologetik*, 2 vols., 1895.

A. Stummer, O.F.M., Cap.: *Manuale theologiae fundamentalis*, 1907.

S. Szydelski: *Prologomena in theologiam sacram*, 2 vols., 1920–21.

C. Vosen: *Das Christentum und die Einsprüche seiner Gegner*, 5th ed. (revised by Weber), 1905; *Der Katholizismus und die Einsprüche seiner Gegner*, 3rd ed. (revised by Brüll), 1885.

S. Weber: *Der alte und neue Glaube*, 3rd ed., 1911; *Christliche Apologetik in Grundzügen für Studierende*, 1907.

A. Weisz, O.P.: *Apologie des Christentums vom Standpunkte der Sitte und Kultur*, 5 vols., 4th ed., 1905.

W. Wilmers, S.J.: *De religione revelata; De Ecclesia; De Fide;* 1897–1902.

Th. Zigliari, O.P.: *Propaedeutica ad s. theologiam*, 4th ed., 1906.[55]

The following authors wrote works designed for a more popular audience:

J. Arts, O.P.: *Bijdragen tot wetenswaardige godsdienstvragen*, 3 vols., 1920–1921.

Th. Bensdorp, C.SS.R.: *Apologetica*, 3 vols., (revised by M. Stoks), 1918–1922.

A. Boulenger: *Manuel d'Apologetiqué*, 1920.

G. Esser and J. Mausbach: *Religion, Christentum, und Kirche*, 3 vols., 5th ed., 1923.

L. V. Hammerstein, S.J.: *Gottesbeweise; Das Christentum; Katolizismus und Protestantismus;* 1891–1894.

E. Huguney, O.P.: *Critique et Catholique,* vol. II, *L'apologie des dogmes catholiques,* 1910.

J. Klug: *Der katholische Glaubensinhalt,* 4th ed., 1920; *Lebensfragen,* 1913.

M. Morawski, S.J.: *Abende am Genfer See. Grundzüge einer einheitlichen Weltanschauung,* 1926.

R. V. Oppenraay, S.J.: *Apologie van het Christendom,* 1922.

F. Sawicki: *Die Wahrheit des Christentums,* 1918.

D. Sloet: *God, Christendom en Kerk,* 2 vols., 1890.

W. Wilmers, S.J.: *Lehrbuch der Religion,* 4 vols., 8th ed. (revised by J. Hontheim), 1928. He edited various works of apologetics: *Apologetische Vereeniging Petrus Canisius.*

The following authors produced exclusively books of dogmatic theology:

B. Bartmann: *Lehrbuch der Dogmatik,* 2 vols., 7th ed., 1928.

F. Diekamp: *Katholische Dogmatik,* 2 vols., 3rd to 5th ed., 1921.

L. Döry: *Compendium theologiae dogmaticae specialis,* 1926.

P. Einig: *Institutiones theologiae dogmaticae,* 6 fasc., 1896.

J. Herrmann, C.SS.R.: *Institutiones theologiae dogmaticae,* 2 vols., 6th ed., 1926.

J. Hervé: *Manuale theologiae dogmaticae,* 4 vols., new ed., 1949–51.

E. Hugon, O.P.: *Tractatus dogmatici ad modum commentarii in praecipuas quaestiones dogmaticas divi Thomae Aquinatis,* 3 vols., 1927.

L. Janssens, O.S.B.: *Summa theologica ad modum commentarii in Aquinatis Summam, praesentis aevi studiis aptatam,* 9 vols., 1899–1921.

J. Katschthaler: *Theologia dogmatica Catholica specialis,* 5 vols., 1877.

G. Noggler (P. Gottfried a Graun) O.F.M.Cap.: *Institutiones theologiae dogmaticae specialis p. Alberti a Bulsano recognitae,* 3 vols., 1893.

B. Otten: *Institutiones dogmaticae in usum scholarum,* 6 vols., 1922–1925.

A. Paquet: *Disputationes theologicae seu commentarium in Summam theologicam,* 6 vols., 1893.

J. Pohlet: *Lehrbuch der Dogmatik,* 3 vols., 1910.

E. Rolfes: *Die Wahrheit des Glaubens,* 3 vols., 1910.

A. Sanda: *Synopsis theologiae dogmaticae specialis,* 2 vols., 1916, 1922.

M. Scheeben: *Die Mysterien des Christentums,* 3rd ed. (revised by A. Rademacher), 1912. English translation: *The Mysteries of Christianity,* translated by Cyril Vollert, S.J.

Vacant-Mangenot: *Dictionnaire de Theologie Catholique,* 1903.

Among the more recent manuals of theology the following are noteworthy:

F. Diekamp: *Theologiae dogmaticae manuale,* 4 vols., 3rd ed. (Latin version by A. Hoffman, O.P.), 1949.

A. Ferland: *Commentarium in Summam D. Thomae,* 4 vols., 1936–43.

P. Parente and A. Piolanti: *Collectio theologica Romana,* 7 vols., 3rd ed., 1947.

Spanish Jesuits (various authors): *Sacrae theologiae summa* (B.A.C.), 4 vols., 1952.

Introduction to Fundamental Theology

Before presenting a treatment of fundamental theology it is proper to make a few preliminary remarks about the aim, method, and prerequisites of that division of sacred theology.

1. Aim

Fundamental theology, as already noted, deals with those truths on which the entire structure of sacred doctrine rests. It deals with the truths which all other divisions of theology presuppose as already known and proved, namely, the actual existence of a revelation and its infallible preservation by the Church. Fundamental theology is, therefore, *the study of those matters which one must know before undertaking the study of special theology.* It includes four treatises:

1. The True Religion (Apologetics);
2. Christ's Church (partly apologetical, partly theological);
3. Sources of Revelation (strictly theological);
4. Divine Faith (strictly theological).

The first treatise deals with *The True Religion.* This treatise undertakes to prove that there exists on earth one religion which has been revealed by God and meant for all men. That religion is the one brought to us by Jesus Christ, an authentic messenger from God; and that religion is, in the concrete, the religion professed by the Catholic Church.

The second treatise considers *Christ's Church.* In this treatise it is demonstrated that Christ instituted a Church which truly merits the name "Church," namely, a visible society, and that He entrusted to that Church His doctrine and bestowed upon her His own divine mission of saving souls. After studying the structure and characteristics of this Church founded by Christ, fundamental theology goes on to identify it with the Roman Catholic Church. This section of the treatise is apologetical. The next section studies the different hierarchical ranks within the Church, the Church's infallible magisterium, and the Church viewed as Christ's Mystical Body. This section is theological.

The third treatise is entitled *The Sources of Revelation*. It deals with the two streams from which the Church draws her doctrine and her theologians their arguments, namely, inspired Scripture and sacred Tradition.

The fourth treatise deals with *Divine Faith*. It is concerned with the act whereby men believe, or the assent with which men embrace the truths revealed by God.

It must be noted that fundamental theology has been developed as a special branch of theology only in the last two centuries,[56] and does not have fixed and precise boundaries. A number of theologians reserve a large part of their treatment on the Church and the whole of their treatment on Faith to dogmatic theology. The dogmatic treatment of the Church is generally put after the treatise on God the Redeemer.

2. The Method Used

The choice of a method is necessarily dictated by the goal one has in view. The goal in this treatment of fundamental theology is twofold: the first and major objective is to gain a deeper and more precise knowledge of the arguments which guarantee certitude in religious matters, and a better understanding of the reasonableness of faith; the second is to learn how to show unbelievers the truth of the Catholic Religion and to solve their difficulties.[57] If either of these ends is to be attained, we must, at least at the outset, avoid strictly theological arguments (that is, arguments drawn from revelation), and proceed by way of arguments of the natural order, whether they be philosophical or historical, until such time as the truth and infallibility of the Catholic Church have been demonstrated. Thus, the treatment, at least in the first part, will not be strictly theological, but will be for that reason all the more useful.

Yet even in this scientific investigation of the foundations of the faith, the theologian or the student of theology does not by any means forget that he is a Catholic. It is not, therefore, as one still groping for the truth that he approaches this treatise, but as one who already possesses that truth and is merely seeking a deeper and wider knowledge of the arguments on which it rests.[58]

That is why, even from the outset of this treatise, *The True Religion*, the pertinent *theological notes* will be annexed to the theses—for the truths which will be demonstrated with natural arguments, the divine origin of Catholic doctrine, the truth of the

(xlviii)

Church, and so forth, are at the same time dogmas of the Faith. As often as it is convenient, definitions from the ecclesiastical magisterium will also be introduced, not indeed to prove the theses, but rather to show what Catholics are theologically bound to hold about the subject, and also because in any branch of knowledge it is right to listen to those who are especially skilled.[59]

3. Prerequisites:

In ecclesiastical seminaries the men who begin the study of fundamental theology have already completed *ex professo* studies in the field of philosophy; for this reason good order demands that the matter they have already studied in philosophy should not here be repeated, but rather taken for granted.

One may therefore begin with all the basic truths of sound philosophy admitted as true, and in particular the following: a. *the ability of human reason to arrive at truth* in the metaphysical, moral, and historical orders. This point is absolutely basic. It must be clung to especially against the assaults of the Modernists who adhere to agnosticism. Agnosticism is the philosophical system which maintains that the only object of our intellectual knowledge is phenomena, namely, things which are within the reach of our sense organs.

Agnosticism, consequently, denies that man can either know or prove the existence of any supra-sensible being, such as God, or the soul, by the thought-processes of his intellect.

b. *The existence of the one, infinite God* who is distinct from the world and from whom all things in the universe proceed and towards whom they tend, and by whose ineffable providence they are all governed and conserved in being.[60]

c. *The genuine liberty of man.* It should be obvious that these points are necessary preambles, not merely to faith, but to all religion, even natural religion. Unless these three points are already admitted, any discussion of religion, natural or supernatural, is useless and even absurd.

Finally, one must presuppose as admitted the historic or human authority (that is, the authenticity, truthfulness, and substantial integrity) of the *Books of the New Testament,* and especially of the *Gospels.* It is true that a demonstration of the divinity of the Christian revelation and of the truth of the Church in largest measure rests upon these books, but it is the universal custom to deal *ex professo* with the historic authenticity of these books in a

(xlix)

special branch of ecclesiastical science, namely, *Introduction to Sacred Scripture.*

The Connection Between Philosophy and Theology

Since the tract on faith [61] deals expressly with the relationship obtaining between faith and reason, the bonds of union between philosophy and theology will be indicated only briefly here.

Philosophy's principal job in this connection is to make clear the reasonableness of the assent of faith, and then, as a necessary consequence, the duty of clinging by faith to the tremendous mysteries which divine authority proposes — mysteries which are worthy of trust indeed (Ps. 92:5) by the very wealth of external criteria which serve as a guarantee of their intrinsic truthfulness.

Theology has a far different task to perform. It rests on the divine revelation itself and makes more solid in the faith those who rejoice in the glory of being honored with the name of Christian. Certainly no Christian ought to be arguing that the doctrine which the Catholic Church believes with her heart and professes with her lips may not be true; rather, always holding on without any hesitation to that same faith, loving it and living by it, he ought humbly to seek, in so far as he can, the reasons why it is true. If he can understand, let him thank God; if he cannot, let him instead of throwing his head back to bellow, bow his head to adore (Pius X, Encyclical, *Communium rerum,* April 21, 1909, DB 2120).

Special Bibliography for the General Introduction to Theology and the Introduction to Fundamental Theology

Works useful for an historical study of systematic theology:

Congar M-J.: DTC 15.1 (1946), no. II: "La Théologie: étude historique," cols. 346–447. This article is remarkable for presenting a *synthetic* picture of the development of the science of theology *without sacrificing a sense of history* to the needs of systematic presentation.

Grabmann, Martin: *Geschichte der katholischen Theologie seit dem Ausgang der Väterzeit* (1933)

Hurter, H.: *Nomenclator Literarius,* 5 volumes (1913).

(1)

Straubinger, H.: *Apologetische Streitfragen: Kritische Unter-suchungen zu den religions-philosophischen und apologetis-chen Bestrebungen der Gegenwart* (1925).
Werner: *Geschichte der apologetischen-polemischen Literatur der katholischen Kirche*, 5 volumes (1861).
Der heilige Thomas von Aquin, 3 volumes (1858).
Franz Suarez und die Scholastik der letzten Jahrhunderte, 2 volumes (1861).
Die Scholastik des spätern Mittelalters (1881).

Brief historical outlines are given by: Sheeben: *Katholische Dog-matik*, I, no. 56 ff; Pesch: *Praelectiones dogmaticae*, I, no. 32 ff; Tanquerey: *Synopsis Theologiae Dogmaticae*, II (26th ed., 1949), 1–67; Diekamp: *Theologiae dogmaticae manuale*, I (3rd ed., 1949), 90–110.

Particular works for a study of the pre-scholastic period:
de Ghellinck, J.: *Le Mouvement Théologique du XIIᵉ siècle* (2nd enlarged ed., 1948).
Landgraf, A.: *Einführung in die Geschichte der theologischen Literatur der Frühscholastik* (1948).
Paré, Tremblay, Brunet: *La Renaissance du XIIᵉ siècle: Les écoles et l'enseignement* (1933).

For individual studies on various little-known early scholastics consult the various excellent monographs by specialists in the field like: A. Landgraf, R. M. Martin, T. Eschmann, O. Lottin, et al.

In English, C. H. Haskin's *The Renaissance of the Twelfth Cen-tury* (1933) is a classic as a survey of the general culture of the period, but it is relatively scanty on theological information. Two excellent reviews, *Medieval Studies* (University of Toronto) and *Speculum* (Harvard University), contain from time to time val-uable articles on medieval theology.

Special Bibliography for theology as a science:
St. Thomas Aquinas: *Summa Theologiae, Prima Pars*, q. 1, 1–8.
Congar, M-J.: *"La Théologie Science,"* in DTC, 15.1 (1946) cols. 459–61.
Ferland, A.: *Commentarium in Summam D. Thomae*, IV, *De Deo Uno et Trino* (1943), 1–12.
Gardeil, A.: *Le donne révélé et la Théologie*, 2nd ed. (1932).

Garrigou-Lagrange, Reginald: *De Revelatione per Ecclesiam Catholicam proposita*, 4th ed. (1944).

d'Herbigny, M.: *La Theologie du revele* (1921).

Kreling, G. P.: *De aard der H. Godgeleeröheid* (1928).

Nicolau, P. and Salaverri, P.: *Sacrae theologiae summa*, I, 2nd ed. (1952), 15–28.

Parente, P.: *Collectio theologica Romana*, I, *Theologia Fundamentalis*, 3rd ed. (1947), Appendix 2, *Introductio in S. Theologiam*, 232–42.

Rabeau, G.: *Introduction a l'etude de la theologie* (1926).

Schultes, R. M.: *Introductio in historiam dogmatum* (1922).

Van Laak, H.: *Institutiones theologiae fundamentalis*, tract. I, *De theologia generatim*, fasc. I (1910).

In English the following works are noteworthy:

Burke, Eugene: "The Scientific Teaching of Theology in the Seminary," *Proceedings* of the Catholic Theological Society of America (1949), pp. 129–73.

Donlan, T.: *Theology and Education* (1952).

Fenton, Joseph C.: *The Concept of Sacred Theology* (1941).

Garrigou-Lagrange, Reginald: *Reality*, translated by P. Cummins (1950). See in particular Chapter 6, "The Nature of Theological Work," 61–70.

Journet, Charles: *The Wisdom of Faith*, translated by R. F. Smith (1952).

Mersch, Emil: *The Theology of the Mystical Body*, translated by Cyril Vollert (1951). See Chapters 2 and 3, pp. 27–74.

Scheeben, Matthias: *The Mysteries of Christianity*, translated by Cyril Vollert (1946). See in particular Chapter 28, "Theology as Science," 733–61.

Theological reference and source books available in English:

Attwater, D., *A Catholic Dictionary*, 2nd ed., 1949.

Parente, P., *Dictionary of Dogmatic Theology*, 1951.

Palmer, P., *Sources of Christian Theology*, 1955.

Plumpe, J. and Quasten, J., *Ancient Christian Writers*, 1946ff.

Quasten, J., *Patrology*, 1950ff.

Notes

A General Introduction to Theology and the Introduction to Fundamental Theology

1. See St. Thomas, *S. Th.*, I, q. 1, arts. 2 and 8; R. Gagnebet, "La nature de la théologie speculative," in *Revue Thomiste* (1938), no. 1 and 2, 78, and (1939), pp. 108–47; M-J. Congar, DTC, 15.1 (1946) "La Théologie science," cols. 459–61. Although Scotus holds that theology is a science, he does not agree with St. Thomas that it is a science in the strict Aristotelian sense of the word. For a brief presentation and rebuttal of Scotus' position see P. Parente, *De Deo Uno et Trino* (1943), pp. 4–5.

2. See St. Thomas, *op. cit.*, a. 6.

3. M. Scheeben presents an excellent analysis of this point in the following analogy:

> The domain of natural things is formed by a circle of truths which links together created natures as such. It embraces only such things as concern created nature itself, its development, and its essential relations. Objectively, of course, God also is the center of nature and the natural order, inasmuch as created nature proceeds from Him by an act of His will, and is drawn back to Him as its final end. *But God is to be considered here not immediately and in Himself,* but only in His relations to the creature, and moreover *the eye which contemplates the entire order is in the creature.* Natural things form, so to speak, an eccentric circle with two centers, created nature on the one hand and God on the other, in the first of which is located the eye that surveys the whole order.
>
> The supernatural truths, on the contrary, are grouped directly not around the created nature, *but around the divine nature.* . . . Consequently, to survey this order our eye must, as it were, be located in the divine center of the circle, since we can perceive it only by belief in God's revelation, and so we must contemplate it with an eye that is indeed ours, *but must look through God's eyes.* Hence the sphere of the supernatural order is a simple circle with one center (*Mysteries of Christianity,* translated by Cyril Vollert, S.J. [St. Louis: B. Herder Book Company, 1946], Ch. 28, "Theology as Science," pp. 737–38).

4. If, then, fundamental theology receives the name "theology," the term theology is being used in a broad sense. In this broad sense of the term, theology includes studies which are united to dogmatic theology only by an external bond. Examples are: apologetics in the strict sense, Biblical introduction and Scriptural exegesis, Church history, sacred archaeology, patrology, the various histories of liturgy, Christian art, dogma, councils, heresy, and so on. In a word, all the sciences which in university-studies are grouped together under the label of the department of theology.

Sometimes, on the other hand, the term theology is used in a very restricted sense to designate exclusively that portion of revealed doctrine which treats of God alone. Consequently the Fathers of the Church sometimes divide all sacred doctrine into theology and economy. The latter term refers only to the works of God produced outside of God, and particularly the works of the Incarnation and the Redemption. See H. van Laak, *De theologia generatim,* p. 6.

5. See RCF (1919), 98, p. 321 and 100, p. 416.

6. This knowability is called *historico-philosophical*. Insofar as it proves the existence of a communication (an historical fact) it pertains to the *field of history;* insofar as it demonstrates that this communication has God as its author, it seeks the cause of a thing, and such an inquiry properly belongs to the *field of philosophy.* See van Laak, *op. cit.,* p. 7.

7. This knowability is *historico-philosophical;* for to demonstrate that the Church has always and clearly claimed to be the guardian and teacher of a revelation pertains to the *field of history.* To demonstrate the truth of this assertion (or the Church's divine origin) by means of various miracles is to search out the adequate cause of those miracles, God. Such an inquiry properly belongs to the *field of philosophy.*

8. Notice that God, strictly speaking, does not teach theology as such: He teaches the principles on which theology is built.

9. That is why modern unbelievers are perfectly consistent in demanding that universities should abolish the department of theology as such and should relegate its subject matter to other departments, particularly the departments of literature and philosophy. For if faith is removed, there is no room for any strict science of theology; there remains simply the science and history of religion.

10. J. B. Becker has an excellent treatment of the meaning of this Anselmian adage in PhJ, 1906, pp. 115 ff. The axiom does not mean that all knowledge rests upon faith; neither does it mean that all the revealed truths accepted on faith may be understood in positive fashion and are capable of being demonstrated by the principles of reason. Its real meaning is this: if anyone desires to gain some understanding of mysteries, an understanding that will enable him to see that it cannot be proved that mysteries entail a contradiction, he ought to start with humble faith, the faith whereby he mentally assents to those mysteries and assents to them in the precise sense in which the Church teaches them. The understanding of the mysteries which he will gain will enable him to see that the mysteries are perfectly consistent with one another and that a number of arguments from the viewpoint of fitness and analogies drawn from nature lend credibility to the mysteries.

11. *S. Th* I, q. 1, a. 3.

12. Because fundamental theology treats of general questions which touch upon individual revealed truths, many authors call it *general theology;* because it is a systematic defense of all revealed religion, others call it *apologetics.* It is also called the *introduction to theology* or *theological principles.* Less correctly, however, quite a few authors call it *general dogmatic theology* or *fundamental dogmatic theology.* But this terminology is not exact enough: fundamental theology does not lay the foundation for dogmatic theology alone; it lays the foundation for the entire field of theology. See Ottiger, *Theologia fundamentalis,* I, 12; J. Lebreton, "Les origines de l'apologetiqué chretienńe," in RPA, VII, 564–801; VIII, 178–346.

13. See A. Tanquerey, *The Spiritual Life,* p. 5, no. 11.

14. Some modern authors deliberately restrict their division of theology exclusively to a division by method such as is given above. See A. Ferland, *De Deo Uno et Trino,* 1943, art. 2, "De divisione theologiae," p. 21, no. 1. We prefer, however, to keep also the division according to matter given by Van Noort because it so aptly underscores the over-all unity of theology and

prevents beginners from erroneously misconceiving large branches of theology as though they were totally independent and unrelated disciplines.

15. In the 17th century one sometimes finds the term dogmatic in place of positive theology; it is in this sense that Géner, for example, entitled his work: *Theologia dogmatico-scholastica.*

16. Even though the terms apologetical and polemical signify the same thing etymologically, in customary usage they are employed with the following distinction: *apologetics* (strictly so-called) argues mainly against those who refuse to admit the divine origin of Christian revelation, whereas *polemical* theology argues mainly against heretics or schismatics.

17. See Martin Grabmann, *Geschichte der scholastischen Methode,* 1911.

18. In accord with Kleutgen's dictum: "Scholastic theology begins where positive theology ends. At that precise point it speculatively analyzes the facts which positive theology has dug out of theological sources in order first of all to acquire a wider knowledge and secondly to extract from that accumulated, wider knowledge a deeper and fuller comprehension." *Theologie der Vorzeit,* final volume, no. 12.

19. See Sixtus V, Bull: *Triumphantis,* 1588; thesis no. 4 subscribed to by Bonnetty in DB, 1652; Leo XIII, Encyclical *Aeterni Patris* (August 4, 1879), and *Depuis le jour* (September 8, 1899). Finally, the Vatican Council itself describes that partial "understanding of mysteries" which scholastic theology seeks as "extremely fruitful" (Const. *De fide catholica,* ch. 4). See also St. Pius X, Encyclical *Pascendi* (September 8, 1907); *Motu Proprio: Sacrorum Antistitum* (September 1, 1910), and *Praeclara,* on the study and teaching of St. Thomas (AAS, 1914, p. 336).

20. The patristic era in the West extends up to Gregory the Great (d. 604) or Isidore of Seville (d. 636); in the East it extends to John Damascene. See Johannes Quasten, *Patrology,* I, *The Beginnings of Patristic Literature* (Westminster, Md.: The Newman Press, 1950).

21. See F. Diekamp, *Theologiae dogmaticae manuale,* I (3rd edition, 1949), 93; M-J. Congar, however, points out that patristic theology was not exclusively defensive: a secondary but real motive was the "spontaneous need" of the believer to think about his Faith and align it harmoniously with his general level of human knowledge and culture. See DTC 15.1 (1946), cols. 348 ff.

22. See Diekamp, *ibid.*

23. In brief, the Gnostics sought to replace faith by knowledge and to substitute philosophy for revelation. See F. Cayré, *Manual of Patrology,* I (1935), 101; J. Quasten, *op. cit.,* I, 254: "The Gnostics endeavored to create a Christianity which, fitting into the culture of the time, would absorb the religious myths of the Orient and give the dominant role to the religious philosophy of the Greeks, to leave but a small place for revelation as the foundation of all theological knowledge, for faith, and for the Gospel of Christ."

24. Cayré, *op. cit.,* II, 327.

25. Diekamp, *op. cit.,* p. 94.

26. For a full, scholarly description of theological work during the pre-scholastic period see J. de Ghellinck, *Le Mouvement Théologique de XIIᵉ Siècle* (2nd edition, 1948), I, "La préparation théologique," 1–112. For a

very brief but accurate summary of the theology of the same period see C. Sheedy, "The Eucharistic Controversy of the Eleventh Century," in SST, ser. 2, 1947, pp. 1–32.

27. See de Ghellinck, op. cit., pp. 44–45.

28. See Sheedy, loc. cit., p. 5.

29. See Diekamp, op. cit., p. 96.

30. See Sheedy, loc. cit., p. 5.

31. That John the Scot was no "rationalist" (as some have claimed), but thoroughly Christian in his outlook, despite his errors, is the position of a number of modern scholars. See Cayré, op. cit., II, 385; Sheedy, loc. cit., pp. 18–19.

32. DTC, 15.1, col. 360.

33. See Sheedy, loc. cit., p. 10.

34. The complete Aristotelian corpus was recovered only gradually. During the first half of the 12th century only his logical works were available; his Metaphysics and Ethics were not available until the close of the 12th century. See Ch. Haskins, The Rise of the Universities, p. 346; Paré, Tremblay, Brunet, La Renaissance du XIIe siècle: les écoles et l'enseignement, pp. 31–32.

35. J. de Ghellinck admits, though with cautious restrictions, the enormous influence of Abelard in the development of scholastic theology. See Le Mouvement Théologique, pp. 132, 173ff; Paré, Tremblay, Brunet, op. cit., p. 307, state unequivocally: "Abelard and St. Anselm were thus the creators of scholastic theology, that outstanding product of the philosophical renaissance of the 12th and 13th centuries." It should be noted here that Paré and his associates are viewing the 12th and 13th centuries as one unit in linking together the names of Abelard and St. Anselm. Actually, St. Anselm's work was largely ignored in the 12th century by contemporary masters; only in the 13th century would he come into his own when his works were enthusiastically studied and welcomed by Alexander of Hales, Bonaventure, and St. Thomas. See J. de Ghellinck, op. cit., pp. 83–86.

36. The term "theology" was not used at all in the first half of the twelfth century until Peter Abelard used it in his Introductio ad theologiam. The terms used instead were sacra pagina and sacra doctrina. During the Carolingian era the term sacra pagina was a very apt term to describe the theology of that period which was literally an explanation of the "sacred page" of the Bible. Robert of Melun and Peter the Lombard continued to use the term sacra pagina, but with a wider connotation than it had in the Carolingian era. St. Augustine had used the term sacra doctrina and the term continued to be used as late as the time of St. Thomas. Abelard's use of the term theology was an innovation which did not win general approbation for some time. For a history of the term theology see the work of de Ghellinck and that of Paré, Tremblay, and Brunet, previously quoted.

37. Abelard did not, however, make as many mistakes as are usually attributed to him. As J. Cottiaux has aptly pointed out, much of the confusion about Abelard's position stems out of a failure to consider his method. The different aspects of his thought counterbalance one another by their opposition like arches in a roof. Unfortunately, since Abelard struck out in many directions, he did not often stop to harmonize his viewpoints. Consequently, if one considers his work in separate sections, he is liable to make him out to be both a rationalist and a fideist, an Arian and a Sabellian. See J. Cottiaux, "La con-

ception de la théologie chez Abelard" in RHE, 28 (1932), 247–295; 533–551; 788–828. Some of his theories, like that of Trinitarian appropriation, were to be adopted by the masters of the 13th century. See R. M. Martin, "Pro Petro Abelardo. Un plaidoyer de Robert de Melun contre saint Bernard," RSPT, XII (1923), 308–333.

38. Etienne Gilson sums up the question of Abelard's supposed rationalism neatly in the following passage:

It is a curious thing that precisely because of the passionate yearning with which he desired knowledge of God, men should want to make of Abelard a rationalist. He is neither a rationalist in intention, since he declares the mystery impenetrable, nor in fact, since he never asserted that his comparisons were exact equivalents of dogmatic realities. He attempts to discover for us, not a complete comprehension (*le sens*) of revelation, but some comprehension (*un sens*), and that is exactly what is necessary to prevent formulas from being reduced to mere words devoid of meaning when we utter them. It hardly needs to be mentioned that Abelard could not explain the comparisons he was using without having the air of wanting to explain the dogma itself; and yet, it is not his reason which absorbs his faith when it sets about discovering in the human sphere realities that are analogous to those that dogma reveals; on the contrary, it is his faith which absorbs his reason and restrains it from attempting tasks for which it was not made. "Le sens du rationalisme chrétien," *Etudes de philosophie médiévale* (1921), p. 25. On this same point see Paré, Tremblay, Brunet, *op. cit.*, pp. 280–295; de Ghellinck, *op. cit.*, pp. 171–175.

39. See Abelard's own description of the purpose of *De unitate et trinitate divina* in his *Historia calamitatum*, ML, 178.140; and his explicit use of the term *summa* (. . . *aliquam sacrae eruditionis summam* . . .) in the prologue to his *Introductio ad theologiam*, ML, 178.979.

40. ". . . the famous *Sic et non* . . . for a very long time gave him [Abelard] the reputation of a sceptic, when actually the work is an arsenal of apparently contradictory patristic texts designed for the work of reconciliation by students." J. de Ghellinck, *op. cit.*, p. 46; see Paré et al., *op. cit.*, pp. 289–290.

41. See DTC, 15.1, cols. 366–371. For a presentation of the gradual development of the *lectio, quaestio,* and *disputatio* see Paré et al., *op. cit.*, pp. 125–131.

42. See de Ghellinck, *op. cit.*, pp. 51ff.

43. See Diekamp, *Theologiae Dogmaticae Manuale*, I, p. 99.

44. See C. Suermondt, "Conspectus operum S. Thomae" in ETL (1925), p. 236; Garrigou-Lagrange, *Reality* (1950), pp. 1–22.

45. See *S.Th.*, I, q. 2, Introduction; much information can be found in De Groot, *De h. Thomas v. Aquino;* see M. Grabmann, *Einführung in die Summa Theologiae des hl. Thomas von Aquin* (2nd ed., 1928); Garrigou-Lagrange, *op. cit.*, pp. 1–22.

46. See Mandonnet, *Les écrits authentiques de St. Thomas d'Aquin* (1910), p. 155.

47. See Diekamp, *op. cit.*, p. 102.

48. *Ibid.*, p. 103.

49. DTC, 15.1, col. 417, no. 3: "Continuation et developpement de la scholastique médiévale."

50. See Garrigou-Lagrange, *op. cit.*, p. 24.

51. *Ibid* p. 26.

52. *De Kath.* (1921). His real name was Dionysius van Leeuwen. He was born in Ryckel near Trudonopolis and lived at Ruremunde.

53. See DTC, 15.1, cols. 407–410, "Appreciatión sur la theologíe de la periodé scholastique."

54. The third part of this work, "Les Dogmas du Credo," contains some opinions, for example, the knowledge of Christ-as-man, which should not be approved; see *Etudes* (1878), pp. 205ff.

55. For other works, see the list given by Bainvel, *op. cit.*, p. 5; DAFC, I, 215–250; DTC, 1.1511ff; Buchberger, *Kirchliches Handlexikon*, I, 280.

56. For a history of fundamental theology and apologetics, consult the following: Langhorst, in *Stimmen*, vols. 18–20; Schanz, *Apologie*, I, 3rd ed., 22ff; A. de Poulpiquet, "Apologetiqué et Theologíe," in RSPT (1912), p. 708; M. le Bachelet, "Apologetiqué, Apologie," in DAFC, pp. 189–251; L. Maisonneuve, "Apologetiqué," in DTC, 1, cols., 1511ff; Aigrain, "Histoire de l'Apologetiqué," in *Apologetiqué* (1937), pp. 950–1011.

57. See J. Steffes, "Wie kann mann den Wahrheitscharakter der Religion erweisen?" in *Munsteř Pastoralblaat* (1923), p. 117.

58. We do *not*, then, investigate the foundations of our religion in an attitude of doubt (which George Hermes (d. 1831) recommended as the proper attitude of mind for students undertaking theological studies). This advice was both unreasonable and wicked. See the Vatican Council, Constitution *De Fide Catholica*, ch. 3, DB, 1794, 1815). We do so to find corroboration. In other words, we wish to turn our popular certitude into philosophical certitude. Both types of certitude are genuine because they indicate firm intellectual assent and both are backed up by sufficient motives; but in philosophical certitude the motives are perceived more fully, more distinctly, and above all more reflectively.

59. See B. Durst, "Zür theologischen Methode," in *Theologische Revue* (1927), pp. 293–361.

60. Modernists speak of a need of the *divine* and not of *God* because they are unwilling to acknowledge a *personal* God. See Beijsens, *Theodicée*, I, 7 and 323; G. Michelet, *Dieu et l'agnosticisme contemporain*, 4th ed. (1920); Garrigou-Lagrange, *Dieu*, 5th ed. (1928); I. J. M. van den Berg, *Introductio in theologiam naturalem* (1927).

61. See nos. 331ff of this book.

A Scientific Analysis of Religion in the Abstract

Chapter I. ON RELIGION IN GENERAL

Article I

THE OBJECTIVE FOUNDATION OF RELIGION
AND THE OBLIGATION TO PRACTICE IT

I. *The Objective Foundation of Religion:*

    1. Modern misconceptions can be reduced to this: religious feeling is the beginning of all religion. Man creates religion to fulfill a subjective need.

    2. This misconception disregards the following truths:

        a. religion can possess an objective foundation, the objectively true knowledge of God;

        b. historically, religion has possessed such an objective basis.

II. *The Obligation to Practice Religion:*

    PROPOSITION 1: Man is strictly bound by the natural law to practice religion.

    Proof: 1. from the metaphysical order (man's rational nature);

        2. from the general agreement of mankind.

    PROPOSITION 2: Man is also bound by the natural law to practice some external worship.

    Proof: 1. from the nature of worship;

        2. from the necessity of external worship as a means to sustain internal worship.

    PROPOSITION 3: Men are also bound by the natural law to worship God publicly.

    Meaning: society as such has an obligation to worship God.

    Proof: society depends on God for its existence just as does the individual.

    Scholion: The duty of religion is the most important of all duties and the foundation of all morality.

Treatise on the True Religion

Special Bibliography

In addition to the authors previously cited who have published works covering the entire field of fundamental theology, the following authors are worthy of note:

J. V. Bainvel, *De vera religione et apologetica* (1914).

A. de Broglie, *Problemes`et conclusions de l'histoire des religions,* 4th ed. (1896).

A. de Broglie, *Religion et Critique* (1896).

H. Dieckmann, *De revelatione Christiana tractatus philosophico-historicus* (1930).

A. Dorsch, *De religione revelata* (1916).

Reginald Garrigou-Lagrange, *De Revelatione per Ecclesiam Catholicam proposita,* 4th ed. (1944).

J. L. Gondal, *La religion* (1893).

J. Herrmann, *Tractatus de vera religione,* 3rd ed. (1903).

P. Nicolau, and P. Salaverri, *Sacrae theologiae summa,* v. 1, *Theologia fundamentalis,* 2nd ed. (1952).

J. Ottiger, *De revelatione supernaturali* (1897).

P. Parente, *Theologia fundamentalis,* 3rd ed. (1947).

W. Pohl, *De vera religione quaestiones selectae* (1928).

S. Schiffini, *De vera religione* (1908).

H. van Laak, *Institutiones theologiae fundamentalis, tractatus II, De religionis revelatione in abstracto considerata* (1908).

G. Yelle and R. Fournier, *Apologetica* (1945).

G. Zaccherini, *De vera religione* (1905).

For studies in comparative religion in English the following may be consulted:

W. Koppers, *Primitive Man and His World Picture* (1952).

R. H. Lowie, *Primitive Religion* (1924).

Arthur P. Madgett, *Christian Origins,* v. 1, 2nd ed. (1941).

E. C. Messenger, *Studies in Comparative Religion* (1934).

Eva Ross, *Social Origins* (1937).

W. Schmidt, *The Origin and Growth of Religion* (1931).

Sir Bertram Windle, *Religions Past and Present* (1927).

The True Religion

Preliminary Note

No one, not even an atheist, is ignorant of the existence of religion. Religion is as commonplace as trees, and like trees it grows in an endless variety of shapes, sizes, and colors all over the world. And as some trees are gigantic in size and others small; some flowering and some stunted; some beautiful in form and others grotesque, so too is it with the variant forms of religion.

To one man the term "religion" will evoke the image of a venerable rabbi with a long beard and black skullcap patiently perusing the scrolls of the Old Testament; to another, the image of a Catholic priest saying Mass or entering a confessional box; to another, the image of congregational singing at twilight in a small chapel; to another, the image of a muezzin in his tower summoning Mohammedans to prayer; to another, the image of a Buddhist priest in his temple; to yet others, the image of African natives and their medicine man engaged in a religious dance.

Because religion, as manifested in various parts of the world, exhibits such an endless variety of forms, the exact scope of the demonstration of the true religion must be made clear from the outset.

The study of comparative religion is both scientific and philosophical. Both aspects, the scientific or empirical and the philosophical, are necessary for an adequate study of the science of religion. They should complement, not contradict, each other. The scientific or empirical side of the study is concerned with the discovery of various historical data about religion as it has appeared throughout the ages. It does this by the aid of such special sciences as anthropology, pre-history, archaeology, and ethnology. The various facts unearthed by these studies are to be compared in order to note their agreement and differences.

The philosophy of religion is not concerned with the discovery of historical facts, nor with comparison of the various ritualistic forms under which religion may appear. Its aim is to investigate, in the light of such facts, the common nature of religion underlying all these fragmentary cultural forms. It seeks the ultimate causes of religion, the answers to questions such as these: why is man religious at all? has religion an objective or merely a subjective foundation? is religion something of pragmatic value only, or is it necessary? Finally, in comparing religions one with another, it wants to know whether there is one objectively true religion or whether all religions are partially true and partially false.

It is necessary to keep these two aspects of the science of religion constantly in mind, lest the discussion of religion become hopelessly confused.

(3)

The distinction here suggested between the science and the philosophy of comparative religion is a very important one indeed. In the first place, the distinction provides us with a proper and fair distribution of the subject-matter of the study as a whole. Thus, the questions of the ultimate origin of religion, and of its validity, belong to the Philosophy of religion. On the other hand, the question of the history and development of particular religions belongs to the Science of religion. Now, as these two distinct branches of Knowledge, Science and Philosophy, have their own problems to solve, so also they have their own appropriate methods to be used in their solution.

Thus, a "scientific" problem must be determined mainly by an appeal to facts, or by the various methods which may generally be called "empirical." A "philosophic" problem, on the other hand, must be determined mainly by the *a priori,* or metaphysical, method of abstract reasoning on the necessities of the case. It would be quite out of place to employ a metaphysical method in the determination of a "scientific" question of fact; it would be equally out of place to employ an "empirical" method for the solution of a philosophic problem. Yet this distinction of method has unfortunately not always been observed, and scientists and philosophers have been equally guilty in this respect (E. C. Messenger, *Studies in Comparative Religion,* [London: The Catholic Truth Society, 1934], I, p. 18).

The study of comparative religion is, then, in its entirety, a vast and separate science which deserves to be studied with its own proper techniques. Here no attempt is made to study the various forms in which religion has appeared over the ages; the interested reader is referred to the bibliography on page 2. Further, the philosophy of religion is taken up here only insofar as it is a preliminary matter to the apologetical demonstration of the existence of one revealed religion.

References, therefore, to the empirical side of the study of religion will be incidental and only made when they are necessary to refute objections based either upon false historical data or upon interpretations of correct data which are vitiated by the acceptance and *a priori* application of false philosophical principles.

The Correct Concept of Religion

1. Etymological meaning
2. Definition

3. The practice of religion involves the $\left\{\begin{array}{l}\text{intellect}\\\text{will}\\\text{emotions}\end{array}\right.$

4. Some acts of religion are
   a. essential to the virtue;
   b. merely prescribed by it.
5. Religion may be considered
   a. subjectively, as a virtue;
   b. objectively, as the sum total of theoretical and practical truths pertaining to God and to our relationship to Him.

The Correct Concept of Religion

Etymological definition. The word *religion,* according to Cicero and others, is derived from the Latin term *relegere,* which means "to do much reading," or "to study closely." If this derivation is accepted, religion signifies an attentive and deep study of matters pertaining to the worship of God. Other authors, taking their cue from Lactantius, derive the word from *religare,* which denotes that one "unite himself," or "bind himself fast" to God. Finally, but with far less probability, some take the lead of Augustine and derive *religion* from *re-eligere.* In this case religion signifies that one "chooses once more," the God whom he has lost by sin.

Real definition. Apart from its etymological derivation, *religion* signifies man's relationship to God.[1] This does not refer to the ontological relationship by which everything in the universe depends on God for its whole being; it designates rather the moral relationship by which a rational creature, who recognizes his dependence on God and the duties which follow from that dependence, pays honor to God both in theory and in practice. Since honor accompanied by submission is called worship, religion may be defined as *the virtue whereby we offer God the worship that is rightfully His because of His supreme excellence.*[2]

The definition given above considers the subjective aspect of religion, regarding it as a virtue or constant attitude of mind inclining man to offer God the worship that is His due. Although this treatise is primarily concerned with the objective nature of religion, it is necessary first to clarify a few points pertaining to the subjective element of religion.

The virtue of religion is not practiced exclusively by acts of

(5)

the intellect or exclusively by acts of the will, or exclusively by emotions and feelings; it is practiced by all of these activities together. The acts of the intellect and will, however, are the principal acts of religion; emotional reactions are only subsidiary. Thus, those who teach that religion consists exclusively in intellectual activity (Hegel, Spencer, E. V. Hartmann, O. Pfleiderer), or exclusively in acts of the will (Kant, Fichte, Ritschl, Herrmann, Schopenhauer, Achelis, Caird, Paulsen, Wundt, Tolstoi), or exclusively in emotional activity or feeling (Schleiermacher, Jacobi, James, the Modernists), are badly mistaken. The emotions depend in large measure on physiological conditions and, unless guided by reason, can completely destroy religion.

In addition it must be noted that some religious acts are necessary to the virtue of religion and are brought into being by it; others are merely prescribed by it. Acts which are necessary to the virtue of religion are those which directly and of their very nature honor God: for example, adoration, thanksgiving, and petition. Acts which are merely prescribed by the virtue of religion are acts proper to other virtues: for example, the virtues of temperance or mercy. Insofar as actions proper to these virtues are directed towards God's glory and are prescribed by religion, they are said to belong indirectly to the virtue of religion.[3]

All that has been said thus far pertains to the subjective element of religion. Religion, in its objective sense, embraces all those duties by which we must worship God, or *the sum total of theoretical and practical truths pertaining to God and our relationships to Him.* This sum total of duties is accurately and succinctly summarized in the formula: *creed, code, cult.*

In this treatise, attention will be directed mainly to the objective aspect of religion. The first section of the treatise will contain a scientific *analysis of religion in the abstract;* the second section will contain an application of that theory of religion to demonstrate *the actual existence and the truth of the Christian-Catholic religion.*

The Correct Concept of Religion

Notes

1. See *S.Th.,* IIa-IIae, q. 81, a. 1, c; Schanz: *Apologetik des Christentums,* I, 4th ed., no. 4, 2.

2. We shall not give here a list of all the erroneous notions of religion that exist, but a few common examples may be of interest.

1. Thomas Huxley: Religion is Reverence and Love for the *Ethical Ideal,* and the desire to realize that Ideal in Life.
2. Immanuel Kant: Religion consists in our recognizing all our *duties* as divine commands.
3. Solomon Reinach: Religion is a *sum of scruples* which impede the free exercise of our faculties.
4. A. N. Whitehead: Religion is the *vision* of something which stands beyond, behind, and within the passing flux of immediate things; something which is real, and yet waiting to be realized; something which is a remote possibility, and yet the greatest of present facts; something that gives meaning to all that passes, and yet eludes apprehension; something whose possession is the final good, and yet *beyond all reach;* something which is the ultimate ideal, and the *hopeless* quest.

The first definition excludes the notion of God as the Supreme Power on which all things depend, reducing religion to a humanitarian search for wholesome ethical ideals. The second reduces religion to one of its consequences. The third not only does not acknowledge creed, code, or cult, but makes religion a neurotic disease. The fourth is uttered in poetic prose, but states that religion is an impossible ideal. (The first three definitions are cited in Messenger, *Studies in Comparative Religion* [London: The Catholic Truth Society, 1934], I, p. 5; the fourth is found in Whitehead's book, *Science and the Modern World* [New York: The New American Library, Mentor ed., 1948], ch. XII, "Religion and Science," p. 191).

Many writers describe a sense of dependence on any sort of being whatsoever as religion. D. F. Strauss says: "The fundamental ingredient of every religion is the feeling of absolute dependence. Whether we call it God or the Universe, the fact remains that we undoubtedly do feel ourselves to be dependent on one or the other" (*Alter und neuer Glaube,* p. 142).

To see how far an abuse of terminology has proceeded and what vast confusion exists about the very notion of religion, consult V. Cathrein's article, "Moderne Religion," in *Stimmen,* 68 (1905) 53. Some excellent examples of weird conceptions about both God and religion currently abroad in America may be found in V. Sheppard, *Religion and the Concept of Democracy* (Washington: The Catholic University of America Press, 1949), especially chapter 4, "The Modern Cult of Democracy," pp. 50–70; R. Mohan, S.S., *A Thomistic Philosophy of Civilization and Culture* (Washington: The Catholic University of America Press, 1948), "Religious Anti-Rationalism," pp. 55–59.

3. See S. Th., IIa-IIae, q. 81, a. 1, ad 1; a. 4, ad 2. Here is found an exposition of the sense in which morality is distinguished from religion, and in what sense it is included in that concept.

SECTION I

A Scientific Analysis of Religion
in the Abstract

There are two types of religion: natural and super-natural. Natural religion stems necessarily from the very nature of God and of man, is known and regulated by reason, and leads to a natural goal. Supernatural religion rests upon some sort of revelation. Note, however, that supernatural religion does not destroy, or take the place of natural religion, but is added to it and perfects it.

On Religion in General

The principles established in this chapter are necessarily valid for any natural religion and conditionally valid for a supernatural religion. The condition for the latter is the actual existence of a divine revelation.

Article I

THE OBJECTIVE FOUNDATION OF RELIGION
AND THE OBLIGATION TO PRACTICE IT

I. The Objective Foundation of Religion

In this modern day a great many men adhere to philosophical 1a
monism, subjectivism, or positivism. They deny that there is a God who is distinct from the world, or at least that He can be known by reason. Such persons maintain that all religions lack any objective foundation and rest ultimately on purely subjective experience, a sort of psychological sentiment. They claim that men are religious, not because they know by objectively valid arguments that God exists and that they depend on Him, but because they are driven by their own personal disposition (either a blind instinct about the existence of suprasensible realities, or the awareness of their own helplessness coupled with a desire for help and happiness, or a categorical imperative) to manufacture a god or gods for themselves. Hence we should look for the origin of religion not in man's intelligence, which recognizes God making Himself known either naturally or supernaturally, but in the human heart, emotions, and will. Modernists teach practically the same doctrine. Following, as they do, the principles of agnosticism or immanentism,* Modernists claim that the origin of religion is to be found in a subjective need

---

* Agnosticism holds that the human mind is incapable of knowing anything about a suprasensible world, even its existence. Immanentism teaches that the origin and deepest explanation of every religion and of all aspects of religion is to be found in man himself, namely, in the intrinsic disposition and desires of the human soul.

of the divine which lies hidden beneath our conscious mental activity, or in the subconscious mind. Given a favorable opportunity, this subconscious need bursts forth from its hidden recess and a man begins to *feel* how vehemently his heart pants after God. *This religious feeling*, which is called "faith," is for them the *beginning of all religion*.[1]

Once this assertion is granted, it is easy to accept their other dictum: men have manufactured deities and fabricated diverse relationships between gods and men and developed different religious duties all in accord with their own peculiar subjective or objective circumstances.[2] This is the explanation, according to the Modernists, for all the diversity of religions, past and present. Most Modernists add, finally, that religion has to be changed from time to time to keep pace with the progress of science, human culture, personal views of morality, and so forth.

Against this theory, which makes man the creator of God rather than God the Creator of man, the following is to be maintained here:

1b   **1. Religion can possess an objective foundation,** namely, the objectively true knowledge of an existing and governing God. This fact flows spontaneously from the points proved in the philosophical sciences of criteriology and theodicy. For criteriology demonstrates that we can have objectively valid knowledge of metaphysical realties, and theodicy demonstrates the existence of one God who is Creator and Lord. This is the first and major assertion, since it suffices to safeguard the rights and objective legitimacy of religion as such.

2. Historically, religion has possessed such an objective foundation. It cannot be denied that there have been, and still are, false religions—religions containing many doctrines, moral practices, and forms of worship, which sound reason neither teaches nor approves. In spite of this, when it comes to a question of the substance of religion—the conviction that one is obliged to worship some god, and the genuine will to worship him—we can say, in general, that it rests upon the certitude, even though it may be a common-sense certitude, that some real god actually exists. The same point is a conclusion of theodicy, which demonstrates that a constant and morally universal conviction of the entire human race regarding the existence of God is marked with such characteristics that it must be considered the result of sound reason. In other words, when normal intelligence stops to examine the actually existing world, it arrives by a natural and almost spontaneous process of reasoning

(12)

at the knowledge of some supreme being. That this reasoning process is not merely a subjective way of thinking, but has objective validity can be seen by applying the principles used in criteriology to refute subjectivism and positivism.

II. The Obligation to Practice Religion 2

After the question of the objective foundation for religion, or the possibility of a religion which is more than a mere spawn of psychological sentiment, arises the query: is there any moral obligation to practice religion? That there is a real and strict obligation to honor God by religious worship is denied not only by the men whose views were attacked in the preceding section, but also by all who profess absolute indifference in religious matters. Such people hold that God does not really care whether we worship Him or not; consequently they consider all religion as something useless and unprofitable.[3] Against them the following three propositions are made:

PROPOSITION 1: *Man is strictly bound by the natural law to practice religion.*[4] This proposition is *certain*.

Proof of the proposition. 1. *From the metaphysical order.* Man, 3 since he possesses intelligence and will, ought to assent intellectually to the ontological order of things, and ought to conform to it in practice through his free actions; but the very order of nature demands that the highest honor, complete subjection, and complete love should be offered to God; therefore, man ought to acknowledge in theory this demand of nature, and ought to follow its dictates in practice—in other words, man is bound to practice religion.

The major should be obvious. Who, indeed, would say that man, simply because he enjoys freedom of choice, may neglect or even pervert the order of nature?

As for the minor, nature and reason alike teach that excellence should be honored, that sovereignty should be obeyed, that a goal should be pursued and loved. But in God we find supreme, indeed infinite, excellence, "insofar as He infinitely transcends all things from every possible viewpoint" (*S.Th.*, IIa-IIae, q. 81, a. 4, c.); therefore the highest honor or adoration belongs to God.[5] God is the supreme Sovereign of all things, since all things completely depend on Him as their Creator, Preserver, and Provider; therefore to God is due complete subjection and utter obedience. God is the goal of all things, because they are ultimately ordered to Him. Hence He should be desired above all other goods and loved above all other things. Very rightly did Leo XIII say:

> Of all the duties of mankind, that is without doubt the greatest and holiest duty which orders men to worship God lovingly and religiously. That duty follows necessarily from the fact that we continue to exist by God's power, and are governed by God's will and providence. Since we have come forth from Him, we ought to return to Him (encyclical *Libertas praestantissimum,* in the *Allocutions of Leo XIII*, Desclée ed., III, 108).

The fact that God has no need of our worship, and that He does not gain any additional happiness or profit from it, does not change matters at all. That God does not need our worship does not mean that He forfeits thereby His right to that honor, or that man is excused from his obligation. For who would say that a beggar is dispensed from the duty of gratitude, just because that gratitude would bring hardly any profit to a powerful benefactor? Neither can one pretend that God has yielded His rights in this matter. Since God cannot contradict Himself, He must will His creature to operate in conformity to the very nature He has given him. Finally, let it be noted that we do not worship God "for His profit, but for His external glory and for our profit" (*S.Th.*, IIa-IIae,q. 81, a.6, ad 2).

4   2. Proof of the obligation *from the general agreement of mankind.* All peoples, from all parts of the earth, whether they exist today or have existed in the past, have always professed some sort of religion. Granted that the type of religion practiced may often have been of a very superstitious sort, the fact remains that all kinds of people, not merely civilized nations, but even, and especially, primitive ones have always practiced religion. What some authors have alleged about finding tribes completely without religion is simply not true.* How explain this fact? This

---

* "The question whether anywhere on earth there has ever been discovered a tribe having no religious notions or ideas may be answered definitely, 'No!' " (O. Peschel, *Völkerkunde*, 6th ed., p. 273). "We can now affirm definitely that in spite of all investigations, no human beings anywhere have been found who did not possess something which was recognized by them as a religion" (Max Müller, *Ursprung und Entwicklung der Religion*, p. 88). See Schanz, *Apologie*, v. I, 4th ed., no. 3. Note also that it is incorrect to point to widespread Buddhism as an example of irreligion; for wide-spread Buddhism, that is, popular Buddhism, is not atheistic.

unwavering and universal agreement of mankind in a moral matter which puts a check on man's passions cannot be adequately explained by prejudice or education. Neither can it be sufficiently explained on the grounds that rulers or priests tricked people into practicing religion, or that it was due to ignorance of the natural sciences, or to irrational fears, or to veneration for the dead. This universal fact can be adequately explained only on the grounds that all peoples in this matter were following the dictates of sound reason. As Cicero puts it, "Nature recognizes that God should be worshipped, and there was never any man born who lacked this natural law which orders him to worship" (*Oratio pro Flacco*).[6]

The fact that many people in our day profess no religion or even deny openly that there is any obligation to worship God in no way destroys the validity of this argument. In the first place, many who belong to no church or sect do not thereby necessarily wish to abandon all religion, internal as well as external.[7] Secondly, even those who stubbornly deny the obligation to worship God in any way whatsoever, granted that they may be sincere in their conviction, are still so few that they do not destroy the universal conviction of the human race.[8] No one maintains that man is religious by an inescapable necessity or that the dictates of reason may not be misdirected because of prejudice and passion. Finally, those who have rejected all religion are not particularly noted for virtue, nor are they usually very happy, as is often shown by their falling into spiritualism, or by the fanatical hatred they frequently exhibit against religion.

PROPOSITION 2: *Man is also bound by the natural law to practice some external worship.* This proposition is *certain.*

Religion consists, above all, in the acts of the intellect and will with which we acknowledge and love God's excellence. This is internal worship. A secondary, but nonetheless necessary, part of

5

The idea that somewhere there ought to be found peoples who were naturally atheistic was not the product of scientific research into the history of religion, but the a priori theory of nineteenth century comparative religionists who sought to apply the theory of biological evolution to the field of religion with the utmost rigor. In accord with their a priori reasoning, religion ought to be found in its purest form, monotheism, where man has reached his highest development and in its crudest form where man was very primitive. And somewhere in the dim twilight beyond that stage one might possibly hope to find peoples who were atheistic or totally lacking religion. As a matter of fact, religion as found among the earliest men is monotheistic and quite elevated; only later did it degenerate into such aberrations as fetishism, animism, totemism, magic, etc. See No. 10 of this book, *Scholion*, p. 25.

religion is external worship, or the honor we pay to God through the external actions of our body. Some people who admit in general the obligation to practice religion and consequently the obligation to pay internal worship, make it a point to deny that there is any natural obligation to worship God externally. Man is, however, bound to practice some sort of external worship. The question whether or not man is bound by the natural law alone to practice this or that special act of worship is of no concern here.[9]

6 *Proof of the proposition.* 1. *Worship by its very nature* demands an external expression. The entire man is dependent on God, and so the entire man, not merely his soul, but also his body, ought to take part in acknowledging this dependence. "Worship of God is twofold," says Aquinas, "interior and exterior. Since man is composed of both body and soul, both should take part in the worship of God. The soul should pay interior worship and the body exterior" (*S.Th.*, Ia-IIae, q. 101, a. 2, c.).

It is not hard to see that external worship is necessary *as a means to sustain internal worship.* Man is obliged to pay God the most perfect internal worship he can. It follows that he is also bound to take the means by which those internal acts of religion may be aroused, sustained, and strengthened. But our nature is so constructed that our internal activities are stimulated, strengthened, and rendered more vivid through the motions and actions of our senses.[10] According to St. Thomas:

The human mind, if it is to be joined to God, needs the helping hand of the senses. That is why in divine worship it is necessary to make use of some material things which act as a sort of signpost to stimulate man's mind to those spiritual activities by which it is joined to God. Hence it is that religion looks upon external actions as somewhat secondary and as geared towards the production of interior acts (*S. Th.* IIa-IIae, q. 81, a. 7, c.).

Again he writes:

Men make use of a number of corporeal actions . . . such as prostrations, genuflections, audible cries and songs. We do these things, not because we think that God needs such signs, for God knows all things. We do them for our own sake so that by these corporeal actions our will may be directed towards God and our affections may be kindled; and in so doing we at the same time acknowledge that God is the author of both our soul and body and accordingly render to Him both spiritual and bodily submission (*S.C.G.*, III, 119).

PROPOSITION 3: *Men are obliged by the natural law to offer public worship to God.* This proposition is *certain.*

Men must worship God not only privately, as individuals, but **7** publicly, as members of society. This means that society as such is obliged to worship God. It is evident that this public worship is external. Therefore, the demonstration of this proposition furnishes additional proof for the necessity of external worship. Opponents of this proposition are liberals and, above all, socialists. They both assert that "religion is a private affair," although in practice they frequently attack even private religion with all their power.

Proof of the proposition. Just as its individual members, so society as a whole continues to exist by God's sustaining power, is ruled by God's providence, and totally depends on God. Who would maintain that men are subject to God in their private lives, but not in their social or political lives? Consequently, man as a social being, or society as such, must acknowledge and profess its dependence upon God.

Pope Leo XIII says:

> The very same law of nature and reason which orders men as individuals to honor God in a holy and religious fashion, because we are in His power, and because we must return to Him from whom we have come forth, likewise binds the civil community. For men living in society are no less in God's power than men living as individuals. And society no less than individuals ought to pay thanks to God who is its author and preserver, and from whose generosity it receives the countless goods by which it is enriched (encyclical *Immortale Dei, Allocutions of Leo XIII,* Desclée ed., III, 149).

Scholion. The duty of religion is the most important of all duties and is the foundation of all morality.

1. Reason itself points out that man has duties towards God, **8** towards himself, and towards other men. It must be evident that of all these duties the most important and holiest are those which man owes to God, who is the first cause and last end of all things.

2. Note, also, that religion is the foundation stone of all other duties, the basis of all morality.[11] In fact, once the obligation of

honoring God through subjection to His will is admitted, the other duties of morality find an unshakable basis, the will of God the law-giver, whose authority binds all men. Those who deny either the existence of God or the obligation of serving Him simply cannot find any reason why men should really and strictly be obliged to lead a moral life.[12] Such persons appeal either to the dictates of conscience or civil laws. Their appeal to the dictates of conscience, or to an innate sense of what is decent, or to love of order is futile. Unless conscience be viewed as a sort of herald which makes known the divine law, it can have no real binding force. No one can be obliged to any duty except by a superior. But conscience or reason is not superior to man, since it is but one of his own faculties. Hence, to proclaim that reason is the final court of appeal actually amounts to proclaiming that man is free of any real obligation.[13] Such people also appeal to civil laws. Without mentioning any other arguments, it should be obvious that a merely human legislator who is not sanctioned by divine authority cannot impose any obligation that really deserves the name.

No matter what people may protest to the contrary, to preach a morality cut off from religion, a morality which they call "independent" or "free," amounts in fact to the destruction of the entire moral order.[14] This gives a fresh argument for the necessity of religion: for if it is an evil thing to undermine morality (and the conclusion that morality has no binding force proceeds logically, once religion is excluded), then the basic necessity of religion must never be denied.

It is also untrue to assert that a morality which is dependent on another's will is unbefitting man's dignity. As man cannot be independent in the ontological order, neither can he be so in the moral. But it is one thing to *be dependent* on a supreme legislator, and quite another to fulfill his commands out of *purely slavish fear.*

Notes

1. See DB 2074 ff.

2. F. Paulsen states: "Religion does not spring from the intelligence, nor from logical-metaphysical speculation, nor from the evidence of history; it springs from the heart" (*Philosophia militans*, p. 46). "The intellectual garments in which religion gets dressed up, the conceptual formulae in which philosophy and theology try to corner it, are an injury and a disgrace to religion" (*System der Ethik*, 5th ed., p. 406).

W. Wundt remarks that religion "has not died out of the human soul."

Religion is "nothing but the concrete expression of the moral ideal. The yearnings and challenges, the highest emotional sanctions which man meets with in his consciousness, he sets before himself as a goal, and, still more, as a sort of universal frame of reference in which to interpret the existing world outside himself. Man then divests his religious conceptions of their imaginative force in order to grasp the real meaning of the commands of conscience" (*System der Ethik*, II, 3rd ed., 104).

3. For example, Kant wrote: "I accept the following point as an axiom which needs no demonstration: everything, with the exception of good conduct, which man pretends to do to learn how to become pleasing to God is purely religious-compulsion and sham-service of God" (*Religion innerhalb der Grenzen der Vernunft*, Werke VI, Hartenstein ed., p. 353).

4. M. Serol, *Le besoin et le devoir religieux* (1908). The author does not always correctly distinguish between revealed positive religion and purely natural religion.

5. See L. Roure, "La religion du Dieu Createur ou la place de l'adoration dans la religion," in *Etudes* (1928), 194, 513.

6. See M. Lagrange, "La religion de Cicéron d'après le *De natura deorum*," in ETL (1928), p. 413.

7. A Sabatier: "People confuse hostility directed against an exterior religion, or against a dogma, or against a church, or against a tradition, with atheism and irreligion. Nothing could be more false . . . the only atheist and the only irreligious man is the frivolous man who uses his very frivolity as a cover-all weapon and disguise for a vain and brutal egotism" (*Esquisse d'une philosophie de la Religion*, pp. 27–28).

Against those who assert that knowledge of natural science puts an end to religion, see Kneller, *Das Christentum und die Vertreter der neueren Naturwissenschaft* (1912); Emeyieu, *La part des croyants dans le progrès de la science au XIX siècle* (1920). Emeyieu has "listed the names of 432 scientists of distinction. Setting aside 34 whose religious views are unknown, he tabulates them as follows: Atheists 16; Agnostics, 15; Believers 367. Selecting out of this total some 150 original thinkers and scientific pioneers, he finds among them only 5 Atheists and 9 Agnostics compared with 123 Believers—the views of 13 are unknown" (B. Conway, *The Question Box*, [New York: The Paulist Press, 1929], p. 113).

Sir Bertram Windle, himself a lifelong student of science, has edited a series of biographies of distinguished Catholic scientists (*Twelve Catholic Men of Science*) who found no contradiction in accepting both rational and revealed truth. The twelve scientists are: Linacre, Vesalius, Stensen, Galvani, Laënnec, Müller, Corrigan, Secchi, Mendel, Pasteur, de Lapparent, and Dwight. See Conway, *op. cit.*, p. 144.

A change in the either/or attitude about religion and science, so rampant in the nineteenth century, is strikingly indicated by the president of Harvard University, Dr. Pusey, who pleads for a return of theology to the university as a major science. See "Religion Now" in *Harper's*, December, 1953, and the comment about the article by G. Gustafson in *The Priest*, January, 1954.

No one has better indicated than Pius XII how valuable is the contribution of science to religion when the two work hand in hand. He says: "For [you men of science] by your research, your unveiling of the secrets of nature, and your teaching of men to direct the forces of nature towards their own welfare, you preach at the same time, in the language of figures and formulae and discoveries, the unspeakable harmony of the work of an all-wise God.

"In fact, according to the measure of its progress, and contrary to affirmations advanced in the past, true science discovers God in an ever-increasing degree—as though God were waiting behind every door opened by science. We would even say that from this progressive discovery, which is realized in the increase of knowledge, there flow benefits not only for the scientist himself when he reflects as a philosopher—and how can he escape such reflection?—but also for those who share in these new discoveries or make them the object of their own considerations" (Address to the Pontifical Academy of Science, Nov. 22, 1951, translated in *The Church and Modern Science* [New York: America Press, 1951], p. 31).

For a sample of the opposite mentality still prevailing among a small group of die-hard, anti-religious scientists, still consumed by a nineteenth-century mentality, see Gordon Child, who writes: "For *convenience only* we distinguish magic in which impersonal mystic forces are directly controlled from religion in which the forces are personified, and can therefore be influenced in the same way as men by entreaties or flattery. *But really there is no sharp distinction*. Most rituals are designed also magically to coerce, or at least assist, the gods. That is the sense, for instance, of the numerous ritual dramas and also of the meals and beer given to the gods" (*Man Makes Himself* [New York: The New American Library, Mentor ed., 1951], pp. 178–179; see also pp. 186–187). The same mentality, less blatantly expressed, is found in G. Gaylord Simpson, *The Meaning of Evolution* [New York: The New American Library, Mentor ed., 1951], pp. 132, 135, 179.

8. When we say that such persons are only a handful compared with the whole human race, we mean the human race considered not merely in the twentieth century, some two and one half billion people (see *Information Please Almanac*, 1954, p. 732), but the whole human race considered during the entire span of its existence, variously estimated as somewhere between 50,000 and 500,000 years (see Gordon Child, *op. cit.*, p. 11).

9. St. Thomas solves the objection, "Ceremonial acts are not demanded by natural reason," by the following general answer: "Natural reason does demand that a man do *something* to show reverence for God, but that a man do *precisely this or that* is not demanded by natural reason, but by regulations laid down by divine or human law" (*S. Th.*, IIa-IIae, q. 81, a. 2 ad 3). Elsewhere he teaches that "the offering of sacrifice pertains to natural law" (*Ibid.*, q. 85, a. 1). Perhaps these two viewpoints can be reconciled by saying that the offering of sacrifice is not indeed strictly ordered by the dictates of natural reason, but that it is suggested by it.

10. Conversely, internal sentiments, especially the livelier ones, tend spontaneously to burst forth in external gestures. That is why internal religion, provided it is sincere, will almost necessarily manifest itself through external worship. For just as external worship without internal would be hypocrisy (for one dissimulates what is in reality lacking), so, too, a purely internal worship without any external worship would be crippled, feeble, and contrary to nature.

11. Morality, insofar as it is distinguished from religion, means the sum

total of duties by which a man has obligations towards himself and towards other men, considered both as individuals and as members of society.

12. See Franon, *Les fondements du devoir*, 1916; Beysens, *Ethiek of natuurlijke zedenleer*, I, 582ff. E. Bruneteau, "Peut-il y avoir une morale sans Dieu?" in RPA, XVI (1913), 801–811.

13. Rousseau says: "People would like to establish virtue on purely rational grounds—but in vain; what basis could they offer for it? Virtue, they say, is love of order. But really could such a love of order, in fact should it, take preference in me over the love of my own happiness? Let them give me a reason for preferring love of order to self-love. If God does not exist, the wicked man is the only reasonable man; the good man is really a fool" (*Emile*, I, 4).

Did not Friedrich Nietzsche, by applying to human society "the-struggle-for-life" theory, grant to the superman the right to trample underfoot all weaklings so that he might reach supremacy (*Herren-Moral*)? How savage morality can become when based on the State as its ultimate norm has been tragically illuminated for the modern world by the concentration camps of Nazi Germany and the purge-trials of Soviet Russia. Stalin merely put into practice that perfect disregard of the dignity of the human person uttered in theory by Karl Marx: "If I speak of individuals, it is only insofar as they are personifications of economic categories, and representatives of special class relations and interests" (*Das Kapital*, quoted by R. Mohan, *op. cit.*). Perhaps the most futile attempt to construct a morality apart from religion is that proposed by George Gaylord Simpson, who wishes to use *evolution* as the ultimate basis for morality. After stating: "Man is the result of a purposeless and materialistic process that did not have him in mind. He was not planned. He is a state of matter, a form of life, a sort of animal, and a species of the order of Primates, akin nearly or remotely to all life and indeed to all that is material. It is, however, a gross misrepresentation to say that he is *just* an accident or *nothing but* an animal," he attempts to give some suggestions for a new, relative morality based upon the process of evolution as re-directed by "a species of the order of Primates" (*op. cit.*, p. 179).

14. In practice, the men who have liberated morality from "the props" of religion are usually not outstanding for good morals; still, one should not make too great generalizations in this matter. If actually a number of men manage to lead a morally upright life without the help of religion, they bear out strikingly the observation of A. Balfour: "Biologists tell us of parasites which live and can only live within the bodies of animals more highly organized than they. So it is with those persons. Their spiritual life is parasitic: it is sheltered by convictions which belong, not to them, but to the society of which they form a part; it is nourished by processes in which they take no share. And when those convictions decay, and those processes come to an end, the alien life which they have maintained can scarcely be expected to outlast them" (*Foundations of Belief*, 1895, pp. 82–83).

Article II

THE UNITY OF THE TRUE RELIGION

I. *This Article is directed against those who favor relative indifference in religious matters.*

II. *Preliminary remarks.*

PROPOSITION: The objectively true, legitimate, and good religion is one and the same for all men.

Meaning: Not all religious duties are the same for all men, but those which are absolute and those which are hypothetically universal.

Proof: a. for absolute duties;

b. for hypothetically universal duties.

Scholion: The theory of progressive religious evolution must be rejected.

Article II

THE UNITY OF THE TRUE RELIGION

The point-of-view of those who favor a relative indifference in religious matters is next to be examined. Although such persons concede that there is some obligation to practice religion, or at least admit the usefulness of religion, they assert that all religions are good and legitimate. Some, however, restrict their assertion to cover merely the various forms or sects of Christianity.

They defend their assertion in a variety of ways. Some, among them the Modernists,[1] rest their case on an error previously discussed, namely, that religion is merely a product of psychological sentiment. Furthermore, they assert that a particular form of religion is useful only insofar as it satisfies the needs and aspirations of the human heart. They conclude, logically enough, that any religion is good, at least for its own time and place. When it ceases to satisfy the desires of its adherents, it is cast aside completely or is changed, unless kept alive unjustly by force. Other proponents of religious indifferentism rest their case on the assumption that all truth is relative and, as a consequence, changeable. Finally, others admit that there is only one objectively true religion and that all others are false; but at the same time they maintain the impossibility in practice to distinguish the true religion from the false ones, and hence conclude that all religions are, in practice, good.

However, if one grants that religion rests on an objective foundation which is an objectively true knowledge (natural or supernatural) of God, it follows of necessity that only that religion can be true which teaches the truth about God, about our relations with Him, and our duties toward Him. On the contrary, any system of religion which proposes false teachings on these points, or mingles falsehood with truth, is certainly a false religion. A thing is morally good only if completely good; morally evil, if even partially defective. Precisely insofar as any religion lacks objective truth, to such an extent must it also lack legitimacy and goodness. A religion is legitimate only if it is in harmony with the law, that is, with the will of God; a religion is good only if it worships God as He ought to be worshipped and if its practice tends of its very nature to man s ultimate goal.

Later it will be shown that one can distinguish the true religion from false ones, employing the criteria of revelation. In practice, however, this task of distinguishing the true religion from the false is not an easy matter for everyone. It can happen, and indeed does happen, that some men mistakenly, but sincerely, embrace a false religion as the true one. If such people practice a false religion in good faith, they are acting rightly from a subjective point of view and, all else being equal, can gain merit.*

But, objectively speaking, the religion they profess still remains in itself false, illegitimate, and evil. Here there is no question of establishing precisely just what may be subjectively licit or even obligatory for a man who has innocently fallen into error. The whole aim of this chapter is to determine which is the objectively true religion, the religion which all men are objectively bound to practice and should seek out to the best of their ability.

PROPOSITION: *The objectively true, legitimate, and good religion is one and the same for all men.* This proposition is *certain.*

Explanation. This affirmation of the unity of the true religion does not mean that all religious duties are the same for all men; it deals only with those duties which are absolute and those which are hypothetically universal.

Absolute religious duties are those which necessarily flow from the very nature of God and of man, for example, the obligation of acknowledging that there is but one true God and Lord, and of honoring Him internally by gratitude and love and externally by some sort of worship. These absolute duties are the same, not only for all men of a particular age, but for all men of all times. *Hypothetically universal* duties are those which, granting the existence of the absolute duties, are based upon some fact of

---

* This fact is not denied by the condemnation of proposition 15 of the *Syllabus* of Piux IX: "Every man is free to embrace and profess the religion his reason has led him to believe to be true" (DB 1715). The proposition was condemned *in the sense intended by its author,* F. Vigil, of Peru. He meant that man is not obliged to consider even the possibility of a revelation, and consequently is not obliged to inquire whether any revelation has taken place; but he is free to embrace that religion whose teachings strike him personally as being more in conformity with reason. He may, therefore, safely reject any religion whose intrinsic truthfulness is not easily apparent to himself. See Tosi, *Vorlesungen über den Syllabus,* p. 52; Heiner, *Der Syllabus,* p. 89.

importance for the whole human race. According to Catholic teaching such facts are: the elevation of mankind to a supernatural order; the revelation made by Christ and His Apostles; the foundation of the Catholic Church. Although these hypothetically universal duties are the same for all men, they are not necessarily the same for all ages. They have binding force only since the historical occurrence of the fact upon which they are based. It must be noted, in addition, that there can be, and indeed are, many hypothetically particular duties which pertain to the true religion. These are the duties which rest on some divine or human fact binding, not all men or all societies, but only some men and some societies. Such duties, as is obvious from their very nature, can differ, not only for different ages, but also for different men living in the same time. Thus, for example, had there existed nothing but a purely natural religion, it should have been set up by a legitimate human authority in different ways for diverse peoples. Again, the Mosaic Law was divinely imposed on Israel alone. In the Catholic religion itself, because of varying human factors, particular churches are obliged to particular ritual forms and particular disciplinary laws; clerics and religious have their own special duties proper to their state of life, etc.

Proof of the proposition. 1. In regard to absolute duties. We have stated that these duties are such that they flow from the very nature of God and of man. But neither divine nor human nature changes; hence, it is impossible that the relationships which stem directly out of these natures, and the duties which correspond to these relationships, should be altered.

2. With reference to hypothetically universal duties. From what has been said it is clear that the fact on which these duties rest equally affects all men. It is consequently impossible, once the fact has occurred, that the very duties flowing from that fact should not be the same for all men. For example, is it not obvious that all men, after a revelation has been made which is designed for all men and after God has established a universal religious society, are equally obliged both to accept this revelation by faith and to enter this society?

Scholion. The theory of progressive religious evolution must be 10
rejected. Many people exclude any supernatural activity of God in the world; some, indeed, cast aside any objective foundation for religion. Die-hard evolutionists, they apply the theory of continuous progress even to the field of religion.[2] Such people teach that all

religions which have ever existed or now exist form just so many stages through which the human race moves upward, little by little, to the perfect religion, which is, in their opinion, one purely natural. According to some, the human race is gradually tending to that point at which it will finally be liberated entirely from the "disease" of religion! It is from the same religious instinct, the same religious consciousness, in accordance with differing internal and external circumstances of various peoples, that different religious conceptions, judgments, practices—in a word, different religions, arose. Since these individual religions suited the temperament, culture, and aspirations of their followers, they were judged as legitimate and good in their own time and place; but, objectively, they differed vastly from one another in their degree of perfection. Consequently all founders and reformers of religions, even though their claim to a special mission from God was based on illusion or pious fraud, are equally worthy of praise because each in his own way championed continuous religious progress.[3]

Although various groups of evolutionists have their own pet theories as to precisely which stage of religion (fetishism, magic, animism, totemism, etc.) came first,[4] they are nearly all agreed that humanity was originally more or less atheistic:

> For they argue that man cannot have had any high form of religion when he first emerged from the animal state from which they think man evolved, and they postulate for man a pre-logical existence, when he could have had no conception of a deity at all (From *Social Origins* by Eva J. Ross, published 1937 by Sheed and Ward, Inc., New York, p. 71).

Since there is neither space nor time to trace out these divergent evolutionary theories in detail, it must suffice to examine, merely as a sample, the once popular theory which held fetishism to be the initial stage of religious evolution. The other theories follow the same thought pattern, but eliminate or vary some of the stages in the total process.

The road traveled by the human race according to the fetishistic theory was roughly this: after a period in which no religion at all existed, or only some barbaric form of religion as yet undiscovered, there arose first fetishism. In fetishistic religion a number of particular material objects,[5] a particular boulder, or shell, or tooth, were thought to possess personality or at least mysterious powers and as a consequence came to be worshipped. Next came animism.[6] Man, becoming conscious of his own soul, began to attribute souls to all nature, animate and inanimate. Thus he began to worship souls or spirits which he believed to be residing in things such as the moon, or the wind, or a local mountain. After that arose totemism. In totemistic religion various classes of animals like bears, or eagles, or snakes, were thought to have some sort of hereditary link with a particular group or clan of people. They thought that their ancestors either descended from the animal or at least had some special connection with it. The animal thus exemplified some trait like bravery or cunning which they associated with their own clan. The clan, therefore, held the animal in reverence and gradually came to worship it.*

Then came schamanism. The schamani, or magic-working priests, sought to placate for a time spiritual beings which were hostile to mankind. Next came polytheism. Then dualism, which acknowledged a twofold principle behind all reality, one good and the other evil, one light and other darkness. Finally, there arose monotheism which some present-day prophets predict will finally give way to atheistic monism.

After the discussion in preceding sections, it will scarcely be 10a necessary to point out how far this theory of progressive religion is removed from the truth.

a. It gratuitously and wrongly rejects the existence or even the possibility of a revelation.

b. If one admits the objective validity of human knowledge, it is asinine to maintain that all religions are legitimate; for it is

---

* More recent writers, as a matter of fact, stress the essential differences and real opposition between both animism and totemism on the one hand and religion on the other, even though the two may be found side by side in the same culture. Sir James Frazer, the outstanding authority on totemism, expressly admits: "Pure Totemism is not in itself a religion at all; for the totems as such are not worshipped, they are in no sense deities, they are not propitiated with prayer and sacrifice. To speak therefore of a worship of totems pure and simple, as some writers do, is to betray a serious misapprehension of the facts" (*Totemism and Exogamy*, 4th ed. (1910), p. 27, cited in E. C. Messenger, *Studies in Comparative Religion*, I, no. 1 (1934), 12). W. Schmidt asserts the same opposition between totemism, magicism, and animism on the one hand and religion on the other: "The spiritualism of the totemistic, magic-working men can in fact be directly contrasted with religion, can even be considered hostile to religion; for where true religion is practiced, magic is, whether instinctively or consciously, always felt to be at the opposite pole, and as such to be avoided and even persecuted" (*The Religion of the Primitives*, cited in Messenger, *op. cit.*, I, no. 3, 18).

evident that in many and even most fundamental doctrines they mutually contradict one another. It does not help matters to make a comparison between the variety of religions and the variety of languages, which latter, though varied in their perfection, are all nonetheless good. A comparison can indeed be drawn between various languages, or systems of arbitrary signs selected to express ideas, and religious *rites* and *ceremonies* which are themselves for the most part arbitrary signs, capable of determination now one way and now another by competent authority. For just as the same truth may be expressed by diverse sounds and words, so the same teaching and the same religious emotions can be symbolized by various religious rites. But the essential meaning of religious teachings is a different case entirely. Unless these teachings express the relationship actually obtaining between God and man, they are false and unprovable. The same sort of distinction suffices to dissolve another analogy frequently used: namely, that just as a ruler is pleased if his subjects honor him in diverse ways, so too God is pleased by a variety of religions! Would a ruler really be pleased if his subjects exhibited the honor due to himself to pretenders, or if false ideas of his government were spread among his people, or if the court ceremonial sanctioned by himself were omitted or despised? Granted that his subjects acted in good faith, a ruler could accept the intention of those who are mistaken, but he would not approve the false veneration in itself.

c. The evolution of religion, such as is proposed by disciples of progressive religion, is not the result of patient historical inquiry, but the bald assumption of an atheistic theory of evolution. As a matter of fact, intense, modern, scientific research into the question has boomeranged against the evolutionist theory of religion. Beginning with the work of Andrew Lang, *The Making of Religion* (1908), down to the monumental work of W. Schmidt, *Der Ursprung der Gottesidee* (1912–49), numerous scholars [7] have completely demolished this quaint nineteenth-century theory of religion's slow upward rise through a series of steady surges. Actually, religion as found among the earliest men is monotheistic and quite elevated; it is only in later stages of culture that it degenerated into the perverted forms labeled fetishism, animism, manism, totemism, and so on.

If we now glance back over the whole picture of man's oldest religion, as we have been able to draw it by means of the

historical correlation of Ethnology and Prehistory, we are immediately impressed by the strong contrast between our findings
on the one hand and the *a priori theorisings* of the old progressive evolutionists on the other.

The development of religion must have started from inferior
beginnings, it was affirmed; but moral monotheism appeared to
them as an intrinsically high form of religion, as indeed it is;
therefore, the *a priori* argument ran, this could only be the
result of a long and complicated development, which finally
produced monotheism in the latest times. *In actual fact, however, it is just in the oldest stages of culture that we find monotheism pure and simple* whereas . . . it is precisely in the later
cultural stages that monotheism recedes further and further
before the onrush of naturism, animism, manism, magicism
(W. Schmidt, "The Religion of Earliest Man," in Messenger's
Studies in Comparative Religion, I, 25).

When one considers the additional fact that there exist widely
diffused traditions among the primitives which stress some sort of
communication with God as the starting point of their religion, the
Catholic thesis about the original monothesim of the human race
(which is accepted on the basis of divine revelation), far from
being in conflict with natural scientific investigation, is corroborated
by it.

Some scholars, indeed, are so impressed by the nobility and
purity of the religious concepts found among primitive peoples
that they feel no sufficient explanation can be given for such nobility except by postulating some sort of primordial revelation.

To what can we trace back the immemorial faith in God? All
are agreed that our primitive races have not invented or evolved
it on their own. Nor do they claim that their forebears did so.
They only say that the latter handed on this belief to them
together with many other things. What was the source from
which those forebears drew their knowledge? . . .

. . . Is it not highly improbable that the least developed and
mentally most primitive beings should by the unaided light of
their own intelligence have been able to recognize, and even
to a certain extent to define, the purpose of man's existence
and that of the world surrounding him? We may well doubt it.
We *must* even do so, when we consider how comparatively
uniform as regards fundamentals is the religion of all these
primitive peoples. Were we dealing with knowledge acquired

by human efforts in the course of time, then these correspond-
ences would indeed be hard to explain; and since, as we have
seen, there can be no question of later borrowing, we are left
no choice but to place the origin of these religious conceptions
far back, somewhere near the beginning of our race, and to
acknowledge that the lofty purity by which they are characterized can hardly be conceived as the result of simple human
endeavour (From *Primitive Man and His World Picture* by
Wilhelm Koppers, published 1952 by Sheed and Ward, Inc.,
New York, pp. 181–184).

With J. Ridderbos we may rightly conclude:

Contrary to the law of evolution, Holy Scripture shows us
another law, namely, that the first light enkindled by God was
darkened more and more through the sin of man, but through
God's grace grew into greater clarity; and so is unfolded before
our eyes the great world-drama, the history of God and man
developing and progressing, not from polydemonism into monotheism, or even from animal to man, but from the first to the
second Adam, from the earthly Paradise to the heavenly
(*Studien*, 85 [1916], 516).

Notes

1. See DB 2077, 2082, 2083.
2. See DB 2094.
3. And thus Christ our Lord, *who is, over all things, God blessed forever*
(Rom. 9:5), is put into the same category with Confucius, Gautama, Mohammed, and Luther. The theory explained above is followed, if not completely,
at least for the most part, by numerous Protestant theologians who are
described as modern. And these theologians, in order to deceive Christian
people, continue to use the term "revelation," and to describe Moses and the
Prophets as "messengers from God," and to call Christ "the Son of God and
Redeemer of the world," but all the while they give a new meaning to the
traditional terms.
4. Fetishism (De Brosses, A. Comte, Sir John Lubbock); Magic (Sir
James Frazer); Animism (E. B. Tylor, R. R. Marett); Manism (H. Spencer);
Totemism (McLennan, S. Reinach, Robertson Smith, Durkeim, Freud); Nature
myths (W. Schwartz, A. Kuhn, M. Müller, B. Bréal). See W. Schmidt, *Primitive Revelation* (1939), "Theories as to the Origin of Religion," pp. 116–124·
E. Ross, *Social Origins* (1937), pp. 71–95.
5. E. Haeckel considered the Catholic veneration given to relics and
images a vestige of fetishism!
6. The concepts of *animism* and *totemism* are not as yet perfectly defined
and are understood by some in one way and by others in another. See Prat,
La science de la religion et du langage d'après Max Müller, p. 18; Al.

Borchert, *Der Animismus oder Ursprung und Entwicklung der Religion aus dem Seelen-Ahnen und Geisterkult* (1900); Th. Mainage, *Les religions de la Préhistoire* (1921).

7. In addition to Schmidt, the works of Pinard de Boullaye, W. Koppers, E. C. Messenger, A. Leroy, E. Eyre, J. M. Cooper, R. H. Lowie, Mänchen-Helfen, and numerous others, are quite valuable. For a discussion of the various pioneers in the field of historical ethnology, see W. Koppers, *Primitive Man and His World Picture* (1952), pp. 9–41.

CHAPTER II

Revealed Religion

REVELATION IS POSSIBLE, NECESSARY, AND RECOGNIZABLE

Article I
REVELATION IS POSSIBLE

I. *Notion of Revelation: the Disclosure of Truth Made by God to Man Beyond the Normal Course of Nature.*

II. *Divisions of Revelation:*
   a. private and public;
   b. mediate and immediate;
   c. modally supernatural and essentially supernatural.

III. *Notion of a Mystery: a Truth which by Its Very Nature Lies Completely Beyond the Grasp of Unaided Human Reason.*

IV. *Division of Mysteries:*
   a. relative;
   b. strict.

Corollary.

PROPOSITION 1: It is possible to have some sort of revelation.
   Proof: 1. It does not involve a contradiction on God's part.
   2. It does not involve a contradiction on man's part.
   Some objections answered.

PROPOSITION 2: A revelation containing mysteries is possible.
   Proof: Arguments essentially the same in nature as those used in proving Proposition 1.
   Some objections answered.

PROPOSITION 3: Mediate revelation is possible.
   Proof: Arguments essentially the same in nature as those used in proving Proposition 1.
   Scholion: The suitability of mediate revelation.

(33)

CHAPTER II

Revealed Religion

---

11   It has been already demonstrated that the natural law itself obliges man to practice religion and that the true religion is necessarily one and the same, in the sense described above, for all men. From these facts it follows that man is bound in conscience to search diligently for the true religion, and to make use of the proper means to find it. Since the duty of practicing religion is the greatest of all duties, the obligation to seek the true religion is a very serious one.

If a religion is presented which, with some real plausibility claims to be revealed by God, men must investigate that religion seriously and embrace it, should its claims be proved. For man must practice that religion which God has taught and prescribed by positive revelation.

Before undertaking the direct proof of Christian revelation, it will be necessary to discuss the views of those who assert that a supernatural revelation is impossible, useless, or unknowable.

These opponents of Christian doctrine, however else they may differ, agree in maintaining that human reason is the only yardstick for measuring truth and falsehood. In consequence, these men declare that nothing above nature is knowable. They are usually called rationalists, naturalists, and Modernists.*

Article I

REVELATION IS POSSIBLE

12 ## I. Notion of Revelation

Revelation, a word derived from a Latin verb meaning "to remove a veil," has the general sense of making known some truth to another. In an active sense it is the operation whereby someone

* Strictly speaking, naturalists teach that nothing beyond the order of nature *exists;* rationalists teach that nothing beyond the order of nature *is knowable.* Most of the time, however, the terms are used synonymously. Modernists, in clinging to the tenets of agnosticism, completely eliminate any

discloses a truth to another; in an objective sense it is the truth disclosed. When theologians use the term, they always mean a divine revelation: the disclosure of a truth by God to an intelligent creature, particularly to man.

God can bring a truth to man's attention in two ways:

1. *Naturally.* This is done through the creation of the visible universe and the gift of intelligence. Such a manifestation of truth is called *natural revelation.* Since God is the author both of man's intellectual powers and of the created universe from which man draws his knowledge, it is not absurd to say that He reveals the truths which are acquired by the use of natural powers. Nevertheless, in speaking of a natural revelation, the term "revelation" is used only analogously. Natural revelation and supernatural revelation may not be compared with one another as though they were species of one and the same genus.[1]

2. *Supernaturally,* in a way to which man has no right. Such a revelation is accomplished by a communication which completely transcends the normal course of nature. This is a *supernatural revelation,* and it alone is truly worthy of the name revelation. Supernatural [2] revelation may be defined as *the disclosure of truth made by God * to man beyond the normal course of nature.*[3]

II. Divisions of Revelation

Revelation may be divided as follows:

1. **Private and public.** This is based on a consideration of the people for whom the revelation is intended. A private revelation

revelation, strictly so-called, by entirely perverting its genuine concept. (See DB 2072.) For an excellent short treatment of the basic principles, spirit, and evil consequences of rationalism and naturalism, see Garrigou-Lagrange, *De revelatione,* v. I, 4th ed. (1944), VII, "De rationalismo seu naturalismo in genere," 206–218.

* When God is said to speak to men, this should not be so crudely misinterpreted as to mean that God, who is pure spirit, uses a mouth or tongue. On the other hand, this phrase should not be interpreted merely metaphorically. God is described as "speaking" by an analogy of proper proportionality: as human speech is related to its proper effect, so is divine revelation related to its proper effect. (See Garrigou-Lagrange, *De revelatione,* I, p. 142.) To put it more simply, God is said to speak because He can produce in the listener the ordinary effects of human speech. (See Yelle and Fournier, *Apologetica,* p. 255; *S.Th.,* IIa-IIae, q. 173, a. 2.) In this way it is clear that revelation does not do violence to God's immutability: "It should be noted that *active* revelation is the divine action *formally immanent in God,* namely, the divine essence, and at the same time *virtually transient* insofar as it produces an effect outside of God" (Garrigou-Lagrange, *op. cit.,* I, p. 158).

is one destined for one or several individuals; a public revelation is one destined for a society.

2. **Immediate and mediate.** This is based on the manner in which the revelation is made known. An immediate revelation is one given to a person directly without the intervention of any other man (although an angel may be an intermediary agent); a mediate revelation is given to men indirectly through some other man appointed as a messenger by God for this purpose.

3. **Modally supernatural** (*supernaturale quoad modum*) **and essentially supernatural** (*supernaturale quoad substantiam*). This is based on the type of truth revealed. If the truths revealed do not by their very nature transcend the comprehension of reason, it is at least physically possible for man to discover their existence without the aid of a revelation. Then the revelation is supernatural only in the manner in which the truths are made known. This is called modally supernatural. If, on the other hand, a revelation lays down positive commandments or regulations which do not necessarily stem from the relationship between God and man, or truths of the intellectual order completely transcending the grasp of reason (mysteries), such a revelation is not only modally but also intrinsically supernatural. This is called essentially supernatural revelation.[4]

III. The Notion of Mystery

14   A mystery, in the popular sense of the term, means something hidden. In theological usage it denotes a *truth which by its very nature lies completely beyond the grasp of unaided human reason.*

Completely: There are many things, such as light, electricity, atomic energy, the attributes of God, whose existence are known without a perfect understanding of their nature and manner of operation. These truths are in a relative sense beyond the grasp of our intelligence, but they are not, at least in the theological sense, mysteries.[5]

By its very nature: Consequently, truths which are only accidentally, or because of some external obstacle, beyond the grasp of our knowledge should not be considered mysteries. Such truths would be, for example, the exact number of the stars or the grains of wheat in a field.

In addition to this, there are some truths that completely and by their very nature transcend the powers of human reason only with regard to their existence. Others are beyond the grasp of reason, both with regard to their existence and their essence (their intrinsic possibility).

A truth whose existence cannot be known with certitude without a revelation, but whose intrinsic possibility may be positively grasped at least after revelation, is called a relative mystery (*mysterium secundum quid*). Such truths are exemplified in the existence of angels, the creation of the world, and the last judgment. To this category may be added divine commandments and regulations which depend exclusively on God's free choice, over and above the natural order of things. Examples of this are the choice of a special day, the Sabbath, for the fulfillment of the third commandment, or the institution of the Church as a perfect and infallible society (also called second-class mysteries).

A truth whose existence cannot be known without revelation and whose intrinsic possibility (the intrinsic harmony of its various elements) cannot be positively comprehended even after its revelation is called a strict mystery (*mysterium simpliciter*).[6] Such, for example, are the mysteries of the Blessed Trinity and the mystery of the real presence of our Lord in the Eucharist.

The qualification "positively comprehended" is important. It is one thing to see the harmony of the various factors involved, and quite another not to see any necessary disharmony among them. In the latter instance, we grasp, in a negative way, that the thing is possible. Since a mystery, though above reason, does not contradict reason, its possibility can be grasped in such a manner. In other words, reason cannot demonstrate that there is any intrinsic contradiction involved in the concepts expressing the meaning of the mystery. If a contradiction were involved, obviously there would be not a mystery, but rather an absurdity. But if, as a matter of fact, a mystery implies no contradiction, reason cannot discover any.

Corollary:

1. No mystery, whether first- or second-class, can be discovered by reason without a revelation, or demonstrated by reason even after its existence has been revealed. If reason, on purely rational grounds, could ever demonstrate with coercive arguments that a revealed truth simply had to be so, such a truth, strictly speaking, could also be discovered by reason.[7]

2. A strict mystery (*mysterium simpliciter*) can neither be

discovered by reason, nor demonstrated, nor completely comprehended even after its revelation.

15 PROPOSITION 1: *It is possible to have some sort of revelation.* This
proposition is *of faith (de fide).*

This proposition defends the possibility of revelation in general
and, consequently, the possibility of that type of revelation which
presents the least difficulties. Such a revelation would be one that
is immediate and only modally supernatural. This would amount
to no more than a fresh promulgation of natural religion and the
natural law.

This proposition was declared a dogma of faith by the Vatican
Council: "If anyone should say that it is impossible or unbecoming
for man to be instructed about God, or the worship due God, by
means of a revelation, let him be anathema" (DB 1807).

16   *Proof:* A revelation about religion and the natural law could
only be called impossible if it involved a contradiction on the part
of God, or on the part of man. But:

1. It involves no contradiction on the part of God. Certainly
God lacks neither perfect knowledge of the natural law, nor the
power to communicate His knowledge to men in a supernatural
way. Furthermore, He can do this in such a way that man can be
certain he is being instructed by God. Such a revelation would
have a goal worthy of Gods wisdom. Even though it is physically
possible for man to learn the truths under discussion without a
revelation, a revelation would make them known more easily and
more definitely, and the commandments would carry more weight.
Furthermore, God would manifest His goodness in a new way and
would Himself be honored greatly by the closer union of man with
God which would result. At the same time, a revelation does not
demand, to prevent its being superfluous, that a nature lack any
perfection rightly its own, but simply that the nature be capable
of additional perfection. Finally, if it is no offense to the *majesty*
of God to create man and even microscopic animals, such as
amoebae and paramecia, by what right may rationalists declare
that it is unworthy for God Himself to instruct man?

2. Revelation involves no contradiction on the part of man.
Since it is normal for man to learn many truths through human
teachers rather than through his own discovery, it is obvious
that to have God as his teacher, who possesses infinite knowledge
and authority, offers no insult to man's dignity. If it is no disgrace

for a man to believe other men, why would it be a disgrace for him to believe God? It is not true to say that the human soul, in receiving a revelation, is unnaturally reduced to absolute passivity,[8] since the ideas which God communicates by His immediate action require the concurrence of the act of human intelligence.

Some Objections Answered:

Some object that revelation destroys the autonomy and independence of reason.[9] But it is absurd to speak of reason—a power that always operates in a necessary manner, being determined either by its proper object or by the will—as autonomous. If the objection means that the human will is so autonomous that it is not obliged to move the intelligence to consent to a revelation which it knows has definitely come from God, such a conception of the autonomy of the will must simply be rejected.[10]

Others object that a revelation interferes with the continuous evolution of human knowledge. Still, God, who causes all things to take place in an orderly fashion, gave His revelation in such wise that by His gentle providence He disposed and prepared the human race to receive it. Do not even the rationalists seek to explain the whole history of the Mosaic, Prophetic, and Christian revelation by a natural evolution? They try in vain; but even so, attempts of this kind would not even be possible if God, in revealing, had in no way taken into account the aptitude, the aspirations, and the circumstances of those who were to receive His revelation.

PROPOSITION 2: *A revelation containing mysteries is possible.*

This proposition, insofar as it covers a revelation which is essentially supernatural, has been defined as a *dogma of faith* by the Vatican Council:

> If anyone says that man cannot be raised by God to a knowledge and perfection that is above his natural capacity, but can and ought to arrive finally at the possession of all truth and goodness by the exercise of his own powers and without any interference, let him be anathema (DB 1808).

By the term "mysteries" is here meant whatever is divinely added over and above natural religion and the natural law. Hence, commandments which depend exclusively on God's free will, second-class mysteries, and first-class mysteries are included. There is *a priori* certitude that some second-class mysteries can exist, for

17

who would contend that God can make no free decrees? And such decrees could not be known unless they were revealed.

A posteriori, that is, from the very data of revelation, we know that mysteries of the first class actually exist; here we maintain simply one point: no one can prove *a priori* that such mysteries are impossible. In what possible way could reason show that there cannot be any reality in God which completely transcends the grasp of our reason? Is not God an infinite Being whose nature is known only analogically and very imperfectly? Additional force is added to this argument by the consideration that many facts about finite realities, whose existence is known naturally, remain obscure to men of the highest intelligence even after prolonged study.

18

Proof: Since the arguments adduced in the preceding thesis can be easily applied here, it will be enough simply to dissolve the difficulties which rationalists oppose to the revelation of mysteries, especially the revelation of first-class mysteries.

Some Objections Answered:

1. There cannot be any mysteries or truths which completely exceed the grasp of the human intellect, because the object of the intellect is all being, all truth.

The object of the human intellect is indeed all being, but a distinction is required. All being is the object of the human intellect if a proportion exists between the being and the intellect, or if the being is suitably presented. In this sense, the objection is valid. But if one of the two conditions mentioned is lacking, the objection has no force. In the present life the only realities which are proportioned to the human intellect are corporeal things, together with such knowledge as can be gleaned from them. There is no argument to prove that from corporeal reality one can gain the knowledge of all truth.[11]

2. Mysteries are said to be above reason; actually, they are contrary to reason. Everyone grants that mysteries are not suitable subject-matter for reason. Consequently, mysteries must be unsuitable for, or contrary to, reason.

Mysteries are not positively suitable for reason in the sense that reason can discover, or demonstrate, or completely comprehend them. Granted. But it does not follow that they are in consequence positively unsuitable, or contrary to reason in the sense that reason can find in them an obvious contradiction.

3. The revelation of a mystery is a contradiction in terms: to

reveal means "to remove a veil," but the Vatican Council states that even after revelation mysteries "remain covered with a veil and wrapped . . . with a kind of darkness" (DB 1796).

In the revelation of a mystery the veil is moved aside far enough to make known the existence of the reality, but not far enough to disclose the intrinsic possibility of that reality. This distinction dissolves the sophism: a mystery cannot be revealed, otherwise it would cease to be a mystery.

4. The Author of reason does not want us to abdicate reason. Any man, however, who assents to propositions that are neither proved nor provable does abdicate reason; but it is just such propositions that are called mysteries.[12]

The statement, "mysteries are propositions which are neither proved nor provable," can be understood in different ways. The proposition in its correct sense means that mysteries cannot be proved by internal arguments in such a way that their truth is clearly apparent to reason. It is false to extend it to the sense that mysteries cannot be proved by external arguments, testimony historically certain and eminently trustworthy: divine testimony. To acknowledge obscure truths on trustworthy testimony is not to abdicate reason, but to follow it.

> For just as an ordinary man would be very stupid to assert that facts proposed to him by a philosopher were false solely on the grounds that he could not personally grasp them, so too a man would be guilty of an even greater stupidity who would suspect truths revealed by God to be false solely on the grounds that they could not be investigated by reason (St. Thomas, S.C.G., I, 3).

Nor is it correct to think that only practical truths, or rules for practical living, can be imposed by external authority, and not truths of the intellectual order:

> Man totally depends on God, his Creator and Lord, and created reason is completely subject to uncreated Truth. Consequently, we are obliged to offer to God, when He speaks, the complete homage of our intelligence and will by an act of faith (DB 1789).

Insofar as the modern mind shuns this obligation, it refuses to God a homage that is naturally due Him.

5. God does not do anything useless. But it would be useless to 18a

(41)

teach men propositions which offer no meaning that is intelligible. However, it is propositions of this nature that are called mysteries.

It is one thing for the truth of a proposition to be imperfectly clear to the mind, and quite another for a proposition to offer no meaning of an intelligible character, that is, for a proposition to be utterly devoid of meaning. The first case occurs whenever the fitness of a given subject to a given predicate cannot be seen. This certainly is the case whenever there is at least a first-class mystery. The second instance of unintelligibility would occur only if the very concepts themselves, in the subject and predicate, or in either one of them, were *purely negative*. The concepts in which mysteries are couched, since they are derived from created reality which only imperfectly mirrors divine realities, are indeed analagous concepts, and hence positive-negative concepts,* but they are far from being purely negative.[13]

Even though such concepts cannot be perfectly adequate, they are still distinct enough and clear enough to be distinguished correctly

---

* See Jacques Maritain, *Formal Logic*. The imperfection of analogical knowledge is beautifully expressed by Gutberlet in these words:

> Analogous ideas are like silhouettes. If we could not gaze upon the actual world itself, but had to arrive at an understanding of it by means of shadows cast by real objects and from the positions and mutual inter-relations of those shadows, how many facts of the real world would have to remain unknown to us? Anything that failed to cause a change in the shape and size of the shadows would completely escape us. Many other facts would be quite bewildering to us, as the penetration of one shadow into another: this phenomenon would lead us to deny the incompenetra-bility of bodies (*Lehrbuch der Apologetik*, II, 2nd ed., 18).

Nevertheless, projected shadows do exhibit at least some likeness to the bodies they represent and some likeness of the relationship of these bodies to one another. Think, for example, of the shadows cast by a tall man leading his small daughter by the hand. Even from shadows we can glimpse at least some knowledge, however imperfect, of the bodies themselves. This example may help us to grasp how completely different is an analogical idea from a mere algebraic symbol which exhibits no likeness at all to the thing symbolized, and thus cannot produce any knowledge of the thing in itself.

For a good, brief statement of the role of analogy in metaphysical knowl-edge see Gerald B. Phelan, *St. Thomas and Analogy*. For a much fuller treat-ment of the same subject see James Anderson, *The Bond of Being;* Cajetan, *Scripta philosophica, De nominum analogia* (ed. P. Zammit, Rome, 1934).

For the role of analogy in theology see T. Penido, *Le rôle de l'analogie en théologie dogmatique;* Garrigou-Lagrange, *The One God*, pp. 382–415; J. de Rohellec, "Cognitio nostra analogica de Deo," in *Divus Thomas* (Plac.), 1927, pp. 298ff; A. Ferland, *Commentarium in Summam D. Thomae, De Deo Uno et Trino* (1943), pp. 112–117; P. Parente, *De Deo Uno et Trino*, 2nd ed. (1943), pp. 56–58; T. Penido, "Sur l'analogie des noms divins: L'analogie métaphorique," in RSR, 38 (July-December, 1952), 161–188. An excellent diagram of the various types of analogy is found in Parente, *op. cit.*, p. 57.

one from another. It is not true to say that the content of such concepts is reducible to mere metaphor or to anthropomorphism. For the reality that is expressed, when purified of the imperfections inherent in analogous concepts, is genuinely verified in God formally, or according to its proper definition, although in a more eminent way.

Thus, even in mysteries we grasp the meaning of the proposition, or that which is proposed for us to believe, in such a way that we are able to express the mystery in correct terms and distinguish it from every other proposition. Since we are certain, by reason of God's testimony, that the subject and predicate do not contradict each other, we truly grasp, through the revelation of a mystery, a truth that is not otherwise accessible to us.

Nor is knowledge of this sort completely useless to mankind.

a. It is true that mysteries, since they cannot be positively understood or demonstrated from the principles of reason, even after revelation, are not known scientifically through their causes. Even though it is better to understand a truth than merely to know of its existence, still, knowledge of the latter type should not be despised, since "even a very imperfect knowledge of realities which are themselves sublime bestows on the soul a very high degree of perfection" (S.C.G., I, 5).

b. It is also true that mysteries cannot be incorporated into the system of any science. Nonetheless, they do not contradict any science, nor do they split [14] the human mind into two contradictory compartments. Leaving intact all the truths which human intelligence can master by its own power, mysteries go on to instruct man in matters which exceed his natural capacity.

c. Even if it were true that mysteries do not contribute anything to the advancement of the sciences, this would prove nothing against the usefulness of their revelation.[15] God did not give His revelation for the sake of scientific progress; He gave it for the sake of religious progress. By the revelation of mysteries man is led to a deeper knowledge of the majesty and goodness of God, and this promotes reverence, gratitude, and love toward Him. One need but consider the mysteries of the Trinity, the Incarnation, the Redemption, and the Holy Eucharist.

PROPOSITION 3: *Mediate revelation is possible.* This proposition is *certain.* 19

Since a number of rationalists attack particularly that type of revelation which is called mediate, in which truths destined for a nation or for the whole human race are revealed directly to only a few men who then communicate them to the others in the name, and by the authority, of God, it is necessary to demonstrate *ex professo* the possibility of mediate revelation (either modally or essentially supernatural).

The possibility of a mediate revelation will be dependent upon the condition that God clearly marks such a revelation with definite characteristics to signify its divine origin. The nature of these characteristics will be described shortly.

20 *Proof:* The possibility of mediate revelation must be granted, unless it is intrinsically contradictory either to God's nature or to man's nature. But:

1. It involves no contradiction on God's part. Who could deny that God has the right to appoint a number of men to act as His messengers and agents in instructing other men in religious matters? Who could deny that God has the power to provide for the incorrupt preservation of that revealed doctrine even through long centuries, and to make that doctrine exhibit unmistakable signs of its divine origin?

We cannot say that God, if He willed to make a revelation, would be obliged by His own wisdom and goodness to teach individual men immediately and directly, because a mediate revelation would spread throughout the world only very slowly, and would also be rejected by many. Even though arguments of this sort show that immediate revelation is preferable to mediate on this point, it still remains true that even mediate revelation is a magnificent gift of God. God is not bound, especially when it is a question of supernatural gifts, to select the better gifts.[16] As for those who, without fault of their own, refuse to acknowledge a mediate revelation, either because it has not yet been propagated in their countries, or for other good reasons, they do not thereby merit punishment. Even if a great number of men were to reject such a revelation through their own fault, the error could not be ascribed to God. From another point of view there are good reasons, worthy of divine wisdom, why God should prefer to make a mediate rather than an immediate revelation. Notice, too, that the difficulty alleged on the score of the slow spread of a mediate revelation would definitely not hold true of a revelation granted by God to the first parents of the human race—if God did grant such a revelation.

2. It does not involve a contradiction on man's part. On the one hand, human beings are capable of acting as messengers in communicating to other men truths received from God. That holds true even of mysteries. On the other hand, men are usually docile enough to accept instruction from other men, even in matters pertaining to God. This should be clear from the very ease with which the most diverse peoples have, as a matter of fact, accepted religious doctrines from men who claimed, rightly or wrongly, to have a divine mission. Nor would it be impossible for men to have moral certitude (which suffices in matters of this kind) about the divine origin of a mediate revelation, in the supposition that God had sealed it with His own trademark. Finally, mediate revelation involves no contradiction, simply because we receive a doctrine from men and are obliged to believe God; for the men in this instance do no more than propose divine doctrine on divine authority.[17]

Scholion: The suitability of mediate revelation.   21

Mediate revelation is not only possible, but also quite suitable. Three reasons will suffice to show this:

a. By a mediate revelation God follows the same procedure He employs in natural affairs. Just as God makes use of secondary causes to produce a vast number of natural events which He Himself could directly produce, so, too, in the hypothesis of mediate revelation, some men would communicate divine truth to others. On this point St. Thomas says:

> Since God always acts in an orderly fashion, it was fitting that He manifest the truths of the faith in an orderly manner; namely, that some men should receive these truths from God directly, and that others should be instructed by these in their turn, and so on in an orderly manner even to the very last (*S.C.G.*, III, 154).

b. By a mediate revelation a supernatural religious society springs up connaturally and spontaneously, whereas in the hypothesis of a revelation made directly to every individual no such religious society would necessarily result. Men could indeed, even in this latter hypothesis, be joined together by certain sacred bonds, but the union would be both less natural and less binding.

c. By a mediate revelation the door is opened for a far wider opportunity to exercise the virtues of humility and obedience in accepting the revealed doctrine, and of charity in making it known to others.

Notes

1. The Reformation denied that there was any natural revelation, but it did not deny supernatural revelation. Rationalists, if they use the term "revelation," always mean by it natural revelation in accord with the dictum of A. Schopenhauer: "There is no other revelation than the thoughts of a wise man" (*Parerga*, II, no. 177). To the Modernists revelation means nothing more than a man's experimental consciousness of his relationship to God (see DB 2020).

2. The customary definition of the supernatural includes everything that exceeds or surpasses the essence, needs, and powers of any created being. The supernatural must not be confused with: a. whatever surpasses the power of the senses and can be reached only by reason; b. any sort of teaching about God, for God can be known by the unaided reason; c. anything that is contrary to nature; for what is unnatural destroys or injures nature, whereas the supernatural perfects nature beyond its needs.

3. It makes no difference whether the signs God uses to manifest a truth directly affect the external senses, the imagination, or the intelligence: corporeal, imaginative, intellectual revelation. Regardless of the means God uses in making a revelation, He not only manifests a truth, but also makes those receiving the revelation absolutely sure that the truth(s) communicated come from God. See *S.Th.*, IIa-IIae, q. 173, a. 2. Many authors prefer a definition which states more clearly that the disclosure of truth is caused by a formal utterance on God's part, so as to exclude creation, miracles, infused knowledge, and the beatific vision. See Van Laak, *De theologia generatim,* p. 2; Mannens, *Theologia fundamentalis,* 2nd ed., p. 32; W. Wilmers, *De religione revelata,* p. 47; Garrigou-Lagrange, *De revelatione,* I, pp. 132, 135, 136; G. Yelle and R. Fournier, *Apologetica* (1944), Art. I, "An recte revelatio dicatur locutio Dei?," 254–256; M. Nicolau and J. Salaverri, *Sacrae theologiae summa,* I, 2nd ed. (1952), 93, no. 53, and 96–97, no. 58.

4. Some authors refer to a revelation which is only modally supernatural (*supernaturale quoad modum tantum*) as *formal* revelation, and to an intrinsically supernatural revelation (*supernaturale quoad substantiam*) as *material* revelation.

5. See M. Gossard, "Le mystère religieux et le mystère scientifique" in RPA, XIII (1912), 344. Van Laak, *op. cit.,* p. 20, describes the opinions of those who either deny the existence of mysteries or pervert the concept of mysteries.

6. To put the same thing another way we can say: a mystery loosely so-called exists when reason cannot see that the predicate is actually in harmony with the' subject; a mystery strictly so-called exists when reason not only does not see the actual harmony of the subject and predicate but also cannot see how the predicate could be in harmony with the subject.

7. Note the qualification "coercive" arguments. It is one thing to demonstrate a truth with coercive arguments, and quite another to illustrate a truth

or make it sound plausible by using arguments from fitness or by analogies. This latter task, and not the former, is what the scholastic theologians embark upon when dealing with mysteries.

8. This is what D. F. Strauss (*Christliche Glaubenslehre*, I, 140) and many others imagined to take place.

9. See P. Thone, "Le principe d'autonomie" in RCF, 59 (1909), 188; Garrigou-Lagrange, *Le sens commun, la philosophie ˆde l'etre et les formules dogmatiques* (1909), in *Revue Thomiste* (1909), pp. 164, 259, 566, and in *De revelatione*, I, 4th ed. (1944), Ch. 7, no. 4, "De spiritu rationalismi, juxta Ecclesiam," 212–216.

10. See the Vatican Council's constitution *De fide catholica*, can. III, 1, DB 1810.

11. See Van Laak, *op. cit.*, pp. 23ff. Garrigou-Lagrange, *De revelatione*, I, 353–357, gives a correct distinction between *proper* and *adequate* object of the human intellect.

12. This objection and the following one was advanced again in our century by E. le Roy, "Qu'est-ce qu'un dogme," in *Quinzaine* (April 16, 1905) and in the book: *Dogme et critique*. See *Revue Thomiste* (1905), p. 438, where le Roy's entire doctrine is refuted by Th. Pegues. See also J. Bittremieux, "Der pragmatische Dogmabegriff," in ThGl (1912), p. 277. For a more complete list of objections against the possibility of mysteries see Garrigou-Lagrange, *op. cit.*, I, 372–376.

13. See St. Thomas, *De potentia*, q. 7, a. 5.

14. See the decree *Lamentabili*, prop. 57, DB 2057.

15. The contrary-to-fact condition "even were it true" is important. For, as we shall see in a future volume (*Divine Faith*, no. 336), faith actually enriches reason by liberating it from errors, and by conferring on it much additional knowledge, even with regard to secular sciences.

16. It is quite impudent, therefore, for J. J. Rousseau to say: "I would prefer to have heard God myself; it would not have been any more difficult for Him, and I would have been protected from deception. Why should there be men standing between God and me?" (*Emile*, book IV).

17. See Van Laak, *op. cit.*, pp. 25ff.

Article II

THE NECESSITY OF REVELATION

I. *Preliminary Remarks.*

PROPOSITION: Once men began to worship false gods, a suitable knowledge of natural religion was morally impossible without the aid of revelation.

Meaning: 1. moral impossibility;
2. suitable knowledge of natural religion;
3. the human race, not individual men;
4. once idolatry had a firm grip;
5. without a revelation: unless God used some other supernatural means.

Proof: 1. Pagan peoples did not possess a suitable knowledge of natural religion and the natural law.
2. Given the natural means at their disposal, it was morally impossible for them to rise to such knowledge.

Scholion 1. A note about modern philosophers.

Scholion 2. Revelation is not man's right, but something eminently fitting for him.

Since God out of pure benevolence elevated man to a supernatural order, that is, designed for man a supernatural goal to be
reached in a way suitable to a rational creature, and since man
cannot even know about this goal by his own natural reason, it
follows *in this hypothesis,* and consequent to this economy set up
by God, that an *essentially* supernatural revelation is an absolute
necessity. That is why the Vatican Council says:

> Revelation must be said to be absolutely necessary . . . because
> God out of His own infinite goodness has destined man to a
> supernatural goal which is to share in divine goods completely
> surpassing the understanding of the human intellect (DB 1786).

But please notice, we are not for the present concerned with
that hypothetic necessity just described above; here we are exclusively concerned with the question of whether, from any point of
view at all, men need a revelation (granted it be only modally
supernatural) in order to have sufficient knowledge about *natural*
religion and the natural law. For the purpose of this inquiry is not
to conclude from the acknowledgment of some sort of necessity for
a revelation to the actual existence of a revelation, but simply to
point out from reason itself the very great usefulness of a revelation against the rationalist position that it is, at least, 'not fitting
for man to be taught about God and the worship due Him by a
divine revelation" (DB 1807).

PROPOSITION: *Once men began to worship false gods, a suitable
    knowledge of natural religion was morally impossible without
    the aid of revelation.* This proposition is *certain.*

1. **Moral impossibility implies a physical possibility.** A phys-   23
ical impossibility exists when the physical power to obtain or produce a given effect is missing. It should be obvious that a knowledge, even a perfect knowledge, of natural religion is physically
possible for man; otherwise it could not be called a "natural"

religion.[1] A moral impossibility exists when the physical power to do something is at hand, but the work is impeded by so many and such great obstacles that in reality it never, or rarely, will be accomplished.

2. A suitable knowledge of natural religion and the natural law is morally impossible. Suitable knowledge is knowledge that enables a man to think correctly about God and the worship due Him and to regulate his entire life according to the norms of natural goodness. The following are definitely *not* suitable knowledge.

a. The knowledge of only one or two religious truths. What is required is a rather full and developed knowledge of theoretical and practical truths: the knowledge of the one true God, Creator and Provider of all things; of the way to worship Him; of the immortality of the soul; of the primary and secondary principles of the natural law and their clear-cut application to problems peculiar to each man's state of life. It is, however, just as impossible to define with mathematical precision what is "suitable" knowledge in individual cases as it is to define exactly how much food and what kinds of food a man needs to live healthily. b. A knowledge which is doubtful or mere guess-work, or permeated with errors of all kinds. What is required is a knowledge that is sure and at least free from gross errors. c. A knowledge of religion gained only after many years, or acquired almost at the end of life. What is demanded is a knowledge acquired early enough so that a man may use it wisely in the direction of his entire life.[2]

3. The human race, not individual men. The moral impossibility of suitable religious knowledge must be understood in reference to the entire human race, not this or that particular individual. If it were a question of individuals, even those endowed with the highest intelligence and placed in very favorable circumstances, a suitable knowledge of religious truths could not be called morally impossible; but a *perfect* knowledge would appear to be impossible without revelation. One must consider the human race as it is, with all its weaknesses and defects.

4. Once idolatry had a firm grip. The discussion also considers the human race only after it had begun to worship false gods. According to ethnologists and historians, the cult of false gods, accompanied by a vast corruption of morals, reigned supreme among all nations, the Jews alone excepted, before the time of Christ. The same wretched condition still exists wherever Christian doctrine has not yet been preached.[3] We do not say that the human race always lived in such a state, or that it fell into it by necessity. We simply say: once idolatry had been introduced and had a firm grasp, a suitable knowledge of natural religion was morally impossible for the human race.[9]

5. Without a revelation: unless God used some other means. Once the moral impossibility described above has been established, there immediately arises the moral necessity of some supernatural help. Naturally, it must be admitted that God in His providence could have afforded some extraordinary remedy other than a revelation to supply man's need. Consequently, the words, "without the aid of revelation," are to be understood in the hypothesis that God had not elected to give any other type of assistance.

The proposition is *certain* and is contained in the statement of the Vatican Council: 24

> It is due to divine revelation that in the present condition of the human race those truths about God which are not of them-

[9] For this discussion, it is not necessary to answer the question: "What caused this wretched condition of the human race and the consequent moral impossibility of reaching a suitable knowledge of religion?" Even the purely historical-cultural approach to the study of religious origins strongly proves that polytheism and idolatry were not the original condition of men.

God, as a matter of fact, raised the human race in the beginning to the supernatural order and gave it a (primeval) revelation. It was definitely possible, not only physically but also morally, for the human race to keep this revelation (substantially) intact. But the various peoples, by yielding to lust and vice, lowered their moral life and even fell into idolatry. This condition was caused by men's free will, but with the assistance, so to speak, of concupiscence and the weakness of intellect. Concupiscence and the weakness of intellect were not man's original condition, but came as a result of the sin of Adam. It is quite evident that the moral impossibility of gaining suitable religious knowledge results in its totality from the fault of the human race.

Would such a moral impossibility have been present in a state of pure nature? In the hypothetical state of pure nature our first parents would have been created in a perfect condition and would consequently have possessed suitable religious knowledge from the very moment of creation, or at least they would have gained it for themselves immediately by a special, but natural, help from God. It would have been morally possible for their children to preserve this knowledge. Would their children, though, in actual fact preserve this knowledge? We simply do not know. Theologians, however, are of the opinion that the preservation of religious knowledge in the hypothetical state of pure nature would have been easier than it was in the state of fallen nature. They argue that concupiscence and the weakness of reason would not have been so great, or that extrinsic difficulties caused by the assault of the devil would not have occurred, or that God in His providence would have provided more powerful aids, even though these would have been purely natural.

selves beyond the grasp of human reason can (now) be known by all men readily, with firm certitude, and with no mixture of error. And yet, it is not for this reason that revelation must be said to be absolutely necessary, but because God out of His own infinite goodness has destined man to a supernatural goal . . . completely surpassing the understanding of the human intellect (DB 1786).[4]

Proof:

25   **1. Pagan peoples lacked a suitable knowledge of religion.** Since this fact is unquestionable, it will suffice merely to point out a few highlights. The pagans erred grossly about the unity of God by admitting the existence of many gods. They erred grossly about His nature and attributes by referring to their gods the most evil desires and crimes. They erred about the worship of God by taking part in orgies of drunkenness, lust, and human sacrifices all under the guise of honoring the gods. They erred about man's destiny, either by doubting the immortality of the soul, by believing in metempsychosis, or by dreaming up a foul paradise unworthy of man. In a similar way, they erred greatly in moral matters. One need but recall the brutal slavery, the hatred of foreigners, the rejection of new-born babies, the abandonment and murder of weak or crippled children, the fornication, and other even worse practices which were ratified by common and inveterate custom and were not considered vices.

Such actions were allowed and propagated publicly, with government officials, priests, and philosophers showing the way. They were favored, and frequently ordered, by the civil law. This took place, not merely among barbarians and the uncivilized peoples, but even among the more civilized nations which sometimes erred all the more grossly in religious and moral matters the more they excelled in political and military matters, in science and the arts.

26   **2. The pagan peoples, morally speaking, were incapable of rising to a suitable knowledge of religion.** They had at their disposal only two means of arriving at such a goal: their own personal investigations, and the help of philosophers. But neither the one nor the other was morally sufficient for the task.

a. *Their own personal investigations* were not adequate to the task. To acquire a suitable knowledge of religion by oneself requires diligent and constant investigation. Most men are prevented from such an investigation by native inability, by the pressure of family matters, by laziness, or by lack of interest. Consequently only a handful of men investigate religious truths studiously and persever-ingly. And even they arrive at the discovery of the truths mentioned above only after a long time: to reach the knowledge of such deep truths by the road of reason alone requires both a long application of the intelligence and much prior knowledge. In addition, man, in his youth, is disturbed by passion and consequently less ready for investigations of this type. Finally, this late knowledge on the part of a handful of men is often filled with doubts and errors, because the probative force of a demonstration is sometimes lost very easily, and a merely probable argument or even a sophism is accepted as a demonstration.[5] Therefore, by their own individual efforts only a very few men at best, and those by way of exception, would reach a suitable knowledge of religion. No nation, let alone the entire human race, could, morally speaking, ever arrive at such knowledge.

b. *The assistance of philosophers was not adequate to the task.* The pagan philosophers, although some of them did pass on excel-lent knowledge in some matters, did not themselves, as history testifies, arrive at a suitable knowledge of religion.

> For you know how often they taught false and distorted doc-trines about the true nature of God, and how many uncertainties and doubts they passed on about the nature of God, the first origin of things, about God's knowledge of future events, about the cause and principle of evil, about the ultimate destiny of man and eternal happiness, about virtue and vice. Yet there is nothing more necessary to the human race than a true and sure knowledge of these truths. (Leo XIII, Encyclical *Aeterni Patris,* in the *Allocutions of Leo XIII,* Désclee ed., I, 96).

Then, again, they were unwilling to teach the people the healthier doctrines which they themselves attained. On the whole, these were reserved for the learned: either because they agreed with Horace's dictum: "I hate the stupid rabble and stay away from them,"[6] or because they agreed with Plato[7] and Varro[8] that the false religion of the fatherland must be upheld at all costs. Finally, even if they had wanted to teach them, they would not have been able to do so. Since they disagreed among themselves on so many points, and by their lives and morals contradicted even their own teaching, the people did not look on them as authoritative guides.

All this is confirmed by the fact that no nation, without the help of a revelation, ever arose from its abyss of ignorance and error.

27 *Scholion 1. A note about modern philosophers.* What has been briefly indicated above about the errors of pagan philosophers in religious matters is generally true also of those modern philosophers who have rejected the Christian religion. Which of them has taught the natural truth about God, or about our relationship to Him, or the goal of mankind, without falling into serious errors? Have not almost all of them become skeptics, agnostics, or monists (either idealistic or materialistic)? Clearly, then, if the human race were today still wrapped up in the darkness of error as formerly, it would never arrive at a suitable knowledge of natural religion by the aid of philosophers. As for the fact that many modern philosophers far excel the ancients in the moral doctrine they teach, that is to be attributed not so much to their own genius, as to the Christian revelation on whose truth they were themselves nourished, or by which they were at least surrounded on all sides, and from which they have consciously or unconsciously borrowed many teachings.

28 *Scholion 2. This necessity of revelation which has been established does not prove that the human race, even after the Fall, had a right to a revelation. It simply proves that it was eminently fitting for God to give such a revelation.*

This follows from the fact that we are speaking, not of a physical impossibility, but of a moral impossibility. In addition, the moral impossibility under consideration regards a suitable knowledge, not the minimum knowledge strictly required to reach a natural goal. It must not be forgotten that the moral impossibility to attain a suitable knowledge of religion was caused by man's own fault. Who would claim that a wise and just God is bound to rescue the human race with a supernatural remedy when it has freely and guiltily cast aside its original knowledge or distorted it?

A benefactor who refuses to heap more gifts upon a beggar who has already abused generous gifts and injured his patron cannot be called hard-hearted. Similarly, it is folly to try to draw any other conclusion from the necessity of revelation than that it was indeed quite *fitting* for God in His goodness . . . to heal human misery by the help of revelation; and that man . . . ought to hope for a revelation with intense longing and, if one

is given, . . . seek zealously to discover it and . . . embrace it
(Ottiger, *Theologia fundamentalis,* I, 147).

Notes

1. Traditionalists and fideists exaggerate the necessity of revelation. They
hold that a divine revelation is unqualifiedly and absolutely necessary because
no religious truth, not even the existence of God, can be known by man
naturally. See Egger, *Enchiridion theologiae dogmaticae generalis,* 5th ed.,
no. 70; the propositions signed by Bautain and Bonnetty, DB 1622ff, and
1649ff; J. Beysens, *Ideologia,* p. 195; Roger Aubert, *Le problème de l'acte de
foi,* 2nd ed. (1950), 1st part, III (art. 3), "Rationalisme et fidèisme," 102–127.

2. Notice that the "suitable" knowledge under discussion is not simply
synonymous with such knowledge as would strictly suffice to reach a natural goal.
(Here the question of what knowledge is required to reach a *supernatural* destiny
is not even touched upon.) Although many of the theoretical and practical truths
required for man to reach his final goal in fitting fashion do belong to a suitable knowledge of natural religion, they could be completely, but sincerely,
ignored without causing an utter impossibility of reaching that goal. Certainly
anyone who faithfully follows the dictates of his conscience, even though he has
defective knowledge and consequently makes many mistakes, will not be
deprived of his final end. . . . The suitable knowledge here described holds a
place midway between perfect knowledge and a knowledge which, strictly
speaking, is sufficient to reach the final goal.

3. Mohammedans, for example, have borrowed much from both the
Mosaic and Christian revelations.

4. That the Council at this point was discussing neither an altogether
perfect knowledge of natural religion, nor a very minimum of religious knowledge, but a suitable measure of knowledge is the conclusion reached by
Granderath from an analysis both of the words of the Council and of its
preliminary debates on the question. See Granderath's work, *Constitutiones
dogmaticae Concilii Vaticani ex actis explicatae,* p. 78. The Council referred
to the human race as it actually exists when it declared that the (present)
moral possibility of attaining suitable religious knowledge is due to revelation.
Therefore without revelation no such possibility exists; a suitable knowledge of
religion is morally impossible. The Council added the words "in the present
condition" to show us that the moral impossibility which it affirms is not
present necessarily, but accidentally as a result of a contingent historical fact.
What that contingent historical fact is the Council did not say. Many
theologians seem to think that it was the sin of our first parents, but they
have not yet proved their point conclusively. We prefer to say that the moral
impossibility arises both because our first parents sinned and because universal
idolatry developed shortly afterwards. The opinion which states that the moral
impossibility arises exclusively from the state of fallen nature is, at least, not
taught by the Vatican Council, and seems to be contrary to the mind of the
Fathers of the Council. In the preparatory meeting, the Very Reverend Chair-
man turned down a proposed amendment with the statement: "When we
speak of the present state of man, we do indeed also mean man fallen through
sin" (*Collectio Lacensis,* VII, 136). "We *also* mean:" therefore, they did not

mean the state of fallen man exclusively and without any addition, but something additional. What can that something additional be except the universal defection from the worship of the true God?

5. See St. Thomas, *S.C.G.*, I, 4.

6. *Odes*, Bk. 3, 1.

7. *The Republic*, Bk. IV.

8. See St. Augustine, *De civitate Dei*, Bk. VI, chs. 27 and 31.

Article III

THE RECOGNIZABILITY OF REVELATION

Preliminary Remarks.

I. *Criteria of Revelation: Motives of Credibility.*
   a. Warning: these cannot be determined *a priori.*
   b. Division:
      1. internal and external;
      2. negative and positive.
   c. Enumeration and application of criteria:
      1. internal—a doctrine's truthfulness, moral goodness, sublimity.
         a. negative;
         b. positive.
      2. external—the holiness of the doctrine's herald; effects and history of doctrine; miracles; prophecies.
         a. negative;
         b. positive.
   d. Mutual comparison and evaluation of criteria.

II. *Miracles.*
   a. Notion: an effect perceptible by the senses and beyond the range of all nature.
   b. Division:
      1. with reference to the nature of the effect produced;
      2. with reference to the subject in which miracles are produced;
      3. with reference to the manner of their production.
      Relative miracles.
      Purpose of miracles: a special type of divine testimony.
   c. The possibility of miracles.
   PROPOSITION: If God's existence is granted, miracles are possible.
      Proof: 1. by positive argument;
            2. by refuting the objections of adversaries.
      Scholion. The fittingness of miracles.
   d. The recognizability of miracles.

PROPOSITION 1: Some miracles can be known with certitude both by eye-witnesses and by posterity, even by those who live many centuries later.

Historical truth of a miracle: it really happened.

Philosophical truth of a miracle: it was beyond the range of all nature.

Proof: 1. The effect was not produced by unknown powers of nature or by the cleverness or trickery of men.
Established by:
a. the nature of the effect;
b. the manner of its production.
Answer to objections.

2. The effect was not produced by the help of evil spirits.
Established by considering:
a. the work itself;
b. the circumstances surrounding it.

Scholion: Sometimes the character of one marvelous event enables us to gauge the character of other marvels.

e. The probative force of miracles.
Relevant truth of a miracle: it was performed either directly or indirectly for the set purpose of guaranteeing a doctrine.
Answer to objections.

f. Miracles of the moral order.
1. notion;
2. possibility;
3. recognizability;
4. probative force.

III. *Prophecies.*
a. Notion: the sure and definite prediction of some future event which could not be foreseen through natural causes.
b. Prophecies are possible.
c. Prophecies are recognizable.

Epilogue
1. The Method of Immanence: a method of persuading men that a religion is revealed primarily by arguments drawn from the deepest needs of human nature, adapted to their volitive powers.
2. Critique of this method.

THE RECOGNIZABILITY OF REVELATION

A divine revelation would be worthless unless man could recog- **29** nize it as such. If indeed God willed to reveal certain truths, He undoubtedly stamped such revelation with certain marks whereby it could be definitely recognized and unmistakably distinguished from all doctrines falsely claiming a divine origin. Just as a man is not excused on any pretext from the obligation of accepting a revelation which he definitely knows to be from God, so it would be offensive to right reason and to God's will, as known to us through natural means, were a man to accept a doctrine as divine without being sure that it had really come from God.

The signs or marks by which one may recognize the divine origin of a doctrine are called the *criteria of revelation* or the *motives of credibility*. They are called the criteria of revelation, because they enable man to judge clearly and determine whether such or such a doctrine has truly been revealed by God; they are called motives of credibility, because they move the intellect to make the following judgment: since it is clear that this doctrine has its origin in God, it is reasonable to believe it by divine faith (judgment of credibility).[1]

The purpose, then, of such criteria is not to demonstrate directly the truth of some body of doctrine, but to demonstrate its divine origin, to establish the fact that it has been revealed.

I. A General View of the Criteria of Revelation

Note: Human reason, of itself, cannot determine precisely the **30** methods whereby God, were He to reveal truths, would make His revelation recognizable. Consequently, the existence of most of the criteria to be discussed is known only from the history of revelation. There is no other aim in view at this point than to make known the usefulness and effectiveness of the criteria of revelation.

Division of criteria.[2] The criteria of revelation may be divided **31** into internal and external. Internal criteria are those intrinsic to the doctrine itself, for example, the general tenor of the message whose revealed character is being determined. External criteria are distinct from the doctrine itself and consist of historical facts which precede, accompany, or follow the disclosure of some doctrine.

Both internal and external criteria may be subdivided into negative and positive. Criteria are negative if they show that nothing precludes a given doctrine from having God as its author, but do not give any positive indications of its divine origin. Criteria are positive if they point out (with probability or with certitude) that a certain doctrine has in truth come from God. A positive criterion which proves the divine origin of a doctrine only with probability is by itself ineffective and must be classified as inadequate. Such a criterion, however, may be very useful when linked to other criteria.

32   Enumeration and application of criteria: 1. Internal criteria include the truthfulness, the moral goodness, and the sublimity of a doctrine.

a. *Negative.* A religious doctrine which is in no way opposed to sound reason and moral goodness, contains no contradictions, and does not clash with another revelation known definitely to be divine, may have been revealed by God. If even one of these conditions is lacking, the doctrine cannot be from God.[3]

b. *Positive.* A doctrine satisfying the negative criteria, teaching natural religion and natural law with sufficient fullness, certitude, and purity, independent in doctrine from any prior revelation, should be judged with great probability to be divinely revealed. This probability is all the greater, the more fully and more perfectly natural religion is taught. The reason for saying this is based on the tremendous difficulty, even moral impossibility, of knowing natural religion so perfectly by reason alone. Since it is not altogether impossible for a man of great genius to attain such knowledge by his own power, this criterion, of itself, is not coercive or adequate.

If such a doctrine should, over and above the teaching of natural religion, neatly solve questions which perturb the human mind in matters of religion,[4] prescribe commandments and practices splendidly suitable for man's present state of life and very effective for fostering piety, moral goodness, and the welfare of society, and thereby correspond to the needs and legitimate aspirations of human nature, the presumption in favor of its divine origin is greatly increased, although certitude cannot be given from such indications alone. The basis behind the opinion just given is this.

CRITERIA (signs) of revelation

I. in general

1. internal (intrinsic to doctrine itself)
   - a. truthfulness } negative
   - b. moral goodness } negative
   - c. sublimity } positive

2. external (extrinsic to doctrine)
   - a. holiness of herald } negative
   - b. effects and history of the doctrine } negative
   - c. miracles } positive
   - d. prophecies } positive and coercive

II. in particular

1. miracles
   - a. physical
   - b. moral } evaluated for { historical, philosophical, relevant } truth

   received by:
   - a. corporeal vision

2. prophecies
   - b. imaginative vision
   - c. intellectual vision } evaluated for { historical, philosophical, relevant } truth

(61)

On the one hand, thoughtful people would hardly grant that human intelligence, whose weakness in matters of this kind is well known, could manage to bring forth from its own storehouse such splendid and such salutary doctrine. On the other hand, it cannot be demonstrated by compelling arguments that such a doctrine could have come only from God, especially as an apt or apparently true solution to difficult questions may not necessarily be true.

33   2. External criteria include the holiness of the herald who announces the revelation, the effects and history of the doctrine, and above all, miracles and prophecies. By a "herald" of a revelation is understood its first witness, the man or men who are chosen by God to spread the revelation for the first time.

a. *Negative*. A doctrine which has a herald who is sane in mind and decent in morals, but not in any extraordinary manner, a doctrine which could point to some fine examples of devotion and moral goodness, but not in any sense exceptional, a doctrine whose diffusion and preservation can be explained by honorable, but natural means, *can* have a divine origin, but *need not* necessarily.

Contrariwise, if a religion has as its founder a vicious man, it is improbable, indeed exceptionally improbable, that its origin is divine. Although it is not intrinsically contradictory for God at some time or other to speak through evil men, it is incredible that the all-holy and all-wise God would choose to use such for the establishment of a new religion. Who would believe that God Himself would directly choose for so sublime and extraordinary a mission a man who was hateful and evil? The man's very way of life would create a tremendous prejudice against his religious teaching and would render suspect even the miracles he might perform.[5]

Again, a religion which is perceived to induce by its very nature the perversion and dissolution of morals is unquestionably not from God.

A doctrine, finally, which is propagated or supported by fraud and other dishonorable means,[6] unless it is evident that such practices go against the grain of the religion itself and are happening somewhere merely by accident, is at least badly suspect. If its first champion practiced fraud and trickery, mankind could be certain that he was not God's messenger.

b. *Positive*. A doctrine claiming to be divinely revealed, whose herald is outstanding for purity of life, a doctrine which produces outstanding models of virtue and spreads and lives on beyond all normal expectation, probably, indeed very probably, comes from God.

If, furthermore, either the herald s holiness, or the fruits produced, or the spread and continuance of the doctrine is so exceptional that it cannot be explained solely by natural powers but should be attributed to a special help given by God, proof granting full certitude will be at hand for the divine origin of such a doctrine. In a case of this kind a moral miracle has taken place. This will be described later.

Finally, miracles and prophecies, provided they are joined with the doctrine in question in a proper way, are positive and coercive criteria.[7]

A comparison of the criteria one with another. From the previous discussion it is clear that negative criteria are extremely useful for detecting a religion which falsely claims a divine origin. But they are not so helpful when it comes to recognizing a religion which is true in its claim to come from God. **34**

Of the positive criteria the external far outweigh the internal. This is true for three reasons: 1. A judgment about the utility, excellence, and sublimity of a religion does not of itself solve the matter completely. 2. Such a judgment presupposes a diligent investigation of various religions and can consequently be made by only a handful of men. 3. Such a judgment is influenced not a little by the subjective dispositions of the investigator.[8]

The use of internal positive criteria is, however, usually extremely helpful, both because such criteria dispose uneducated people to examine external arguments more readily, and because they can be used as a corroborative argument of a demonstration already given on historical grounds. In fact, internal arguments are sometimes genuinely necessary in order to remove the prejudices of people who refuse to listen to external arguments, either because they are convinced beforehand that the religion under discussion is outdated or replete with absurdities, or because they are convinced that no religion could be credible or true in their own eyes, unless it could be shown that it meets the needs and aspirations of their own hearts. That external arguments, objectively considered, far outweigh internal arguments should be clear from the fact that a divine revelation is an historical reality and as such should be proved mainly on historical grounds.

Of all external arguments by far the best are miracles and prophecies.

In the light of the above discussion, the following words of the Vatican Council can be easily understood: [9]

> In order that the assent of our faith should be in accord with reason, God willed that there should be joined to the internal inspirations of the Holy Spirit external proofs of His revelation. Such external proofs are divine facts, in particular, miracles and prophecies. Since these brilliantly bear witness to God's omnipotence and infinite knowledge, they are the surest signs of a divine revelation and are accommodated to the intelligence of all men (DB 1790).

II. Miracles *

I. Notion and division of miracles

35 *Notion:* St. Thomas teaches:

> The term miracle comes from the Latin word *admiratio,* which means admiration or wonder. Wonder arises when effects are visible, but the cause is hidden. For example, a man may wonder when he sees an eclipse of the sun and is ignorant of the cause. The cause, though, of some visible effect may be known to one man, but be unknown to others. As a consequence some event may be a cause of wonder for one man and not for others. A rustic, for example, is filled with wonder at the sight of an eclipse, but an astronomer is not. A miracle receives its name because it is completely wonderful; because it has a cause which is absolutely hidden from all. In reality the cause is God. For this reason those effects which God produces in a manner over and above the causes known to us are called miracles (*S.Th.,* I, q. 105, a. 7).†

An angel may be the hidden cause of effects which surpass the normal course of visible nature. In this case the cause would not be absolutely unknown to all beings, but only to men. Effects of this kind, produced by a superhuman agent, are called miracles in

---

* See special bibliography on pages 102–103.
† God is called a strictly hidden cause, not as though His existence were unknown, but because God's mode of operation is far beyond human knowledge. Miracles receive different names depending upon the different points-of-view from which they are considered. In themselves, as effects surpassing nature's power, miracles are called powers; as symbols manifesting something supernatural, they are called signs; considered from the point-of-view of excellence inasmuch as they excite awe and amazement, they are called portents or prodigies. See *S.Th.,* IIa-IIae, q. 178, a. 1, ad 3.

a broad sense of the term, miracles from the point-of-view of men (*miracula quoad nos,* relative miracles).[10]

Definition of a miracle. An absolute miracle is defined as *an* **36** *effect perceptible by the senses and beyond the range of all nature.* The effect lies directly within the range of the senses, or at least it is manifested externally in a way perceptible by the senses. Unless the effect were outwardly disclosed, no wonder would result. It is for this reason that transubstantiation is not considered a miracle in the customary use of the term. Even if imperceptible effects surpassing the range of nature were listed among miracles, it would cause no great confusion.[11] Miracles of that type, however, would be useless for proving the divine origin of a religion.

Beyond the range of all nature means that something is produced in a manner surpassing all the ways whereby created realities operate. Since all the powers and possibilities of every creature are included in the range of nature, a miracle is an effect which surpasses the productive power of all creatures.

A miracle is often described as an extraordinary effect, not precisely because it is rare, but because it supersedes the normal course of nature (*extra ordinem*). That is why St. Thomas says: "Even if blind men were to receive sight every day, it would still be a miracle" (*II Sent.,* d. 18, q. 1, a. 3, ad 2).* Not every effect which has God as its exclusive author is a miracle; only those that take place beyond the natural order, effects which in some sense are opposed to such order and are exceptions to it. That is why neither the creation of the universe, whereby the order of nature was first established, nor the conservation of the universe in existence, nor the daily creation of rational souls, something pertaining to the normal course of nature and demanded by it,[12] is classified as a miracle.

The Author of Miracles. Obviously an effect which surpasses **37** all created power can have only God as its author, its principal cause. Moreover, since the very concept of miracle demands that it

---

* Some authors understand the term "extraordinary" to mean that a miraculous effect must take place in a way surpassing every kind of order established by God. Thus a miracle would have to surpass not only the natural order, but also the normal order of grace. If such is accepted as the true notion of a miracle, then there is one more reason for not considering justification through baptism or transubstantiation as miracles, since they take place according to the law normally observed in the supernatural order of grace. Still, it seems far better, when describing the general doctrine about miracles, to consider them exclusively in reference to the order of nature.

take place in a way beyond the mode of operation of any creature, creatures can give nothing of their own to the physical performance of a miracle. For to whatever extent a created agent would function as an efficient cause of a miracle, to just that extent would the effect produced not be beyond all modes of operation native to creatures. Evidently, then, a creature cannot even act as a genuine or physical instrument in working a miracle. God alone, and nothing else, satisfies the requirements for a true, efficient cause of miracles. It is not true, however, that creatures can play no role in miracle-working. Angels and men can cooperate in a twofold manner: either morally, by moving God by their prayers to work a miracle; or potentially (*potestative*) by doing something simultaneously, namely by presenting the divine command to nature and thus imposing on nature the proximate necessity of being the subject of a miraculous change, the change itself being caused by God alone. In this sense a man or an angel may be called the instrumental or ministerial cause of a miracle. Actually a man who under the impulse of God makes a divine command known to nature, or who, under the impulse of God, persistently implores a miracle, does in some fashion fulfill the notion of a divine instrument in the working of miracles.[13]

38   **Division of miracles.** The best division of miracles is based on a *consideration of the manner in which they surpass the power of nature.** Miracles may surpass nature's power in one of the following three ways (See *S.Th.*, I, q. 105, a. 8):

a. In respect to the *very nature of the effect* produced (*quoad substantiam facti*). Some miracles so far exceed the power of creatures that nature herself could not possibly produce them in any way or in any subject whatsoever. Examples are the mutual compenetration of two material bodies and the glorification of the human body.

b. In respect to the *particular subject* in which the effect is produced (*quoad subjectum in quo fiunt*). These are effects which nature can cause, but not in this particular subject matter. Examples are the resurrection of a dead man (nature can produce life in a fetus, but not in a corpse) and the restoration of sight to a blind man (nature does give sight to a child).

c. In respect to the *manner of production (quoad modum).*

* Another division of miracles, based on the various ways in which effects are opposed to the order of nature or repugnant to the native bent of natural agents, is found in St. Thomas, *De Potentia*, q. 6, a. 2, ad 3.

This is a question of effects which nature can bring about in the same particular subject matter, but not in the same way or by the same means. An example is the healing of a serious wound or disease suddenly, without proportionate remedies—to cure blindness, not by an operation, but by a simple command.

Note: This division explains what is meant by saying that one miracle is "greater" than another. Since an effect is called a miracle precisely by a comparison with the natural power it surpasses, a miracle which greatly surpasses the powers of creatures is rightly said to be greater than another which surpasses the powers of creatures to a less notable extent. Thus it is that of all miracles those hold first place which exceed the order of creation with reference to the very nature of the effect produced (*quoad substantiam facti*), whereas effects which surpass created powers only in the manner of their production hold last place. No miraculous effect, however, may be said to be more wonderful than others by making a comparison on the basis of the divine power employed; this remains exactly the same in all.[14]

Relative miracles (miracula quoad nos). Since pure spirits are included within the ambit of all nature, they cannot perform absolute miracles.[15] Still, they can produce effects which are wonderful in man's eyes. Because they work invisibly and can with the utmost ease and swiftness make use of the powers of the universe, which they understand more perfectly than men, they can do many things which surpass the normal course of visible nature, things which corporeal nature, left to her own, or put to work merely by man, would either not be able to do at all, or could not accomplish with such great perfection. Two points must be made in regard to miracles of this kind.

1. Such miracles differ from absolute miracles not simply in degree, but in kind. Absolute miracles (*miracula simpliciter*) take place by God's will alone and without the operation of a created agent. Relative miracles, on the other hand, are always produced by the application of created power and hence, strictly speaking, are not beyond the order imprinted in creation by God, but are in accordance with it, even though they seem to take place beyond that order. That is why St. Thomas teaches that wonders worked by created spirits take place not after the fashion of a miracle, but after the fashion of an art (*De Potentia*, q. 6, a. 3).

2. Even though created spirits can work relative miracles by their own power, they can work them only insofar as God com-

mands or allows them to do so. Angels, no less than other creatures, are completely subject to the rule of divine providence. Even though man cannot determine precisely what God can or does allow angels to do, two principles are evident: a. God could not allow created spirits to disrupt the normal order of the visible universe by performing miracles almost daily at their own choosing. This fact is demonstrated by experience itself. b. God could not permit spirits to work prodigies in such fashion and in such circumstances that men would thereby be irresistibly driven into some error contrary to religion or good morals. Such permission on the part of God would be contrary to His divine wisdom.

40 *Purpose of miracles.* The all-wise God does not operate in a fashion completely beyond the order of all nature without a very special purpose. The special purpose of a miracle is not to be found within the natural order. If one were to admit that nature's order required from time to time the working of miracles for its own preservation, he would attribute to God a failure of foresight. The purpose of a miracle, then, belongs to a higher order of divine providence. Its purpose is to serve as a supernatural manifestation by God; to be a very special sort of divine testimony. Every miracle is by its very nature a testimony to divine omnipotence, since it shows that God's power is not shackled to the order of nature. In consequence, such a display of power can be used by God to serve as a testimony of special benevolence or anger towards someone, as a recommendation of some virtue, as a manifestation of some person's holiness, or as a guarantee of some religion. To discover which of these motives prompted the miracle one must examine the circumstances under which it occurred. Because of this quality of purposiveness a miracle is considered by everyone to be a divine sign or trademark, and is frequently referred to simply as a *sign.*

The angels, because of their close union with God, never interfere with the normal course of the visible universe, unless ordered or permitted to do so by God. If, then, a good angel works a wonderful deed in favor of some person or religion, his act will always and necessarily include God's testimony in favor of this person or religion. Thus a work performed by a good angel over and beyond the normal course of visible nature is equivalent to an absolute miracle under its aspect of being a divine trademark (*ratione signi divini*). For this reason, wonderful events which exceed the power of visible nature, but not the power of a created spirit, so long as it is clear that they are produced, if not by God Himself, at least by good angels, are frequently called true miracles, though they are minor and merely relative miracles.[16]

Note the qualification, "provided it is clear that those events are worked at least by good angels." Prodigies performed by devils, even though they cannot occur without divine permission, can in no wise be adduced as a divine trademark or testimony. Wonders performed by devils are never described without qualification as "miracles," but are called prodigies, demoniacal miracles, or false miracles.

Catholic teaching on miracles is summed up in these words of 41 the Vatican Council:

> If anyone says that miracles cannot take place and, consequently, that all accounts of them, even those contained in Sacred Scripture, ought to be rated as fables or myths: or [if anyone says] that miracles can never be known with certitude, or that the divine origin of the Christian religion cannot be legitimately proved by them, let him be anathema (DB 1813).

II. The possibility of miracles. Those who deny the existence of a God who is distinct from the universe logically enough deny the possibility of miracles. Such are all atheists and pantheists. Rationalists, however, even though they grant the existence of a personal God, contend that miracles are impossible. Indeed, they are so stubborn on this point that they are led by their preconceived opinion to reject all books containing miraculous accounts, especially the Gospels.[17] Only absolute miracles will be discussed in this section; for, once their possibility is admitted, there is no need to consider the other classes of miracles.

PROPOSITION: *If God's existence is granted, miracles are possible.* 42 The Vatican Council declared this possibility a *dogma of faith.*

Proof. 1. By positive argument. The order of secondary causes was established by God according to His own free choice and not by any necessity of nature, for He could have established another order of things. Consequently God is in no way bound to the order of things once selected and brought into being, but He can

> act in a fashion over and above the order instituted when He so chooses, for example, by producing effects without the agency

of the secondary causes which usually produce them, or by producing other effects beyond the range of secondary causes, . . . or by restraining the activities of natural agents to prevent them from doing what they were designed to do (*S.Th.*, 1, q. 105, a. 6; *De Potentia*, q. 6, a. 2).

43 **2. By the refutation of objections.** Before considering and refuting the individual objections offered by rationalists against the possibility of miracles, the fundamental source of those objections should be pointed out. That source is a hostile attitude of mind rather than a reasoned conviction. Even the assertion that God could intervene in the world's affairs (whether He actually does do so or not) is resented by those who want man to be the center of the universe and man's reason to be the sole criterion of truth and moral goodness. The possible intervention of God in His world is considered rather as an affront than a benefit to men. Rationalists, therefore, instead of searching into the facts of history, start from a quasi-religious first principle that God must not interfere in human affairs. In short, rationalists bitterly oppose the possibility of miracles, not because the very concept of a miracle is in itself something contradictory and hence ridiculous, but because they make it a dogma that man may not be hindered in the management of his affairs. Their subsequent objections to miracles are merely a *post-factum* searching after a rational basis which can bolster up their original, irrational dogma. Perhaps no one has described their position so accurately as G. K. Chesterton. He writes:

> . . . my belief that miracles have happened in human history is not a mystical belief at all; I believe in them upon human evidence as I do in the discovery of America. Upon this point there is a simple logical fact that only requires to be stated and cleared up. Somehow or other an extraordinary idea has arisen that the disbelievers in miracles consider them coldly and fairly, while believers in miracles accept them only in connection with some dogma. The fact is quite the other way. The believers in miracles accept them (rightly or wrongly) because they have evidence for them. The disbelievers in miracles deny them (rightly or wrongly) because they have a doctrine against them. The open, obvious, democratic thing is to believe an old apple-woman when she bears testimony to a miracle, just as you believe an old apple-woman when she bears testimony to

a murder. . . . If it comes to human testimony there is a choking cataract in favour of the supernatural. If you reject it, you can only mean one of two things. You reject the peasants story about the ghost either because the man is a peasant or because the story is a ghost story. That is, you either deny the main principle of democracy, or you affirm the main principle of materialism—the abstract impossibility of miracles. You have a perfect right to do so; but in that case you are the dogmatist. It is we Christians who accept all the actual evidence—it is you rationalists who refuse actual evidence, being constrained to do so by your creed (Reprinted by permission of Dodd, Mead and Company from *Orthodoxy* by G. K. Chesterton, pp. 279–280.)

Rationalists have three principal arguments against miracles. These are:

a. Those who say that God can make exceptions to the physical order should logically conclude that He can also make exceptions to the moral order, for example, by making perjury morally good, or murder, or adultery. After all, God is equally the author of both orders.

There is no parity in this example. God can make exceptions to the physical order not precisely because He is its author, but because He instituted it in such a free fashion that He could also have fashioned another. The moral order, or the natural law governing morals, was not freely instituted by God, but flows necessarily from the moral attributes of God. There is nothing strange about this. The physical order governs the mutual relations existing among creatures. Those relations could have been altogether different without destroying in the slightest degree the necessary relations which exist between creatures and God Himself. The moral order, on the other hand, governs the free actions of creatures in reference to their final goal, God Himself. If that relationship should be destroyed, rational creatures would no longer be directed towards God, surely a result that would be contradictory both to God's wisdom and to His sanctity.[18]

b. A miracle would destroy the immutable laws of nature (physical laws).[19] Physical laws, or the native tendencies of things to act in a definite way, are indeed immutable, as long as the natures of those things with which the tendencies are identified remain unchanged. But those tendencies do not come into play unless there are present at the same time all the conditions requisite for their action. Such conditions are not present by necessity, but

(71)

may be impeded, modified, or completely removed, either by the influence of secondary causes, or by the positive action of God Himself.

When a miracle takes place, the natural tendency of a thing to act in a definite way is neither destroyed nor changed. God directly and personally causes some condition on which the exercise of the native tendency depends to remain unfulfilled. In what precise fashion God does that, is not known. That He can do it is beyond cavil because of His omnipotence. Certainly if man by erecting Grand Coulee Dam can stem back a tide of water, what could prevent God, in exercising divine power, from holding back the waters of the Red Sea without destroying the law of gravity? If man can launch a rocket missile far into the atmosphere, what could prevent God's power from lifting up the body of Christ on the occasion of His ascension into Heaven? If man by use of chemicals can make a thing temporarily incombustible, why could God not protect the three youths in the fiery furnace while at the same time the flames retained their natural tendency to ignite? [20]

Since it is true that created things, so long as all the requisite conditions are fulfilled, always operate in accord with their natural tendency, in the case of miracles there is really no change or suspension of the physical law itself. The effect of the law is suspended or changed in a particular case because some condition required for its operation is absent. Since this occurs without the intervention of a natural cause, it is correct to say the course of nature is altered in that particular case.

It is stupid to say that, if God can alter the course of nature, all human foresight and all science are rendered impossible. For God does not alter the course of nature either widely or frequently; He does so rarely, only in particular instances. Who would be so foolish as to doubt that a man who wanted to walk on the water would sink, merely because Peter once walked upon the Sea of Galilee?

c. The occurrence of a miracle would contradict God's immutability and wisdom. It would contradict His immutability, because the defenders of miracles are forced to admit that God is no longer satisfied with the order of nature which He first instituted. It would contradict His wisdom, because those who admit miracles ought either to grant that God changes the course of nature at whim and without reason, or does so to correct defects which happen in nature contrary to His will. This would certainly show a failure on the part of God's providence. [21]

A miracle does not contradict God's immutability. By one and the same eternal decree God established the normal course of nature and simultaneously decreed to allow exceptions to it from time to time by performing miracles.

From all eternity God foresaw and chose to do whatever He has done in time. Therefore He established the course of nature in such wise that whatever exceptions He should make from time to time to that course would have been preordained by His eternal will (*De Potentia,* q. 6, a. 1, ad 6).

Consequently there is no change in God's will.

Neither does a miracle contradict God's wisdom. It is not claimed that God makes exceptions to the order instituted by Himself without good reason, or that He does so to repair something He had fashioned poorly to begin with; rather He makes such exceptions for reasons very worthy of His wisdom, as indicated above (See no. 40).[22]

Scholion. The fittingness of miracles.   **44**

From the purpose of a miracle, which is to show that God's power is not shackled to the order of nature, one can understand why it is not only possible but even very fitting for God to work miracles from time to time. St. Thomas says:

There is no better way of making it obvious that the whole gamut of nature is subject to the divine will than for God from time to time to do something over and beyond the order of nature. By so doing He makes it clear that the order of creation flows from Himself not by any necessity of nature, but by His own free will. Nor should we deem it frivolous that God should perform something in corporeal nature in order to manifest Himself to the minds of men, since all corporeal creatures are directed towards an intelligent nature as towards their goal. But the goal of an intelligent nature is to know God. There is nothing strange, then, in having an occurrence in corporeal nature serve as a means of bringing knowledge about God to intelligent beings (S.C.G., III, 99).

St. Augustine writes:

Because He [God] is not the sort of substance which can be seen with the eyes, and because those miracles whereby He rules the whole universe and provides for every creature have

(73)

grown so stale by custom that scarcely anyone bothers to notice the marvelous and stupendous works of God found even in a grain of seed, He has in His mercy reserved some works for Himself which He performs at an opportune time over and above the normal course and order of nature so that men might grow awe-struck by seeing, not greater, but rarer works than those which daily occurrence has rendered commonplace (*Tractatus 24 in Joannem no. 1*).

45   **III. The recognizability of Miracles** [23] Recognizing the futility of arguments adduced against the possibility of miracles, once God s existence has been granted, a number of rationalists seek another subterfuge: they say that miracles are not impossible, but that they can never be recognized with certitude, or at least that up to this time no miracle has been definitely established.[24] The leaders of the "Higher Criticism" movement of the late nineteenth century afford an example of this mentality. Renan wrote: "We do not say: a miracle is impossible. We say that up to this time no miracle has been proved" (*Histoire des origines du Christianisme*, I, *Vie de Jesus*, 19th ed., 96). Harnack stated: "The historian is in no position to deal with a miracle as with an established historical event. . . . Each individual miracle remains quite doubtful from the viewpoint of history, and the sum total of doubtful occurrences can never add up to certainty" (*Dogmengeschichte*, I, 3rd ed., 63).

Others maintain that the miraculous fact itself, considered purely as a fact (*materialiter sumptum*) can never be definitely established, especially for men of a later generation. In other words, it can never be definitely settled whether the extraordinary effect which may be a miracle ever took place in reality. Here the question turns on the historical truth of miracles.

Finally, others assert that the supernaturality of the cause of the miraculous fact can never be established. This means that man cannot demonstrate that the effect was produced by God or by a good angel, and not by the unknown powers of nature, or by the deceit of man, or by the devil. Here there is a question of the philosophical truth of miracles.

46   PROPOSITION 1. *Some miracles can be known with certitude both by eye-witnesses and by posterity, even by those living many centuries later.* The Vatican Council declared this proposition a *dogma of faith.* (See above, no. 41.) [25]

This proposition deals exclusively with the historical truth of miracles, omitting for the present all discussion of their supernatural character. Note, too, that in the present discussion one must beware of the paralogism used by some moderns: they say that a miracle, by the very fact that it is supposed to be miraculous, that is, produced by a cause *unknown* to us, cannot be "demonstrated." It is indeed impossible to prove the genuinity of a miraculous effect by means of its causes (a demonstration of why a thing is so, *demonstratio propter quid*). But it by no means follows that the *existence* of such an effect cannot be known with certainty.

The existence of the effect can be known to eye-witnesses by their own sense perception; it can be known to posterity by trustworthy testimony. Even though these methods do not grant us strictly scientific knowledge, they do grant us a genuine certitude (a demonstration that the thing is so, *demonstratio quia*).[26] This is a moral certitude, which is the only kind of certitude possible in historical matters. Nor can such certitude be gained about every single miraculous event which is asserted to have ever happened, but only about some, those which have been passed on to us in proper fashion.

Proof. 1. With reference to *eye-witnesses.* For eye-witnesses to gain sure knowledge of a miraculous fact, nothing else is required except that the witnesses have normal sensory faculties and pay sufficient attention. Surely a miraculous event, considered simply as an event, can be perceived by the sense organs just as easily, clearly, and definitely as an ordinary event. It can be perceived clearly not only by educated persons but also by simple, ordinary men whose sensory powers are as good as those of the educated. Then, also, the very strangeness of the occurrence provokes greater attention, and stimulates the bystanders to explore the matter more diligently. Would it really be impossible or difficult to find out with certitude whether a man, one's own fellow citizen, had been born blind and afterwards received sight? that Lazarus had been four days in the tomb and then was restored to life?—Those unbelievers are acting petulantly who demand that a miracle must always be announced beforehand, and that the event must be reviewed under a legal form of examination or judged exclusively by specialists.

2. With reference *to posterity.* For posterity to gain certitude about a miraculous fact that has been legitimately examined by eye-witnesses, what is required and suffices is that the fact be transmitted and preserved by trustworthy testimony. If there are

witnesses who know the facts, who are competent, truthful, and in agreement, there is no reason why one should value their testimony to a miraculous fact less than their testimony to ordinary facts. This is particularly true in light of the fact that very strange events usually provoke doubts and further investigations among those that hear of them, so that if some should believe too readily, there are others equally prone to doubt. This is all the more true when it is of great importance to both listeners and witnesses to spot false-hood in the matter. Nor is the long passage of centuries an obstacle to certitude. Though a recent event usually strikes the imagination to a greater degree, tradition, provided it possesses the requisite conditions, does not lose its value by the mere passage of time.

47   There are two chief objections.[27]

1. They say that it is physically impossible for a miracle to occur, whereas it is only morally impossible for even a thousand witnesses, otherwise quite trustworthy, to make a mistake or to practice fraud; therefore the moral certitude in favor of a miracle is always cancelled out by the physical certitude to the contrary. Similarly, they maintain that the experience of one man, testifying that a corpse came back to life, must yield to the experience of a thousand men who maintain that the dead do not come back to life. Thus it is with every miracle: against the lone witness rise a thousand who assert the opposite.

For merely natural causes to produce a miracle, by definition an effect surpassing nature's powers, is indeed physically impos-sible. But for the First Cause, God, to produce a miracle is in no way impossible; in fact, it is altogether possible, as has been demonstrated (see nos. 42–43–44). The objection, therefore, is specious. For factually one is not confronted with the problem of two opposed certitudes: the one physical, the other moral.

Neither is the experience of a small number of men who witness to the resurrection of a corpse rendered useless by the contrary experience of thousands of others. Since their experiences do not revolve about the same event, they are not mutually contradictory.

When David Hume, the inventor of this objection, said: "Every superstition is necessarily overthrown by this argument," he added with good reason: "if it be a legitimate argument"! (*An Inquiry Concerning Human Understanding*, I, 10).

47a   2. They argue: it is at least certain that Christian men have been quite gullible about admitting miraculous occurrences.

It must be admitted that some Christians, and indeed in some ages most Christians, like the other men of their time, have been over-credulous. For that very reason learned men who rely on the aid of critical investigation to sort the true from the false perform an excellent service for religion itself. But it by no means follows that no miracle can be known with certitude, or that all miracles which Christians have accepted were received without question. Let critical norms be applied, but let them be sober and honest rules of criticism. Just as gullibility should be avoided, so too should quibbling.[28]

Our adversaries are illogical when they conclude that an over-eagerness in this matter of belief is necessarily and inextricably entwined with belief in revelation, because some men of the Middle Ages were guilty of extreme credulity. Such gullibility was connected with faith purely by accident. It arose from a lack of the critical sense, which is easily understandable in the case of men who were not accustomed to the exactitude of the natural sciences and who were short on documentary evidence. If the men of the Middle Ages sinned frequently by gullibility, the learned men of our age often err in the opposite extreme. They apply the methodology of the physical sciences to the field of history, especially religious history, or they exclude a priori the possibility of miracles, at least in practice, and conclude with Renan that all accounts of supernatural events necessarily indicate either gullibility or fraud.[29]

PROPOSITION 2: *At least some genuine miracles can be clearly dis-* 48 *tinguished from merely natural marvels and from diabolical prodigies.* The Vatican Council declared this proposition a *dogma of faith.*

Once the historic truth of an event has been established, one must investigate closely its miraculous character, the philosophical truth of a miracle. This can be done both by eye-witnesses and by later investigators. By the term true miracles are meant not only absolute miracles, but also relative miracles worked by good angels; for these, as has been said above (no. 40), are equivalent to absolute miracles from the point of view of their serving as a divine trademark.

Only this is asserted here: true miracles can *sometimes* be recognized with certitude. And it should not be considered strange that the matter may at times remain more or less doubtful. When a miracle occurs, not as a proof of some doctrine, but simply as a manifestation of special love towards a particular person, there is no necessity for the person himself to be absolutely certain that he was rescued by a miracle strictly so-called.

Proof. The proposition can be proved by exclusion. If a given effect cannot be explained by the powers of the visible universe or by the activity of devils, obviously a true miracle has occurred.

49   *Part I.* Careful attention given to the nature of the effect and to the manner in which it occurred is often all that is needed to know for certain that a remarkable event has not been accomplished by the unknown powers of nature or by the cleverness or trickery of men.

1. *The nature of the effect.* Some effects by their very nature obviously surpass all the powers of material creation and all human ingenuity in regard either to the essence of the fact or to the subject in which they occur. For example, the resurrection of a corpse, the multiplication of loaves of bread, walking on water, etc.

2. *The manner of production.* An effect which nature herself can produce in a given subject can definitely not be referred to nature's powers whenever it is clear that no equipment at all has been used or that the means at hand were woefully inadequate to produce the effect. Examples of miracles in which no equipment at all is used are the curing of leprosy or the silencing of a storm by the mere command of the miracle worker. Examples of miracles in which the means at hand are inadequate are the restoration of sight by the application of mud to the eyes of a blind man, the instantaneous cure of paralysis by the touch of a hand, etc. Every type of secondary cause must use proportionate means.

Objections against this proposition are many.

50   a. Some maintain that man does not yet know the precise extent of nature's power, as is attested by the stupendous inventions of our own times.[30]

Certainly man does not always know the extent of nature's powers, but he does know a lot. For example, he knows in a negative way that no natural power can produce certain effects, such as the restoration of life to a corpse.[31] At times man knows in a positive way just how nature's powers will necessarily operate in a given set of circumstances, since many natural laws are very well known. Does not the human body burn by necessity when surrounded by flames? Does not the human body tend to sink by necessity in water? To gauge the occurrence of a miracle one need not know the absolute limits of all natural powers in all possible circumstances; it is enough to know that the powers actually employed in a given set of circumstances were utterly incapable of producing such an effect. Who could possibly maintain that a bit of mud or a drop of saliva can restore sight instantly, or that a touch of the hand is equal to the task of healing instantaneously an amputated ear? *

b. Maybe the miracle-worker cleverly made use of some force of nature unknown to the rest of men.

How would the miracle-worker have known of this mysterious power which was unknown to the rest of mankind prior to, during, and even after his own lifetime? How could he have applied it so cleverly without the use of technical apparatus of any kind, or instruments? If such a gratuitous assertion is to be granted, then the miracle in question is avoided only by having recourse to another miracle. We might add that miracle workers are usually not professors of the physical sciences.

c. Why could not the miracle-worker have been aided by some chance occurrence of some unknown power of nature?

It seems absurd to suppose that a miracle brought about by an unknown force should happen to coincide by chance not once, but many times with the wonder-worker's beck and call. And even if it were a question of but a single miracle, unless there were some other way to prevent misunderstanding, divine providence itself, to which even chance happenings are subject, could not permit a charlatan to be aided by such a fortuitous coincidence as a guarantee of a false religion.

d. Perhaps there was some fraud used and it was undetected.

One can, it is true, imagine circumstances under which a faked miracle would be possible. When, therefore, the character of the miracle-worker, the circumstances, and the purpose of the miracle give rise to some suspicion of fraud, the rules of criticism come into play. Unless they can completely allay the suspicion of fakery, the event must not be accepted as a miracle. But in many cases the

---

* It is in this way, too, that we solve the trite objection that our ancestors judged that it was impossible for a man to make the journey from Holland to America in ten hours, or for a man living in Amsterdam to talk with a friend in New York and so on. Our ancestors judged it to be impossible for anyone to do these things through the means available in their day; and they judged rightly. They had no jet-planes and no transatlantic telephones. When we examine a miracle, we are not asking whether or not at some future date means will perhaps be found proportionate to produce such an effect; what we are asking is whether the means actually at hand or those that could have been on hand could reasonably account for the effect.

very circumstances of the event exclude any suspicion of fraud or deceit: think, for example, of the multiplication of the loaves of bread, the resurrection of Christ, to mention but two.

e. How many marvels are wrought by the power of the imagination and hypnotism!

It cannot be denied that the imagination and hypnotic suggestion can produce extraordinary effects, particularly in women and sick persons, and that even some diseases arising from a disordered nervous system can be healed by them. For that very reason some men exaggeratedly and deceptively, but not without all foundation, praise "the faith which heals." [32] When it comes to a question of judging cures of this sort, one has to be extremely cautious. But, even prescinding from such marvels as the resurrection of the dead, the multiplication of the loaves of bread, or the calming of the storm, it is quite certain that many diseases, especially those involving some serious lesion of the organs, simply cannot be cured by the imagination alone or by hypnosis, or at least cannot be cured instantaneously:

> Faith-healing . . . is the popular name for cure by suggestion. The more accurate term for it is *psychotherapy* . . . let us call to mind the obvious limits of this method of cure, even when supported by the most accurate medical knowledge and scientific procedure: *it cannot be used at all in the majority of the ills which afflict mankind.* Wounds, ulcers, lesions of nervous and muscular tissues, cancers, diseases caused by pathogenic microbes—these and all other organic diseases are quite outside its scope (A. P. Madgett, *Christian Origins* [Cincinnati: Xavier University, 1941], I, 210).

The same author relates that an eminent American psychiatrist, Dr. M. H. Hoffman, Clinical Director of the psychiatric division of Eloise Hospital, Eloise, Michigan, in discussing cures brought about by psychotherapy emphasized the length of time required to effect such cures:

> He [Dr. Hoffman] gave an instance of what was considered a most exceptional case. The patient, a purely mental case, had become completely helpless as far as normal human activity was concerned. He administered metrazol shock treatments, and after five of these, covering a week's time, the patient began to show signs of improvement. Within a few months she was able

to resume some of her normal activities. Within a year (!) she was quite normal (*Ibid.*, p. 212).

The facts of hypnosis, in general, strengthen rather than weaken the case. For the startling results of hypnotism (those which are authentic) have not been produced by the simple command of a will or voice, but by the use of psychic means whose proportion to the effect desired is already known or at least considered probable by medical men:

Always and everywhere I have held and written that suggestion is a psychical treatment adapted to a psychical case, which must be a simple functional auto-suggestive disturbance, not created by organic development that is toxic or affects the brain, like meningitis, uraemia or mental defect. These are not answerable to psychotherapy (*Ibid.*, p. 211, quoting Bernheim, *Hypnotism and Suggestion*).

But whenever one finds authenticated effects which, upon investigation, cannot be attributed to the powers of nature, the activity of a super-human agent must be acknowledged.

Part II. To establish with certitude that some marvel which is **51** recognized as being beyond the powers of visible nature has not been worked by the help of evil angels, it is usually enough to examine carefully the work itself and its circumstances, especially its moral circumstances.

1. *The work itself.* There are some works which either by their very nature, or by the subject in which they occur, or by the manner of their production completely surpass the power of a created spirit. Such works are those which are definitely known to be incapable of realization either by simple local motion, or by the application of some natural power. For example, the resurrection of a dead man (provided it be certain, for example by the stable possession of new life, that we dealing with a genuine resurrection). The devil could, strictly speaking, assume the appearance of a corpse. Other examples are instantaneous cures of damaged organs, such as the eyes, the limbs, the lungs, etc.

2. *The circumstances.* God's works must be honorable, good, holy, and wholesome for man. Consequently, something evil or treacherous will usually be detected in the works of an evil spirit.

a. If the wonder-worker is evil, proud, light-headed, or desirous of praise, the work performed should not be considered miraculous. God does not usually choose such people as His instruments, especially when there is question of the first announcement of a revelation.

b. If the manner whereby the marvels are wrought betrays anything shameful, obscene, ridiculous, irreverent, violent, or cruel, if the wonder-worker is wildly excited and mentally unbalanced, God's approval should not be regarded as given. If the wonders are unaccompanied by a profession of religion and do not foster religious purposes, considerable suspicion should be attached to their value.[33]

c. If the goal or effect of the work is either evil or unworthy of God, if the work is merely fuel for human curiosity, if it nourishes pride, disobedience, or discord, if it favors a break-down of morals, if it is performed to bring favor on a false, irreverent, or indecent doctrine, or a doctrine contrary to a prior revelation already definitely known as coming from God—then God is not its author. The same holds true if men have been warned beforehand against prodigies of this sort by a genuine messenger from God,[34] or if the prodigy is destroyed by a higher power.[35]

Divine providence cannot permit demons to use their native power in producing prodigies in such a way that honest men, because of such works, would be almost irresistibly led astray in the business of salvation. At least when it is a question of the approval of some religion, means will never be lacking to distinguish diabolical prodigies from true miracles.

52 *Scholion. Sometimes the character of one marvelous event enables man to gauge the character of other marvels.*

Suppose there is a man who claims he is a messenger from God. Suppose he has done something which is beyond all doubt a true miracle and at the same time worked other marvels which he himself claims as divine signs, but whose miraculous character is not in itself equally clear. All those other marvels can and ought to be considered true miracles. The man's *divine mission is already proved,* and he is certainly not a deceiver. As often, therefore, as he seemed to be working miracles, he actually was working genuine miracles.

On the contrary, if it has been proved of a man that he once performed a prodigy by the aid of the devil, or by trickery attempted to simulate a miracle, all other actions performed as a guarantee of the same cause, no matter how marvelous they may seem, should not be accepted as miracles.

IV. The probative force of miracles.[36] It is somewhat super- 53 fluous to demonstrate *ex professo* that miracles fully and coercively prove the point for which they are worked. It is quite obvious that the all-wise and all-holy God can never guarantee a false assertion by His exclusive trademark. This probative force belongs not only to absolute miracles, but also to relative miracles worked by a good angel. As God Himself cannot perform a work to foster false-hood, neither can He order or approve such action on the part of angels. It is easy enough to grasp that a miracle, even one, is sufficient to establish complete proof of a thing forever. The objection that the modern mind does not accept miracles as proof and is offended rather than convinced by them proves nothing against the objective value of any argument based upon miracles.[37]

If a religious doctrine is to be proved by miracles, it should be definitely established that the miracle was wrought either directly or indirectly for the purpose of guaranteeing that doctrine. A king's seal does not guarantee the authenticity of a document unless it is stamped upon it. Neither does a miracle, however historically and philosophically true, guarantee a doctrine unless it can be shown that it has been worked for that purpose. This is what is known as the relevant truth of a miracle.

A miracle is worked directly as a guarantee of a doctrine if a man or an angel asserts in clear words, or equivalently, by his manner of acting, that he is about to perform a miracle for the express purpose of making known to all the divine origin and hence the truth of such or such a doctrine. Thus Christ, before healing the paralytic at Capharnaum, stated: *"But that you may know that the Son of Man has power on earth to forgive sins . . ."* (Matthew 9:6; see Mark 2:1ff; Luke 5:17ff).

A miracle is worked indirectly in favor of a doctrine if it is directly worked in favor of a man who claims to be a messenger from God, and that man in turn appeals, openly or equivalently, to the miracle as a guarantee of his divine mission. So St. Paul defended the truth of his claim to be an Apostle by appealing to the wonders that had accompanied his labors (see 2 Cor. 12:12). The miracle, by directly proving the divine mission of the messenger, indirectly proves the divine origin of the doctrine he preaches. It is unthinkable that God would permit a genuine messenger of His to propose a doctrine as divine which actually is false or non-divine in origin.

Objections. The difficulties raised by unbelievers against the probative force of miracles are groundless. They say:

54

a. Miracles, since they are historical facts, cannot prove the intrinsic truth of a doctrine.

The Church does not maintain that miracles directly prove the intrinsic truth of a doctrine. A miracle does prove the divine origin of a doctrine, the fact that God has spoken, and this, in the supposition that God is truthful, suffices for a judgment of credibility.

b. The argument from miracles involves a vicious circle. First of all the truth of the miracle is established from the character of the doctrine with which it is connected; then from the very same miracle is established the truth of the doctrine (see nos. 51, 2, c).

The opponents are mistaken. There is no vicious circle if the character of the doctrine, which is analyzed by reason, sometimes serves as a negative criterion for judging the philosophical truth of a miracle, and the miracle in turn serves as a positive confirmation for the divine origin of that doctrine. The negative base (namely, the absence of a patent contradiction and of depravity in the doctrine) on which the genuineness of a miracle is partially judged is one thing; the positive conclusion (namely, the divine origin of that doctrine) which is reached once the reality of the miracle has been established is quite another.

c. Practically all religions, even the most perverted, boast about miracles.

This can be easily understood. In doing so they testify to the universal agreement of mankind that a religion ought not to be considered divinely revealed if it lacks miracles, and that miracles definitely do prove a religion to be divine in origin. Moreover, it is obvious that the probative force of miracles is not destroyed by the mere fact that many falsely appeal to them:

> I hope we may dismiss the argument against wonders attempted in the mere recapitulation of frauds, of swindling mediums or trick miracles. That is not an argument at all, good or bad. A false ghost disproves the reality of ghosts exactly as much as a forged banknote disproves the existence of the Bank of England—if anything, it proves its existence (Chesterton, *Orthodoxy,* pp. 283–84).

If the miracles appealed to by false religions are examined critically, the following conclusions will be discovered: either they lack historical foundation; or, if they did factually occur, they were not real miracles (they were not philosophically true), or else they were not worked as a guarantee of those religions (they lacked relevant truth).[38]

V. Miracles of the moral order. *Notion of a moral miracle.* **55** A moral miracle is *an action or series of actions, preceptible by the senses, so difficult that man's moral powers are unable to accomplish them (with God's normal concurrence).* A sufficient explanation for such an act can be found only in the postulate of a special help from God. Some examples of moral miracles are the following: the holiness of Christ, the extraordinarily swift spread of Christianity, the heroic constancy of the martyrs.

A moral miracle is like a physical miracle in that both exceed the powers of nature and take place in a way beyond or outside their respective laws. But a moral miracle differs from a physical miracle in many ways.

a. In a physical miracle the effect exceeds the physical powers of creatures, and takes place in a fashion beyond the laws governing the activity of physical things, so that without the intervention of God it would be physically impossible. In a moral miracle the effect exceeds not the physical, but the moral powers of men, and occurs in a fashion beyond the normal laws of human behavior, that is, beyond the constant and uniform fashion in which human liberty reacts in given circumstances, so that without God's intervention it would be not physically, but morally impossible.

b. In a physical miracle the effect is wrought by God alone without the mediation of a secondary cause; in a moral miracle the effect proceeds directly from a secondary cause, from the human will, but only with God's special help.*

* The nature and characteristics of a moral miracle are excellently described by R. von Nostitz-Rieneck:
Supernatural influences on the spiritual life of men and especially what we call "moral miracles" stand in an altogether different relationship to the natural laws of individual and social ethics than that of physical miracles to natural and physical laws. The latter tend to run counter to the laws; the former seem to conform to them. Moral miracles take their supernatural or superhuman character from the fact that in the actions and events surrounding them intellectual and ethical forces are applied in a manner, and with a perfection, that produces results which seem to lie far beyond the usual, moral strength of men, considered as individuals or as a class. But when is this the case? When can I say that deeds which actually have men as their authors and are in conformity with moral laws

56   *Possibility.* The question whether moral miracles are possible or not does not offer any special difficulty. What is there to prevent God from so increasing the power of a man's will by a special help, directly or indirectly, that the man wills and does things he would never will to do and never would accomplish if left to himself?

57   *Recognizability.* In this regard a twofold judgment must be made. In the judgment of the existence of the fact (the historical truth) there is nothing special to be remarked. But in making a judgment about the miraculous character of the fact (the philosophical truth of the miracle) human behavior must be carefully weighed. One must determine, for example, how men in situations of a similar kind, and amid similar obstacles, and with similar helps, constantly behave. It is in this way that one learns what men can or cannot morally do when left on their own. The laws or fashions of human behavior are only morally constant and hence admit of exceptions, even though rare, in particular cases. To make a prudent judgment that there is present a special help of God generally requires that a large number of men depart from the usual manner of acting in a given situation,[39] or for one and the same man to make such a departure frequently. To have sufficient proof of the philosophical truth of a moral miracle a rather large number of cases, larger or smaller in proportion as the act is more or less difficult, is demanded.

58   *Probative force.* The probative force of a moral miracle, granting it possesses relevant truth, is no less than that of a physical miracle. It is obvious that God cannot cooperate in a special way to guarantee a false doctrine or an evil institution.

III. Prophecies [40]

59   **I. Notion and definition.** The word "prophecy" comes, according to the common opinion of modern [41] scholars, from the word

---

and ethical ideals surpass human power such as it has been created? In our opinion, we may say so particularly in two cases. First, if, in their performance, moral force of unprecedented excellence is at hand. Second, if through these deeds extremely noble social effects are produced, effects which have no proportion to the means used. In both instances the superhuman character must follow as a conclusion from the unparalleled uniqueness of the deeds. But what can be called "unprecedented" or "unparalleled"? That which lies beyond the frontiers of all historical experience; that which has never happened anywhere before in this manner, or with this perfection (*Stimmen*, 60 (1901), 132).

prophanai "to speak for another," or "to speak in the place of another." This accords with Augustine's dictum: "A prophet of God is nothing more than a proclaimer of God's words to men" (*Quaestio 17 in Ex. 7:1*). That is why Scripture, in a broad sense of the term, calls all men prophets who by God's impulse speak about divine matters, either by interpreting the Scriptures, or by exhorting the people, or by praising God.[42]

Because the men who were moved to speak by divine impulse very often made known hidden realities, the term prophet in a more restricted use began to mean those who manifested hidden things, whether past, present, or future.[43] Finally, because future realities are the most hidden of all, a prophet in a very restricted sense of the term is a man who foretells future events. It is in this last, technical, and apologetical sense that the term prophecy is now used.

Definition: A prophecy may be defined as *the sure and definite* 60 *prediction of some future event which could not be foreseen through natural causes.* The qualification "sure" is inserted to exclude both mere guesses or suspicions and assertions that are indeed apodictical, but clearly rash, assertions which would not be accompanied by sure foreknowledge. Prophecy consists principally in knowledge.

The prediction must be "definite," because ambiguous predictions which could be twisted in any direction or applied to any event, such as those of the pagan oracles,[44] do not deserve the name of prophecy. It is not necessary, however, for future events to be predicted with the maximum of clarity. A prediction can be definite and yet more or less obscure because of metaphors and parables, especially before the event occurs.

It must deal with future events which could not be foreseen by natural causes. If the thing predicted could not be naturally known by any created intellect whatsoever, there results what is known as an *absolute* prophecy, one which proceeds from a knowledge that is superior to all created intelligence. But if the prediction is something which is beyond the powers merely of the human mind, there arises what is known as a *relative* prophecy, or a prophecy from the point of view of human knowledge (*quoad nos*).[45] If such a prophecy is uttered by the aid of the devil, it is not described unqualifiedly as a prophecy, but it is called a false prophecy, or divination.

Prophetic knowledge (considered *theologically*).[46] God does no 61 violence to those creatures He uses as instruments for working supernatural effects, nor does He use them in a way contrary to their natures. To prophesy, however, without any understanding of the things which are spoken is opposed to human perfection. Such a manner of acting belongs to idiots and dreamers. Hence, both the Fathers and the theologians consider as certain that true prophets never utter their revelations in a delirious state, but always grasp intellectually the things they prophesy.[47]

Excluding that peculiar and imperfect form of prophecy in which the person who speaks is not considered a true prophet (as in the person of Caiphas, cf. John 11:51), one finds that prophets understand to some extent, even though at times very inadequately, what God wishes to announce through them, and know that God has given them their message. The words "understand to some extent, even though at times very inadequately, what God wishes to announce," are added because "the mind of the prophet is a deficient instrument in relation to the principal agent; even genuine prophets do not understand everything that the Holy Spirit intends to convey through their visions, words, or deeds" (S.Th., II-II, q. 173, a. 4).

There are two elements in prophetic knowledge. First, the reception or representation of the realities to be announced. This requires an infusion of some sort of species into the mind of the prophet. Second, a judgment about the realities represented. This judgment is made by the light of the intellect, as given added strength by God Himself.

The representation of the realities may be made to the senses, to the imagination, or to the intellect. A sense-vision occurs when the prophet perceives something by eye or ear (see Daniel 5); an imaginative-vision, when nothing is perceived by the external senses, but when God either imparts completely new images to the imagination or rearranges in a completely new way images previously gathered from the senses (see Acts 10.10ff); an intellectual-vision, when God directly puts new intellectual ideas into the intellect (as happened to the Apostles when they received infused knowledge). On this basis, prophecies are divided into corporeal (or sensible), imaginary,[48] and intellectual.

The judgment about the revelation received means that the divinely strengthened intelligence of the prophet decides with infallible certitude both the meaning of the revelation and the fact that it has been given by God.

This judgment is the major factor in prophetic knowledge:

because judgment is the terminating point of knowledge. Consequently a man who receives a representation of things from God through the means of imaginary likenesses, as did Pharaoh (Gen. 41), and Nabuchodonosor (Dan. 4), or through the means of bodily likenesses, as did Balthassar (Dan. 5), is not considered a prophet unless his mind is also enlightened to make a judgment. On the other hand, a man will be considered a prophet if he receives only the intellectual light needed to make a judgment of the visions granted to the imaginations of other men, as is clear in the case of Joseph, who explained the dream of Pharaoh. As Augustine says (*De Genesi, ad literam,* XII, 9), however, the greatest type of prophet is the man who excels in both respects; the man who sees personally the images signifying bodily realities and penetrates their meaning with great intellectual acumen (*S.Th.,* II-II, q. 173, a. 2).

II. **Prophecies are possible.** If the existence of God is granted, **62** the possibility of prophecies cannot be denied. Two considerations are enough to prove this: 1. philosophy demonstrates the fact that God knows all future realities of any sort whatsoever; 2. it has been already demonstrated that God can communicate His knowledge to men.

The best argument that rationalists can offer against the possibility of prophecy is that prophecy would force a man or a people to perform whatever has been predicted. Since it is incredible that the all-kind and all-holy God would foster fatalism and destroy man's liberty, prophecies are impossible.[49] This argument, however, does not even consider those prophecies whose fulfillment does not depend on the exercise of human freedom; for example, that God will perform such or such a miracle. Moreover, even in the case of a prophecy whose fulfillment requires human cooperation, the prophecy itself in no way destroys or limits human freedom. The event foretold takes place, not because it was prophesied, but it is prophesied precisely because it will actually take place.[50]

III. **Prophecies are recognizable.**[51] True prophecies, just as **63** true miracles, can sometimes be known with certitude both by eye-witnesses and by others who are removed either by space or time from the prophetic event.

1. The historic truth of the prophecy can be seen easily. For this it is sufficient to know that the event was predicted beforehand

in a positive and definite way and that the event took place afterwards.

2. The philosophical truth of the prophecy can be grasped easily. To be certain that some event, which was predicted and then actually happened, proceeded either from God Himself or from some good angel who acted at Gods behest or with Gods approval, it is sufficient to show that such an event can be referred neither to human foresight, nor to the devils, nor to the rashness of a man favored by chance. The very nature of the event predicted or at least the circumstances under which it occurred preclude alternative explanations.

a. The nature of the event itself usually shows that the fulfilled prediction cannot be explained on the grounds of human foresight. Future events which depend exclusively on God's own free choice can in no way be known beforehand by men. In addition, there are a large number of events which (either totally or partially) depend on the free choice of men. Such events could not be foreseen even with probability by human foresight, especially if one consider not only the events themselves, but also the various circumstances of time, manner, and place in which the events take place. Even in the case of future events which do not proceed from the activities of free causes, there are a great number which are clearly beyond the power of human foresight. Examples of these are found in such matters as contagious diseases and storms which occur, long after they have been predicted, in a definite place and at a definite time. Here we may also include in a general way all events that take place by chance.

b. That a fulfilled prediction was not the work of devils is clear either from the very nature of the event foretold or from the circumstances.

The devils certainly had no role to play when there is question of an absolute prophecy. No created intelligence can foresee with certitude events of the future which depend on the exercise of God's free will or the free will of men. The devil, possessing great intelligence and long ages of experience, can predict with greater or lesser probability some free actions of men by an analysis of man's nature and habitual way of acting. But there are many other free acts about which he cannot make even a probable guess. Such acts are those that are free in the fullest sense of the word, or vastly improbable in a given set of circumstances, or not due to occur until the far distant future.

The circumstances of the prophecy also can help determine whether the activity of the devil should be considered.[52] For when we are dealing with an event which surpasses the knowledge of men but not of devils (a *relative* prophecy), an investigation of the circumstances, of the person of the prophet and his manner of acting, or the purpose and effect of the prophecy, are often enough to disclose whether the prophecy should be attributed to God or to a good angel, or to the devil. God, in His wisdom and holiness, could not allow a demoniacal prediction to be of such character that it would lead, almost of necessity, men astray in the matter of religion. When, therefore, there is question of a prophecy given as a guarantee of a religion, means will not be lacking to distinguish true prophecies from divination.

c. That a fulfilled prophecy cannot reasonably be explained on the grounds of a chance occurrence can usually be demonstrated with ease. When the event foretold is, by its very nature, utterly uncertain or wildly improbable, it is unreasonable to expect that chance brought about its fulfillment; this would be doubly true of an event impossible in the order of nature. Who could believe the assertion that the prophecy of a virginal birth or of the resurrection of a dead man was fulfilled by mere chance? If the same person were to prophesy not only one but many events, or even one event along with its attendant circumstances, to attribute the fulfillment of such prophecies to chance would be plainly stupid. "If a pig," says Cicero, "were to scratch out the letter A on the ground with his snout, would you therefore conclude that he could write the story of Ennius' *Andromache?*" Finally, Divine Providence, which controls even chance happenings, could certainly not permit a false religion to be strengthened and made highly plausible by prophecies which came true because of chance.

What has been stated above in regard to the probative force of miracles can be applied without any difficulty to prophecies.

Epilogue   63a

The Method of Immanence. The whole aim of traditional apologetics is to prove the fact of revelation by objective arguments, in particular by external ones, and thereby prepare the way for a judgment of credibility. Toward the close of the nineteenth century, however, a school of philosophers and theologians, especially in France, maintained that this method is not effective. They claimed that traditional apologetics is of little value, if not absolutely and in itself, at least in the concrete world of facts, because it does not satisfy modern mentality. Such opinions still have a large body of supporters.

The modern mind, according to this school, grows impatient with truths imposed on it from without (extrinsicism); it is not attracted by purely historical arguments that prove the fact of revelation (historicism), but yearns to find in itself and in its own vital action the beginning of the truth it ought to embrace (immanentism). The modern mind has a horror of abstract dialectic, of arguments which belong exclusively to the speculative reason (intellectualism); it is captured far more easily by arguments which appeal to the whole man, which appeal in a very special way to man's volitive powers, to his emotions and will. In pursuing religious and moral truth the modern mind gives a primacy to the will (voluntarism, moral dynamism).

To meet this modern mentality the new school[53] urges that apologetics should begin by way of a *psychological* approach rather than a philosophical-historical one. It urges the use of the *Method of Immanence,* whereby apologetics should seek its fundamental arguments for embracing a revealed religion in man's nature itself, in the deepest needs and yearnings of human activity. This apologetics of immanence may be defined as "*a method, of persuading men that a religion is revealed, based primarily on arguments drawn from the deepest needs of human nature, and adapted to their volitive powers*" (J.'V. de Groot, *Summa,* p. 13).

63b   The procedure followed in this type of apologetics embraces two steps:

1. If anyone examines attentively the intimate make-up of man as he is and carefully studies his thoughts, desires, and actions in their entirety, he will find that man is anything but self-sufficient in spiritual matters. Every man who has not deliberately crushed the noblest aspirations of his nature yearns after an evolution and perfection of religious and moral life which he cannot attain by his own native intelligence and power. There is, therefore, in man as he now exists a vague yearning and an inescapable need for a truth and a virtue surpassing his nature, for a supernatural truth and help; in short, for revelation and grace. Apologetics should, then, diligently seek the reasons behind this need and awaken men to a consciousness of them. The purpose of apologetics should be, not to summon from man's own nature a supernatural reality or to determine precisely what that supernatural reality should be, but

to make man realize that he ought to love and desire as his own proper good and as a need of his own life that supernatural reality should it be offered. Indeed, if the personal experience of this need is the point where the natural and the supernatural meet, then this experience is a necessary condition for man's acceptance, under the guidance of his will, of the supernatural reality offered from without.

2. Once these things have been accomplished, let the apologist propose that supernatural reality, namely the Catholic Church, together with her doctrines and institutions. Above all let him picture the rich spiritual life to which the Church has always guided and still guides the best of her children. Let him point out that the doctrines and institutions of the Church perfectly correspond to human needs and aspirations; that they are extremely useful for attaining a full growth of spiritual life, and that they make possible a life which one ought to yearn for with all one's heart, a life of incomparable richness which may be found nowhere outside the Church.[54]

Even if it should turn out that a man who has been stirred by the deep longing of his heart to embrace Christ and His Church later encounters the difficulties which rational criticism can raise, he will still cling faithfully to Christ and His Church, because he is joined to them not by the dry bonds of reasoning, but by the living embrace of his entire soul. Still, one may present to him the historical arguments which traditional apologetics usually advances.

Criticism. This apologetics according to the Method of Im- **63c** manence ought in our opinion neither to be rejected as totally useless or erroneous, nor ought it to be approved wholeheartedly.

a. The urgent need for supernatural truth and supernatural help is conceived in relation to man such as he now is. We do know that man is destined for a supernatural goal and has been elevated to the supernatural order. Provided, therefore, that the origin of the need for the supernatural which is asserted is not sought for in the very principles of human nature itself,[55] but in the impulse of the Holy Spirit summoning man to his actual goal, there will be no confusion of the natural and supernatural orders. One might well doubt whether the grace of the Holy Spirit actually arouses in all men, or in most men, particularly in those who are not baptized, a true desire and a genuine need for a strictly supernatural good, or whether it is actually possible to lead all men, or at least most men, to a consciousness of this urgent need. In addition, there is always the danger that the apologist may imagine he sees in the souls of men who are, so to speak, neutral, his own deep realization of Christianity.

b. One must certainly approve strongly whatever can be offered to point out that the dogmas and practices of the Church correspond to the noblest aspirations of the human heart, and such dogmas and practices confer a grandeur on human life, both individual and social. Arguments of this sort carry weight with cultured and morally good men and at times, with the help of Gods gráce, achieve the desired end. It must be admitted, though, that such arguments are suitable for only a relatively small group of men. In addition, the evaluation of such arguments depends to a large extent on the subjective and variable dispositions of those to whom they are addressed. For this reason one might fear somewhat for the constancy of a conversion that results from these arguments alone: the greater the role of the emotions in a conversion, the greater the danger of inconstancy.

If it is asked whether arguments of this sort, taken by themselves, suffice to prove the divine truth of the fact of revelation with certitude, the answer is, we think, no. For they do not directly prove anything except the eminent utility or goodness of the Catholic religion. But to be able to conclude with certitude from the goodness of a religion to its divine origin, it should be established that this goodness, this suitability to human nature, this power to perfect human living is so great that it completely excludes any possibility of mere human invention.

To prove this point beyond doubt is no easy matter. And, as a matter of fact, the immanentists themselves pay little attention to doing so. The arguments that they offer may present valid presumptions; they may accidentally suffice for some men; but they do not appear to be strictly sufficient arguments for proving the fact of revelation. Unless the fact of revelation is established with certitude, divine faith, that is, an assent given because of the authority of God revealing, becomes impossible.

The apologetics of immanence can, therefore, be employed with some usefulness among cultured men. In fact, in the case of men guided by the modern mentality, as described above, such an apologetics may perhaps be necessary to dispose them for the acceptance of the philosophico-historical arguments. But by itself it does not lead to a judgment of credibility which is fully and strictly established. It can, therefore, by no means be substituted in the place of traditional apologetics; nor can the latter be condemned as useless and obsolete. The patrons of the method of immanence, however, from time to time imply and even assert openly that this should be done.

It is customary to praise the apologetics of immanence as some- **63d** thing specially suitable for men who have swallowed the Kantian prejudices about the inability of the theoretical reason to reach objective truth. In fact, its main proponents either subscribe to or favor a moral dogmatism. In so far as the new apologetics is motivated by Kantian principles, it loses all intrinsic and objective value and can be used only as an argument *ad hominem.* Anyone who holds that the theoretical reason is unable to know objective truth can only grant such power to the practical reason by a bald lack of logic.[56]

Certainly, if the conclusions of the theoretical reason give nothing but subjective necessity, if they do not establish a thing to be necessarily so, but only necessarily to be *thought* so, can the postulates of the practical reason generate objective necessity? Why should they not also be reduced to subjective norms of thought? Therefore, just as often as you shall show by the arguments of the Immanentists that the truth of the Catholic religion is a postulate of the practical reason or of the religious consciousness, *if you likewise acknowledge the theory of the impotence of the theoretical reason,* you will have captured a Kantian, but you will not have moved one foot towards proving the objective truth of the Catholic religion.

Notes

1. The criteria of revelation and the premises to faith (*i.e.,* God's existence and truthfulness) are similar in that both are prerequisites for anyone to attain faith; they differ in that the criteria of revelation prove that God has spoken or given testimony.

2. See A. de Poulpiquet, "Le solidarité apólogetique des motifs de credibilité," in RPA, 13 (1912), 81, 161.

3. Not every assertion of philosophers or scientists is to be accepted as an irrefutable axiom of sound reason. As the philosopher A. Whitehead notes: "Science is even more changeable than theology. No man of science could subscribe without qualification to Galileo's beliefs, or to Newton's beliefs, or to all his own scientific beliefs of ten years ago" (*Science and the Modern World,* Mentor ed. (1948), p. 182).

A divine revelation can contain truths which surpass the grasp of unaided reason. From the two points mentioned above it is clear how wrong is the assertion of rationalists that the sole criterion of a genuine revelation is its perfect harmony with the principles of reason. How could such a criterion be the sole criterion of revelation since, of its very nature, it cannot prove the "divine origin" of any revelation, but solely the truthfulness of a doctrine, and since it cannot possibly be applied to mysteries?

4. For example, the origin of man, our subjection to evil, retribution to God offended by sin, the immortality of the soul.

5. This position is by no means weakened because of Balaam (Num. chs. 22–24) or Caiphas (John 11:49–52). There is simply nothing in common between these men and founders of new religions. Nor can the assertions made about the first herald of a revelation be applied with the same force to later promulgators or ministers of that religion once it has been established. The latter are not chosen directly by God Himself, and they do not cause so great a prejudice against a religion whose revelation has already been established. It goes without saying, however, that such men do immense harm to the authority of the religion they teach when they live wickedly.

6. The use of armed might is as equally disreputable as fraud. The employment of this sort of coercion is contradictory both to the normal course of God's providence, which treats every man with great reverence, and to the very nature of religion, which is of no value unless it rests upon conviction and is freely exercised. Here the only point in question is the acceptance of God's revelation. Obviously God, as Creator and Supreme Lord, has the right to punish man for his crimes. That He has exercised that right, directly or indirectly, is abundantly clear from the Old Testament and portions of the New Testament (see Acts 5:1–11).

7. Orthodox Protestants consider miracles and prophecies vehicles of revelation rather than criteria of the truthfulness of revelation. As a consequence they say that the power of working miracles ceased once the Christian religion had been established. See H. Bavinck, *Gereformeerde Dogmatiek*, I, 2nd ed., 349, 353, 361.

8. See A. de Poulpiquet, "Quelle est la valeur de l'apologetique 'interne?" in RSPT (1907), p. 449.

9. See also Canon III, 3, DB 1812. The canon was directed against those sole or primary way of discerning the divine origin of a religion is based on internal experience, religious feeling, private testimony received from the Holy Spirit, the direct certitude of faith, and other criteria of the same sort.

10. Whenever we make mention of purely spiritual creatures, whether good or evil, we are speaking hypothetically, that is, on the hypothesis that such creatures exist. In speaking of them we shall describe them according to the doctrine commonly held by all who admit the existence of created, pure spirits.

11. See St. Thomas, *S.Th.*, I, q. 105, a. 7, ad 3; *De potentia*, q. 6, a. 2, ad 2.

12. The production of a rational soul does not in every way transcend the effective power of nature, as the generative action of parents does in some sense cause the soul of the child. It does not do so, however, efficiently, but dispositively.

13. If we read in the lives of some saints that they were endowed with the "gift of miracles," or were distinguished by having the "grace of powers or cures," we should not conclude that those saints had some power, natural

or supernatural, which remained in them habitually, to be turned on or off at will. Such assertions simply mean that God frequently stirred those saints by a transient motion to cooperate, either by prayer or by some external action, in working a miracle. See St. Thomas *loc. cit.*, and S.Th., IIa-IIae, q. 178, a. 1, ad 1. See also ZkTh (1918), p. 748.   14. *S.Th.*, I, q. 105, a. 8.

15. See St. Thomas S.C.G., III, 102; de Tonquédec, *Introduction à l'étude du merveilleux et du miracle* (1916), pp. 239ff.

16. Many modern authors, taking miracle in this broader sense, define it as an effect perceptible by the senses, produced by God or a good angel, and surpassing the normal course of visible nature. . . . Ecclesiastical tribunals themselves, in causes of canonization, acknowledge as true miracles even such effects as good angels are thought to be able to produce by their own native power. See Benedict XIV, *De beatificatione et canonizatione servorum Dei*, IV, 1, no. 17.

17. D. F. Strauss: "Certainly one can have no clear sense of history without an insight into the solidly linked chain of ultimate causes, and a realization of the impossibility of miracles" (*Leben Jesu*, 3rd ed., Einleit, p. 86).—E. Renan: "That the Gospels are in part legendary is obvious from the very fact that they are full of miracle-accounts and of the supernatural" (*Histoire des origines du Christianisme*. I, *Vie de Jésus*, 19th ed., 48). . . . See E. Bruneteau: "De quelques théories éliminatrices du miracle," in RPA, XVIII (1914), 499, 561; XIX (1915), 225, 362.

18. See *De potentia*, q. 6, a. 1, ad 3.

19. P. Périer, "Le miracle est-il une violation des lois de la nature?" in RPA, XXX (1920), 18ff.

20. See *De potentia*, q. 6, a. 1, ad 20. Ch. Renouvier, himself no lover of Christianity, writes: "The knowledge we possess of natural laws cannot be legitimately pushed to the point of allowing us to affirm that a supra-mundane will has never produced such a phenomenon, but simply that the spontaneous development of these laws has never produced one. Neither reason nor our knowledge of nature's laws obliges us to deny the possibility of miracles. Neither have we the right to say that we may banish miracles from history in the name of constant experience and that up to this point no miracles have ever been proved" (*Philosophie analytique de l'histoire*, II (1898), 366).

21. Thus, as Wegscheider maintains (*Institutiones theologiae Christianae dogmaticae, Prolegomena*, 1, no. 12), it is not surprising that men of a less learned age, who were more prone to consider divine power than divine wisdom, easily admitted the possibility of miracles; for they were not paying attention to the fact that in extolling divine omnipotence they were themselves derogating from God's infinite wisdom.

22. It is, therefore, plainly unreasonable for Paulsen to write: "Miracles are *contrivances* whereby the universe gets put back in order again from outside" (*System der Ethik* (1889), p. 343).

23. On this point read Garrigou-Lagrange, *De Revelatione*, II, 4th ed. (1944), art. 3, 58–92.

24. See Kneller, "Wunder und Evangelienkritik," in *Stimmen*, v. 54 (1898) p. 117; G. Mattiussi, "Cognoscibilità del miracolo," in *La scuola cattolica* (1908), pp. 277, 435, 608, 704; J. Guibert "Pour voir un miracle," in RPA, v. 7 (1908), p. 439; Garrigou-Lagrange, *op. cit.*, v. II, pp. 89–92.

25. The proposition signed by Bautain (Sept. 8, 1840) also pertains to this point: "The proof of the Christian revelation drawn from the miracles of Christ which astonished the senses and minds of eye-witnesses has not lost its power or brilliance for later generations. The same proof is found in the oral and written tradition of all Christians. It is by this twofold tradition that one must demonstrate the Christian revelation both to those who reject it and to those who, without admitting the fact, are searching for it" (DB 1624).

26. See Beysens, *Critériologie*, 2nd ed., pp. 320ff, R. P. Phillips, *Modern Thomistic Philosophy*, II, 271.

27. J. Tonquédec "La critique du témoignage en matière du merveilleux," in RSR (1916), p. 50.

28. Well worth reading on this point is de Smedt, *Principes de la critique historique.*

29. Renan: "We shall, then, stand by this principle of historical criticism, that an account of supernatural occurrences cannot be admitted as such, because it always implies either gullibility or fraud" (*op. cit.*, p. 98).

30. See RAP 38 (1924), 344.

31. See Beysens, *Cosmologie*, pp. 275ff.

32. J. Charcot, in his little work, *Faith-Healing*, states that a perfect trust, engendered by natural means, that one will recover health is sufficient to explain all the cures which have actually occurred on pilgrimages and the like. . . . On the power of the imagination see St. Thomas, *S.Th.*, III, q. 13, a. 3 ad 3; *S.C.G.*, III, 99; *De potentia*, q. 6, a. 3 ad 7; *De malo*, q. 4, a. 8, ad 13.

Worth reading are Gutberlet, *Lehrbuch der Apologetik*, II, 2nd ed. 115–128, and J. B. Kettenmeyer, "Wunder und Suggestion," *Der Katholik* (1911), p. 344.

In English, for an excellent treatment of this whole problem see L. de Grandmaison, *Jesus Christ*, III, 142–150. For case histories of weird phenomena, whether produced by supernatural, preternatural, or psychic causes, see the eminent authority Herbert Thurston, *The Physical Phenomena of Mysticism* (1952). This work is more concerned with presenting data than explaining it. For a brief treatment of the usefulness of suggestion in psychotherapy see *Psychiatry and Catholicism*, by J. H. Vandervelt and R. P. Odenwald (1952), Ch. VI.

As a sample of the absurd arguments used by some champions of unbelief in their attempts to abolish miracles we shall quote from Renan's *Vie de Jésus*: "Practically all the miracles that Jesus is believed to have worked would appear to have been miracles of healing. Medicine in the Judea of his era was in the same state as it still is today in the Orient, that is, completely unscientific. In such a state of knowledge, the presence of a superior man who treats the sick person with gentleness and assures him by some visible signs that he will recover is often enough a decisive remedy. Who would dare to say that in many cases, and especially those without well-defined lesions, that contact with an exquisite person is not as powerful as the resources of a medicine-chest? The very pleasure of seeing such a person cures! He gives what he can: a smile, a hope and it is not in vain"! (*Origines du Christianisme*, I, 270).

33. See A. Bros, "Comment constater le miracle," in *Annales de philosophie Chrétienne*, 77 (1906), 250.

34. See, for example, Matthew 24:24; Mark 13:22; Deuteronomy 13:1–3.

35. See, for example, Exodus 7:8–12; 8:16–19.

36. See H. Lesêtre, "La valeur probante du miracle" in RCF 56 (1908), 257; Garrigou-Lagrange, *De Revelatione* II, (1944), 94–97.

37. Evidently, when dealing with people of such mind, one should proceed prudently. At least in the beginning one should use other arguments better suited for them. See G. J. J. Louwerens, *Thaumatophobie of Wondervrees,* 1912.

38. Even though God does not usually make use of men who follow a false religion to work a miracle, strictly speaking He can do so provided it is apparent from the circumstances that the religion of the wonder-worker is not given God's guarantee by that miracle. Consequently, Benedict XIV approved the following conclusions: "He [God] worked a genuine miracle in confirmation of the man's personal faith; therefore that man had true faith." But by no means was the following conclusion approved: "He [God] worked a miracle; therefore the faith professed by that man is the true faith" (*De canonizatione,* 1.IV, c. 4, no. 6); see S.*Th.,* II-II, q. 178, a. 2, and 3; Garrigou-Lagrange, *op. cit.,* II, objection no. 6, p. 97; RPA, XIII (1912), 479; *Pastor Bonus,* XXVII (1915), 392 and 449; DAFC under the heading, "Guérisons miraculeuses."

For a treatment of the prodigies at the tomb of the deacon, de Paris, see DAFC under the heading "Convulsionnaires." For the remarkable accounts of Aesculapius see *Studien* 59 (1902), 367; RCF (1917–18). Many miraculous healings are narrated of John Serguieff, commonly known as Father John of Cronstadt, a Russian priest. That the facts are historical is not absolutely certain, but even if they are genuine, they at least do not prove anything in favor of schismatic doctrine, but simply in favor of those truths which the Russian Church has retained of the Catholic religion; see Jean de Cronstadt, *Ma vie en Jésus-Christ,* published by A. Staerck.

39. This manner of acting is, of course, presumed to be morally good from every point; otherwise any special help of God is excluded *a priori.*

40. See St. Thomas S.*Th.,* IIa-IIae, q. 171–174; *De veritate,* q. 12; J. Touzard, *Comment utiliser l'argument prophétique* (1911); C. Pesch, *Theologische Zeitfrage,* V, 82–115; Garrigou-Lagrange, *De Revelatione,* II (1944), XX, 98–124.

41. St. Thomas less correctly derives the term prophet "from *pro,* which is *procul* [from afar] and *phanos,* which means an apparition, because far-off things become apparent to them [the prophets]" (S. *Th.,* IIa-IIae, q. 171, a. 1).

42. See Numbers 11:25–26; 1 Corinthians 11:4–5; 14 *passim.*

43. That is the explanation, for example, of the usage in Matthew 26:68: "*Prophesy to us, O Christ! who is it that struck thee?*"

44. Some examples of ambiguous prophecy are: "Croesus, in crossing the Halys River, will overthrow the vast power of wealth" (his own wealth, or that of his enemies?); "I say that you, Aeacida (Pyrrhus), can conquer the Romans" (the same sentence, since it is in the accusative with infinitive construction in Latin, can also be translated: "I say that the Romans can conquer you, Aeacida"). Worthy of note are Cicero's remarks about the Oracles of Apollo: "Chryssipus has filled a whole volume with your oracles [the oracles

of Apollo], which are, in my opinion, partly false and by chance partly true, as happens frequently in any sort of utterance. Some of the oracles are double-meaning and so obscure that the interpreter himself needs an interpreter, and the response of the Oracle must be resubmitted to the Oracles; and some of them are ambiguous and must be submitted to dialectical analysis" (De divinatione, II, 56). Even though the pagan oracles were usually combinations of ambiguity and fraud, they should not all be attributed to the wiles of the pagan priest, since they were also uttered frequently by the aid of devils. See Acts 16:16; Minucius Felix, Octavius, n. 26ff; Cyprian, De idolorum vanitate, c. VII; Cicero, De divinatione, I, 9.

In regard to the Sibylline Books the following points are important. Sibyll (Sios = Dios boulē = God's wisdom?) was thought by the pagans to be a nymph who announced the gods' decisions relating to nations and king-doms. At first there was but one Sibyll, but by Cicero's time some ten Sibylls are mentioned. The collection of oracles which once circulated among the pagans under the name of the Sibylls, have all perished except for a few frag-ments which we find in Plutarch and others. The twelve Sibylline books extant today (I-VIII and XI-XIV) were written at different times between 200 B.C. and 300 A.D. by unknown writers, some of whom were Jews and others Christians. See Kirchenlexicon under the heading "Sybillinische Bücher"; RB (1904) p. 627; Pastor Bonus XXXI (1919), 337; Scholastik (1929), p. 54; DAFC under the heading "Sibylles."

45. It is thus apparent that a prophecy is a miracle, not of power, but of knowledge. It is an intellectual miracle and may be either absolute or relative.

46. See S.Th., loc. cit., q. 173, a. 2; RSPT (1914) p. 218.

47. Suarez: "The gift of prophecy perfects a man in a way that is both human and perfect: but to speak without any understanding of what one is saying does not confer anything to human perfection; rather it is characteristic of those who are temporarily deranged, or are dreaming, and sometimes of those who lack the use of reason entirely" (De fide, d. 8, s. 4, no. 1).

48. An imaginary vision has joined to it a disengagement from sense-perceptions. St. Thomas, S.Th., IIa-IIae, q. 173, a. 3. It is clear that this disengagement from sense-perceptions, which occurs in states of ecstasy and rapture, is diametrically opposed to mental disorders.

49. Wegscheider mentions this opinion in his Institutiones theologicae, I, c. 2, no. 50.

50. These points about prophecy itself and God's foreknowledge we have mentioned precisely insofar as they are knowledge. We are not unaware of the fact that God's knowledge together with His will is the cause of things. In fact, God not only foresees future events, He also prepares them to come to pass. Even in so doing He does not destroy human liberty. Divine provi-dence regulates not only the effects but also the causes of those effects and the particular ways in which they will be produced. Just as God provides that I do something at a particular time, so also He provides for my doing it freely. See St. Thomas, S.C.G., III, 93. Let none be disturbed by the manner of speech employed in Sacred Scripture: this was done in order that the prophecy might be fulfilled (see Matthew 1:22; John 19:36). The scriptural manner of speech should be explained in this wise: first, God decreed that this event should some day take place; then, because He had so decreed, He fore-

told its occurrence; and after foretelling it He brought about its accomplishment both in order to carry out His own design and at the same time to manifest that He tells the truth and is faithful to His promises, without, however, in any way destroying man's free will.

For a full treatment of the problem of reconciling God's foreknowledge and man's free will, see works directly interested in that problem, for example, Van Noort's *De Deo Uno et Trino*, no. 70–98.

51. Since we are dealing with the recognizability of prophecy insofar as it acts as a criterion of revelation, we restrict our discussion exclusively to those prophecies which have been fulfilled by the event. For a prophecy which has not yet been fulfilled is of no use in demonstrating the fact of a divine mission or of a divine revelation. However, the philosophical truth of a prophecy that is still to be fulfilled can sometimes be known with certitude. For example, think of a prophecy backed up by a miracle, or of a prophecy uttered by someone whose divine mission has already been established on other grounds.—A prophecy which does not tally with events is by that very fact proved false, unless there is question of a conditioned prophecy, such as is often the case with prophecies of a threatening nature (see Jonas 3:4; Isaias 38), even though the condition may not be expressed as such. See *S.Th.*, IIa-IIae, q. 174, a. 1; *S.C.G.*, III, 155.

52. See above, no. 51. Read, for example, 2 Esdras 6:12ff. . . . Consequently, in the case of visions or predictions brought about by trances, hypnotism and spiritualism, the intervention of God or of a good angel is ruled out by the very circumstances. Certainly God is not in the habit of using hypnotists as His instruments, nor do they themselves maintain that they are being aided by God. The manner whereby spiritualists conduct their performances is often enough morally blameworthy, or at least indecorous. As a final point, supernatural gifts are not fuel for human curiosity or vanity, nor are they given that their recipients may make money. Whatever is certainly genuine in the shows of spiritualists must be explained on natural grounds, or if it is morally certain that purely natural means cannot explain what takes place, then the work of an evil angel must be taken into account.

But, as Ottiger sanely observes, among the matters alleged to be revealed in a hypnotic state, or by spiritualism, one finds nothing the knowledge of which would surpass all created intelligence. Rather, all such items are founded upon the knowledge of things already existent, but hidden, or at most upon such things as could be known by relative prophecy. (*Theologia fundamentalis*, I, 252).

Worth reading on this point are Gutberlet, *Lehrbuch der Apologetik*, II, 2nd ed., 147–200 and Reinhold, *Theologia fundamentalis*, I, 206.

53. M. Blondel, *L'Action* (1893); *Lettre sur les exigences de la pensee contemporaine en matiere d'apologetique* (1896); Ch. Denis, *Esquisse d'une apologie philosophique du Christianisme* (1898); Laberthonniere, *Essais de philosophie religieuse* (1903), etc.

Worth reading on this matter are: Schanz, *Neuere Versuche der Apologetik* (1897), and the Tübinger *Quartals.* (1903); Pesch, *Theologische Zeitfragen*, I, 66; le Bachelet, *L'Apologetique traditionnelle et l'apologetique moderne* (1897); J. v. de Groot, *Summa apologetica*, 3rd. ed. p. 10; H. Mazzella, *Praelectiones scholastico-dogmaticae*, III, 3rd ed., 626; Gardeil, *La' credibilité et l'apologetique,* 2nd ed. (1928); DAFC under the headings "Apologetique" and "Immanence"; DTC under the heading "Apologetique"; J. de Tonquedec, *Immanence* (1913, written against Blondel); *Rev. de philosoph.* (1913), p. 286; *Studien,* 62 (1904), 382; 63 (1904), 427; 72 (1909), 259, 555; RPA XII (1911), 641, 837; XIII (1912), 270, 749; A. de Poulpiquet, *L'objet integral de 'L'apologetique* (1911).

For more recent treatments of the same subject see Garrigou-Lagrange, *op. cit.* I, 121–128. On page 128 he gives a list of articles written by himself in which he has critically examined the more recent publications of Blondel: *La pensee* (1934), *L'Etre et les etres* (1935), and *L'action* (2nd ed., completely revised), v. I (1936), v. II (1937).

See also Nicolau and Salaverri, *Sacrae theologiae summa,* I, 2nd ed. (1952) no. 138, 150–154.

For an excellent historical review of the milieu in which the method of immanence took root, together with a judicious appraisal of what is worthwhile in the movement, see Rogert Aubert, *Le probleme de L'acte de foi,* Part 2, c. 3, "Les controverses autour de la methode d'immanence," 2nd ed. (1950), pp. 265–392.

54. Some writers, like Olle-Laprune (*La prix de la vie*) and G. Fonsegrive (*Le Catholicisme et la vie de l'esprit*), are in agreement with the immanentists only insofar as they personally prefer "the intellectual and moral suitability of Christianity" and its "identity with the laws of life" to all other criteria. In short, they admit the ontological priority of the speculative reason over the practical, and its ability to reach truth with certitude; they admit the objective validity of the proof by external criteria, but simply have a preference for the internal criteria as a means of bringing modern men to the Church. See *Studien,* as cited above; Garrigou-Lagrange, *op. cit.,* I, 114.

55. This idea was already condemned by St. Pius V (see DB 1021, 1024, under the errors of Baius), and St. Pius X condemned any method which attempts to demonstrate that a need for the supernatural order is inherent in human nature:

> But here we must once more bitterly lament the fact that there are Catholics who, though rejecting Immanence as a doctrine, employ it *as a method of apologetics* and do so with so little caution that they seem to admit that there is in human nature not merely a capacity and suitability for the supernatural order (something that Catholic apologists have always noted, but with proper reservations) but an inborn need truly deserving the name need (Encyclical *Pascendi,* DB 2103).

56. See, for example, Beysens, *Criteriologie,* 2nd ed., pp. 240ff; Phillips, *op. cit.*

Special Bibliography for Miracles

St. Thomas: *Summa theologiae,* I, q. 105, articles 6–8. *Summa contra gentiles,* III, 98ff. *De potentia,* q. 6. G. Sichirollo has gathered together various texts of St. Thomas on miracles in his *Nomenclatura tomistica nella teoria del miraculo* (1909).

Ales, A. d': Article "Miracle" in the *Dictionnaire apologetique de la foi Catholique.*

Garrigou-Lagrange: *De revelatione*, II, 4th ed. (1944), 32–97.

Grandmaison,' Leonce de: "Les signes divines et les miracles" in *Recherches de science religieuse* (1914), p. 105.

Hove, A. van: *La doctrine du miracle chez S. Thomas et son accord avec les principes de la recherche scientifique* (1927).

Michel: Article "Miracle" in the *Dictionnaire de 'theologie catholique.*

Poulpiquet, A. de: *Le miracle et ses suppleances* (1913).

Sortais, G.: *La providence et le miracle devant le science moderne* (1905).

Tonquedec, J. de: *Introduction á l'etude du merveilleux et du miracle,* 3rd ed. (1923).

Tessen-Weisierski, F. von: *Die Grundlagen des Wunderbegriffs nach Thomas v. Aquin.*

Zacchi, A.: *Il miracolo* (1923).

English Works:

Chesterton, G.: *Orthodoxy,* pp. 278–284.

Knox, Ronald: *The Hidden Stream,* especially chapter 11 "Miracles."

Lattey, C. and Manson, A.: "Miracles," *Religion and Science* (Cambridge Summer School Lectures, 1939).

Lewis, C. S.: *Miracles* (1947).

Messenger, E. C.: "The Miraculous Element in the Bible," *Catholic Commentary on Holy Scripture* (1951), nos. 87a–91c.

Newman, J. H.: *Essay on the Miracles of Scripture* (1870).

Phillips, R. P.: *Modern Thomistic Philosophy,* II (1950), 352–363.

SECTION II

The Truth of the Christian-Catholic Religion

I. *Preliminary Remarks: Definition of Terms.*

II. *Divisions of this Section:*

    a. The sublimity of the Christian-Catholic religion;

    b. Christ's own divine mission;

    c. The divine origin of Christ's work, that is, of the Christian-Catholic religion;

    d. The divine prophecies about Christ and His work.

Chapter I. THE SUBLIMITY OF THE CHRISTIAN-CATHOLIC RELIGION

Preliminary Remarks.

PROPOSITION 1: From no viewpoint is Christian-Catholic doctrine unworthy of God. Moreover, it is so sublime that it seems to be altogether beyond the power of human invention.

Proof of the first point: Catholic doctrine is not unworthy of God.

1. The sublimity of Catholic doctrine.

    a. It is a complete and full system of religion.

    b. It is an extremely holy system of religion.

    c. It is a very beautiful system of religion.

    d. It is an extremely wholesome system of religion.

    Corollary.

2. This sublimity cannot be attributed to mere human genius.

    a. It teaches natural religion fully, surely, truly.

    b. It adds to natural religion.

    c. It contains many mysteries, yet does not contradict reason.

    d. It is suitable for all minds, all nationalities; and it is extremely wholesome.

The explanations based on evolution from:

    1. Jewish religion, and

    2. syncretism

are inadequate.

The Truth of the Christian-Catholic Religion

Now that the preliminary questions have been clarified, it **64** remains to prove that there actually exists in the world a religion revealed by God: *Christianity as professed by the Catholic Church.*

The Christian revelation was not completed and perfected except through Jesus Christ, from whom it takes its name. That revelation can, in a certain sense, be traced back to our First Parents.[1] Using the term "Christian religion" in a broad sense, one may distinguish three eras.

1. *The primitive religion.* This was based on the revelations made to the First Parents and the Patriarchs, to whom Christ was promised, however obscurely. This is called the era of the natural law.*

2. *The Mosaic religion.* This belonged to one nation alone, the Jews. Moses was the divine messenger who brought this religion to his people, and the prophets developed and enriched it. Its main purpose was to prepare the way for the coming of Christ and the universal religion He would establish. This is known as the era of the Mosaic Law.

3. *The Christian religion* in the strict sense. This was promulgated by Christ and His Apostles for the entire world and for all time. In the concrete it is none other than the religion of the Catholic Church. This, the era in which we live, is called the era of the Gospel Law.

The ideal method of procedure here would be to demonstrate **65** individually the divine origin of the primitive, of the Mosaic, and of the Christian religion. This approach is the most scientific, but it is also the most lengthy. On that account, the demonstration of the primitive and Mosaic religions will be omitted here.[2] After the

---

* The phrase "era of the natural law" does not mean that the people of that time lived exclusively under the natural law. Such a meaning would exclude entirely any revelation. The phrase is used to distinguish it from the era of the Mosaic Law. The era of the natural law lasted up to the promulgation of the Gospel Law for such peoples as did not belong to the Israelite nation. See W. Schmidt, *Die Uroffenbarung als Anfang der Offenbarungen Gottes,* 5th ed., Kempten, 1923.

proof of the divine origin of the Christian religion in the strict sense, a brief discussion of those preparatory revelations which Christ Himself acknowledged and confirmed as divine in origin will be added in an appendix.

The demonstration of the Christian religion will make it clear that the divine religion instituted by Christ is none other than the religion of the Catholic Church. In short, the demonstration of the Christian religion will be at the same time a demonstration of the Catholic religion.

It is one thing to show that the *religion* professed by the Catholic Church is the divine religion established by Christ; it is quite another to explore the establishment and constitution of the Church as an ecclesiastical society. Here the discussion centers on the first point; the second is left for a separate work, *Christ's Church*.

The opponents of this thesis are not only orthodox Protestants who deny the divine origin of the Catholic religion, but also liberal Protestants and Modernists, who deny Christ's divinity and maintain that He taught no definite body of doctrine, but started a sort of religious movement that was adapted, or should be adapted, to varying ages and places.[3]

The subject-matter of this section embraces four chapters. The first proves the divine origin of the Christian-Catholic religion by internal criteria; the others demonstrate the same fact by external criteria, each in a different way. The second chapter presents arguments which directly prove Christ's own divine mission and thereby affords a brief and provisory proof of the divine origin of the Christian-Catholic religion. The third chapter offers arguments to prove directly the divine origin of Christ's work, which is the Christian-Catholic religion. Chapter four corroborates both Christ's own divine mission and the divine truth of the Catholic religion by a consideration of the Messianic prophecies.

66 The Catholic Church claims that her doctrine comes from the divine revelation promulgated by Christ and His Apostles. She maintains that Christ was sent by God to found a religion and that she has truly received a mandate from Christ to guard and preach that religion to the end of time.

Chapter 1. The sublimity of the Christian-Catholic religion

The teaching of the Catholic Church, if examined attentively, is found to be so marvelously sublime that it is altogether credible, and indeed quite probable, that it has come from God. At a minimum, every fair-minded man has an obligation to investigate more closely the arguments which her defenders offer in behalf of her divine origin.

Chapter 2. Christ's own divine mission

It is clear from both oral and written tradition that Christ claimed to be a divine messenger. This claim is proved by the extraordinary holiness of Christ Himself, the fulfillment of His prophecies, the miracles wrought by Him, and His resurrection from the dead. Since Christ's claim to be a divine messenger is true, then the religion founded by Him is divine in origin. Christ's religion was entrusted to the Catholic Church, and to it alone, for its guardianship and promulgation.

Chapter 3. The divine origin of Christ's work (the Christian-Catholic religion)

The Catholic Church claims that she was founded by Christ as the guardian and teacher of His revelation and that the religion she preaches is Christ's own divine religion. This claim is proved by many miracles in the physical order, the wonderful spread and preservation of Christ's religion, the magnificent harvest of sanctity which it has produced, and the remarkable heroism of its martyrs. Consequently the religion of the Catholic Church is truly divine in origin, and Christ's own divine mission is indirectly confirmed, as He was the founder of this divine religion.

Chapter 4. The divine prophecies about Christ and His work

Long before the coming of Christ there were written in the sacred books of the Jews various promises about a certain extraordinary messenger of God and about the universal and indestructible spiritual kingdom He would establish—the Messianic prophecies. Those prophecies have been fulfilled in Christ and in the Catholic religion. Their fulfillment shows that they were true prophecies, uttered under divine inspiration. They validly corroborate both Christ's own divine mission and the divine truth of the Catholic religion. That man whom God Himself has approved as His own messenger is truly a genuine one, and that religion is certainly a divine work which has long beforehand been promised as the kingdom of His Messias.

CHAPTER I

The Sublimity of Christian-Catholic Religion

The argument derived from the sublimity of Christian doctrine **67** can be presented in either of two ways. 1. One can describe only those points of the Christian doctrine which all Christians have received from Christ and thereby conclude that such a doctrine is in a general way beyond the power of human invention and that it was certainly beyond the power of Christ to invent, since He was not even an educated man. 2. One can examine the entire doctrine taught by the Catholic Church (omitting for the time being the question whether or not the whole body of doctrine in all its parts comes from Christ) and thence conclude that such doctrine, no matter who its original author was, cannot be a product of mere human genius.

Those who follow the first method can present only an incoherent doctrine, as there are a vast number of things which are occasions for disagreement among the various Christian sects: did Christ Himself teach this or not? did He mean this doctrine to be understood in this sense or in another? To avoid these inconveniences and to present our argument as one directly in favor of the Christian-Catholic religion, this presentation will follow the second method of approach. The purpose of this chapter is to show that Catholic doctrine, considered in its sublimity, is at least quite probably divine in origin. The words "at least quite probably" are used because an appreciation of internal criteria depends to some extent on the subjective temperament and disposition of the examiner. Consequently one could not grant these criteria a strictly demonstrative power. The principal aim of the present chapter is to prepare the mind to discuss the external arguments more readily and to weigh them objectively and justly.

PROPOSITION: *From no point-of-view is Christian-Catholic doctrine* **68** *unworthy of God; indeed, it is so marvelously sublime that it seems to be altogether beyond the power of human discovery.*

The proposition has two parts. By applying negative internal criteria, the first shows that the doctrine in question could have a divine origin. By applying positive internal criteria, the second renders the divine origin of that doctrine at least highly plausible, even if it does not absolutely demonstrate such a divine origin.

Proof of the first point: Christian-Catholic doctrine is not unworthy of God

The doctrine of Christ, within a few years of its origin, spread even to the more civilized nations, and waxed strong among those peoples who far surpassed others in civilization and in the pursuit of knowledge. Furthermore, Christ's doctrine always found numerous and fierce opponents, of whom many were exceptionally brilliant.[4] Though this doctrine was subjected to the strictest sort of examination a thousand times, no one could ever prove that it was in any way contrary to sound reason or good morals. In fact, with the exception of those who were so incensed by their passions or blinded by prejudices that they did not even refrain from obvious calumny, its opponents usually granted that nowhere were the theoretical and practical truths which belong to natural religion taught in purer form than in Christianity. Rationalists, of course, by common consent sneer at all truths not positively clear to reason and term them contrary to reason; in this, however, they are following not reason, but prejudice. The particular arguments by which rationalists try to show that some Christian dogmas, such as the Blessed Trinity or the Holy Eucharist, are contradictory to reason are dealt with in their own proper places in the course of dogmatic theology. They cannot be treated adequately here, because they require a much more accurate exposition of dogma. It is enough at this point simply to make the following general observation: the semblance of a contradiction between the teachings of the faith and the conclusions of reason will almost always be found to take its origin from the fact that

> . . . either the dogmas of the faith have not been grasped and presented according to the mind of the Church, or that opinions and guesses have been mistaken for axioms of reason (DB 1797).

69 Proof of the second point: Christian-Catholic doctrine seems to be utterly beyond the power of human discovery

To prove this it must be shown that: 1. Christian-Catholic doctrine is actually sublime; and 2. it is so sublime that it could hardly, indeed, in no wise, be attributed to merely natural causes.

I. The sublimity of Catholic doctrine

a. It is a complete and full system of religion. In addition to teaching a complete system of natural religion with great purity and certitude, it also supplies abundantly for the lacunae that are found in natural religion (for example, its teachings on the manner in which God should be worshipped, about the way of obtaining forgiveness of sins, etc., and it solves with great adroitness the deepest problems which trouble every human mind. One need merely point out its doctrines about the origin of the world, the common origin of all from one parent, the cause of misfortunes in the life and the internal struggle common to all men, the doctrine about man's condition in the life to come, and many others. With good reason St. Thomas could assert:

Not one of the philosophers before the coming of Christ, no matter how hard he struggled to do so, could learn as much about God and matters necessary for eternal life, as one poor old lady can know by faith after Christ's coming. Hence it is said in Isaias 11:9: *the earth is filled with the knowledge of the Lord* (*Expositio symboli,* art. 1).[5]

b. It is an extremely holy system of religion. Consider its standard of sanctity. Presenting the noblest doctrine about God as the all-loving Father of all men, it offers as the supreme standard of all morality: *"Thou shalt love the Lord thy God with thy whole heart . . . and thy neighbor as thyself"* (Matt. 23:37, 39). From this standard flow all man's duties to God, to his neighbors, and to himself.

Duties towards God. Man is taught to seek His glory in all things and before all else, to seek Him with love and awe, to place in Him perfect confidence, casting aside anxiety about earthly affairs, to imitate His infinite perfections with all his human strength.

Duties towards neighbors. Man is commanded to love his neighbors for the sake of God with a brotherly love that excludes all injustice, all harsh words, and even unkind judgments. This love is to embrace not only benefactors, friends, and fellow-citizens, but it is to include also foreigners, enemies, and persecutors. This is to be a practical love which will move him to run to the aid of the poor and downtrodden. What is more, it will move him to lay down his life for his brothers, if need be.

Duties towards self. All men are commanded, in acknowledgment of their own dignity, to abstain from the vices of the world, to bear misfortune patiently, to avoid vainglory, to treat their bodies with the reverence fitting God's temples, and to place the care of their souls before all other interests. These injunctions, in proportionate measure, are given to all Catholics as necessary commandments.

To foster a still higher form of perfection and to attract generous souls to the very heights of sanctity there are added to the commandments the counsels of obedience, poverty, and chastity, which open a fuller and safer road to Christian perfection.[6]

Consider the means of sanctity. It is deeply impressed on individuals that to be able to lead a life worthy of the Christian name there is always at hand power from high, ready to supplement the weakness of human strength. This power is the manifold grace of God which Christ, dying on the cross, merited for all men, which He constantly offers to individuals in many ways, especially in the Holy Sacrifice of the Mass. Man is ordered to come with confidence to the throne of grace that by frequent prayer he may obtain help at an opportune time. To make up for his poor dispositions and at the same time to give a sort of visible guarantee that grace has been received, there are the sacraments which admirably correspond to all the necessities of the spiritual life.

Consider the stimuli to sanctity. Before the eyes of all are held up the most perfect Model of sanctity, Christ Himself, and the strongest sanction possible. The good have promised to them in this life peace of conscience and spiritual joy; in the hereafter a life which is eternal, whose pure delights, worthy of both God and man, are such that eye has never gazed upon, nor ear heard, nor mind ever imagined their like. On the other hand, to inculcate a saving fear in evil-doers, eternal punishment is threatened.[7]

71   c. It is a very beautiful system of religion. This beauty derives from the unity and perfect consistency of its doctrines.[8] Its speculative dogmas are indissolubly interlinked with one another in such a way that one flows from the other, one calls for and presupposes another. Think of the mystery of the Redemption which gives life to all Christianity. This mystery supposes, on the one hand, the mysteries of the Trinity, the Incarnation, and the privileges of the Blessed Virgin Mary. On the other hand, it supposes the dogmas concerning original sin and the elevation of man to the supernatural order. Similarly, from the dogma of the Redemption are

derived the doctrines concerning the Church, the Mystical Body of Christ, the Eucharistic Sacrifice, the sacraments, and the adoption of men as sons by God (an adoption now imperfect by grace, to be made perfect by glory). Again, the dogmas mentioned above in many ways presuppose, are related to, and throw light on, truths of the natural order. The mystery of the Trinity necessarily supposes a God who is purely spiritual, having infinite intelligence and will; the dogma of the Redemption admirably demonstrates the justice, wisdom, and goodness of God, and holds as already evident the freedom of man; the doctrine of original sin necessarily implies the common origin of all men from a common parent and offers an explanation for the miseries of this life; the doctrine of glorification includes the truths that the soul is immortal and that man's final destiny consists in the knowledge and love of God. Because of this deep consistency of doctrine, heresies usually tend by their own weight to fall into dissolution: the rejection of one truth or of a few truths makes the whole edifice of doctrine begin to totter.

There is an indissoluble connection between the theoretical dogmas and the moral precepts. The latter either arise from the former, or are strengthened by them, or receive their sanction from them. Usually born of the theoretical truths of natural religion, the moral precepts receive new and extremely valid motives of obligation from the mysteries. What could more stir a man to love God above all things than the dogmas of the Incarnation and adoptive filiation? What could more strongly urge a man to love his neighbor than the common redemption of all men through Jesus Christ? What could more powerfully move a man to sobriety and chastity than a reflection on the Eucharistic blood received into our very bodies, and on the Holy Spirit dwelling within us? With good reason, then, can one compare Christian ethics without Christian dogma to a house without a foundation.

Christian-Catholic doctrine is sublime because it is suitable to every type of mind and every nationality. It is so profound that even after nineteen centuries it offers to learned men inexhaustible material for thought and meditation, always opening up new vistas to their minds, ever attracting their hearts with new delights. Yet, at the same time, it is so simple that even the uneducated may easily learn it and love it sincerely. Do not little children have the deepest mysteries explained to them in a few words? Do not unlearned men receive a sure and clear solution of the deepest problems which even the greatest geniuses cannot discover on

(115)

their own? Do not business men, manual laborers, and housewives, the healthy and the handicapped, old people and school children approach Holy Communion with a devotion equal to that of the learned theologian? [9] For this reason Christian doctrine has been compared to a river in which both the lamb may gambol and the elephant swim. [10] It is suitable also for all nationalities, because all its dogmas and all its commandments refer equally to all nations; no nation is preferred to any other. Furthermore, Christianity has no regulations which bind it to any particular place—it sharply distinguishes religion from politics—nor is it shackled to a particular form of government.

72   d. It is an extremely wholesome system of religion, admirably designed to promote the happiness both of individual men and of society. What has been said already goes far to establish this matter. A religion which is suitable to every type of mind, which satisfactorily answers the legitimate questions of the human intellect and at the same time strikingly fosters human holiness is definitely a happy religion. Otherwise one must concede that what aptly fits mans nature does not lead men to happiness. How could a religion fail to foster the happiness of individual men, when that religion teaches a man to resist his passions and concupiscences, to bear the hardships of life with manly courage, to be content with life's necessities, and to acknowledge the governance of a fatherly providence in all things? How could a religion fail to foster the happiness of society, when that religion strongly urges those very virtues that establish peace and harmony among men: humility, patience, obedience? When it commands all to lend aid to their neighbors, defends the full sanctity of marriage, vindicates the legitimate use of both domestic and public authority, and at the same time forbids every abuse of that same authority with a warning about the strictest sort of judgment by a Divine Avenger?

72a Corollary

In these days especially, some people object that Christianity, or at least Catholicism, offers an obstacle to gracious living and economic progress because it prescribes "flight from the world," praises poverty, and so forth. This objection is utterly groundless. Christianity, in teaching man his absolutely final goal—to serve God in this life, and to enjoy Him in the next, by no means excludes other goals, even though they are intermediate and subordinate.

But it is perfectly legitimate for men continually to aspire to a more perfect use and exercise of all their powers, both bodily and spiritual, and to be busy constantly about the job of subjecting material things more fully to their control. Are we not clearly instructed that man, the image of God, was made by God to be lord over all irrational creatures? That is why the Catholic religion neither discredits nor condemns anything designed to serve the well-being of people. Indeed, precisely because it so deeply understands that men in general are greatly hindered from the pursuit of virtue by indigence and poverty, the Catholic religion ardently longs for all to have a decent share of temporal goods. Catholicism forbids only the immoderate or disordered use and pursuit of earthly goods.

If it is asked whether Catholicism also gives a positive motive for a more intense pursuit of material goods, a distinction must be made. Catholicism does not directly and *ex professo* urge men to pursuits of this sort. And quite rightly, for it is a religion to which was entrusted the care not of temporal, but of eternal affairs. Men rarely need any urging to make them pursue earthly goods with great zest. Indirectly, though, the Church does a great deal to foster economic progress by condemning sloth, carousing, extravagance, and avarice, by instructing every man about the duties of his state in life, by ordering all men to practice justice, honesty, and charity. That is why, all else being equal, a society dedicated to materialism, and thirsting exclusively after material goods, may amass more abundant riches, but a Christian society will more successfully promote the common prosperity of its citizens. Even if one consider exclusively material goods, it does little good for a country to have its wealth immensely increased by multiplying and perfecting its means of production, unless at the same time all classes of society obtain a proportionate share of the wealth.

But the Catholic Church applauds poverty! True; but what does this mean? She does not praise or yearn for a social milieu in which the majority of the citizens would be oppressed by poverty. She does praise voluntary poverty; that is, she praises those who put aside all zeal for earthly riches and live only for God and their neighbor. These people, although despised by a number of men who ridicule what they fail to understand, do a great service to human society. They help society by the works of charity they undertake, or by the prayers, penances, and example with which they soften God's anger and restrain other men from a disordered desire for things of this earth.*

73 **II. Catholic doctrine is so sublime that it cannot be referred solely to the discovery of human genius**

a. Catholic doctrine teaches natural religion with great fullness, with perfect certitude, and without any error. So perfect a knowledge of the entire field of natural religion is so difficult a task that it seems morally impossible, at least in the broad sense of the term, for any human intelligence to attain it. (See number 23.) It is at least certain that outside of Christianity no school of philosophy and no religion has ever arrived at such knowledge. In fact, a large number of Christian sects which separated from the Catholic Church have erred in teaching even natural religion: early Protestantism did so when it denied man's free will; Calvinism (and Jansenism) did so when they taught that God arbitrarily precondemned some men to hell, thereby attributing to God an obvious injustice.

b. By the teachings which the Catholic religion has added to natural religion it has aptly supplied for the lacunae of natural religion. It has adroitly solved the deepest sort of problems which have troubled mankind in religious matters, and has strikingly advanced men's holiness. Once again, therefore, human genius seems to be ruled out as a satisfactory explanation. If it is so terribly difficult to know even natural religion satisfactorily, would it not be even more difficult to add such points as seem quite clearly to perfect natural religion?

* Note that the Catholic Church does not acknowledge a double standard of sanctity, one for monks and the other for the laity, nor does she identify Christian perfection with the monastic life. Christian perfection for people in all walks of life consists in love of God and neighbor; the religious vows (poverty, chastity, and obedience) are nothing more than means to sanctification, but means of very great value for certain people. On the one hand, any man in any walk of life can arrive at perfection without the observance of the vows; on the other hand, not all of those who dedicate themselves to a life in religion actually arrive at perfection. The religious state, considered in itself and purely abstractly, is the quickest means to perfection and can be spoken of as the state of perfection, *i.e.*, a way of life professedly dedicated to the pursuit of perfection (see *S.Th.*, IIa-IIae, q. 184). It is erroneous to conclude from this that the monastic life is the best route to perfection for each and every man considered in the concrete situation. *Each one has his own gift from God, one in this way, and another in that* (1 Cor. 7:7).

(See A. Tanquerey, *The Spiritual Life*, III, 153–203; Garrigou-Lagrange, *The Three Ages of the Interior Life*, I, chapter 8, 144–159 and 12 and 13, 196–213.)

c. Catholic doctrine contains many mysteries which border on certain truths of the natural order. Even though vast progress has been made in the natural sciences long after the origin of Christianity, not one of these new discoveries (this means, of course, definitely established truths, not wild guesses) has been found to contradict any Christian dogma. The more carefully and more profoundly learned men investigate the Christian religion, the more they marvel at the perfect harmony of that system; the more they marvel at the perfect coherence of the super-rational truths in relationship to one another and in relation to natural truths, and at the extraordinary appropriateness of the mysteries in themselves. Now if this teaching about mysteries were nothing but the product of man's imagination, it would of course, be nothing more than a ridiculous imposture. If this were so, would it not be utterly incredible for some man to have knit together a series of lies in matters of this kind with such extraordinary dexterity that even after innumerable and exacting examinations no falsehood would ever have come to light? Again, it can be easily shown that all the people who, over the course of the centuries, have dared to "reform" the Christian-Catholic religion, either by adding or subtracting something, have always destroyed something honorable or introduced something dishonorable, and have lessened its over-all harmony. If the Catholic religion were a purely human invention, it would be difficult to explain why it could never be improved upon by men and why every change has always turned out for the worse.

d. Catholic doctrine is suitable for every type of mind and every nationality, and at the same time is an extremely wholesome doctrine.[11] This fact greatly supports the preceding arguments. A doctrine which is wholesome for all kinds of men and at the same time is very worthy of God, the loving Father of all mankind, seems by that very fact to be beyond the power of man's genius. Every purely human doctrine in precise proportion to its depth and sublimity, gets beyond the reach of the common multitude of men; and practically all the other religions were tightly bound to one or another particular nationality.

From these considerations one can conclude with at least great probability that Christian-Catholic doctrine is not a human invention. And since no serious minded man would attribute the origin of an extremely holy religion to evil spirits, it is at least quite probable that Christian-Catholic doctrine has good reason to claim a divine origin. If that is so, then every man has the obligation of seriously investigating the various external or historical arguments which are adduced as proof of that divine origin.

To weaken the argument from the incomparable splendor of the Christian religion rationalists try to explain the origin of that religion on the grounds of evolution, to which, in the minds of many of our contemporaries, nothing is impossible.

74 *Scholion. The origin of the Christian religion cannot be explained either as an evolution of Judaism, or as a syncretism of the Jewish religion with pagan superstition and Greek philosophy.*

1. The Jewish religion did indeed contain several dogmas and precepts of Christianity. Some can be found expressed clearly; others are found only in germ. Because this is so, Christianity is rightly called the final fulfillment of the Mosaic religion. Did not our Lord Himself say: *"I have not come to destroy, but to fulfill"* (Matthew 5:17)? Do not all the Fathers and Doctors of the Church agree with the saying of Augustine: "in the Old Testament the New is concealed, and in the New the Old is revealed" (*The First Catechetical Instruction*, ACW translation, IV, no. 8, 23)?

Christianity, nevertheless, is so vastly superior to Judaism and contains so many doctrines which are foreign to and even opposed to Judaism such *as it was professed at the time of Christ,* that Judaism can in nowise be said to have given birth to Christianity by a natural evolution. The fundamental Christian dogmas of the Trinity, Incarnation, and Redemption through the death of the Messias, of justification by faith without the works of the Mosaic law, were utterly foreign to the minds of Christ's contemporaries. The moral teaching of Christianity not only abolished the ceremonies of the Mosaic law, which had a strong attraction for the Jews, but also perfected the moral code of Moses, purifying it of the corruptions of the Pharisees, Sadducees, and Essenes. For their external and ritual sanctity it substituted an internal and truly noble one.[12] Certainly the Jews awaited a Messias, but a Messias who was to be a political king and was to restore a temporal kingdom to Israel by conquering the pagan nations. The Messianic prophecies of the Old Testament were truly fulfilled in Christ and in His religion, but they were fulfilled in a manner quite different from the hopes and desires of the Jews of Christ's time. The Jews at the time of Christ were so addicted to religious exclusivism that, as history shows, the narrowness of the early Judaic Christians caused great trouble for the Church, which from the very beginning had a universal perspective.[13]

The Christian religion seemed so novel to contemporary Judaism, and its teachings differed from the ideas current among Jews to such a degree that the leaders of the Jewish nation, with the support of the people, demanded Christ's death on the cross and inaugurated numerous persecutions against His Apostles.[14]

Another answer to the objection that Christianity is a purely natural religion, a further evolution of the Jewish religion, which itself was purely natural, can be given. The seeds of the Christian religion, which were actually contained in the Law and the Prophets, were themselves not the product of man s mind, but revelations given by God.

2. Syncretism maintains that Christianity originally lacked real 74a dogmatic teaching, but little by little gathered together its doctrines, regulations, and practices from very different sources. Syncretism is quite popular among many students of comparative religion today, though there are almost as many varieties of the theory as there are adherents. In fact, many hold that the pagan mysteries were one of the major sources on which Christianity relied.[15]

This theory is not based upon proved, historical data, but is an *a priori* postulate of rationalism, which excludes at the outset all possibility of supernatural intervention by God, and consequently is obliged to find a natural explanation of the Christian religion. For this reason it leaps from very tenuous premises to very resounding conclusions, nor does it hesitate to assert that the most superficial resemblances among religions definitely establish that one religion has borrowed from another. These comparative religionists indicate various sources for Christian doctrine: now the Greeks, now the Persians, now the Buddhists. The variety and inconsistency of their opinions is itself a good argument against the lack of a sound scientific foundation for their conclusions.

Even if the historical possibility of such a multiple derivation of Christian doctrine, or rather the accommodation of that doctrine to the religious and philosophical mentality of varied peoples, were granted, the theory of religious evolution is still faced with two insoluble difficulties. 1. It offers no answer to the question: "How could there arise out of such an evolution a religion that is universal, possessing an extremely consistent body of doctrine?" If Christianity had adapted itself all over the world to the opinions of local peoples by embracing whatever they contain of vitality and worth, it would have had to change its nature in different places. Even if all these varied additions had managed to be strung together by heaven only knows what sort of a unifying principle, it would, at the very least, never have reached that extraordinary unity found in Catholic doctrine. 2. This theory cannot explain why the Christian religion caused such contradiction and fierce persecutions all over the world. Why should the various pagan nations have attacked a religion whose very genius lay in its inexhaustible ability to accommodate itself to various peoples?

The syncretistic theory is historically impossible. The supposed eclectic borrowing could not have been done by Christ or His Apostles. According to the adversaries they were mere men and possessed no supernatural aids. Consequently how could they know of foreign and far-off religions? They were either completely ignorant of Greek philosophy, or at best did not know enough to accomplish such a task. Nor could the borrowing have been done by later Christians. It can be demonstrated unquestionably, from an examination of the books of the New Testament and other ancient documents, that the fundamental dogmas and essential institutions of Christianity were in existence during the second century, and most probably during the first. An examination of these documents shows that these teachings were not, as our adversaries would have it, taken from non-Christian sources during the third and fourth centuries.

The very fact that Christian dogmas did not exist either in their own proper form or even in their essential elements anywhere outside of Christianity shows that the presumed evolution was impossible. If the foreign doctrines assigned as sources for the dogmas of the Trinity, of the Logos, of the Incarnation, of the Resurrection, of baptism and the Eucharist are examined seriously and freed from the wishful interpretations surrounding them, it can be seen that these "sources" have so little in common with the Catholic mysteries that their vague or merely superficial similarity is always accompanied by a far vaster dissimilarity, one that is real and intrinsic.

This does not mean to assert that there is no connection whatsoever between Christianity and other religions.[16] Many of the theoretical and practical truths which the Church professes belong by their very nature to natural religion and consequently are found outside the Church. In the practices and ceremonies of worship some things are so natural to man that it is not at all strange to find them both in the true religion and in false ones: the offering of sacrifice, sacrifical banquets, a type of confession and expiation for guilt, the use of water as a symbol of purification, singing, the use of incense and lights, images, vestments, and many others. Christianity is not the original discoverer of human nature or of religious conscience. Nor is it so far above nature that it disregards it. Not all things in false religions are false; nor are all things in the true religion, Christianity, supernatural.

Notes

1. See St. Augustine, *Retractationes*, I, 13, no. 3.

2. A rather full demonstration of the divine origin of these prior revelations is found in Ottiger, *Theologia fundamentalis*, I, 341–514. For different methods of approach to this matter read Bellamy's book, *La théologie Catholique au XIXe siècle*, p. 210. For an apologetic presentation of primitive revelation, correlating data from ethnology, anthropology, pre-history, and Sacred Scripture, see W. Schmidt, *Primitive Revelation* (translated by J. Baierl, Herder, 1939). For a scholarly, Biblical analysis of the first chapters of Genesis, see *La Sainte Bible*, I, part 1, "Genèse," by A. Clamer.

3. See Decree, *Lamentabili*, propositions 22, 54, 59; DB 2022, 2054, 2059.

4. Most of the objections brought against the Christian-Catholic doctrine by modern adversaries were already known in their main outlines as early as the second century. See J. Muth, *Der Kampf des heidnischen Philosophen Celsus gegen das Christentum* (1899).

5. Th. Jouffroy, *Mélanges philosophiques* (1830), p. 330, has developed this point as follows:

There is a small book which we make little children learn and about which we question them in church. Read this little book, the *Catechism*, and you will find in it a solution to all the problems I have raised; a solution to all without exception. Ask a Christian how the human race arose, and he knows the answer; ask him where humanity is heading, and he knows; how it goes there, and he knows. Ask this tiny child, who has never in his life given a thought to the matter, why he is here on earth and what will happen to him after death. He will give you an answer that is sublime. He will not fully understand his answer, but the answer will not be for that reason any less wonderful. Ask him how the world was made, and for what purpose, and why God has placed on earth animals and plant-life; ask him how the earth was populated, if it was by one family or by many; why it is that men speak different languages, why men suffer, why they fight with one another, and how the whole business will end: he knows the answers. The origin of the world, the origin of the human race, the problem of different races, the destiny of mankind here on earth and hereafter, man's relationships with God, the duties of men to their fellow men, man's dominion over the earth: he is ignorant of none of these matters. And when he grows older he will, moreover, not be in doubt about the natural law, or political law, or international law, for he finds out all those points and expounds them clearly and, as it were, all on his own because of Christianity. There is what I call a great religion. I recognize by it this sign, that it does not leave unanswered any of the problems which are of interest to humanity.

6. Goethe says: "Let spiritual culture stride ever forward, let the human soul expand to any extent it desires, still it will never surpass the sublimity and moral culture of Christianity such as we see it glowing and gleaming in the Gospels." Quoted in Harnack, *Wesen des Christentums*, p. 3.

7. It is unreasonable for E. von Hartmann to maintain that Christian morality should be considered a rather inferior sort of morality because it promises a reward. The reward is nothing other than God Himself, and man's happiness itself glorifies in the most perfect manner possible the God of all things. The attainment of the final goal has by its very nature a twofold aspect: it is simultaneously the glorification of God and the happiness of the creature. Would it not be foolish to neglect this other aspect, which even though secondary is nonetheless a very powerful stimulus for all men, particularly for the less holy? On the other side of the picture, the main punishment of the damned is the loss of God Himself; punishment of loss. See Van Noort's *De gratia*, nos. 149ff.

8. Worth reading on this point are E. Lingens, *Die innere Schönheit des Christenthums* (1914); J. Souben, *L'Esthétique du dogme Chrétien* (1898); V. Cathrein, *Die katholische Weltanschauung in ihren Grundlinien mit besonderer Berücksichtigung der Moral* (1914); J. Gspann, *Schönheit der katholischen Weltanschauung* (1914); G. Menge, *Die Herrlichkeit der katholischen Kirche in ihrer Lehre* (1919); F. Sawicki, *Die katholische Frömmigkeit* (1921).

9. E. Laboulaye: "Put beside Spinoza and Hegel the character of Jesus. Where is the ideal of beauty, of truth, of goodness? Where do you find the doctrine that can entrance the greatest human beings and at the same time comfort the humblest? Where do you find the moral standard for mankind, the standard of duty and of justice for the citizen? Forget your church or your school of thought and simply gaze objectively" (*Etudes morales et philosophiques*, p. 56).

10. What has been said above about Christian doctrine generally is applicable to the prayer which is Christianity's very own: the *Our Father*. This prayer, magnificently simple and plain, by its incomparable richness, satisfies and is eminently suitable for every man. Stökl says:

All that man can ever express in prayer to God is contained in this short prayer and, indeed, in so simple a form that it is accessible to every understanding however limited, and in a style so ingenious and attractive that it must touch the heart of every being, great or lowly, learned or simple, of this or that age or sex. Not everyone can be initiated into the profundity of the prayer of Christ in exactly the same way. But everyone can pray the *Lord's Prayer*. If he says it with attention and in a true spirit of prayer, then he has, as far as the essence of the matter is concerned, offered to God the complete and full homage of prayer. From this focal point emanate all the rays of prayer, and every prayer offered by the Church herself or enjoined upon her faithful represents only a further development of and commentary upon this kernel of all prayer" (*Lehrbuch der Apologetik*, 2, 198).

11. See Billot, *De Ecclesia*, I, 5th ed. (1927), 225–238.

(124)

12. See Matthew 5:17; 7:29; 19:3–31; 21.

13. How badly mistaken was Harnack in denying that Christ Himself had a concept of a universal religion is brought out in *Der Katholik* I (1913), 240–291; Batiffol, *L'enseignement de Jésus,* pp. 297ff; de Grandmaison, *Jésus Christ,* I, 3rd ed. (1928), 370–71.

14. Lagrange says: "Through Jesus, man's religious life enters into a phase that is truly new: Judaism recoils in dismay and refuses to accept this ending of its history because it is not the natural ending looked for. . . . If Jesus had done nothing more than make a synthesis of current Jewish ideas, the Jews would have followed him docilely" (*Méthode historique,* 1st ed., p. 55). Even Renan admits: "Far from Jesus' being the continuator of Judaism, what characterizes his work is its rupture with the Jewish spirit" (*Vie de Jésus,* ch. 28).

15. See I. Rohr, "Griechentum und Christentum," in Bibl Zf, V (1912), p. 8; B. Allo, *L'Evangile en face du syncretisme païen* (1910); B. Heigl, "Religionsgeschichtliche Methode und Theologie," in Bibl Zf, XII (1926), 1; see *Stimmen,* 71 (1906), 376, 500; 72 (1907), 37, 182; 82 (1912), 388, 520; RPA, III (1907), 462, 519; DAFC under heading "Syncrétisme."

16. See A. Deneffe, "Das henologische Prinzip," in *Stimmen,* 83 (1912), 423; A. Pirngrüber, "Synkretismus," in *Stimmen,* 87 (1914), 268.

CHAPTER II

Christi Had a Divine Mission

I. *The Person of Christ.*
   a. His portrait in the Gospels is not a composite fabrication.
   b. Testimonies of Josephus, Tacitus, Suetonius, and Pliny the Younger.

II. *His Own Testimony About Himself.*
   a. Jewish expectations of a Messias;
   b. False Jewish expectations;
   c. Christ declared that He had been sent by God to teach men the truth, that His teaching was divine, and that it must be accepted by men.
   d. He transferred His own mission to others.

III. *We Know that His Testimony Was True Because of:*
   a. His extraordinary holiness;
   b. the fulfillment of His prophecies;
   c. His numerous miracles;
   d. His resurrection from the dead.

CHAPTER II

Christi Had a Divine Mission

I. The Person of Christ

It is an undeniable fact that Jesus of Nazareth, a man possessing the character and activities sketched in the Gospels, historically existed.* This fact is guaranteed by the veracity of the Evangelists, a veracity here taken for granted.† Some historians of comparative religion maintain that the portrait of Christ in the Gospels was based largely on religious ideas current at the time, in particular, on the mythology and mysteries of the pagans. They maintain, in other words, that there already existed on canvas the colors out of which the Evangelists might paint their picture of an "ideal" Christ. This presumption of an idealistic portrait is not only historically untrue but morally impossible. The extraordinary nobility of character, and the utterly pure life of our Lord could in nowise be assembled from those impure and ridiculous myths about Osiris, Attis, Adonis, Dionysius, etc.[1] Even under the supposition that the elements were at hand to be thus selected, purified, and harmonized, how would those simple men, the Evangelists, who were not learned in philosophy, ever have used them to give us that exceeding marvellous portrait which excites admiration in even unbelievers, and of which no later writer has ever been able to produce the equal?

There have come down to our own times two powerful accounts written by pagan writers, attesting to the historical existence of Jesus of Nazareth, the Founder of Christianity.[2]

* Bruno Bauer (1809–1882) denied that Jesus Christ ever existed. Since his wild criticism and that of others equally childish from Reimarus (d. 1768) to Paulus and Strauss are of purely antiquarian interest today, we refer the interested reader to G. Ricciotti's cool, critical analysis of them: "Rationalist interpretations of the life of Christ," found in *The Life of Christ* (1944) pp. 179–216. The only point of importance here is that the same philosophical prejudice—the impossibility of miracles and of the supernatural—which spawned these radical theories of the 19th century "higher critics" still casts a spell over the minds of many contemporary liberal Protestants and prompts them to prate loftily about "the Christ of Faith" and "the Christ of History." The much publicized Albert Schweitzer is a good example of this mentality.

† See the special bibliography on page 134.

Flavius Josephus, who died about 100 A.D., wrote:

At that time lived Jesus, a wise man, if indeed it be right to call him a man. He was a miracle-worker, a teacher of men who are willing to receive truth, and he attracted many Jews and even many Gentiles to himself. This man was the Christ; and although he was handed over to Pilate by our leaders and Pilate had him crucified, those who had first loved him did not cease to love him. For he returned to them alive on the third day in accord with the predictions of the divine prophets made about this marvel and a thousand other marvels foretold of him. And the tribe of Christians, which takes its name from him, exists even to this day (*Antiquities of the Jews,* XVIII, 3, 3).[3]

Tacitus, who wrote during the reign of Trajan in the years 98–117 A.D., has this to say:

To obliterate the rumor [which accused himself of setting fire to Rome] Nero rounded up the guilty ones and subjected them to the most uncommon tortures. The guilty ones were the Christians, who were usually described by the populace as "loathsome" because of their shameful crimes. The originator of that sect was Christ, who during the reign of Tiberius had been put to death by the procurator Pontius Pilate. Even though that deadly superstition was checked momentarily [by Christ's death], it burst out again, and now not only through Judea, where the evil originated, but even in Rome, where all sorts of monstrous and shameless doctrines flow in from all sides and find a following. Thus it was that the ones first caught, who confessed their crime and the large multitude captured by their testimony were condemned, not so much for the crime of arson as for hatred of the human race.[4] And they were made sport of in their dying by being strapped to the backs of wild animals so that they might be torn apart by the fangs of dogs, or were nailed to crosses, or were burned to death, and when daylight failed they were set on fire to serve as lamplight. . . . Nero opened up his gardens for that spectacle and, proclaiming it a sport-circus, he mingled with the people in the dress of a charioteer. So it came about that even though the torments were inflicted on criminals who deserved such because of their most recent crimes, a cry of pity began to rise up that the torments be ended, not so much for the sake of the public good, as against the savagery of one man (*Annales,* XV, 44).

The events narrated took place in the year 64 A.D.

In addition to these witnesses, *Suetonius* also gives historical testimony of the Christians and perhaps of Christ Himself, and *Pliny the Younger* makes mention of both Christ and the Christians.[5]

II. Christ's Testimony About Himself [6] 76

Christ openly and continuously proclaimed Himself before friends, before the general populace, and before the doctors of the law and the public officials, as a messenger from God to men. He also taught that He was the Son of God, and Himself true God. The divinity of Christ is mentioned at this point only because Christ asserted and performed some things which no mere messenger of God could ever dare to assert or do.

1. The Jews at the time of Jesus of Nazareth were expecting a messenger from God, whom, as a prophet without peer, they called the Messias, that is, the Christ.[7]

King Herod inquired of the priests and scribes where the Christ was to be born. And without any hesitation they replied: *"In Bethlehem of Judea"* (Matthew 2:4).

Simeon was *looking for the consolation of Israel . . . And it had been revealed to him by the Holy Spirit that he should not see death before he had seen the Christ of the Lord* (Luke 2:25–26).

John the Baptist sent two of his disciples to ask: *"Art thou he who is to come, or shall we look for another?"* (Matthew 11:3; see John 1:19–36).

Andrew, after meeting Jesus, told his brother Simon Peter: *"We have found the Messias"* (John 1:41). Philip exclaimed: *"We have found him of whom Moses in the Law and the Prophets wrote"* (John 1:45).

The Samaritan woman confessed: *"I know that Messias is coming (who is called Christ), and when he comes he will tell us all things"* (John 4:25).

The people who ate the loaves of bread exclaimed: *"This is indeed the Prophet who is to come into the world"* (John 6:14).

After hearing Jesus speak, the crowd in the temple asked: *"When the Christ comes will he work more signs than this man works?"* (John 7:31).

The Jews inquired of Christ: *"How long dost thou keep us in suspense? If thou art the Christ, tell us openly"* (John 10:24).

2. The Jews pictured for themselves a political Messias who 77 should subject all nations by earthly conquest and in that way extend the kingdom of the one true God. Jesus carefully avoided

anything that might foster and add fuel to such an expectation. Nevertheless, throughout His entire public life He acted as a prophet and often declared, either equivalently or openly, that He was the Messias.

The citizens of Nazareth *took offense at him. But Jesus said to them, "A prophet is not without honor except in his own country, and in his own house"* (Matthew 13:57; see Luke 4:16–21).

Jesus was accustomed to speak of Himself: *"Behold, a greater than Jonas is here . . . behold, a greater than Solomon is here"* (Matthew 12:41). In the parable of the vineyard He exhibited Himself as a son in His Father's household and as greater than all the prophets. (See Mathew 21:33ff; Mark 12:1ff; Luke 20:9ff. Compare these passages with Matthew 13:16–17; John 8:52ff.)

When the disciples of John came to seek His identity, He answered by pointing out His miracles and at the same time by applying to Himself the prophecies which the Jews were accustomed to apply to the Messias: *"Go and report to John what you have heard and seen: the blind see, the lame walk, the lepers are cleansed, the deaf hear, the dead rise, the poor have the gospel preached to them. And blessed is he who is not scandalized in me"* (Matthew 11:4–6).

When the Samaritan woman referred to the Messias, Jesus said to her: *"I who speak with thee am he"* (John 4:26).

To the Jews who demanded, *"If thou art the Christ, tell us openly,"* He replied: *"I tell you and you do not believe. The works that I do in the name of my Father, these bear witness concerning me. But you do not believe"* (John 10:25–26).

When the high priest ordered: *"I adjure thee by the living God that thou tell us whether thou are the Christ, the Son of God,"* Jesus answered: *"Thou hast said it"* (Matthew 26:63–64).

Peter was called blessed because in reply to the question: *"But who do you say that I am?"* he had answered: *"Thou art the Christ, the Son of the living God"* (Matthew 16:15–16).

After the resurrection, when talking with His disciples on the road to Emmaus, He applied to Himself all the things foretold in the Old Testament about the Messias: *"O foolish ones and slow of heart to believe in all that the prophets have spoken! Did not the Christ have to suffer these things before entering into his glory?" And beginning then with Moses and with all the Prophets, he interpreted to them in all the Scriptures the things referring to himself* (Luke 24:25–27).[8]

3. Consequently, Christ declared very clearly that He had been 78 sent by God the Father to teach men the truth, that His teaching was divine and must be acknowledged as such by all men if they were not to suffer the most terrible of punishments.

"For from God I came forth and have come; for neither have I come of myself, but he sent me" (John 8:42).

"This is why I was born, and why I have come into the world, to bear witness to the truth" (John 18:37).

"I have not come of myself, but he is true who has sent me, whom you do not know. I know him because I am from him, and he has sent me" (John 7:28–29; see Matthew 11.:27 and Luke 10:22).

"My teaching is not my own, but his who sent me" (John 7:16).

"He who believes in me, believes not in me but in him who sent me. And he who sees me, sees him who sent me. I have come a light into the world, that whoever believes in me may not remain in the darkness. And if anyone hears my words, and does not keep them, it is not I who judge him; for I have not come to judge the world, but to save the world. He who rejects me, and does not accept my words, has one to condemn him. The word that I have spoken will condemn him on the last day. For I have not spoken on my own authority, but he who sent me, the Father, has commanded me what I should say, and what I should declare. And I know that his commandment is everlasting life. The things, therefore, that I speak, I speak as the Father has bidden me" (John 12:44–50).

For God so loved the world that he gave his only-begotten Son, that those who believe in him may not perish, but may have life everlasting. . . . He who believes in him is not judged; but he who does not believe is already judged, because he does not believe in the name of the only-begotten Son of God (John 3:16–18).

4. Christ transferred His own divine mission to other men who 79 were to propose and promulgate His doctrine with divine authority.

"Amen, amen, I say to you, he who receives anyone I send, receives me; and he who receives me, receives him who sent me" (John 13:20; see Matthew 10:40 and Luke 10:16).

"As the Father has sent me, I also send you" (John 20:21).

"All power in heaven and on earth has been given to me. Go, therefore, and make disciples of all nations, baptizing them in the name of the Father, and of the Son, and of the Holy Spirit, teaching them to observe all that I have commanded you; and behold,

I am with you all days, even unto the consummation of the world" (Matthew 28:18–20).

"Go into the whole world and preach the gospel to every creature. He who believes and is baptized shall be saved, but he who does not believe shall be condemned" (Mark 16:16).

The preceding pages contain a brief outline of Christ's testimony about Himself and His mission. He *was teaching them as one having authority* (Matthew 7:29). He did not teach like the pagan philosophers, nor like the Scribes and Pharisees. *"Never has man spoken as this man"* (John 7:46).

The truthfulness of Christ's testimony about Himself and His work can be proved by:

the extraordinary *sanctity* of Christ Himself: *Article I;*
the fulfillment of His *prophecies: Article II;*
the numerous *miracles* He worked: *Article III;*
His *resurrection* from the dead: *Article IV.*

Special Bibliography for the Life of Christ

Fillion, L.: *L'existence historique de Jésus* (1909).

Graber, C.: *Im Kampfe um Christus* (1927).

Jung, E.: *Die geschichtliche Persönlichkeit Jesu* (1924).

Keulers, J.: *De Pseudo-Christus,* 2nd ed. (1927).

Meffert, F.: *Die geschichtliche Existenz Christi* (1910).

Meyenberg, A.: *Leben Jesu-Werk,* 3 volumes (1922–1928).

Oldra, A.: *Gesù Christo, Studio critico-apologetico,* 2 volumes (1923).

Sanders, N.: *Jesus Christus* (1928).

English Works:

Daniel-Rops: *Jesus and His Times* (translated by Ruby Millar, 1954).

Fillion, L.: *The Life of Christ,* 3 volumes (translated by N. Thompson, 1928).

Fouard, C.: *The Christ, the Son of God,* 5th ed. (1 volume ed. 1945).

Grandmaison, L. de: *Jesus Christ,* 3 volumes (1928).

Guardini, R.: *The Lord* (translated by Elinor Briefs, 1955).

Lebreton, J.: *The Life and Teaching of Jesus Christ Our Lord* (revised ed. 1935).

Prat, F.: *Jesus Christ,* 16th ed., 2 volumes (translated by J. Heenan, 1950).

Ricciotti, G.: *The Life of Christ* (translated by A. Zizzamia, 1947).

Notes

1. See Tromp, S., *"De differentia mysteriorum et Christianismi,"* in *De Revelatione Christiana* (1950), pp. 404–406.

2. Wilmers says:

No sensible man would expect the Romans or Greeks to have written accurately and extensively about Jesus of Nazareth. The province of Judea was too far off from them, and even more remote from their minds was the Jewish race with whom the Christians used to be confused from the very beginning by even the governors and emperors themselves. But with the passing of time, when the grain of mustard seed had blossomed into a mighty tree, even Roman writers were forced to take notice of the author of the new religion (*De religione revelata*, p. 328).

Kurt Linck, a non-Catholic professor, examined the testimony of Josephus, Tacitus, Pliny, and Suetonius about Christ and arrived at this conclusion against Drews: "That Jesus lived is absolutely undeniable!" (*De antiquissimis veterum quae Jesum Nazarenum spectant testimoniis*, Giessen, 1913).

3. The passage quoted is extant in all handwritten and printed codices and was already presented by Eusebius (HE I, 11). Yet there are many who consider the passage either spurious or partially interpolated; for, they say, how could an unbelieving Jew have written in such fashion; furthermore, older apologists failed to cite Josephus. The usual answer to their objection is that Josephus, though indifferent and skeptical about religious matters, could have recorded about Christ, not his own personal opinion, but the common opinion of the people. The argument from the silence of the oldest apologists is a negative argument and proves little. It is at least very improbable that Josephus, who praises John the Baptist and makes mention of James the less and the brother "of that Jesus, who is called Christ," should have been completely silent about our Lord.

Authors defending the authenticity of the passage are:

1. among non-Catholics: Burkitt, Harnack, Laqueur;

2. among Catholics: Gutberlet, Hettinger, Hurter, Kneller, Tricot, Wilmers.

Authors claiming an interpolation are:

1. most rationalists;

2. among Catholics: Batiffol, Schanz, and Funk.

Works of value on this disputed point are:

Felten, J.: *Neutestamentliche Zeitgeschichte*, I, 2nd ed. (1925), 683ff.

Thackeray, H. St. John: *Josephus: The Man and the Historian* (1929). This is a work by a scholar who has devoted most of his life to the problem. He defends vigorously the authenticity of the passage and his testimony is all the more impressive because it was delivered to a Jewish audience as the Jewish prize lecture of the year.

Wohleb, L.: "Das Testimonium Flavianum; ein kritischer Bericht über den stand der Frage," in *Romische Quartals.*, vol. 34 (1927).

4. For hatred of the human race, "that is, for being stubbornly opposed to Roman civilization and Roman religion." P. Allard, *Le Christianisme et l'empire Roman*, p. 16.

5. Suetonius: "The Christians, a tribe of men who follow a new and vicious false religion, were persecuted" *Nero*, c. 16. "The Jews, who at the instigation of Christ [Chrestus] were constantly raising disturbances, he [Claudius] banished from Rome" *Claudius*, c. 25. Even though it is true that

the pagans sometimes called Christ, "Chrest," it is not certain that the Christ (Chrest) mentioned by Suetonius is our Lord. According to Ricciotti:

> There is no reasonable doubt that the epithet *Crestus* used by Suetonius is the Greek term *christos,* the etymological translation of the Hebrew *messiah* especially since even later we find the Christians called *crestiani.* . . . We may therefore conclude that about twenty years after the death of Jesus the Jews living in Rome were given to constant and noisy quarrels regarding the character of "Christ," or Messias attributed to Jesus, some evidently recognizing him as such and others denying him. The former were undoubtedly the Christians, especially those converted from Judaism. Suetonius, who writes seventy years after the events have taken place and who knows very little about Christianity, thinks that his *Crestus* was present in Rome and personally provoked the riots. (*The Life of Christ* (1944), p. 83).

6. See M. Lepin, *Jesus Méssie et Fils de Dieu* (1910); H. Felder, *Jesus Christus* I, 144–290; RPA 34 (1922), 154 and 231.

7. The name *Masiah,* derived from the *verb Māsah* (to anoint), was taken from Psalm 2, 2: *the princes conspire together against the Lord and against his anointed.* See Ph. Freidrich, *Der Christus-Name im Lichte der Altestamentische und Neutestamentische Theologie* (1905).

8. Luke 24:25–27. To deny that Christ actually claimed to be the Messias and hence a Messenger from God seems too much even for rationalist critics, at least for most of them. Harnack himself states: "That Jesus Christ claimed to be the Messias has been denied by some critics. . . . But it seems to me that this portion of the Gospel tradition can withstand even the most searching examination" (*Lehrbuch der Dogmengeschichte,* I, 3rd ed., 63, note). Nevertheless, some rationalists, such as Wellhausen and Wrede, deny this fact. For a refutation of their position read Batiffol, *L'Enseignement de Jesus,* 6th ed., p. 224.

CHRIST'S EXTRAORDINARY HOLINESS PROVES HIS DIVINE MISSION

I. *First Argument: Solution of a Dilemma.*
   1. Christ, in claiming a divine mission, was not deluded by His own imagination.
   2. Neither was He a charlatan.
   Corollary.

II. *Second Argument: A Man Who Possesses Superhuman Sanctity Cannot Possibly Lay False Claim to a Divine Mission. But Christ Possessed Utterly Perfect and Superhuman Sanctity.*
   1. Christ was completely sinless.
   2. He excelled in every virtue.
   Corollary.

CHRIST'S EXTRAORDINARY HOLINESS PROVES HIS
DIVINE MISSION

---

80 **First Argument**

It has been shown how clearly and how frequently Christ declared that He was a messenger from God to men. In making such declarations, Christ was either deluded by His own imagination, or He deliberately and with extraordinary viciousness deceived men, or He spoke the truth. The first and second alternatives are false. Consequently Christ spoke the truth and in reality was a messenger from God to men.

1. Christ, in declaring that He was a messenger from God, was not deluded by His own imagination. Suppose there is a man suffering from hallucinations who, constantly and over many years, in private and in public, before friends and enemies, by words and deeds, acts as though he were a messenger from God, indeed as though he were the Son of God. As a result of this claim he demands absolute trust in and utter devotion to himself. Suppose this man is finally brought before a court because of his hallucinations and willingly submits to a judicial condemnation and a death which he had foreseen. Would not such a person be justly considered out of his mind and in fact insane? The very majesty of His teaching shows that our Lord was not a man of this sort.[1] Furthermore, even the rationalists, usually rate Christ as one of the wisest of men.

It does no good to say that Christ was a gifted enthusiast, since anyone who would be so sadly deluded by enthusiasm must certainly be insane. The truth is that the charge laid against Christ that He was an enthusiast or fanatic is utterly without basis. As a matter of fact, He excelled in moderation, temperance, and meekness.[2]

81 **2. Christ, in declaring Himself a messenger from God, was not a charlatan.** Surely a man mentally sound, who declares falsely that he is a messenger from God, commits a monstrous sin: he is guilty of a hideous irreverence towards God, deceives his fellow

men in a matter gravely serious, and attains the very pinnacle of arrogance. This is precisely what our Lord would have done throughout His entire public life, if this second charge were true!

Recall the manner in which Christ actually recommended Himself and His doctrine. He demanded of all men, under pain of damnation, faith in Himself and in His disciples for all time. He called Himself the way, the truth, and the life, without whose help no one could come to the Father and without whom no one could do anything good. He declared that He was the Son of God, to whom God the Father had committed all judgment; that He will come one day in the clouds of heaven with power and majesty. He claimed to be one with the Father and that all the works of God the Father and all power on heaven and on earth were His very own.[3] Would not a man who deceitfully claimed such prerogatives for himself, and stubbornly persisted in such lies, be clearly deserving of the hatred and contempt of all men?

Yet even the rationalists do not dare to call our Lord a bad man, let alone an extremely vicious one. In fact, they usually describe Him as the finest product of the human race and the glory of mankind.[4]

Now if Christ was neither a lunatic nor a liar, then the testimony He gave regarding Himself must be true. There is no other alternative.

Corollary

Notice how outrageously the rationalists contradict themselves. On the one hand they refuse to believe Christ's lucidly clear words and will not accept Him as the Son of God or a messenger from God; on the other, they praise Christ as the wisest and holiest of all men. Let them lay aside rhetoric * and have the courage to put before themselves and their readers the basic dilemma: Christ was either *a lunatic, a liar, or a messenger from God!*

* As an example of rationalist procedure in this matter, note Renan's statement:

> Jesus went back to Galilee having completely lost his Jewish faith, and full of revolutionary ardor . . . the Law will be abolished; and he himself will do the abolishing. The Messias has come; and he himself is the Messias. The Kingdom of God will soon be manifested, and he himself will do the manifesting. . . . The son of man, after his death, will come again in glory, accompanied by legions of angels . . . the daring of such a conception should not surprise us. Jesus had for a long time been envisaging himself with God as a son with his father. What would in other men be considered insufferable arrogance ought not be considered as outrageous in him . . . Jesus should not be judged according to our

The Second Argument

82   It is impossible that a man who possesses superhuman sanctity should falsely claim to have a divine mission. Christ, however, possessed such superhuman sanctity. Consequently Christ could not have claimed falsely to have a divine mission.

---

petty standards of propriety. His disciples' admiration overwhelmed him and carried him away. It is clear that the title of rabbi, with which he had been content, was no longer sufficient for him; even the title of prophet, or of messenger from God, no longer corresponded with his thought. The role that he was attributing to himself was that of a super-human being and he desired that people should regard him as having a relationship with God more elevated than that of other men. But . . . there was for him no supernatural, for there was for him no nature. . . . On the one hand, Jesus' need for good, general esteem, and on the other hand the enthusiasm of his disciples entailed contradictory notions. . . . An absolute conviction, or, to put it more precisely, the enthusiasm which removed from him [Jesus] even the possibility of doubting, would cover all these audacities. We, with our cold and timid natures, understand very little of the mentality of being completely possessed by an idea which turns people into apostles. For us, conviction signifies sincerity with one-self. But sincerity with oneself does not carry much weight with Oriental peoples who are little accustomed to the critical spirit. Good faith and imposture are terms which, in our rigid conscience, are utterly irrecon-ciliable. In the Orient, there are between the one and the other a thousand nuances and thousand detours. . . . Literal truth has very little value for the Oriental. He views all from the experience of his prejudices, interests, and passions. . . . All the really great events are accomplished by the people; but one does not lead people unless one tolerates their ideas. . . . the man who takes humanity as he finds it with its illusions, and seeks to move it and with it, will not be blamed. . . . There is no great founda-tion which does not rest on legend. The only one deserving blame in such a case is humanity which wants to be deceived (*Vie de Jesus*, Ch. 15).

Another rationalist whose views on this subject are expressed quite emphatically is O. Pfleiderer. He writes:

It is indeed true that Jesus taught no new concept of God. But . . . Jesus felt the idea of the Father-God . . . as the central truth in his personal experience, and . . . in its light he comprehended the destiny of the world and of men . . . this was definitely the new fact which concealed the nucleus of a completely new religious world in its mustard-seed insig-nificance. . . . If Jesus knew and felt that he was in possession of a blessed knowledge and love of the heavenly Father and saw all his brethren walk-ing in error, then it was quite natural, and even necessary, that he share with others the higher life of peace and joy enjoyed by a child of God. . . . And if . . . daily experience showed him that the most effective heal-ing power for sick hearts lay actually in what he communicated from within himself . . . how naturally, then, did it come about that the first faint inkling became . . . a growing certainty that he and no one else was called to initiate the promised era of salvation for his people . . . that he was fated to be their Messias or Savior (*Religionsphilosophie*, II, 2nd ed., 187 and 191).

Proof of the major. Nothing, in the common and correct estimation of men, so powerfully recommends a religious doctrine as the holiness of its founder. Consequently few men would believe that God could permit a false prophet to maintain, for his entire life, the appearance of outstanding virtue. When it is a question, not merely of great sanctity, but of a sanctity which from every point of view is perfect and unique, it is certain that such cannot be found in a false prophet. Certainly this most perfect type of sanctity surpasses the natural powers of any man; everyday life shows that in many respects all men fail. Such sanctity supposes special help from God, indeed, an extraordinary help from God. Were God to offer such help to a man who falsely claimed to have a divine mission, then He, Truth itself, would be furthering a fraud in a way most powerful.

Proof of the Minor: Christ possessed the most perfect and super- 83
human sanctity.[5]

1. **Christ was completely sinless.** It is not perhaps so remarkable that Judas, Pilate, and Pilate's wife declared that Christ was a holy man; [6] but even the Apostles who had lived familiarly with Him for a long time, and had Him continually under their observation, openly testified to His perfect sinlessness.[7] Finally, Christ Himself, who taught all men to pray: *forgive us our debts,* never displayed any consciousness of sin, or asked forgiveness for His sins; even though He was utterly humble, He confidently stated: *"Which of you can convict me of sin?"* (John 8:46), and *"the prince of the world is coming, and in me has nothing"* (John 14:30), and elsewhere He exclaimed: *"I do always the things that are pleasing to him* [the Father]" (John 8:29).[8]

2. **Christ excelled in every virtue.** He excelled in a burning love for God, the fulfillment of whose will was His very meat,[9] and whose glory alone He sought.[10] He excelled in love for men, for whom He spent Himself and all that He had, so that His whole life may be summed up in the brief phrase: *he went about doing good* (Acts 10:38). He excelled in humility and meekness, teaching more by example than by words: *"Learn from me, for I am meek and humble of heart"* (Matthew 11:29). He excelled in obedience both to His mother and to His foster-father,[11] and especially to God the Father to whom He was *obedient to death, even to death on a cross* (Philippians 2:8). He excelled in patience, bearing the rudeness of His disciples, laboring among great sinners, implacable persecutors, and a traitor. He had unconquerable cour-

age whereby He endured the ultimate in mockery and torture without opening His mouth.

How greatly Christ surpassed a merely human measure of virtue is evident from the following considerations:

a. The proportion and harmony of His virtues was so great that one in no way detracted from another. There was majesty about Him, yet He attracted even children by His kindness and friendliness. He was chaste beyond the slightest suspicion, yet He allowed women to care for the necessities of His daily life. He was just without being harsh, indignant without being wrathful, humble without being slavish. Christ alone is the exception to the saying of Thomas a Kempis: "every perfection in this life has some imperfection coupled with it." [12]

b. Though His sanctity is utterly sublime, it does not frighten men by a disagreeable and stifling rigidity. Quite the contrary, it appears to all as something to be loved and imitated. With good reason did Christ assert: *"My yoke is easy, and my burden light"* (Matthew 11:30).[13]

Since Christ's sanctity was not diminished by any defects, nor clouded by any stain, and utterly ideal, we rightly conclude that it was superhuman. It was a miracle of the moral order. It is impossible that God would grant so marvelous a sanctity to a man who falsely pretended to be His messenger.[14]

Corollary
84

There are few people who try to lower the sanctity of our Lord by saying that He was not free enough from affections. They say that He even favored with a kind of blind affection the poor, the sick, and the sinners, and turned His back on the rich, the strong, and the good.

The perfection of sanctity in a human being does not require that one should not have affections or feel them deeply; what it does require is that the rational will should in no way be prevented by the affections from pursuing moral good. But not one example can be adduced to show that Christ's affections ever stopped Him from the pursuit of moral good.

Similarly, it is not contrary to the perfection of sanctity to show one's inner feelings by words and deeds, provided there is a legitimate reason. But our Lord manifested His affections not because of any softness, but for the instruction of mankind. It is absurd to state that Christ, out of blind affection or out of human respect, favored some and turned His back on others. Christ pursued His goal, which was to save all men, in ways accommodated to the background of His listeners. With those who were conscious of their ignorance and their spiritual poverty, He was usually gentle; with those who put too much stock in themselves and seemed in their own eyes brave, holy, and wealthy, but despised or envied others, He was usually austere and sometimes stern. He was so, not that He might drive them away, but that He might destroy their sense of pride and self-sufficiency, which was the greatest obstacle in the way of a Messianic salvation. At times, our Lord treated even His Apostles and friends sternly, though He certainly had no aversion for them; He did so in accord with the seriousness of His task and as circumstances demanded.[15]

Notes

1. Simply recall how many principles of surpassing beauty and depth Christ gave; how many parables of delightful simplicity; how many answers, full of wisdom, to the most erratic questions. Read, for example, Matthew, chapters 5–7; Luke, chapter 20:20–40.

2. Our adversaries attempt to show that Christ, both by word and by deed, showed Himself mad, insane, mentally unbalanced, immoderate, etc. To back their assertion they point out the following places in the Gospels:

a. Mark 3:21: *But when his own people had heard of it, they went out to lay hold of him, for they said, "He has gone mad."* Even though *some* of Christ's relatives may have thought Him mad, their opinion proves nothing. The whole Gospel story cries out that Christ was neither out of His mind, nor out of control. We cannot conclude, either, from the actual Greek text, that Christ's relatives themselves thought Him mad. It may be that they went out to protect Him from those who did lay such a charge at His feet. Moreover, the Greek words actually signify "He was beside himself," and do not necessarily imply a condition of insanity.

When some modern critics (John Weisz, O. Holtzmann) state that a "Messianic consciousness" can only be explained psychologically as a result of a deranged imagination, they are obviously making such a statement on the gratuitous assumption that a *genuine* mission from God and genuine divine sonship—indeed any supernatural fact—is *a priori* impossible. See Ph. Kneib, *Moderne Leben—Jesu-Forschung unter dem Einflusse der Psychiatrie* (1908), p. 46.

b. These words of Christ, say our antagonists, prove that He was mentally unsound: *"If anyone comes to me and does not hate his father and mother . . . he cannot be my disciple"* (Luke 14:26); *"if someone strike thee on the right cheek, turn to him the other also"* (Matthew 5:39); *"Therefore do not be anxious, saying: 'What shall we eat?' or, 'What shall we drink?' or, 'What are we to put on?' "* (Matthew 6:31); *"But do not you be called 'Rabbi' . . . And call no one on earth your father . . . Neither be called masters"* (Matthew

23:8–9), and so forth. These sayings, we must remember, were uttered hyperbolically to suit the Oriental mentality and an epigrammatic fashion of speech. That they should be considered as hyperbole is usually clear from the context or from other places in the Gospels. Could Christ really want us to hate our parents, when as a matter of fact He orders us to love even our enemies (Matthew 5:24)? Apply Christ's own dictum: *the letter kills, but the spirit gives life!* When Christ calls the Scribes and Pharisees "hypocrites" and a "brood of vipers" (Matthew 12:34), the context shows that no hyperbole is intended. He uses sharp language, perfectly justified both by the deeds of those whom He addresses and by His own mission. It is always necessary to keep the context and the group addressed in mind.

c. The deeds of Christ pointed to by our adversaries as showing that He lacked moderation are the following: the expulsion of the merchants from the Temple (John 2:13; Matthew 21:12; Mark 11:15; Luke 19:45) and, above all else, the cursing of the fig tree (Mark 11:13; Matthew 21:19). Christ was stern towards those who violated the holiness of the Temple, but He did not act wildly; certainly He had a valid reason for so doing—*"The zeal for thy house has eaten me up"* (John 2:17).

All agree that the cursing of the fig tree was a symbolic action, signifying the rejection of the synagogue, which outwardly exhibited leaves of legality and zeal, but inwardly lacked the fruit of genuine holiness. See CCHS (1951) p. 880, no. 711c-d. The writer there pertinently remarks: "There is no impatience in the words since he [Christ] expected no fruit and it would be a curious sentimentality that could read cruelty there . . . especially as the insentient tree becomes a signpost for man." An example of such "curious sentimentality" is found in Philip Wylie's treatment of the incident in *Generation of Vipers*. Wylie accuses Christ of acting peevishly. He apparently accepts the incident as true and we can only wonder what sort of mind it is that can say, not what power Christ must have, but only how peevishly he has acted.

3. See John 3:16–18; 5:19, 22ff; 10:30; 14:6; 15:5; Matthew 24:30; 28:18–20; Mark 16:15–16.

4. Thus Renan writes: "He [Jesus] is the common glory of all who have a human heart" (*Vie de Jesus,* Introduction).

5. On this point read Hettinger, *Apologie,* 18er Vortrag (Lecture): "Die Person Jesu Christi," 10th ed., p. 465; H. Felder, *Die Heiligkeit Jesus* (1921); and *Jesus Christus,* II, 180–285.

6. Matthew 27:4, 19, 24.

7. Peter: *"But you disowned the Holy and Just One"* (Acts 3:14); *You know that you were redeemed from the vain manner of life handed down from your fathers . . . with the precious blood of Christ, as of a lamb without blemish and without spot* (1 Peter 1:18–19); *"Who did no sin, neither was deceit found in his mouth"* (Ibid. 2:22); John: *"We have an advocate with the Father, Jesus Christ the just* (1 John 2:1); *Sin is not in him* (Ibid. 3:5); St. Paul teaches the same doctrine: *For our sakes he made him to be sin who knew nothing of sin* (2 Corinthians 5:21); *Holy, innocent, undefiled, set apart from sinners* (Hebrews 7:26).

8. Bougaud marvels over the sublime sinlessness of Christ. He writes: This unique fact elevates Jesus Christ to a height of grandeur immeasurably above the rest of the great men of the world. For which of them

was without sin? Which of them has given his own immaculate purity as the foundation for a work of 1900 years? Which of them has so identified his own life with moral beauty that to swerve away from that life is to swerve away from moral good, and to copy his life is to attain to good? From this viewpoint Jesus Christ has no equal, no rival. He is unique, and by this one fact of his immaculate purity, he appears to us in the midst of other men as in a sublime solitude (*Jésus-Christ*, p. 94).

9. See John 4:34.

10. See John 8:50.

11. See Luke 2:51.

12. *The Imitation of Christ*, Bk. I, 3, 4. Heinrich writes:

Even in the saints we find traces of human frailty; in Christ alone do we find light without shadows. There lies even in the *virtues* of men at times an element of imperfection. We are such limited beings that frequently our very strength is our weakness. Virtue is much like talent: we develop one virtue, to some extent, at the cost of others. Gentleness suffers with the growth of forcefulness, dignity with that of humility, the interior life with that of zealous, external activity. Even in the case of saints one virtue stands out above all the others. Now and then the heroism of their virtue frightens us because of an apparent excess and violence of which no doubt their virtue had need in order to carry off the victory over human imperfection. But in Christ we gaze upon a phenomenon absolutely unique in mankind. In Him are joined in a fine harmony what are apparently the most contradictory of attributes and virtues: childlike simplicity and marvelous wisdom; an incomparable gentleness and tenderness side by side with unflinching forcefulness; the most perfect humility and the most exalted dignity; restless activity and the most profound inner life; burning zeal and a heavenly peacefulness; an all-embracing love and compassion coupled with the highest earnestness of holy righteousness. It is precisely this marvelous unity and harmony which bestow on Him that incomparable moral beauty which everyone observes in Him. . . . Just as in white light all the colors of the rainbow shine in their undivided unity, so are all the virtues of the wise and the just, all the holiness of the saints with the greatest completeness and purest beauty joined together in the perfection of Christ as in their ultimate source and divine archetype (*Dogmat. theol.* I, 2nd ed., 438).

Dr. A. Pierson praises the extraordinary harmony of Christ's virtues in this manner:

In the Son of Man we find more than one man: the stern preacher of penance as well as the preacher of love; the ascetic denying all bonds of blood as well as the bridegroom who prepares for his companions pure joy; the hero full of enthusiasm who sees "Satan falling down like lightning from heaven," as well as the supremely patient friend of man who compares his preaching to the slowly growing seed; the heavenly-minded man who criticizes all concern for earthly things, as well as the founder of a religion who is not afraid to put upon the lips of his followers, as often as they take their place before the Infinite, this prayer: "Give us this day our daily bread" (*Geschiedenis v. h. Roomsch-Catholicisme tot op het Con. van Trente*, I, 5).

13. Heinrich again states:

In this ideal perfection of Jesus lies also the reason why He can be the model and the object of the highest veneration and also of the most trusting love for *all* men, without distinction of time, nationality, degree of culture, or personal characteristics. All find in Him the purest and most beautiful human nature. . . . As Jesus once won the hearts of highly cultured Greeks, so does He today win the hearts of the poor savages of the South Seas, who with wondering astonishment hang on the very words of the missionary who presents to their minds the picture of Jesus, of this man who has never had an equal (*op. cit.*, p. 434).

Even Rousseau's testimony here is amazing: He confesses:

If the life and death of a Socrates are the life and death of a wise man, the life and death of Jesus are those of a God. Shall we say that the history of the Gospel is a tale invented to please? My friend, one does not invent in such fashion. . . . At bottom, this is to fall back in the face of the difficulty without resolving it. It would be more inconceivable for several men to have harmoniously fabricated this book than for him to be the only one who furnished its subject matter. Jewish authors would never have created either this tone or this moral grandeur; and the Gospel has characters so real, so great, so striking, so perfectly inimitable that an inventor of them would have to be more striking a character than its hero (*Emile*, Bk. I, IV).

14. It is not necessary to mention what a horrible monstrosity he would conjure up for the moral order who would think that it could be admitted that a man who displayed such tremendous sanctity in all things should nonetheless have been a vicious fraud.

15. See, for example, Mark 8:33; 9:32–33; Luke 10:41; 23:27–30; 2:49. See Hennemann, *Die Heiligkeit Jesu* (1898).

Article II

CHRIST'S PROPHECIES PROVE HIS DIVINE MISSION

I. *Christ Foretold Events to Come, Events Which Later Actually Happened.*
1. facts about Himself;
2. facts about His disciples;
3. facts about the destruction of the Holy City.

Corollary: On the same plane are statements revealing His knowledge of things far off or hidden.

II. *Christ's Predictions Do Not Admit of Natural Explanation.*
1. The events foretold were:
   a. numerous;
   b. complex;
   c. contingent on the free will of God or of men.
2. They were, moreover:
   a. sure;
   b. accurate;
   c. crystal clear.

III. *Christ Made These Prophecies as a Guarantee of His Mission.*
1. In a general way: "These very works that I do bear witness to me."
2. Now and then Christ made a specific assertion to this effect.

Corollary: The Apostles evidently so considered His knowledge of hidden things.

CHRIST'S PROPHECIES PROVE HIS DIVINE MISSION

In order to construct a valid argument on the basis of Christ's prophecies three facts must be demonstrated: 1. Christ foretold events to come, events which later actually happened (historical truth); 2. Christ's foreknowledge of these things was no natural knowledge (philosophical truth); 3. Christ made these predictions in confirmation of His mission (relevant truth).

85 I. Christ Foretold Many Things which Later Actually Came to Pass [1]

1. Facts about Himself. *He began to tell them what would happen to him, saying, "Behold, we are going up to Jerusalem, and the Son of Man will be betrayed to the chief priests and the Scribes; and they will condemn him to death, and will deliver him to the Gentiles; and they will mock him, and spit upon him, and scourge him, and put him to death; and on the third day he will rise again'* (Mark 10:32–34; see Matthew 20:18–19; Luke 18:32–33). The Old Testament had indeed foretold that the Messias would die a violent death, but at the time of Christ none of the Jews understood these passages as applying to the Messias. As a result, the idea of a suffering and dying Messias was foreign even to the minds of the Apostles.[2] Furthermore, none of the circumstances enumerated in detail in His prediction, namely, that He would be betrayed to the leaders of the Jews, that He would be mocked, spat upon, and scourged by them, and finally, that He would rise on the third day —none of these circumstances had been clearly foretold by any Old Testament prophet.—The precision with which all these predictions were fulfilled is well known.

86 2. Facts about the disciples. a. *He sent two of his disciples, and said to them, "Go into the village opposite you, and immediately on entering it you will find a colt tied, upon which no man has yet sat; loose it, and bring it. And if anyone say to you, 'What are you doing?' you shall say that the Lord has need of it, and*

immediately he will send it here" (Mark 11:2–3; see Matthew 21:2ff).–And so it happened.

b. *And he said to them, "Behold, on your entering the city, there will meet you a man carrying a pitcher of water; follow him into the house into which he goes. And you shall say to the master of the house, 'The Master says to thee, "Where is the guest chamber, that I may eat the passover there with my disciples?"' And he will show you a large upper room furnished; there make ready"* (Luke 22:10–12). And immediately therafter: *And they went and found just as he had told them* (Luke 22:13).

c. *And while they were eating, he said, "Amen I say to you, one of you will betray me."* . . . *And Judas who betrayed him answered and said, "Is it I, Rabbi?" He said to him, "Thou has said it"* (Matthew 26:21, 25).

d. *Jesus said to him* [Peter], *"Amen I say to thee, this very night, before a cock crows, thou wilt deny me three times"* (Matthew 26:34; see Mark 14:30). For the fulfillment, see Matthew 26:69–74, and the parallel passages.

e. *And while eating with them, he charged them not to depart from Jerusalem, but to wait for the promise of the Father, "of which you have heard,"* said he, *"by my mouth; for John indeed baptized with water, but you shall be baptized with the Holy Spirit not many days hence . . . you shall receive power when the Holy Spirit comes upon you, and you shall be witnesses for me in Jerusalem and in all Judea and Samaria and even to the very ends of the earth"* (Acts 1:4–5, 8; see Luke 24:29). It is true that the pouring forth of the Holy Spirit had been foretold by Joel,[3] but no one before Christ had made the precise prediction that this Spirit would come upon the Apostles and that this would take place within a short time after the Ascension. The fulfillment is recorded in Acts 2:1ff.

3. **Facts about the destruction of the Holy City.** Daniel had 87 predicted the ruin of the city of Jerusalem and of the Temple.[4] However, our Lord's prophecy was so freshly original that it has led many rationalists to conclude that the Gospels of Matthew and Luke must have been written after the actual fall of the city.

a. The destruction of the Temple would definitely not coincide with the end of the world. This was a bit of news altogether opposed to Jewish expectations: *"Jerusalem will be trodden down by the Gentiles, until the times of the nations be fulfilled"* (Luke 21:24).

b. The city would be hemmed in by ramparts: *"Thy enemies will throw up a rampart about thee"* (Luke 19:43). Josephus and Tacitus [5] testify that this is precisely what was done by Titus: "Caesar Titus decided to use earthworks and ramparts in attacking this city and its populace" (*Hist.*, bk. 5, c. 13).

c. The Jews would experience extreme distress: *"They will shut thee in on every side"* (Luke 19:43). *"For there will be great distress over the land, and wrath upon this people. And they will fall by the edge of the sword"* (Luke 21:24). The frightful fulfillment of this prophecy is described by Josephus: "The number of those that perished during the whole siege was one million, one hundred thousand. The majority of these were indeed of the same nation, but did not belong to the city itself; for they had come up from the whole country to the feast of unleavened bread. They were all of a sudden hemmed in by an army, and so tightly that first a pestilence broke out among them, to be followed in short order by a famine" (*Wars of the Jews*, bk. 6, c. 9, 3).[6]

d. The Temple and city would be completely devastated: *"Dost thou see all these great buildings? There will not be left one stone upon another that will not be thrown down'* (Mark 13:2). They *"will not leave in thee one stone upon another'* (Luke 19:44). As a matter of fact, Titus had the Temple burnt to the ground.[7] The foundations and the remaining ruins were not quite completely demolished, since the Jews, at the instigation of Julian the Apostate, tried to rebuild the Temple. "During the night there was a great earthquake, which shook loose the rocks which had been torn away from the old foundations of the Temple and scattered them all, and the neighboring buildings with them" (Socrates, *Historia Ecclesiastica*, bk. 3, c. 2). "Fearful globes of fire bursting forth near the foundations in frequent attacks made the place unapproachable, and actually consumed some of the workmen; thus kept at a distance by the quite stubborn fire, they gave up the task before it was fairly begun" (Ammianus Marcellinus, *Re R. gest.*. bk. 23, c. 1).

Josephus states that "those who destroyed it, so thoroughly laid the city even with the ground that those who came thither could scarcely believe that it had ever been inhabited" (*op. cit.*, bk. 7, c. 1, 1).

e. The Jews would be scattered throughout all nations. Jerusalem, as the capital of the Jewish nation, and hence a symbol of that nation itself, would not be rebuilt: *"And they . . . will be led away as captives to all the nations. And Jerusalem will be trodden down by the Gentiles, until the times of the nations be fulfilled"* (Luke 21:24).

Indeed, after the capture of the city by Titus, very many of the Jews were sold into captivity;[8] those who stayed in Palestine were conquered once more by Hadrian and were deported to many different places, even as far away as Spain. From that time henceforth they have been scattered over all the face of the earth. Under the same Hadrian Jerusalem was, it is true, rebuilt and given the name Aelia Capitolina, but the Jews were never in possession of the new city.[9]

Corollary 88

One may also consider as prophecies those statements of Christ which revealed His knowledge of things far off or hidden. *"When thou wast under the fig tree, I saw thee* [Nathaniel]" (John 1:48). *"Thou has had five husbands, and he whom thou now hast is not thy husband"* (John 4:18). *"Lazarus, our friend, sleeps. But I go that I may wake him from sleep"*. . . . *Jesus said to them plainly, "Lazarus is dead; and I rejoice on your account that I was not there, that you may believe"* (John 11:11-15). *"Go to the sea and cast a hook, and take the first fish that comes up. And opening its mouth thou wilt find a stater"* (Matthew 17:26).

II. Christ's Predictions Do Not Admit of a Natural   89 Explanation

It is apparent to any reader of the Gospel that Christ foretold many events, which were at times quite complex, which depended on the free will of God or of men. And His predictions were sure, accurate, and crystal clear. Many of the events were of such a nature that they could not even have been guessed in advance, and some were completely beyond the capacity of any created intellect. Therefore, it is certain that Christ could have foreseen all these events, considered in their ensemble, only by means of divine power. And if the same conclusion does not hold good for each prediction as such, it does so for at least some individual predictions.

III. Christ Made These Prophecies as a Guarantee   90 of His Mission

1. In a general way Christ alleged all His marvelous works as proof of His mission: *"These very works that I do bear witness to me, that the Father has sent me"* (John 5:36).

(151)

2. In addition Christ now and then made a specific assertion that He was foretelling a particular event for the precise purpose of gaining belief in His divine mission. For example, after His prediction of Judas' treason, He went on: *"I tell you now before it comes to pass, that when it has come to pass you may believe that I am he* [the Messias]" (John 13:19). Similarly, after having foretold the ruin of the city, He added, "[They] *will not leave in thee one stone upon another, because thou hast not known the time of thy visitation"* (i.e., because you have refused to accept me as the promised Messias) (Luke 19:44).

Corollary

The Apostles themselves quite evidently looked upon our Lord's knowledge of hidden things as a proof of His divine mission: *"Now we know that thou knowest all things, and dost not need that anyone should question thee. For this reason we believe that thou camest forth from God"* (John 16:30).

Note: At this point the objection is usually raised that Christ foretold as quite near at hand His second coming (*Parousia*) and the end of the world. As this is a matter for quite lengthy discussion, it will receive more complete consideration in *Appendix II*.

Notes

1. In order to avoid any cavil about the philosophical truth of this or that prophecy, we deem it wise to omit Christ's predictions about those things already foretold in the Old Testament, except for those prophecies to which He gave new precision or a fresh application. See F. Schmid, *Christus als Prophet;* RPA, XVII (1914), 801; XVIII, 5 and 161.

2. See John 12:34; Luke 18:34.

3. Joel 2:28; see Acts 2:16–17.

4. Daniel 9:17–27; see no. 157ff.

5. *Wars of the Jews,* bk. 5, 12, 2; bk. 6, 8, 1.

6. Hettinger remarks that Josephus is not always reliable when it comes to reporting numbers (*Lehrbuch,* 2nd ed., p. 358). See also H. St. John Thackeray, *Josephus, the Man and the Historian* (New York, 1929).

7. Josephus, *op. cit.,* bk. 6, 4–6.

8. *Ibid.,* bk. 6, 9, 2.

9. See Granderath, "Die Trümmer des Israelitischen Volkes," in *Stimmen* XVII (1879), 42ff. Many theologians in their treatment of this passage draw additional arguments from Matthew 24:2–14 (and the parallel passages). But since exegetes are not agreed as to whether the things there set forth by Christ were meant as signs which would precede the destruction of the city, these passages cannot form the basis of a sure argument. There are, in fact, four main views on these verses:

a. They list the signs which will herald the destruction of the city.

b. They give the signs that will precede the final judgment.

c. We have in this passage signs pointing to both disasters simultaneously. These signs will be realized fully before the destruction of the world and partially before that of the city.

d. Christ here gives warnings rather than real signs. It is as though He says: "You ask me about the time and the sign, but it is much more important to be alert and to take care that no one lures you from your faith in me. For impostors, wars, disasters, persecutions, and all kinds of ills are on the way, and you must stand unshaken in the midst of all this. Come what may, my Gospel will be spread throughout the whole world." See Knabenbauer, *op. cit.,* pp. 315ff.

CHRIST'S MIRACLES PROVE HIS DIVINE MISSION

I. *Christ Worked Many Miracles. This Truth is Established:*
    1. by the testimony of the Evangelists.
        a. If their testimony is acceptable in other matters, it is trustworthy in this matter also.
        b. Remove the miracles and the whole Gospel story crumbles.
        c. They are vastly different from those recorded in the Apocrypha.
    Note: Christ's foes, too, admitted the truth of His miracles.
    2. by the testimony of non-Biblical writers of antiquity.

II. *The Prodigious Deeds of Christ were Real Miracles. They Cannot be Explained by:*
    1. occult natural forces (trickery, deceit, chance);
    2. the intervention of an evil spirit.
    The only explanation left is that He performed them by divine power.

III. *In the Performance of His Miracles Christ Intended to Prove His Divine Mission.*
    1. This is true in general of all His miracles, considered *in toto.*
    2. At times He made special mention of the purpose of a miracle.

CHRIST'S MIRACLES PROVE HIS DIVINE MISSION [1]

I. Christ Performed Very Many Miraculous Works.   91

There is no need to catalogue the miracles performed by Christ. The Gospels recount more than forty individual miracles, and they refer to many more in general terms.[2] For outstanding examples, representative of the three main classes of miracles, read the accounts of the multiplication of the loaves,[3] of the cure of the man born blind,[4] and of the raising of Lazarus.[5] For Christ's miracles can be reduced to three chief categories. Some had as their subjects irrational creatures, others men, and still others spiritual beings (as in the casting out of evil spirits).

This prepares the way for an examination of the historical truth of Christ's miracles in general. The argument is based, not on one or another individual miracle, but on all taken together.

The fact that Christ performed miracles is established:

    1. by the testimony of the Evangelists, and

    2. by the testimony of non-Biblical authors.

1. The testimony of the Evangelists. The historical trustworthiness of the Evangelists is assumed as proved. It would be well to point out here the inconsistency and unreasonableness of those who reject the testimony of the Evangelists in the matter of miracles and accept their testimony on all other points. Such a position is logically impossible. The following considerations may help to show why it is:

    a. It is not any more difficult to verify miraculous facts than others. If anything, miracles attract more careful attention. If the sacred authors are accepted as trustworthy in other matters, it is unreasonable to reject their witness to miracles.

    b. The miracles are so closely connected with the other facts and teachings recounted in the Gospels that, if they were removed, the whole Gospel story would have to be rejected. Without miracles the story loses its special character and lacks all logical consistency.[6]

    c. The character of Christ's miracles is vastly different from the character of those described in the apocrypha. They are not hollow shows of power or tales to feed men's curiosity, but they are instances of mercy and charity.

The historical truth of Christ's miracles, according to the testimony of the Evangelists, was admitted not only by His disciples but also by His foes.[7]

92   **2. The Testimony of non-Biblical writers of antiquity.** No one can deny that in the first years of Christianity, everyone, Christians, Jews, and Gentiles alike, admitted the miracles of Christ as historically certain.

a. Quadratus, in his defense of the Christians addressed to the emperor Hadrian (117–138), wrote about those whom Christ had healed or raised from the dead:

> These people were seen by everyone, not only at the time they were healed or recalled to life, but in the ensuing years as well. Nor was it only during the earthly life of the Saviour that they remained alive, but for a long time after His departure; indeed, some have survived even to our own day (quoted by Eusebius, HE, bk. 4, c. 4).[8]

St. Justin Martyr, recalling Christ's miracles, remarks: "That Jesus did these things you may learn from the *Reports* drawn up by Pontius Pilate" (*Apology*, bk. 1, c. 48).

Tertullian, in his account of the life, miracles and death of Christ, states: "Pilate, who was himself a Christian as far as his conscience was concerned, reported to the reigning emperor Tiberius all these matters touching Christ" (*Apologeticum*, 21, 86–87).[9]

b. It has already been said (no. 75) that Flavius Josephus referred to Christ as a "wonder worker." And how little the Jews, whether during Christ's lifetime or later, dared to deny His miracles is clear from the fact that they tried to explain them away as tricks of magic which He had learned in Egypt (such is the explanation offered by the *Talmud*) or as having been performed by the power of the name YHWH * pronounced with its proper vowels, which He would have learned deceitfully (so states the *Toledoth Jesu*).[10]

---

* YHWH is the sacred Tetragrammaton, being the four consonants of the Hebrew word "Yahweh," which is generally taken to mean "I am Who am," the answer given by God to Moses when asked what His name was. See Exodus, 3:13–14.

c. Origen makes the following statement in regard to Celsus, a most bitter foe of Christianity:

He admits to a certain extent the miracles which Jesus performed and by which He drew many people to follow Him as the Christ, but he makes the calumnious charge that those miracles were performed not by divine power, but by magical arts (*Contra Celsum*, bk. 1, c. 38).

Julian the Apostate declared:

This Jesus did nothing particularly memorable throughout his whole lifetime, unless one considers it remarkable to cure the lame and the blind and to exorcise some possessed people in the villages of Bethsaida and Bethany (quoted by St. Cyril of Alexandria, *Adversus Julianum*, 6).

On the supposition that Christ's miracles were only the fictions of His disciples, would not their contemporaries, as foes of the Christian religion, have openly and flatly given the lie to such a deceit? Would not later adversaries of Christianity, Gentiles and Jews especially, have unceasingly repeated this rebuttal, particularly in view of the fact that, as history shows, the Apostles and the earliest Fathers and Apologists were always appealing to these miracles as proof of their teaching?

If it is clear on the basis of non-Biblical testimony that Christ was a wonder-worker, then there is absolutely no reason why those who admit the historicity of the Gospels as a whole should reject the miracle accounts that form part of those Gospels.

II. The Prodigious Deeds of Christ Were Real Miracles. 93

If Christ's deeds cannot be explained by appealing to occult natural powers or to the intervention of evil spirits, then the only explanation left is that they were performed by divine power.

1. Any explanation based on an ingenious use of natural forces is impossible.

a. At least several of Christ's miracles clearly surpass any created power, whether one considers the subject on which they were worked (for example, raising the dead),[11] or the manner in which they were performed (for example, the multiplication of the loaves or the curing of the ruler's son from a distance).[12] Miracles of this nature alone suffice to establish our point; but in addition they show that the wonders whose miraculous character is not readily evident were not performed by any natural power (see no. 52).

b. If one considers the great number and the rich variety of the wonders which Jesus worked without any material equipment and openly in public places, crowded streets, in the sight of friend and foe alike, then one cannot have any suspicion of trickery or deceit; nor is any other merely natural explanation adequate. Arnobius asks the pagans:

> Can you point out to us, show us from all those Magi who ever existed through the ages, any one that ever did anything resembling what Christ did, even to the thousandth part? (*The Case Against the Pagans*, ACW translation, I, bk. 1, 43).

Christ, far from acting as a magician, showed by the frequency, variety, and manner of His miracles that He was not only a wonder-worker, but in actual fact the Lord of all creation, animate and inanimate.

c. One has simply to read the "natural" explanation of Christ's miracles advanced from time to time by unbelievers to realize that they are futile, perverse, and ridiculous.* One of their arguments

---

* In this connection, it is interesting to read some of the explanations advanced by rationalists. Renan explains Christ's power to cast out devils in this fashion:
> There were at that time many lunatics in Judea, doubtless because of the great mental excitement then prevalent. Jesus had a great deal of influence over these poor wretches. In this case a gentle word was enough to put the demon to flight (*Vie de Jésus*, Ch. 16).

K. Furrer states:
> People were awaiting the coming of the Messias with feverish impatience. Long-continued hoping and waiting had shattered the nerves of thousands and had caused a whole rash of disease symptoms. What a tremendous impression this intrinsically healthy and holy personality of Jesus must have made on these neurotics! Yes, we understand that hundreds upon hundreds left him with their health restored (*Vorträge über das Leben Jesu* 1902, p. 126).

G. Paulus explains the multiplication of loaves in this manner: Christ and the Apostles fed a few with what little they had. Others who had brought food with them were moved by their example to give part of what they had to others who had nothing. In this way all were fed. Lloyd Douglas gave a modern twist to this theme in his popular novel, *The Robe*. Bernard Weisz, in his *Leben Jesu*, II, 4th ed. (1902), 186, offers practically the same explanation as does Furrer in his work. Renan explains this miracle by saying: "Thanks to an extreme frugality, the holy band was able to subsist there [in the desert]. Naturally people thought they saw a miracle in this" (*op. cit.*, Ch. 12).

Some try to explain the calming of the tempest by assuming that Christ poured oil on the water. Hase thought it was a question of Christ's calming

can be summarized in this manner: at the time of Christ people were so ignorant of the forces of nature that they unhesitatingly cried "miracle!" Perhaps. But did their ignorance keep them from observing the facts and recording them truthfully? Let the learned of the present day explain the recorded data.

2. Any explanation which appeals to the aid of an evil spirit 94 must be rejected for these reasons:

a. some miracles of Christ, such as the raising of the dead, surpass the powers of any created being;

b. the circumstances surrounding His deeds dispel any possible suspicion of diabolical intervention. By circumstances here are meant Christ's eminent holiness and the manner in which He performed His miracles, humbly, not to satisfy curiosity, but to help the suffering; [13]

c. in addition, the purpose and results of Christ's miracles make it clear that no demon could have aided Him. Christ performed His miracles to recommend His teaching, a teaching completely holy and altogether antagonistic to devils. Would an evil spirit willingly have used his power to commend and spread such a doctrine? [14]

III. Christ Performed His Miracles to Prove His Divine Mission.[15]   95

1. This is true in general of all His miracles, considered as a unit. Thus, to the question of the Baptist's disciples, *"Art thou he who is to come, or shall we look for another?"* He answered: *"Go and report to John what you have heard and seen: the blind see, the lame walk, the lepers are cleansed, the deaf hear, the dead rise, the poor have the gospel preached to them"* (Matthew 11:3-5). When the Jews demanded: *"If thou art the Christ, tell us openly,"* He answered: *"I tell you and you do not believe. The works that I do in the name of my Father, these bear witness con-*

---

the minds of the Apostles, disturbed by the storm. Furrer writes: "A few minutes later the storm subsided. It is a peculiar characteristic of storms in that area to come up suddenly and just as suddenly to stop again" (*op. cit.*, p. 129). O. Holtzmann remarks: "The only amazing thing is that the sea actually became calm. But then it could only be a coincidence" (*Leben Jesu*, 1901, p. 209).

Rationalists offer similar explanations for Christ's walking on the sea— or rather, as they say, to the sea! See Ottiger, *Theologia fundamentalis*, I, 759; Fonck, ZKTh (1903), pp. 302ff; Dr. J. Smit, *De daemoniacis in historia Evangelica* (1913).

cerning me. . . . Do you say of him whom the Father has made holy and sent into the world, 'Thou blasphemest,' because I said, 'I am the son of God.'? If I do not perform the works of my Father, do not believe me. But if I do perform them, and you are not willing to believe me, believe the works" (John 10:24–38). Elsewhere He says: *"For the works which the Father has given me to accomplish, these very works that I do, bear witness to me, that the Father has sent me"* (John 5:36. See 15:21–24).

2. At times He made special mention of the purpose of a miracle. For example, on the occasion of the resurrection of Lazarus He said: *"Father, I give thee thanks that thou hast heard me. Yet I knew that thou always hearest me; but because of the people who stand round, I spoke, that they may believe that thou hast sent me."* When he had said this, he cried out with a loud voice, *"Lazarus, come forth!"* (John 11:41–43). Similarly, just before He cured the paralytic, He said, *"But that you may know that the Son of Man has power on earth to forgive sins,"—then he said to the paralytic,—"Arise, take up thy pallet and go to thy house"* (Matthew 9:6).

Hence, anyone who is really sincere can only say with Nicodemus, *"Rabbi, we know that thou hast come a teacher from God, for no one can work these signs that thou workest unless God be with him"* (John 3:2).

96 *Scholion 1. Solution of some difficulties.* Rationalists and Modernists claim at times that Christ Himself held miracles in low esteem, or at least that He did not perform His miracles with a view to leading men to faith. The falsity of the claim is evident from the foregoing remarks, but some difficulties remain.

a. Christ sometimes rebuked those who asked for a miracle; [16] but these were of the type who had not the least interest in learning the truth and wanted to disguise their malice under a mask of ignorance; the type who were always looking for new wonders and especially for "a sign from heaven." But at the same time He foretold what was by far the greatest sign of all, His resurrection. Elsewhere, Christ scolds a bit more gently those who, though not really incredulous, were slow to believe.[17]

b. Again, He praised those *"who have not seen, and yet have believed"* (John 20:29);—but this text has nothing to do with miracles. Rather He is reprimanding those who are not satisfied with legitimate evidence and demand proof which they can verify with their own physical senses. Did not Thomas deserve this gentle reproof when, after Christ's own prediction and the testimony of his fellow Apostles, he refused to admit the fact of the resurrection until he could verify it by seeing with his own eyes and touching with his own hands? [18]

c. Christ habitually required of the sick an act of faith in Himself before He cured them. Indeed it was quite fitting that they who already had sufficient motives for belief on other grounds should prove themselves deserving of His divine bounty by expressing their faith in Him. Still this by no means prevented the miracle from serving as a confirmation of Christ's divine mission, as it could by strengthening the faith of the sick person and by leading others to believe. Rather, this demand of an advance act of faith proves the relevant truth of the ensuing miracle. He who says, "I will cure you if you believe that I am the promised Messias," explicitly shows that the miracle to follow will confirm His mission. Furthermore, Christ did not always demand faith in advance,[19] and quite often He demanded, or at least took into account, the faith, not of the sick person, but of others.[20] It is consequently clear that the belief He looked for in advance of a miracle was not a psychological preparation of the person for a cure, such as a sick person's confidence in his doctor sometimes is, but a purely ethical preparation.

d. If Christ performed, or could perform, only a few miracles in His native district because of the unbelief of His fellow-townsmen,[21] this means only that our Saviour did not wish to lavish His gifts on people who were stubbornly incredulous. Indeed, He could not in all fairness do so, for they were unworthy, and their attitude held out little promise for the future.[22]

e. Finally, one cannot deny the relevant truth of Christ's miracles on the ground that He forbade the publicizing of some of them.[23] Since He was not only a teacher of truth but also a model of virtue, it was necessary that He give, even in this matter, an example of humility. Besides, there may have been special underlying reasons which made inopportune too wide a publication of some miracles. For one thing, Christ wished to continue preaching for some time to come among the Jews and to win men over to true Messianism by weaning them gradually from the idea of a temporal kingdom. But, in the ordinary course of events, He could not have been able to do this if all His miracles, dazzlingly clear from the very beginning, had over-excited the minds of the disciples, dreaming as they were of a Messianic kingdom in the political sense, and had at the same time put too sharp an edge on the hate His enemies bore Him.[24]

97   *Scholion 2. The symbolic meaning of Christ's miracles.* "We must accept the miracles of our Lord and Savior in such a way as to believe in their reality and to learn the lesson they have for us" (St. Gregory, *Homilia 2 in Evangelia,* no. 1). "Let us ask of these miracles what they have to tell us about Christ; for if they are understood, they have such a message. Since Christ Himself is the Word of God, every act of this Word is a word addressed to us" (St. Augustine, *Tractatus 24 in Joannem,* no. 2). In view of these and of other like assertions of the holy Fathers, we may say: .

a. Christ's miracles *as a whole* show symbolically the purpose of His mission, the nature of which they prove. Our Lord's miracles did not simply evoke a sterile admiration; they were positively and eminently advantageous for men. By the greater part of them men were freed from the tyranny of the devil, restored to health, even to life. As enslavement by the devil, temporal calamities and death are nothing other than the results of and the punishment for sin, do not Christ's miracles, by removing the consequences of sin, teach us that Christ was sent to free mankind from sin? From this it follows that Christ's miracles were not irrelevant deeds having nothing to do with His teaching, His "good news." They are intimately bound up with the Gospel and are, as it were, samples and pledges of that perfect liberation and restoration which Christ promised and prepared by His preaching.

b. Many of Christ's miracles illustrated in a special way the doctrines He proposed. He prefaced the discourse on the Eucharist with the multiplication of loaves;[25] He cured the man born blind to show that He was the Light of the world;[26] to strengthen belief in Himself as the Resurrection and the Life He raised Lazarus from the dead.[27]

98 Corollary

Miracles performed by God the Father. On the same plane as the miracles of Christ one can consider those which God the Father, apart from the intervention of Christ's humanity, performed in Christ's favor—like His sending the angels and the star to proclaim His birth,[28] or His rescuing Him from Herod's clutches,[29] or His declaration of Christ's dignity at the baptism in the Jordan,[30] at the Transfiguration,[31] and at the time of His death upon the cross.[32] For it is most evident that God could not have called attention to and recommended by such prodigies a man who falsely claimed to be the legate and the Son of God. All these wonderful works were an eloquent commentary on the words spoken by the Father: *"This is my beloved Son, in whom I am well pleased; hear him"* (Matthew 17:5).

Notes

1. See Felder, *op. cit.*, II, 291–471;
   Fillion, L., *Les miracles de N. S. Jésus-Christ* (1909–1910);
   Jacquier and Bourchany, *La Résurrection de J.-C. et les miracles évangéliques* (1911);
   Watterott, Ign., *Lehre und Wunder des Gottmenschen* (1922); and Dausch, P., "Die Wunder Jesu" in BiZ, V (1912) nos. 11–12.
2. See Matthew 8:16 and Luke 4:40 for examples.
3. Matthew 14:14ff. (See also Mark 6; Luke 9; John 6.)
4. See John 9:1ff.
5. See John 11. The article in RPA 31 (1921), 533ff is good on this point.
6. "The miracle accounts form the substance of the synoptic narrative to such an extent that once you reject them the whole intricate mosaic loses all trace of a recognizable plan, all intelligible meaning. . . . Unless you accept miraculous cures as everyday occurrences there is simply no Gospel story." Holtzmann, *Die synoptischen Evangelien* (1863), p. 509.
7. See Matthew 9:34; Luke 23:8; John 11:47.
8. Philip Sidetes (c. 450) in his *Historia Christiana* relates that Papias remembered persons raised to life by Christ who lived to the time of Hadrian. See Preuschen, *Antilegomena* (1901), p. 58.
9. Neither St. Justin nor Tertullian, who had read Justin's apology, nor anyone else for that matter, indicates that he had personally read or even seen these *Acts of Pilate*. In view of this, many scholars conclude that these apologists merely assumed the existence of such a report only because they were under the definite impression that the Roman procurators sent to Rome a report on all matters of major importance. The extant *Acts of Pilate* were actually composed in the fourth or fifth century. See A. Harnack, *Die Chronologie der altchristlichen Litteratur bis Eusebius*, I, 605–611; Battifol, *La Littérature grecque*, 3rd ed., p. 38; Bardenhewer, *Altkirchliche Litteratur*, I, 409; Quasten, *Patrology*, I, 115-118.
10. See Norbert A. Tux, *Compendium theologiae fundamentalis*, I, 261; Liebermann, *Institutiones theologicae*, I, 10th ed., 422.
11. Rationalists try in vain to rule out miracles involving the raising of the dead by objecting that it is very difficult to determine whether or not a person is really dead. For—and this is just one among many possible answers —how could Christ have been the only one to know, in spite of the fact that everyone testified to the contrary, that Lazarus, Jairus' daughter, and the widow's son were not dead, and this even before He had seen them (at least Lazarus and Jairus' daughter)? Furthermore, in the case of Lazarus, Christ had foretold to the Apostles His friend's death and his imminent return to life. And He had made this prediction while still some distance from Bethany. Read the accounts in John 11; Luke 7:11ff, 8:49ff.

12. See John 4:46ff.

13. Christ Himself excluded the possibility of diabolical intervention. See Matthew 12:25–37.

14. See Luke 11:15–18.

15. Modernists and others deny this. See the decree *Lamentabili*, proposition 28; DB 2028.

16. See Matthew 12:39, 16:1; Mark 8:11; Luke 11:16–29.

17. See John 4:48.

18. See Mark 16:14.

19. See John 9:6, 35.

20. See Matthew 8:13, 9:2, 15:28; John 4:47ff.

21. Matthew 13:58; Mark 6:5.

22. See Billot, *De Verbo incarnato*, 8th ed. (1942), p. 235; J. Huby, S.J., *L'Evangile et les Evangiles* (Paris, 1940), pp. 21–22; Garrigou-Lagrange, *De revelatione* (Rome, 1945), II, 307ff.

23. Matthew 9:30, 12:16ff: He *warned them not to make him known; that what was spoken through Isaias the prophet might be fulfilled, who said, "... He will not wrangle, nor cry aloud, neither will anyone hear his voice in the streets"* See also Mark 1:44.

24. See Wilmers, *De religione revelata*, p. 339; Buzy, *La Sainte Bible*, p. 9 (Paris, 1946); F. Chable, "Die Wunder Jesu, in ihrem innern Zussammenhange betrachtet," STS II, 4, 15.

25. See John 6.

26. See John 9:5ff.

27. See John 11:25.

28. See Luke 2:8; Matthew 2:2.

29. See Matthew 2:13.

30. See Matthew 3:16.

31. See Matthew 17:5.

32. See Matthew 27:51ff.

Article IV

CHRIST'S RESURRECTION PROVES HIS DIVINE MISSION

I. *Christ Foretold His Resurrection.*

II. *He Foretold It As a proof of His Divine Mission.*

III. *Christ Really Died, As Is Evident from:*
1. the unanimous teaching of the Evangelists;
2. the activities of His friends;
3. the activities of His foes;
4. the activities of the officials.

IV. *Christ Really Came Back to Life.*
1. Theories of rationalists:
   a. rejection of the Gospel account of an empty tomb;
   b. apparitions of our Lord merely subjective or objective visions;
   c. belief in the resurrection a result of evolution in Christian consciousness.
2. Proof of thesis is based on:
   a. an exposition of facts;
   b. a refutation of rationalist hypotheses regarding the resurrection:
      1. swoon and subsequent revival;
      2. fraud;
      3. evolution;
   c. a refutation of rationalist hypotheses regarding apparitions:
      1. fraud and deceit;
      2. hallucination.
3. Additional remarks on the evolution theory.

Corollary:
Why did Christ appear only to His friends?

Epilogue:
The Catholic Church continues Christ's mission.

99   CHRIST'S RESURRECTION PROVES HIS DIVINE MISSION

The resurrection of our Lord holds first place among all the arguments advanced to prove the credibility of His claims. The Apostles adduced the fact of the resurrection as the foremost argument of their preaching.[1] St. Paul, in unmistakable terms, made it the keystone of faith: *If Christ has not risen, vain then is our preaching, vain too is your faith* (1 Corinthians 15:14). Throughout nineteen centuries, everyone, adversary as well as proponent, has considered it the basis of the entire faith; and no wonder, for it is a brilliant miracle, intimately related by its very nature with the truth of the mission of Christ the Redeemer. Indeed Christ Himself chose it as the crown of all His marvelous works, as the sublime seal of all His preaching.

Since there is no doubt about the philosophical truth of the fact, that is, about its being truly miraculous, only its historical and relevant truth need to be discussed. The decree *Lamentabili* condemned the following proposition:

> The Saviour's resurrection is not a fact of the historical order, but purely of the supernatural order, neither proved nor provable, gradually deduced from other facts by the Christian consciousness (DB 2036).

The object of this chapter is to demonstrate that the resurrection was not only a miracle but also the fulfillment of a prophecy made by Christ.

100   I. Christ Clearly and Frequently Foretold His Resurrection.

From that time Jesus began to show his disciples that he must . . . be put to death, and on the third day rise again (Matthew 16:21).

Jesus cautioned them, saying, "Tell the vision [the Transfiguration] *to no one, till the Son of Man has risen from the dead"* (Matthew 17:9; see Mark 9:8).

And Jesus said to them, "You will all be scandalized this night.

. . . But after I have risen, I will go before you into Galilee" (Mark 14:27–28).

Christ's words are abundantly clear: *And what he said he spoke openly* (Mark 8:32). It is quite obvious that even His enemies were aware of this prophecy and understood what it meant: The chief priests and the Pharisees went in a body to Pilate, saying, *"Sir, we have remembered how that deceiver said, while he was yet alive, 'After three days I will rise again.' Give orders, therefore, that the sepulchre be guarded until the third day"* (Matthew 27:62–64).

Rationalists have absolutely no reasonable basis for their contention that Christ had in mind some sort of metaphorical resurrection, such as the triumph of His cause, or a spiritual fellowship with His disciples, or assistance to be sent them from heaven, or something else of like nature.[2]

II. Christ Foretold His Coming Resurrection as a Proof of His Divine Mission. 101

1. When, at the beginning of His public life, Christ cleared the Temple of merchants, saying, *"Do not make the house of my Father a house of business"* the Jews, that is, the leaders who had at least tacitly countenanced this profanation, asked: *"What sign dost thou show us, seeing that thou dost these things?"* Since the rightful authorities allow this business to go on, you have no right to stop it unless you can show some clear signs that you are armed with authority from God. Their question amounted to a request for the credentials of His divine mission. Accordingly, *in answer Jesus said to them, "Destroy this temple, and in three days I will raise it up" The Jews therefore said, "Forty-six years has this temple been in building, and wilt thou raise it up in three days?" But he was speaking of the temple of his body. When, accordingly, he had risen from the dead, his disciples remembered that he had said this, and they believed the Scripture and the word that Jesus had spoken* (John 2:14–22).

Although neither the Jews nor the disciples themselves grasped the meaning of the prophecy at that time, Christ actually had in mind the resurrection of His body. He deliberately set up the prophecy in advance to serve later as a proof of His mission.[3]

2. *Then certain of the Scribes and Pharisees answered him, saying, "Master, we would see a sign from thee." But he answered and said to them, "An evil and adulterous generation demands a*

(167)

*sign, and no sign shall be given it but the sign of Jonas the prophet.
For even as Jonas was in the belly of the fish three days and three
nights, so will the Son of Man be three days and three nights in
the heart of the earth"* (Matthew 12:38–40).[4]

It is clear that there is question here of a return from the dead.
That this return is foretold as a sign of the divine mission is evident
from the context. The request of the Pharisees can mean only that
they wanted to see some clear proof that He was in reality the one
He claimed to be. In the ensuing verses (41–42) Christ asserts that
He is greater than Jonas and Solomon, and that as a result the
Jews will be condemned for not believing Him. The preceding
verses (22–37) recount the events which seem to have occasioned
the question of the Pharisees. Christ had cured a possessed man
who was both blind and dumb, whereupon the amazed throng
asked, *"Can this be the Son of David?"*, that is, the promised Messias. The Pharisees countered with the accusation that Christ cast
out devils by the power of Beelzebub. Then our Lord replied that
He cast out devils *"by the Spirit of God"* and, that accordingly the
"kingdom of God" had arrived in their midst. This reply furnished
yet other Pharisees the opportunity to demand a sign from heaven [5]
precisely as confirmation of that divine authority to which He
appealed and which the·throngs ascribed to Him.[6]

3. Moreover, even if Christ had never explicitly proposed His
resurrection as an argument for His mission, its relevant truth
would still be sufficiently clear. He had constantly presented Himself as God's envoy. He had openly declared that He had the power
to lay down His life and to take it up again. He had even asserted
that the Father had willed Him to lay down His life with a view
to receiving it back again.[7] He had been put to death for claiming
to be the Son of God.[8] In the light of all this, is not God's act of
raising Jesus from the dead a perfectly evident confirmation of the
latter's teaching?

102 III. Christ Really Died.

Adversaries have left no stone unturned in their efforts to do
away with the fact of the resurrection. During the modern era
some rationalists—a handful, it is true, and without any support
from the ancient enemies of Christianity—have had the audacity
to claim that Christ did not really die on the cross, but merely
lost consciousness and was later revived by the sharp odor of the
burial spices, or by drugs of some sort (Salvador, G. Paulus, Hase).

Consequently, if the argument that Christ returned to life after His death is to be genuinely effective, the fact must first be established that He neither feigned death nor merely swooned, but that He died a real, physical death.

A consideration of the following points easily shows that Christ really died.

1. **The Evangelists unanimously teach that He died.** One of them, John, was an eye-witness, and wrote: *And bowing his head, he gave up his spirit* (John 19:30).

2. **The action of Christ's friends** prove that He really died. These friends, Joseph, Nicodemus, the holy women, cared for the Lord as they would for a dead person. They entombed Him, something they would never have done had they doubted to the slightest degree the fact of His death. The manner of His burial, which involved wrapping the body in tight cloths, embalming it with approximately one hundred pounds of aromatic spices, and placing it in a walled-up rock tomb,[9] would have certainly caused Christ's death if by any remote chance He had been still breathing. Certainly the burial would not have revived Him. That the Apostles and the other disciples were unquestionably certain of Christ's death is abundantly clear from the subsequent difficulty they experienced in admitting the truth of His resurrection.

3. **The activities of Christ's enemies** furnish further proof. Had they not been sure that Christ was dead, they would never have allowed His body to be taken down from the cross,[10] especially as they were aware of the prediction of the resurrection.[11] If Christ had not really died, they would never have had to take refuge later in the fable of the stolen corpse.

4. **Added proof is furnished by the actions of the officials** who took part in the execution. To avoid leaving the bodies on the crosses over the Sabbath, soldiers were sent to break the legs of those crucified and thereby to bring their sufferings to a speedy end. In fact they did break the legs of the robbers, who still had some life left in them; but, *when they came to Jesus, and saw that he was already dead, they did not break his legs; but one of the soldiers opened his side with a lance, and immediately there came out blood and water* (John 19:33–34). The breaking of the legs, which was really an additional torture, was dispensed with in the case of Christ, precisely because He was already dead, as all could clearly see. Still, in order to exclude any possible doubt about His death, one of the soldiers took his lance and inflicted the

coup de grace. That this lance thrust inflicted a lethal wound is clear when one considers its very purpose, which was to make certain of Christs death on the supposition that He might possibly be still alive. That it achieved its purpose may be gathered from the size of the wound, which was large enough to receive Thomas' hand.[12] The authentic testimony of the centurion corroborates all this: *But Pilate wondered whether he had already died. And sending for the centurion, he asked him whether he was already dead. And when he learned from the centurion that he was, he granted the body to Joseph* (Mark 15:44–45).[13] No, there was no physician there to write a death certificate, but on the basis of the data at the disposal of history, any doctor of any age can judge for himself.[14]

103 **IV. Christ Really Came Back to Life.**[15]

1. Theories of the rationalists— Though only a few rationalists have denied the death of our Lord, all reject His return to life, but not for the same reasons.

a. Some reject completely, or at least partially, the credibility of the Gospels concerning the fact of the empty tomb, and brashly declare that the Apostles and other heralds of the resurrection simply deceived the whole world. Some insist that our Lords body' was stolen from the tomb by the Apostles or by Joseph of Arimathea (Holtzmann), or by the Jewish leaders themselves (Reville),'and that this was done on Pilate's authority (Le Roy). Loisy holds that our Lord's body was never given private burial, but was thrown into the common grave reserved for criminals. Others—and they are by far the majority—grant that the Apostles were fully convinced of the resurrection, but insist that they were victims of hallucination, or that, at the most, through some sort of imaginary vision they saw our Lord living, not in the flesh, but in the spirit.

b. The appearances of our Lord were either subjective or objective visions. They were subjective if, as the result of some abnormal physiological or psychological disposition, the visionary's internal senses were so strongly and vividly affected that he believed these sensory reactions to be stimulated genuinely by some external object (Meyer). They would have been objective, not in the sense that any objective reality acted as a stimulus for these sensory reactions, but in the sense that the experiences themselves and the ensuing judgment passed on them were the immediate effect of direct divine action (Reim, Schweitzer).

(170)

c. Rationalists advance these explanations of the empty tomb and of our Lord's appearances only to account for certain progressive stages of belief in the God who came back to life. But in the name of literary and historical criticism, they flatly deny the fact of the resurrection itself. Following the lead of A. Harnack, they will admit the truthfulness of the synoptic Gospels, but only in the sense that these Gospels record faithfully the legends and the beliefs current at the time of their composition.

Belief in Christ's resurrection, clearly expressed in the Gospels, is nothing but the effect of a gradual process of evolution whose successive stages can still be discerned from a comparative study of the various documents. Four stages took place. 1. At the very beginning any notion of Christ's rising to life after three days in the tomb was simply non-existent. Soon, however, the Apostles, back in Galilee, began to reminisce about their departed Master, and these reminiscences led to faith in Jesus. In this way were laid the foundations for the subsequent hallucinations, which were not long in coming. The Apostles and other disciples of our Lord convinced themselves, in good faith, that they had seen Jesus, even though they had actually seen nothing at all. This original tradition is recorded almost without corruption by St. Paul (1 Cor. 15:3-8). 2. Once Jesus had been seen, the process of evolution entered the second stage, in which He was declared alive. To explain this, the tale that Jesus left the tomb on the third day and that some women found the tomb empty was invented. The witness to this stage of the process is Mark (16:1-8). 3. Then, in order to make Christ's bodily resurrection more readily credible, the Christians composed the stories about the guarding of the tomb and about the doubts the Apostles suffered on this matter, which doubts Christ Himself is supposed to have dispelled. St. Matthew preserves these narratives in his Gospel. 4. The final stage of the evolution is found in the later Gospels of St. Luke and of St. John, who recount the appearances of the risen Lord which took place in Jerusalem near the empty tomb itself.

There is no general agreement on the point of departure for the evolution of belief in the resurrection. Many trace it to faith in Jesus the Messias, others to belief in the immortal life of Him who had been crucified (Loisy), still others to faith in God the Father, and to Jesus' consciousness of His divine Sonship (Harnack). According to the rationalist principles of those who admit a natural evolution in the history of religion, belief in the resurrection is to be explained in the light of Oriental and Greek mythology. The basic notion of resurrection is suggested by what men observe in nature: the sun sets and rises again, the seed decomposes only to germinate, the tree is stripped of its leaves, but later the leaves reappear. This phenomenon of physical nature and plant life dying and being reborn year after year was in time ascribed to some deity or other, or was symbolically represented by some deity, even at times by the sun and moon, and was celebrated under the image of a dying and rising god (Osiris, Adonis, Attis, Persephone, Dionysius).

This explanation becomes much easier, of course, when it is granted that Jesus never even existed (Drews).

103a **2. Proof of the Resurrection**—The fact of Christ's real, bodily return is proved 1. directly, by an exposition of the facts, and 2. indirectly, by showing the weakness of the rationalist theories.

a. *Directly—The exposition of the facts.*

The most important fact, one thoroughly established, is that Christ's tomb, though shut tight by a huge rock and guarded by soldiers, was empty on the third day. This fact, supported not only by the testimony of the angels [16] and the women,[17] but also by the admission of Christ's most bitter foes, could not be explained away merely on natural grounds, as is clear from the desperate reaction of the Jews. *Behold, some of the guard came into the city and reported to the chief priest all that had happened. And when they had assembled with the elders and had consulted together, they gave much money to the soldiers, telling them, "Say, 'His disciples came by night and stole him while we were sleeping.' And if the procurator hears of this, we will persuade him and keep you out of trouble." And they took the money, and did as they were instructed; and this story has been spread abroad among the Jews even to the present day* (Matthew 28:11–15). This clumsy expedient truly merits the mockery of St. Augustine:

> What? You produce sleeping witnesses? Truly, you yourself must have fallen asleep, you who have failed with such far-fetched devices. If they were sleeping, what could they have seen; if they saw nothing, what kind of witnesses are they? (*In Psalmum* 63, no. 15.)

There is the further fact that the risen Christ was seen often, at different times and in many different places under varied circumstances. He appeared to many people, and not only to women but also to men.[18] And not only was He seen; He spoke and took food and let Himself be touched—precisely for the purpose of dispelling every last doubt about the reality and the identity of His body.[19] So it is quite true that *he showed himself alive after his passion by many proofs, during forty days appearing to them and speaking of the kingdom of God* (Acts 1:3).

b. *Indirectly—The weakness of rationalist theories.*

Theories about the empty tomb. None of them can explain how our Lord's body vanished from the tomb or what happened to it. That it did vanish and was not subsequently recovered is quite evident, for otherwise the Jews would have lost no time in producing it to expose the deceit of the Apostles' accounts. The hypotheses of hallucination and of imaginary vision do not even touch this difficulty.[20] The contention of a few rationalists that Christ fainted on the cross and was later revived by the odor of the burial spices or by drugs is directly and openly contradicted by the Gospels.[21] The rationalists appeal to the Gospels to sustain their contention; the Church appeals to those same Gospels to refute it. As a matter of fact, Christ, bound tightly in the burial bands, would have been suffocated by the spices rather than revived. How would He have been able to leave the tomb, closed off as it was by a huge rock? How could the Apostles ever have come to believe that the Master had conquered death? As a matter of fact, the Apostles acknowledged that Christ died, and St. Paul re-echoes the voice of Apostolic tradition by stating *that Christ died for our sins according to the Scriptures, and that he was buried. . . .* (1 Corinthians 15:3).

The theory of fraud is also inadmissible. This theory claims that Christ's body was stolen from the tomb. The Apostles and other friends of our Lord were too despondent to dare attempt such a crime, and even had they been bold enough to try, they would have found it impossible to succeed. It would have been quite an achievement to roll away the large stone and spirit off the body without being detected by the guards, and then to hide it away so perfectly that no one ever discovered it. To accuse the Apostles of engineering or cooperating in such a fraud is to be guilty of gross calumny.

An appeal to an earthquake [22] and a flat statement that Christ's body was swallowed up by the earth is futile. How then explain the fact that the burial bands and headcloth stayed at ground level? [23]

104   One looks in vain for a motive that would explain why the Jewish leaders would have had our Lord's body removed; on the contrary, they had very strong motives for keeping it exactly where it was.[24] And, granting for the moment this groundless supposition, their subsequent procedure is simply inexplicable. When the Apostles began to proclaim Christ's resurrection, they would have made haste to produce His body; and this, of course, they never did.[25] St. Matthew would have been unable to record the lie which the guards told, and he would have been even less able to write: *and this story had been spread abroad among the Jews even to the present day* (28:15). Rabbinic writers do not even so much as hint at such a procedure on the part of the Jews.

If Joseph of Arimathea had removed our Lord's body secretly, having placed it in the tomb near Calvary only temporarily, the Apostles' preaching of the Resurrection would have forced him, either as a friend or as foe of Christ's followers, to reveal his action. But in fact, the words which St. Paul and the Evangelist use clearly bespeak a burial, with all the finality of a burial.

Loisy [26] objects that no one could possibly convince himself that Christ's tomb was empty, for His body was not entombed, but cast into the common grave reserved for executed criminals. The following facts expose the weakness of Loisy's theory. 1. All Evangelists agree in saying that the body of Jesus was buried by Joseph of Arimathea, who had requested and received permission from Pilate to take down the Lord's body—in keeping with the Roman custom. 2. In a document of highest antiquity (I Corinthians 15:3) which, according to modern critics, preserves the original tradition, St. Paul uses the term *etaphe* ('he was buried'), which in New Testament usage always indicates normal, decent burial.[27] St. Paul certainly intended to use the term in this sense; otherwise he could never have written that Christians are *buried together* with Christ through baptism unto death.[28] 3. St. Peter, in the sermon which he delivered on Pentecost,[29] compares the tomb of King David with that of Christ, and contrasts the former to the latter; something he could not have done if Christ's burial had not been honorable. 4. If what the Gospels and tradition narrate about the honorable burial of Christ had not been worthy of acceptance, the preaching of Christ's resurrection would have been impossible and indeed the very account of His honorable burial could not have come into being or have been promulgated.

Those who espouse the theory of evolution assert that the 104a Evangelists' tale of the empty tomb is not worthy of credence, and they base their strongest argument on the fact that St. Paul, in First Corinthians, 15, says nothing about an empty tomb and that consequently neither Peter nor James nor, for that matter, any of the Apostles could have known anything about it.

1. However, it is one thing to be silent about a certain matter and quite another to be ignorant of that matter. An argument from silence is valid only when one of necessity should have spoken and was in a position to do so. For his proof of Christ's resurrection in First Corinthians, 15, St. Paul makes use of a better and stronger argument, the appearances of the risen Christ.

2. St. Paul was well aware that the tomb was empty, for he was an intimate friend of St. Luke, who narrated that fact in his Gospel. St. Paul reveals his knowledge of this fact in his sermons and writings. The succession of expressions in 1 Corinthians 15:3–4: *Christ died . . . he was buried . . . he rose again on the third day*— necessarily demands that Christ rose from the tomb alive and that St. Paul knew that He did so. And how could Christ arise alive on the third day without leaving behind an empty tomb? In fact, St. Paul bases his argument for the Messiahship of Jesus (Acts 13:34–37) on the fact that Jesus did not experience corruption as did David and that, of a consequence, our Lord did not remain in a tomb as did David. The Apostle could not have been so certain, had he been ignorant of what had happened *early in the morning the first day of the week.*

3. St. Peter's Pentecost sermon (Acts 2:24–31) makes it clear that the Apostles knew the tomb was empty. It was not in David, but in Christ, that the words of David found their fulfillment: *you will not abandon my soul to the nether world, nor will you suffer your faithful one to undergo corruption* (Psalm 15:10; see Acts 2:27). St. Peter proves this by pointing to David's tomb and contrasting it to that of Christ. David's body stayed in the tomb and suffered corruption. Therefore Christ, who did not experience corruption, did not stay in His tomb.

The proponents of the evolution theory claim that the fact of an empty tomb was invented after belief in the resurrection had crystallized.

1. The proponents of this theory distinguish in the Gospels a Galilean tradition (Matthew and Mark) and a Judean tradition (Luke and John) which, they claim, are mutually opposed and contrary. They also claim that the fact of the empty tomb was not

yet known in 57 A.D. when St. Paul wrote First Corinthians. But if the fact of the empty tomb was a later invention, how—and especially in such a short time—could it have been incorporated into mutually opposed traditions? For we find it in both the Galilean and Judean traditions.

2. When belief in the resurrection finally produced the fiction of the empty tomb, one would have expected it to state not only the fact but its accompanying circumstances, for example, the precise manner in which Jesus came forth from the tomb. In fact, the apocryphal gospels, notably the Gospel of the Hebrews and the Gospel of Peter, do just that. The forthright simplicity of the accounts in the canonical Gospels is a guarantee of their truth.

3. St. Matthew's narrative (28:11–15) of the Jewish leaders' connivance with the sepulchre guards indicates that at the time he wrote his Gospel the report had already spread abroad that the disciples had stolen Christ's body from the tomb. By publishing this report, the foes themselves (the Jews) stand forth as witnesses that the tomb was empty and that it was empty before the Christians, in the rationalist view, made up the story.

4. Finally, the argument from an invented tale about the empty tomb is absolutely preposterous. Belief in and preaching of the resurrection would have been impossible unless friend and foe alike had been fully convinced of the fact that the tomb was really empty. If these adversaries insist that the preaching of the resurrection was done in clandestine fashion, then they find themselves faced with a fact of history, namely that from the beginning there existed at Jerusalem a Christian community openly professing the resurrection.

105   *Theories about the apparitions.* None of those proposed offers an adequate explanation.

The theory of fraud and deceit is unsatisfactory. In fact, with the exception of a few thoroughly shameless individuals, rationalists as a group admit that the Apostles were not deceivers, but simple, upright men. How could these fishermen, so timid and fearful on Good Friday, have so cleverly invented a situation of such magnitude as to win the adherence even of many of the priests [30] right in Jerusalem—and all this in spite of the rumor of the fraudulent theft of the body? And what had they to gain from spreading such a lie? They certainly knew that lying would win them nothing from God; they knew, too, that this particular lie would win for them the vicious antagonism of men. Notwithstanding all this, they not only designed the most heinous fraud ever; but through a life filled, by reason of this very lie, with hard work and persecution, they maintained it right up to death by martyrdom. Absurd! [31]

The theory of hallucination is inadequate. It claims that first some women, then the Apostles and a few others—all in good faith —convinced themselves that they had seen Jesus, though in reality they had seen nothing at all. This illusion grew chiefly out of the all-consuming confidence with which the disciples expected the resurrection of their beloved Master.[32] Now in truth, neither the fact of such an hallucination nor its psychological explanation is admissible.

1. How could so many people—and not just hysterical women —so often, and in such varied circumstances, have been so deluded by their imaginations as to convince themselves groundlessly that they were looking at Christ, talking and eating with Him, touching Him with their hands? Is one to believe that the whole primitive Church was made up exclusively of psychotics?

2. It is simply not true that the disciples, carried away by an enthusiastic expectation of the resurrection, were quick to believe. On the contrary, after the Lord's death they were quite despondent and loath to believe anything. When Magdalene saw the stone rolled back her first thought was not of the resurrection. Her reaction was: *"They have taken the Lord from the tomb, and we do not know where they have laid him'* (John 20:2). Later she asked Christ Himself, under the impression that she was speaking to the gardener: *"Sir, if thou hast removed him, tell me where thou hast laid him and I will take him away'* (John 20:15). When the women reported the resurrection to the Apostles, these considered their words to be *nonsense, and they did not believe the women* (Luke 24:11). The disciples on the road to Emmaus had apparently found no ground for hope even in the report of the resurrection.[33] The assembled Apostles were disturbed at the sight of Jesus and thought that they were seeing a ghost, so that Christ had not only to show them His hands and feet and to suggest that they touch them but even to eat in their presence. Only then did they believe.[34] The unbelief of Thomas is proverbial.[35] Even when Christ appeared on the mount of Galilee, there were still some who had their doubts.[36] Unbelievers stumble all over themselves when they try to avoid this evidence by asserting that the disciples were indeed despondent and without hope at first, but that they gradually built up confidence and eventually a real conviction about

(177)

the resurrection. Then at last they "saw" the Lord.[37] The fact is that the disciples did not see Christ because they "believed" in His resurrection, but that they believed in His resurrection because they had seen Him alive with their own eyes and had touched Him with their own hands.

The inadequacy of the hallucination theory can be proved against modern critics also. In the original tradition admitted by them (1 Cor. 15:3-8), Paul equates the appearances of the risen Lord to Cephas, James, and all the Apostles with the appearance to himself on the road to Damascus. Now the accounts of this latter appearance in Acts show clearly that St. Paul was far from being psychologically disposed to convince himself in good faith that he saw Jesus, but that he actually did see Him. Consequently, neither can the appearances to the Apostles be explained away as hallucinations.

Unsatisfactory, too, is the theory of imaginary visions, according to which not the risen body of Christ, but only His soul appeared to the disciples, with the help of some sort of picture presented to the imagination.

1. This theory, which satisfies neither Christians nor rationalists, does not explain the facts; for pictures in the imagination cannot be touched and felt.

2. This theory makes Christ responsible for a fraud, because He allowed Himself to be touched, and ate in the presence of His Apostles precisely to convince them that He was not a ghost or a spectre, but a living man.[38]

105a   Additional remarks on the evolution theory of the Resurrection

1. Too short a time elapsed before the writing of the Gospels— between 60 and 70 A.D. according to Harnack—for the aforementioned evolution to have taken place, especially since there were still living many of Christ's contemporaries whose attitude toward Him and the disciples was anything but favorable. Furthermore, the factors alleged as foundation for belief in the resurrection are inadequate to furnish such a foundation, as is clear from what has been said above.

2. The exposition above has already refuted the claim that the Apostles thought they had seen Jesus, whereas they had actually seen nothing at all, or at most the soul of Christ, presented to them by means of a picture in their imagination. The fact that they actually did see the body of the risen Christ is clear from 1 Cor. 15:3-8. This text shows clearly not only the belief and the teaching

(178)

of St. Paul, but also that of the other Apostles. *I delivered to you first of all, what I also received* (v. 3) . . . *Whether then it is I or they, so we preach* (v. 11). The belief and the teaching of St. Paul and of the Apostles were accordingly one and the same, and this was true even at the time of St. Paul's first visit to Jerusalem, which took place three years after his conversion, some three or four years after the death of Jesus. Now the object of St. Paul's belief and teaching was Jesus, living again in the flesh, as is clear from the context and the order in 1 Cor. 15:3–7: *died—was buried—rose —was seen.* He who arose, then, was He who had died and was subsequently buried. This can mean nothing but bodily resurrection. He who was seen was He who arose. What can this mean but the appearance of Him who arose in the flesh? Besides, in 1 Cor. 15:12–16, St. Paul used the fact of Christ's resurrection as a proof for the resurrection of the dead, and he could not have done this if the resurrection of Christ and that of all men were not of the same nature. According to St. Paul, the resurrection of the dead will clearly involve a bodily resurrection (1 Cor. 15:35–44)—consequently it was the body of the risen Christ which appeared.[39]

Granted, then, that the object of St. Paul's belief and teaching was Jesus, living again in the flesh, it follows that the Apostles, too, saw the risen body of Jesus. They all teach the same doctrine. Consequently one could not admit that stage in the evolutionary process in which the Apostles first thought they saw the Lord, but only gradually came to think that He whom they had supposedly seen was actually alive again.

3. Just as the claim that the empty tomb is a fiction must be rejected (104a), so must the opinion which holds that the Christians fabricated at a much later date the initial doubts and incredulity of the Apostles. Such doubt and unbelief, which certainly reflected little credit on the Apostles, could not have been invented or fabricated at a time when the Apostles were held in highest honor by all. But if, in spite of all this, the doubt and unbelief were narrated at this time, one can only conclude that they are based on the truth of the original tradition. Furthermore, the proponents of the evolution theory say that these fables were composed to strengthen belief in the resurrection. Belief in Christ's resurrection, however, is hardly strengthened by these doubts. The enemies of the Apostles could with justice say that the latter had seen merely some spectre of the imagination which they thought was the Messias. Finally, the evolutionists contend that these

(179)

doubts are recorded only in the later Gospels, those of St. Luke and St. John. This is not true, for Matthew mentions them in passing (28:17), and there are indications that Mark, too, intended [40] to narrate the initial doubts and unbelief of the Apostles (16:8). Besides, to have recorded them would have contributed nothing at all to the purpose which Matthew and Mark had in writing their Gospels.

4. The proponents of evolution distinguish among the Gospels. Matthew and Mark, they say, give the Galilean tradition and accordingly relate only those appearances of our Lord which took place in Galilee. Luke and John give the Judean tradition and thus relate also the appearances which took place in Judea and Jerusalem at the tomb of Jesus. Whatever may be the meaning of these words,[41] *he goes before you into Galilee; there you shall see him* (Matthew 28:7; see Mark 16:7), they certainly do not exclude the possibility of our Lord's appearing in Judea.

a. The first appearance, recorded in Matthew s Gospel (28:9–10), was that made to the women early in the morning on the first day of the week. The claim that this text was interpolated is a gratuitous assumption on the part of the critics; for the text is missing in no manuscript and there is no evidence of its being spurious. Besides, St. Matthew indicates (28:16) that the appearance in Galilee was not the first, but that another had preceded it, namely, the one in which the disciples received the order to go to Galilee. Matthew does not record all the appearances, but only those which furthered his set purpose, which was generally apologetic in character. On the other hand, Luke and John set out specifically to convince their readers of the truth of the resurrection.

b. It is clear that St. Mark also knew of the appearances at Jerusalem (see Mark 16:9, 12). In the original Gospel of St. Mark (up to 16:8), the Evangelist records the words: *"He goes before you into Galilee"* and thus shows his awareness of the fact that something kept the Apostles from leaving Jerusalem. That could be nothing other than the resurrection and the appearances of the Lord.[42]. Again, Mark follows in his Gospel the preaching of the Apostle Peter, which, as far as the resurrection is concerned, is the same as that of St. Paul. The latter (1 Corinthians 15:5) sets out to prove from the appearances of Christ that He rose on the third day. But he could not have done this had not some of the appearances taken place on the very day of the resurrection. It is clear from the order in which these appearances are recorded that they were none other than those to Cephas and the eleven. They were still in Jerusalem that day. Hence, the appearances related by St. Paul, with whom the Petrine catechesis and St. Mark agree, took place at Jerusalem.

As for the alleged borrowing of belief in the resurrection from 105b Oriental and Greek mythology or from pagan mysteries, the following must be noted:

1. It should be clear from what has already been said that belief in the resurrection is based upon historical facts and trustworthy testimony. The conclusion is evident.

2. It is simply false to assert that the idea of a real resurrection, in the sense of an historical fact, was a familiar one in pagan circles. For when Paul announced Christ's resurrection to the Athenians, men thoroughly acquainted with the mysteries, they considered the matter absurd and ridiculous.[43] Celsus, in his search for analogies to Christ's resurrection, did not dare invoke these myths, but was satisfied with some secular tales.[44] Why? Was it not because he considered the religious myths complete fables? In fact, the majority of the pagans, especially the better educated, looked upon them as mere symbols of the death and rebirth of nature.

3. As Harnack points out, the resurrection was preached not by Hellenistic Jews from Egypt, but by Palestinian Jews. The latter were unlettered and ingenuous fishermen. How then would men of this stamp have conceived the idea of a Messias rising from the dead, an idea so foreign to the Jewish mind that it was actually a stumbling-block to them? [45]

4. There is a vast difference between the Christian faith in the resurrection and Oriental mythologies. These latter, it is true, recognize a return to life after death; but it is a resurrection which will be followed again by death. Christ, on the other hand, *having risen from the dead, dies now no more, death shall no longer have dominion over him* (Romans 6:9).

Corollary 106

With a view to refuting the fact of the resurrection, rationalists object that this fact rests solely on the testimony of Christ's disciples and friends, and are constantly repeating the words of Celsus: "If Jesus really wanted to make known his divine power, he should have shown himself to his enemies, his judges, to everyone indiscriminately." [46] Here is the answer to that objection.

Had the fact of the resurrection no other witnesses than Christ's friends, it would still be irrefutable. Truthful witnesses are not to be refused a hearing simply because they testify for a friend.

Although the risen Christ, appearing for forty days,[47] was seen only by His disciples, it is not true that the fact of the resurrection rests solely on their testimony. Even the Jews admitted that the tomb was empty. The soldiers testified that they had felt the earthquake and had seen the angel come down and roll back the stone.[48] Hence Christ's resurrection was made known to all, to His friends in one way and to His enemies in another.

It is not our task to determine the reasons which prompted the risen Christ to allow Himself to be seen, *not by all the people, but by witnesses designated beforehand by God . . . to preach to the people and to testify* (Acts 10:40–42). As things are, the truth of the resurrection is proved by arguments that are completely adequate. It is hardly probable that an appearance of Christ would have done any good for men whose obstinate unbelief had failed to yield in the face of so many miracles.

CONCLUSION TO THIS CHAPTER

The claim of Jesus of Nazareth that He was the legate of God was no empty boast; His divine mission stands proved by the arguments given. But if Christ was God's messenger, then the religion which He preached and enjoined upon all men is divinely true. In all confidence one might say with Richard of St. Victor: "Lord, if it is all a huge mistake, then you yourself have duped us; for these matters were guaranteed to us by miracles and prodigies of such magnitude and of such a nature that only you could have been responsible for them" (*De Trinitate*, bk. 1, 2).

107 Epilogue

The Catholic Church continues Christ's mission.

Having ascertained the truth of the Christian religion in the abstract, the argument can proceed to a consideration of the truth of the Catholic religion. There are indeed, besides the Catholic Church, many religious bodies which glory in the title of Christian; but it is impossible to hide the fact that all of them came into existence over the centuries by seceding from the Catholic Church, to which they are all related as lopped-off branches are to the mother tree. It is consequently quite certain that none of them goes back to the time of Christ and the Apostles. How could sects which arose only long centuries after Christ, have been established by Christ as heirs and guardians of His religion? How could a society or institution whose beginnings are centuries removed from the time of Christ have received from Christ the task of continuing

His divine mission? Only the Catholic Church has been in existence over the whole span of centuries stretching from Christ to the present day. Therefore, this Church alone could have received from Christ and His disciples its mission and its doctrine. And so it is that "to the Catholic Church alone belong all those things which God has so abundantly and marvelously bestowed in order to proclaim the credibility of the Christian faith" (DB 1794).

These sects contend that they withdrew from the Catholic Church in order to return to that genuine, pure Christianity from which the Church had strayed. But by speaking in this fashion, these heretics admit that the Catholic Church was truly the original guardian and depositary of the religion of Christ. Granting this fact, any such corruption of this Church is impossible because of Christ's promise. For He not only gave the Apostles and their successors the perpetual charge to preach His doctrine to all peoples but at the same time He promised them His assistance *all days, even unto the consummation of the world* (Matthew 28:20). Now either Christ, the legate and the Son of God, who could certainly not be on the side of those who would corrupt His teaching, was in error, or the Church, enjoying divine assistance, did not distort in the slightest the teaching which He had entrusted to her.[49]

The remarks made in this epilogue will be expanded in the next chapter and are made here only to show that the considerations of the preceding chapter alone would suffice to prove the truth of the *Christian-Catholic religion.*

Notes

1. See Acts 1:22, 2:22–36, 3:15–16, 4:10–33.

2. So, for example, Hase, Wendt, and others. See Wilmers, *op. cit.*, p. 357.

3. Ottiger refutes other rationalistic explanations of Christ's words in his *Theologia fundamentalis*, I, 837.

4. The phrases, "after three days" and "three days and three nights," need not, in view of the Jewish mode of expression, indicate three *whole* days, as P. Jovino demonstrates fully in his *Disquisitio critico-biblica de tempore sepulturae Christi*. The Hebrew word 'ônâ is thus explained by the Gemarists: "A day and a night make up an 'ônâ, and any part of an 'ônâ is considered as a whole one" (Lightfoot, *Horaria Hebraica*).

5. See Luke 11:16.

6. We admit that Christ spoke somewhat cryptically in the passages cited, but on both occasions He was dealing with men who were asking for a sign from base motives. Christ, who showed Himself very fair when it came to giving information, usually spoke to such men in such a way that though they heard they would not hear with understanding. See Matthew 13:13.

7. John 10:17–18: *"For this reason the Father loves me, because I lay down my life that I may take it up again. No one takes it from me, but I lay it down of myself. I have the power to lay it down, and I have the power to take it up again. Such is the command I have received from my Father"*

8. See Matthew 26:63–66; John 19:7.

9. See John 19:39ff.

10. Renan himself admits:

To tell the truth, the best guarantee an historian possesses on a point of this nature [the death of Jesus] is the suspicious hate of Jesus' enemies. . . . At any rate, they had to see to it that he was really dead. However careless the ancients may have been in certain eras about anything connected with legal punctuality and about the exact conduct of business, it is hardly credible that in this instance the interested parties would not have taken some precautions, since they considered the affair so very important (*Vie de Jesus*, Ch. 26).

11. See Matthew 27:63.

12. See John 20:25–27.

13. The reason for Pilate's wonder is of scant moment. It is true that authors of the period when crucifixion was in vogue record cases of men who were crucified and lived for a whole day or more, but these remarks concern men who had suffered very little before being crucified. Christ had suffered so many and such horrible tortures before being nailed to the cross that His dying within a few hours, and before the thieves, seems hardly a matter for wonder. If, nonetheless, Pilate was surprised, we can only say that he either paid little heed to our Lord's preliminary torture or that he half hoped and half feared that Christ would resort to some extraordinary or miraculous expedient.

14. Some exegetes think that the flow of blood and water was a perfectly natural occurrence, but the more common opinion among the Fathers and the exegetes is that they give evidence of a miracle. A natural explanation runs into serious difficulties, particularly with regard to the flow of water. On this point see: Le Bec, Dr. E.: *The Death of the Cross: A Physiological Study* (St. Louis, 1951), pp. 19ff.

Prat, Ferdinand: *Jesus Christ*, II, 394–96;
Ricciotti, Giuseppe: *The Life of Christ*, p. 643;
Der Katholik (1886), II, 585.

On the emphatic assertion found in John 19:35, see V. Kasteren, *Het Mattheus-Evangelie en de Overlevering*, pp. 26–32.

15. Consult the following authors:

Disteldorf: *Die Auferstehung Jesu Christi* (1906);
Jacquier-Bourchany: *La resurrection de Jesus-Christ* (1911);
Ladeuze: *La resurrection de Jesus* (1910);
Muser: *Die Auferstehung Jesu und ihre neuesten Kritiker* (1914); and
Rose: *Etudes sur les Evangiles*, ch. 8. This work is of special interest.

The following articles are also good for this point:

Dieckmann, H.: "Die formgeschichtliche Methode und ihre Anwendung auf die Auferstehungsbericht," *Scholastik* (1928), p. 379; "Die Auferstehungsberichte der vier Evangelien nach ihren Verschiedenheit und Eigenart," *ibid.*, (1928), p. 221;

Lohmann, H.: "Die biblischen Berichte fur die Auferstehung," *ThGl* (1926), p. 154.

16. See Matthew 28:6; Mark 16:6; Luke 24:5–6.

17. See Luke 24:9. Compare this passage with Matthew 16:5–6; Luke 24:5–6; John 20:2, 15.

18. He appeared to Mary Magdalen (Mark 16:9; John 20:11–17); to the women on their way back from the tomb (Matthew 28:9); to Peter (Luke 24:34; 1 Corinthians 15:5); to the disciples on the road to Emmaus (Luke 24:13–33; Mark 16:12–13); to the assembled Apostles minus Thomas (Luke 24:36–43; John 20:19–23; Mark 16:14; 1 Corinthians 15:5); to the Apostles, Thomas included, (John 20:24–29); to the disciples by the Sea of Tiberias (John 21:1–23); to the eleven Apostles on the mount in Galilee (Matthew 28:16); to more than five hundred of the brethren at one time, many of whom were still alive when Paul wrote the First Epistle to the Corinthians, probably in the 58 A.D. (1 Corinthians 15:6); to James (1 Corinthians 15:7); and finally to the Apostles before the Ascension (Acts 1:9ff; Luke 24:50–51).

19. See Luke 24:39–44; John 20:24–29.

20. In fact Renan calls the question, "Where was the place where the worms consumed the lifeless corpse?" idle and unanswerable. He goes on to say: "We shall always be in the dark on this point of detail" (*Les Apotres*, Ch. 2).

21. See no. 102.

22. See Matthew 28:12.

23. John 20:6–7. Tertullian, even in his day, ridiculed the idea that Christ's body had been spirited away secretly: "This is the one whom the disciples secretly whisked off so that they could believe He had arisen, or whom the gardener removed for fear his lettuces would be trampled by the frequent visitors" (*De Spect.*, 30).

24. See Matthew 27:64.

25. See Acts 4:1–22. Dentler writes: "It looks very much as though they [the leaders and elders and scribes] did not yet know at that very moment what' Reville thinks he knows about them today" ("Die Auferstehung Jesu in dem Neuen Testament," Bibl Zf, I [1908], 57).

26. *Quelques lettres sur les questions actuelles et sur dés 'evenements recents, XXXV.*

27. See Luke 16:22; Acts 2:29.

28. See Romans 6:4; Colossians 2:12.

29. See Acts 2:31.

30. See Acts 2:41, 6:7.

31. Those who claim fraud sometimes appeal to the differences of style and order in the presentation of Christ's apparitions by the Evangelists and by St. Paul. They conclude from these differences that the sacred writers contradict one another and are not trustworthy—at least in the matter of the resurrection. But:

    a. Even were it true that the sacred writers actually contradicted one another in these relatively unimportant details, one could not jump to the conclusion that they are unreliable with regard to the main facts of the narrative. There they are definitely in accord.

    b. A real contradiction cannot be proved. No sacred author set out to compose a complete account covering every detail. In the light of individual aims, one writer omitted certain details, another others, or one simply synopsized what another had related at greater length. Since we do not know all the circumstances, and since the very concise method of presentation is sometimes susceptible of various interpretations, it is difficult to determine with precision the exact order in which the events narrated follow upon one another. This is the reason for the different explanations given by exegetes. Worth reading on this point are Le Camus, *Vie de Notre Seigneur*, 6th ed.; A. Cellini, *Gli ultimi capi del Tetramorfo;* Prat, *op. cit.* v. II; Ricciotti, *op. cit.*

   c. We should like to remark in addition that these apparent contradictions themselves clear the sacred writers of any suspicion of fraudulent conspiracy. If they had set out to deceive, they would sedulously have avoided such apparent contradictions.

32. Renan seems to have scaled the heights of impudence with his remark:

The vivid imagination of Mary of Magdala played a leading role in this affair. Ah, the divine power of love! sacred moments in which the passion of a woman suffering hallucinations gives to the world a risen God! (*Vie de Jesus,* Ch. 26).

33. See Luke 24:19–24.

34. See Luke 24:36–44.

35. See John 20.

36. See Matthew 28:17. How does this unbelief of the Apostles fit in with the many prophecies of the resurrection? The Gospel itself gives the answer. After recording the unmistakably clear prediction of the death and resurrection, St. Luke goes on to say: *And they* [the Apostles] *understood none of these things and this saying was hidden from them, neither did they get to know the things that were being said* (18:34). The Apostles knew, of course, what Christ's words meant in their literal sense, but since any idea of a suffering and dying Messias was farthest from their minds, they clearly did not know what to make of such a statement. Perhaps they ended by convincing themselves that the prediction had some allegorical meaning.

37. See C. Rose, *Études sur les Evangiles,* Ch. 8.

38. See Luke 24:36–43.

39. For the meaning of these phrases of St. Paul: *flesh and blood can obtain no part in the kingdom of God* (1 Corinthians 15:50); *what is sown a natural body rises a spiritual body (ibid.,* 15:44); *now the Lord is the spirit* (2 Corinthians 3:17), see Tobac, *Le problème de la justification dans S. Paul,* (Louvain, 1908); Prat, *The Theology of St. Paul,* v. II.

40. Ladeuze, *op. cit.,* p. 51.

41. See *ibid.,* p. 43, and Mangenot, *op. cit.,* p. 269.

42. Ladeuze, *op. cit.,* p. 45. Mark 16:9–16 cannot be used in arguing against critics, since they hold that St. Mark's Gospel ends at 16:8.

43. See Acts 17:18, 31, 32.

44. Origen, *Contra Celsum,* Bk. 3, chs. 26, 31–34. See *Stimmen,* 72 (1907), 46–49.

45. See 1 Corinthians 1:23.

46. See Origen, *op. cit.,* Bk. 2, ch. 63.

47. Note the expression *throughout forty days*. Christ later appeared also to Saul, who was at the time of the apparition definitely not a friend of Christ, but His foe and persecutor (Acts 9:3; see 1 Corinthians 9:1, 15:8; St. Thomas, *S.Th.* III, q. 57, a. 6, ad 3). We may guess, then, what would have happened had Christ appeared to His foes as well. Either they would have believed and be counted by the rationalists among Christ's friends, as is Paul; or they would not have believed and in that case would certainly have found some way to deny the truth of the apparition.

48. See Matthew 28:2-4.

49. From another point of view, if the Catholic Church were assumed to have become corrupt with the passing of the centuries, it would still not at all follow that the mission once entrusted to her by Christ passed on to some sect or other, such as Protestantism. Such a transfer would have to be proved by positive arguments. No sect can produce such arguments; in fact, none even makes the attempt. The logical conclusion would be that the lawful guardian and teacher of Christian revelation had completely vanished; and this conclusion certainly cannot be reconciled with Christ's promise.

CHAPTER III

The Divine Origin of Christ's Work or of the Christian-Catholic Religion

---

The Divine Origin of Christ's Work, or of the Christian-Catholic Religion is proved by:

1. many physical miracles;
2. various moral miracles:
   a. spread and conservation of the Christian-Catholic religion;
   b. its marvelous harvest of holiness;
   c. the marvelous fortitude of its martyrs.

Article I

THE DIVINE ORIGIN OF THE CHRISTIAN-CATHOLIC RELIGION IS PROVED BY PHYSICAL MIRACLES

Sample Miracles from Different Periods of Church's History.
Scholion. General observations about miracles:

1. Critical reading of lives of saints still leaves huge mass of sure miracles.
2. Miracles quite often performed as direct proof of Christ's mission and doctrine.
3. Miracles more common in early days. Why?

CHAPTER III

The Divine Origin of Christ's Work or of the Christian-Catholic Religion

108

All agree that from Apostolic times to our own there has always existed that group of Christians who have been united at least by the profession of the same faith. All agree also that this group, very early in its career, adopted the name "Catholic Church," [1] which has been preserved throughout the ages.

It is also admitted that that church at all times and in the most clear manner has claimed to be the guardian and teacher of the divine religion founded by Christ. So strong have been its feelings on this point that it has always expelled as a heretic anyone who deviated from its teaching on even one point. If such a man stubbornly persisted in his defection, it proclaimed him liable to eternal damnation.[2]

This chapter, then, will answer the question: "Is this solemn and constant claim of the Catholic Church to be a religion divine in origin backed by divine testimony?" It contains the following articles:

1. many physical miracles: *Article I;*
2. various moral miracles (e.g., the marvelous spread and conservation of the Christian-Catholic religion): *Article II;*
3. the marvelous fruit of holiness always produced by the Church: *Article III;*
4. the wondrous fortitude of the martyrs: *Article IV.*

Article I

THE DIVINE ORIGIN OF THE CHRISTIAN-CATHOLIC RELIGION IS PROVED BY PHYSICAL MIRACLES

Even as Christ Himself was shown to be God's messenger to men by miracles, so too is His work, the Christian-Catholic religion. In fact, there has never been a time when the Catholic

109

(191)

Church has not been distinguished as something unique because of miracles. This is so true that to consider even a portion of those miracles would consume a great amount of time. Consequently, this treatment is limited to a few miracles only, taken from each of the more important periods in Church history. These will prove that the faith of the Catholic Church, in every age of its existence, has been stamped with the divine seal of approval. At the same time they will refute the contention of heretics that the ancient Church in this or that century, say at the time of the Eastern Schism or of the Protestant Reformation, had become corrupt through a substantial degradation of her teaching.[3]

110   1. It is well known that the Church was set apart by many miracles at the time of her institution and early expansion. St. Luke, in the Acts of the Apostles, recounts many miracles performed by the Apostles [4] and others.[5] St. Paul, in his First Epistle to the Corinthians, gives eloquent testimony to the frequency of miraculous gifts (charisms) in the early Church (see 1 Cor. 12ff). Near the end of the second century St. Irenaeus wrote: "It is impossible to reckon the number of graces which the universal Church receives from God, and which, in the name of Jesus Christ who was crucified under Pontius Pilate, she uses every day for the benefit of the people" (*Adversus Haereses*, bk. 2, c. 32, 4).[6] In the same passage Irenaeus records various types of miracles and adds that miracles do not take place among heretics.

2. During the period of the Catholic Church's struggle against Arianism many outstanding miracles were wrought to bear witness to her divine origin.

a. When the patroness of Arianism, Justina, the mother of Valentinian II, was persecuting St. Ambrose, a certain blind man, well known in Milan, recovered his sight by touching the relics of Sts. Gervase and Protase, which were discovered at that time (386) as the result of a revelation. This was but one among many other miracles, as is known from the writings of St. Ambrose [7] and of St. Augustine,[8] who was in Milan at the time. Paulinus, a deacon of St. Ambrose, describes the effect of these miracles in this fashion: "Thanks to these good deeds wrought by the favor of the martyrs, the faith of the Catholic Church was growing steadily and the faithlessness of the Arians declined" (*Vita sancti Ambrosii*, 5, 14).

b. In 484, in the forum of Typassa (modern Tefessed, near Algiers), a large group of Christians, unwilling to join the ranks of the Arians, had their tongues and right hands cut off by order of King Hunneric. Victor, bishop of Vita, tells us that:

> when this had been done, a singular favor of the Holy Spirit enabled them to speak as they had always spoken, and they enjoy this power to the present day. But if anyone is unwilling to believe this, he can go to Constantinople, and there he will find one of these favored ones, the subdeacon Reparatus, delivering polished sermons without the least trace of an impediment. And it is for this reason that he is held in such veneration in the palace of Zeno the emperor (*Historia persecutionis vandalicae*, bk. 5, c. 6).

Other witnesses to this miracle are the emperor Justinian I,[9] Aeneas of Gaza,[10] and Marcellinus, Comes of Illyria,[11] all of whom assert that they saw with their own eyes some of these tongueless martyrs speaking quite fluently. Procopius of Caesarea,[12] a contemporary author, says the same thing.

3. After the Greeks, under the leadership of Michael Caerularius, had in 1054 withdrawn from the Catholic Church which they accused of corrupting Apostolic tradition, St. Bernard, Abbot of Clairvaux (d. 1153), a man thoroughly devoted to the Church and to its head, the Roman Pontiff, worked many miracles. One noteworthy case occurred in the region of Toulouse, where St. Bernard was combatting the Petrobrusian and Henrician heretics.

> There is a place in that region called Sarlatum, where at the end of one of his sermons, they brought this servant of God several loaves of bread to be blessed, in accordance with the universal custom. Raising his hand and blessing them in the name of God with the sign of the cross, he said: "This will be a sign of the truth of our teaching and of the falsity of that of the heretics, if your sick regain their health upon eating this bread." But the venerable Bishop of Chartres, who happened to be present and found himself quite close to the man of God, was a bit fearful and said: "If they eat it in good faith they will be cured." The holy father, entertaining not the slightest doubt of God's power, replied: "I should not ordinarily say this, but the fact is that no matter who eats it he will be cured, and this will be a sign to them that we speak the truth and are true messengers of God." Such a great crowd of sick persons grew well after having eaten the bread that the event was spread broadcast throughout the whole province, and when the holy

man tried to make his way back through the neighboring districts he was besieged by such insistent crowds that he turned aside, afraid to pass that way (*Vita Sancti Bernardi,* bk. 3, c. 6, 18).

This is the account of Gaufridius, secretary of St. Bernard, who prefaces his biography of the saint with the words: "Our account deals chiefly with those events at which I was present in person, but I have sometimes included also a few things which I learned on the trustworthy testimony of the brethren who witnessed them." [13]

112   4. At the time of the Reformation, when whole nations deserted the Church to follow the "pure Gospel," the Catholic doctrine found solid approbation in the miracles of St. Francis Xavier, Apostle of the Indies and of Japan (d. 1552). Very many of these miracles, among them the raising of four people from the dead, are recorded in the work of Orazio Tursellini, who in writing the biography of St. Francis used the authentic records prepared by the viceroy of India at the order of the king of Portugal.[14] One outstanding prodigy is taken from the *Bull of Canonization:* [15]

When the servant of God was preaching to the infidels in a certain church at Cape Comorin, and was making no progress at all because of the hardness of their hearts, he brought the sermon to a close and ordered that a tomb be opened in which a man had been buried the day before. He then announced to the people that as proof of the truth of the Christian faith the dead man, by Gods will, would live again. Cutting away the cloth in which the corpse had been wrapped, he commanded the dead man to come to life. To the amazement of all, the dead man came alive on the spot. Moved by this compelling miracle, those who were present, and many others besides, came to believe in God.

113   5. Finally, in our own time, when almost all the sects were accusing the Church of inventing a new dogma, the Immaculate Conception of the Blessed Virgin, many miracles took place just outside the town of Lourdes at the invocation of her who deigned to reveal herself under the title of the Immaculate Conception.[16]

In this connection one may well mention the amazing cure of Peter de Rudder, whose leg, broken eight years before and still broken in spite of all the work of his doctors, was suddenly and completely restored in 1875, when the poor fellow, who lived in the village of Oostacker, implored the aid of the Blessed Virgin of Lourdes.[17]

Although these miracles corroborate more directly the doctrine of the Immaculate Conception, they can be used also as confirmation of the whole Catholic religion. On the one hand, the doctrine of the Immaculate Conception is peculiar to the Catholic Church alone [18] and is intimately connected with the rest of her dogmas, and on the other hand, these cures are obtained only through participation in Catholic belief and worship.

Scholion. Some general observations about the miracles which have 114 *always been a characteristic of the Catholic Church.*

To the very few examples adduced above it would be well to add some observations on the Church's miracles in general.

1. It is a well known fact that not all of the marvelous deeds narrated in the lives or acts of the saints merit belief.[19] There is therefore need of caution, even in laudatory sermons; for Christian people are not to be fed on fables or on tales which are suspect. Setting aside those which are historically or philosophically doubtful, there remains a huge mass of real miracles. It is indeed true that real miracles have never been lacking at any period of the Christian-Catholic Church's history. The matter is so certain that no one who acknowledges the worth of properly certified human testimony could call it into question. It is likewise certain that no other religion or sect stands approved by a like endowment of miracles.[20]

2. These miracles were quite frequently performed as direct proof of Christ's mission and teaching. This we know either from the explicit assertion of the miracle-worker or from the accompanying circumstances (when, for example, preachers of Catholic doctrine performed miracles precisely as such preachers, as happened in the case of the Apostles and generally in the case of missionaries, or when martyrs were favored with miracles because they suffered for Catholic teaching). But although there are a great many miracles which were not performed directly in support of the Church (but rather to prove, for instance, the holiness of this or that person), still their very frequency and unbroken continuity bear witness at least indirectly to the truth of the Catholic religion. For who cannot see that God, by the very fact that He continually works miracles in the Catholic Church, and graces with miracles

the outstanding children of that Church in every age of history, is thereby strongly recommending the Church herself and the religion she teaches? All the saints who were remarkable for their miracles either during their lifetime or after their death acknowledged and loved the teaching of the Church as something divine, and were most avid in their use of the means of sanctification provided by the Church; in a word, they were remarkable for their devotedness to the Church. Who would not, therefore, say that God, by testifying to their holiness by miracles, at the same time set His seal of approval on the Church? For it was to this Church that they rendered honor as the source of their holiness, and it is this Church which claims them as children.

3. All are aware of the fact that miracles took place more frequently during the early years of the Church than in later centuries. St. Augustine recognized that even in his day.[21] St. Gregory the Great thus expresses the chief reason underlying this fact:

> If the faith was to grow, it had to be nourished by miracles, just as when we plant saplings we water them constantly until we can see that they are firmly rooted in the soil. And as soon as they have taken firm root, we stop watering them (*Homilia 29 in Evangelium,* no. 4).

In fact, the more widely the Catholic religion is spread throughout the world and the longer it has been in existence, the less need it has of miracles (on the physical plane). This is true not only because its first advance was retarded by greater difficulties than were its subsequent conservation and further spread, but chiefly because the older and the more widespread the Church becomes, the more easily it can be recognized on its own merits as the work of God. This is due to miracles of the moral order which are a constant phenomenon in the Church.

There may be still other reasons for God's wishing to perform more miracles at one time than at another.[22] It is plausible that the earlier centuries were richer in miracles for the reason that in those days men were more remarkable for their deep faith, especially since the gift of miracles was promised in a special way as a reward for heroically staunch faith.[23] Would not God's punishment have been perfectly just if He were to withdraw the grace of abundant miracles from nations which arrogantly rejected a faith they had once embraced?

Notes

1. We have abundant proof that the title *Catholic Church* was already used at the beginning of the second century. St. Ignatius of Antioch writes:

Where the bishop appears, there let the people be, just as where Jesus Christ is, there is the Catholic Church (*To the Smyrnaeans*, ACW, I, 93).

In an early Christian document, *The Martyrdom of Saint Polycarp Bishop of Smyrna*, we read:

The Church of God which resides as a stranger at Smyrna, to the Church of God residing at Philomelium, and to all the communities of the holy and Catholic Church, residing in any place: *may mercy, peace, and love* of God the Father and Our Lord Jesus Christ *be* yours *in abundance!* (Salutation. ACW, VI, 90).

The whole world-wide Catholic Church (Chapter 8, p. 93).

he [Polycarp] glorifies God and the Father Almighty, and blesses Our Lord Jesus Christ, the Savior of our souls, the Captain of our bodies, and Shepherd of the world-wide Catholic Church (Chapter 19, p. 99).

See also the *Muratorian Fragment* in ML, III, 191; Tertullian's *De praescript.* 30, and St. Cyprian's *Epistola 52 ad Antonianum*, no. 1.

In the middle of the fourth century St. Cyril of Jerusalem wrote:

If you ever stop in [other] cities, do not ask simply where the Lord's House is, for others, impious sectaries and heretics, try to dignify their dens by calling them the Lord's House. Nor should you ask merely where the church is; but ask where the Catholic Church is. For this is the unique name of this holy Church which is mother of us all and indeed the Spouse of our Lord Jesus Christ (*Cat.* 18:26).

And towards the end of that century St. Augustine said:

Whether they like it or not, heretics themselves and schismatics, too, when they are speaking not to those of their own circle, but to people outside of it, refer to the Catholic by no other than its own name, the Catholic Church. For no one would understand them if they did not call it by this name which the whole world uses to designate it (*De vera religione*, Bk. 7, ch. 12).

St. Pacian (370 A.D.) writes:

Under the apostles, you will say, no one was called catholic. Granted! But after the Apostles, when heresies had arisen and were, under various names, striving to tear apart and divide the *dove* and the *queen* of God, did not the apostolic people need a special name to distinguish the unit of the people who had remained uncorrupted. . . . Suppose this very day I were to enter a large city. After running into Marcionites, Apollinarians, etc., by what name should I know the congregation of my own people unless it were named Catholic? . . . Christian is my name, but Catholic is my surname. The former gives me a name; the latter distinguishes me. . . . Consequently our people, when called Catholic, are separated by this appellation from the heretical sects. (*Ep.* 1, 5–6).

See P. Batiffol, *L'Eglise naissante*, 2nd ed., p. 166. We purposely referred to the Catholic Church as "a group of Christians bound together by the profession of at least the same faith." Since we are investigating in this chapter only the truth of the *religion* which the Catholic Church professes, we are deliberately omitting anything having to do with the Church precisely as a society. Consequently we care nothing at present about such questions as whether the Church was endowed by Christ or the Apostles with a fixed and

(197)

immutable constitution, or whether the Church always kept its primitive social structure, etc. We shall have occasion to touch these matters in the treatise on *Christ's Church.*

2. That the Church did excommunicate from the very beginning those who held false doctrine is clear from Titus 3:10–12; 2 John 9–10; the letters of St. Ignatius *To the Trallians* (ACW, I, 75–80) and *To the Smyrnaeans* (*Ibid.*, pp. 90–96). St. Irenaeus tells us how the Apostle John, having caught sight of Cerinthus, left the baths without washing, "because Cerinthus, the foe of truth, was inside," and how St. Polycarp dubbed Marcion "the first-born of Satàn." He continues: "Such was the horror which the Apostles had even of entering into conversation with anyone who perverted the truth" (*Adversus Haereses,* bk. 3, ch. 4).

3. See Wilmers, *De vera religione,* pp. 633ff; Dieringer, *Die Göttlichen Taten des Christentums,* II, 422ff; M. d'Herbigny, "Les arguments apologétiques de S. Augustin; L'Eglise," in RPA, IX (1910), 565.

4. See Acts 3:6, 5:15, 9:40, 14:7, 19:12, 20:10.

5. See Acts 6:8, 8:6–13.

6. See bk. 32, ch. 2 of *Adversus Haereses.* Worth reading are St. Justin's *Dialogue with Trypho the Jew,* no. 30; Tertullian's *Apologia,* bk. 23, 93–97; bk. 37, 126.

7. *Epistola* 22, no. 2 and 19.

8. *Confessions,* bk. 9, ch. 7, *City of God,* bk. 22, ch. 8.

9. *Codex Justiniani,* bk. 1, 27.

10. In *Theophrastus,* or *De immortalitate animae et corporum resurrectione.*

11. In his *Chronicles* for the year 484.

12. *De bello vandalico,* bk. 1, ch. 8. See Hurter, *Opuscula ss. Patrum,* 22, p. 222, and *Stimmen,* 37, 270; 40, 415, where Hurter has a special defense of the philosophical truth of this miracle as well as of its historical truth. These articles are aimed at the Englishman, E. Twistleton, who published in 1873 a short book called *The Tongue not Essential to Speech.*

13. The question of the historical and philosophical truth of St. Bernard's miracles is treated by G. Hüffer, "Die Wunder des h. Bernhard und ihre Kritiker," in *Historisches Jahrbuch des Görresgesellschaft* (1889), p. 748.

14. *Vita Sancti Francisci Xaverii,* 6.1. On the historical truth of St. Francis Xavier's miracles, see *Anal. bolland.,* 16.52, 17.485, 33.107.

15. In *Bullar. Rom.,* 4, Appendix, 3.

16. Dr. Boissairie, *L'oeuvre de Lourdes,* 10th ed. (1909); *Lourdes: Les guérisons,* 3 vols. (1913); G. Bertrin, *Histoire critique des événements de Lourdes,* (1905); J. Bricout, *Les merveilles de Lourdes,* (1910); A. Castelein, *Le surnaturel dans les apparitions et dans les guérisons de Lourdes,* (1912); A. Gemelli, *La lotta contro Lourdes,* (1912); J. P. Baustert, *Lourdes und die Gegner vor dem Forum der Wissenschaft,* (1913); L. Cros, *Histoire de Notre Dame de Lourdes d'après les documents et les témoins,* 3 vols., (1925–1926); Dr. A. Marchand, *Les faits de Lourdes et le bureau des constatations médicales,* (1923); RPA, XII, (1910), 816; *Etudes,* 118 (1909), 161; 174 (1922), 423; 180 (1924), 359; *Rev. de philosoph.,* (1911), pp. 48, 553; NRTh, (1909), p. 129; RAp, 34 (1922), 568.

17. *Récit et étude d'une guérison subite de fracture,* by Drs. Van Hoesten-berghe, Royer, and Dechamps (1899); see *De Katholiek,* 116, 474; Dr. A. Dechamps and Dr. le Bec, *Le cas Pierre de Rudder et les objections des médecins.* On the miracle of St. Januarius see L. Cavenne, *Le célèbre miracle de saint Janvier à Naples et à Pouzzoles* (1908); Dr. C. Isenkrahe, *Neapolitanische Blutwunder,* (1912); L. Silva, *Il miracolo di S. Gennaio,* (1916); G. B. Alfano and A. Amitrano, *Le scienze occulte e il miracolo di san Gennaio,* (1922).

18. Even the Church of Constantinople, in its encyclical of 1895 against the "church of corruption" (i.e., the Catholic Church), upbraids us for holding the doctrine of the Immaculate Conception, or at least for defining it. See J. B. Baur, *Argumenta c. orientalem ecclesiam ejusque synodicam encyclicam anno 1895,* (Innsbruck, 1897), p. 56.

19. See, for example, DTC, under the headings "Acta martyrum," "Acta sanctorum"; Günter, *Legenden-Studien,* (1906).

20. We do not claim that no one outside the Church was ever granted a miracle in answer to his prayers—a matter which would be difficult to investigate. We do claim a. that no undoubted miracle was ever performed in such a manner as to serve as approval for another religion and b. that miracles, if indeed they are found outside the Catholic Church, are extremely rare.

21. *Retractationes,* bk. 1, ch. 14, 5.

22. See Dieringer, *Die göttlichen Taten des Christentums,* II, 448.

23. See Matthew 17:19; Luke 17:6; Mark 6:5.

THE DIVINE ORIGIN OF THE CHRISTIAN-CATHOLIC RELIGION IS PROVED BY ITS MARVELOUS SPREAD AND CONSERVATION

Preliminary Remarks: Spread and Conservation, Though Really Distinct, Are Yet One.

PROPOSITION 1: The far-flung and swift spread of Christianity, taken in conjunction with all its accompanying circumstances, must be acclaimed as a moral miracle.

> 1. Christianity spread throughout the world very quickly:
> a. during the lifetime of the Apostles;
> b. and after their death.
>
> *Corollary:* The Church characteristically preached the Gospel to the poor.
>
> 2. This vast expansion defies explanation on purely natural grounds.
>
> *Proof:* based on a study of the circumstances surrounding the expansion:
> a. very serious obstacles:
> > 1. intrinsic impediments: the very Person of Christ; Christian teaching; exclusiveness.
> > 2. extrinsic impediments: for the Jews; for the Gentiles; for both groups.
> b. natural means at hand pitifully few and poor.
>
> *Conclusion:* An effect of such magnitude demands a proportionate cause. The natural means at hand were almost completely inadequate. Supernatural intervention alone offers an adequate explanation.
>
> *Scholion:* Solution of difficulties:
> > 1. attempts at natural explanations;
> > 2. the wide expansion of other religions: Buddhism, Mithraism, Mohammedanism, Protestantism.

PROPOSITION 2: The conservation of the Christian-Catholic religion throughout all ages, considering all the circumstances, must be acclaimed a moral miracle.

1. Fact of unbroken conservation self-evident, but nature of this stability demands close attention.
2. This unbroken stability cannot be explained on natural grounds.
   a. Extremely grave dangers have always threatened it:
      1. diversity of peoples within the Church;
      2. bitter attacks, heresies, and schisms.
   b. Natural means inadequate to insure such stability.

Conclusion.

Some difficulties answered:

1. natural conservation through principle of authority;
2. long existence of other religions.

Article II

THE DIVINE ORIGIN OF THE CHRISTIAN-CATHOLIC RELIGION IS PROVED BY ITS MARVELOUS SPREAD AND PRESERVATION [1]

---

115   *Preliminary remarks.* The marvelous spread and preservation of Christianity seem to demand distinct treatment, since both are different matters. However, both shall be treated in this article. Although the miraculous character of Christianity's expansion pertains especially to the first three centuries, and its amazing stability more particularly to subsequent times, yet a consideration of both miracles together will clearly demonstrate that the Christian-Catholic religion, throughout the entire period of its existence, has always enjoyed divine protection. In short, this study will show that the Christian-Catholic religion has been supported and approved by a miracle of divine omnipotence for as long as it has been in existence.

By taking both miracles together a common objection of heretics can be anticipated. They indeed admit divine intervention in the early diffusion of Christianity, but claim that this in no way constitutes an argument in favor of the Catholic religion, since the latter and true Christianity are, in their opinion, poles apart. This difficulty is forestalled by a joint treatment of both miracles. Who will be so rash as to claim that God would miraculously conserve a religion which would be only a spurious imitation of the religion miraculously established by the same God throughout the world?

The linking of the miracles of the diffusion and preservation of Christianity is not at all arbitrary; for they are, of their own nature, intimately related. If the wide and swift expansion had not been accompanied by an unshaken stability, one might well conclude that the expansion had not been the work of God. Indeed, one would be hard put to it to convince anyone that a religion which would so quickly fall to pieces had been established with God's help. To put it another way, if the Christian religion needs God's help to be preserved throughout the world, how could it have been spread among the Gentiles in the first place by purely human means? Beginnings are always most difficult.

(202)

PROPOSITION 1. *The far-flung and swift spread of Christianity, taken* 116 *in conjunction with all its accompanying circumstances, must be acclaimed a moral miracle.*

I. Christianity Spread Throughout the World Very Quickly

In particular, this section will consider the spread of Christianity from the time of the Apostles to the end of the third century.[2]

1. **Its spread during the lifetime of the Apostles.** Comparatively few men threw in their lot with Christ while He was still alive, but after Peter's sermon on Pentecost, *there were added . . . about three thousand souls* (Acts 2:41). A short time later there was added a group of *five thousand* (4:4), and in short order *the multitude of men and women who believed in the Lord increased still more* (5:14). Not long after, a persecution broke out in Jerusalem and the Apostles and their aides scattered throughout Judea and Samaria *preaching the word* (8:4). When Paul came to Jerusalem about the year 58 and recounted *what God had done among the Gentiles through his ministry, . . . they said to him, "Thou seest, brother, how many thousands of believers there are among the Jèws'* (21:19–20). This was the situation in Palestine.

That many churches existed outside Palestine, even during the lifetime of the Apostles, is suggested by St. Peter in the greeting of his First Epistle: *to the sojourners of the Dispersion in Pontus, Galatia, Cappadocia, Asia and Bithynia.* The same conclusion is indicated by the accounts of St. Paul s journeys, by his own epistles, and by the Apocalypse wherein St. John is commissioned to send a letter to the *seven churches of Asia; to Ephesus, and to Smyrna, and to Pergamum, and to Thyatira, and to Sardis, and to Philadelphia, and to Laodicea* (Apoc. 1:11). That these primitive churches were in some cases quite large can be gathered from the remarks which Tacitus [3] and St. Clement of Rome [4] make about the church in the city of Rome at the time of the Neronian persecution. Again, St. Paul writes that even in his own time the Christian faith was being preached and was making strides throughout the whole world.[5] Though Paul s expression can hardly be understood literally, it does argue for an expansion which under the circumstances was very broad indeed.

2. **Witnesses to post-Apostolic expansion:** St. Ignatius of An- 117 tioch (martyred 107 A.D.) writes: "Jesus Christ, our inseparable life, for His part is the mind of the Father, just as the bishops, though appointed throughout the vast, wide earth, represent for their part

the mind of Jesus Christ" (Epistle to the Ephesians, 3, 2. ACW, I, 61).

Pliny the Younger, the propraetor of Bithynia, wrote (about 112 A.D.) to the emperor Trajan for advice as to treatment of Christians and remarked:

> I thought the matter called for consideration particularly because of the number of those in danger. For many people of every age, of every social station and indeed of both sexes are being brought into peril of their lives by their accusers; and this dangerous situation threatens to continue. Not only are the cities involved; this contagious superstition has infected even the villages and rural areas. Yet I think it can be checked and corrected. It is certainly clear that the temples, which were formerly almost deserted, have begun to fill again and that the long neglected sacred solemnities are being celebrated once more. Fodder for sacrificial victims is again being sold, whereas until recently scarcely any market could be found for it. It is easy to imagine what a throng of people could be brought round were they given a chance to mend their ways (*Epistolae*, 10:97).

St. Justin Martyr (100–164 A.D.) declared: "There is not a single race of men, whether Greeks or Barbarians, or whatever else they may be called, nomads living in wagons, homeless vagrants or herdsmen living in tents, among whom prayers and thanksgiving are not offered to the Father and Creator of all through the name of the crucified Jesus" (*Dialogue with Trypho the Jew*, no. 117).

St. Irenaeus (125–202 A.D.) mentions churches in Germany, Spain, Gaul, the Orient, Egypt and Libya in his work *Adversus haereses*, bk. 1, ch. 10, no. 2.

Tertullian boasts to the Roman governors of Africa: "We are but of yesterday, and we have filled every place among you—cities, islands, fortresses, towns, market-places, the camp itself, tribes, companies, the palace, senate, forum—we have left you nothing but the temples of your gods" (*Apology*, 37).

In the year 212 the same Tertullian warned the Pro-consul Scapula, who was planning to launch a persecution, that the "majority of Carthage" was Christian:

> What will you do with so many thousands, with such a multitude of men and women, persons of every sex and age and of

every rank who will step forward to surrender themselves to you? How many fires, how many swords will you need? What will be the sufferings in Carthage alone, which you will have to decimate. . . . (*To Scapula*, 5, ML 1. 783).

Clement of Alexandria testifies: "The word of our Master did not remain in Judea alone, as philosophy did in Greece. No, it was spread throughout the whole world, winning over Greek and barbarian nations alike, villages and whole cities, bringing to the truth entire households and individually each of those who heard it, even quite a few of the philosophers themselves" (*Stromata*, bk. 6, c. 18).

Lactantius, describing the condition of the Church before the Decian persecution of 249, said: "It stretched forth its hands to the east and west, so that there was at that time no corner of the earth, howsoever remote . . . , whither the religion of God had not penetrated; no nation so savage that it did not turn to gentle works of justice once it had embraced the worship of God" (*De morte persecutoris*, c. 5).

Maximinus Daza, the emperor, wrote that Diocletian and Maximian had raged against the Christians "because they saw nearly everyone abandoning the worship of the immortal gods and joining the sect of the Christians" (Quoted by Eusebius in his *Historia Ecclesiastica*, bk. 9, c. 9).

Testimonies mentioning the whole world are, of course, to be restricted to the then-known world, and at times even to the Roman Empire. One must also remember that some of the authors cited above sacrificed truth to rhetoric. Even granting all this, it is still abundantly clear that the Christian religion had been very widely spread before the end of the third century, not only within the confines of the Roman Empire but also beyond, so much so that it had reached many, many peoples in widely scattered districts of the (known) world. No one who considers even for a moment the difficulties involved in international contacts at that era of history could possibly deny that this expansion was extremely swift.[6]

Corollary

117a

A special mark of the Christian religion was its regard for the poor and the care taken to preach the Gospel to them. During the early years of its existence there were in fact *not many wise . . . not many mighty, not many noble* (1 Cor. 1:26). However, some of the more well-to-do and better educated are found giving their allegiance to Christ from the very beginning. Among the Jews there were, for example, Nicodemus, Joseph of Arimathea, St. Paul, Crispus, Apollo, and a goodly crowd of priests and several Pharisees. The Epistle of James suggests that many of the Christians were quite well off. Among the Gentiles during the first century are found Cornelius the centurion, the proconsul Sergius Paulus, Denis the Areopagite, and not a few noble women at Thessalonica and Beroea, the consul Flavius Clemens and his wife Domitilla, Acilius Glabrio, also of consular rank, and many others. Burial inscriptions at Rome, around the year 200, testify that quite a few members of the most respectable families had given themselves to Christ.[7] At the beginning of the fourth century Arnobius of Sicca could address these words to the pagans:

> Do not even these considerations give you reason to believe: the fact that through all lands in such a short period of time the sacred doctrines of this great name have been spread abroad; that there is no nation of so wild a character and so impervious to gentle sentiments which has not under the influence of His love softened its harshness, and, adopting tranquility, passed over into peaceful dispositions? that men endowed with great ability—orators, grammarians, rhetoricians, lawyers, and physicians, even those who explore the profundities of philosophy— eagerly seek instruction in these things, having abandoned those to which a little while before they were devoted? (*The Case Against the Pagans,* bk. 2, c. 5, ACW, VII, 117).

With good reason P. Allard writes: "Hardly out of its cradle, Christianity broke down the barriers of race, language and culture; and right from the beginning recruited its disciples and its martyrs from all classes of society. This penetration of society by the Church was no less remarkable than its geographical expansion" (*Dix leçons sur le martyre* (1906), p. 152).

118 II. This Vast Expansion of Christianity Defies Explanation on Purely Natural Grounds

The above statement finds its proof in a consideration of the circumstances surrounding that expansion. Such circumstances were the magnitude of obstacles and the dearth of natural means available to overcome those obstacles.

Very serious obstacles made the spread of the Christian religion extremely difficult. Some of these obstacles were intrinsic; others extrinsic.

Intrinsic impediments were:

a. The very person of Christ. Born of the despised Jewish race and put to death by crucifixion, He was now proposed to men as God, as the object of adoration. This was *to the Jews indeed a stumbling-block and to the Gentiles foolishness* (1 Cor. 1:23).

b. Christian teaching. The doctrine taught by the Christians contained the deepest of mysteries and the moral code accepted and lived by Christians, though chaste and beautiful in itself, put a check on all sinful passions, and for this reason was hated by the perverse and was most difficult for the weak.[8]

c. The unavoidable exclusiveness of Christianity, outlawing as it did every other form of religious worship.

Extrinsic impediments:

a. For the Jews: the expectation of the Messias who would be an all-powerful ruler freeing his people from foreign domination; the deep-seated reluctance to allow Gentiles to participate in religion on an equal footing; the authority of the priests and the Pharisees, entrenched in the Chair of Moses and fiercely defending its inviolability.

b. For the Gentiles: devotion to the religion of their forebears, a devotion made staunch by centuries-long custom. This religion catered to their passions and was furthermore so closely bound to each nation's history, political condition, social and domestic life, laws, institutions, festivals and arts, that anyone who embraced Christianity practically cut himself off from all society.[9] Another important factor was the authority of the pagan priests, whose prestige, social position and livelihood depended on the worship of the local gods. The authority of the civil leaders, themselves either high-priests of pagan superstition or convinced that the well-being of the state depended on the worship of the gods, was an added factor.[10] Finally, there were the philosophers, who taught that Christianity was a deadly superstition, beneath the dignity of a Greek or Roman.

c. Affecting both groups were the calumnies devised against Christians wherever they went—chiefly through the efforts of the Jews [11]—and the frightfully cruel persecutions which, when not actually raging, were always threatening.

2. There is hardly any need to explain that the natural means 119 at hand for spreading the Christian religion were pitifully few and poor. Certainly the Apostles were favored with neither worldly wealth nor influence. They were in no position to promise temporal

advantages to their followers, nor could they rely on erudition and compelling eloquence. They were all members of the detested Jewish race and, at least for the most part, were unschooled and unlettered, quite clumsy in their handling of Greek, the common coin of expression. What intelligent person could honestly believe that this handful of obscure fishermen—burning with zeal, indeed, but completely lacking in the usual natural aids—had the power to effect this remarkably vast and difficult expansion of a new religion? [12]

120   *Conclusion.* There is, on the one hand, an effect of the highest magnitude—the rapid conversion of very many men in diverse parts of the world to a religion which is in itself quite difficult, an object of general hatred, attacked in every possible manner. On the other hand, there is a natural cause, somewhat efficacious, to be sure, but evidently out of all proportion to an effect of such magnitude. Since every effect demands a proportionate cause, and since the natural cause at hand is almost completely inadequate to account for the effect, one must acknowledge the activity of another, and much more powerful cause, namely, the supernatural intervention of God, efficaciously moving men by His light and His grace to embrace Christianity.

121   *Scholion. Solution of difficulties.*

1. Many rationalists, following Gibbon's lead, have tried to offer a natural explanation for the wide expansion of Christianity. Among the more important causes which they allege are the following:

a. The promise of eternal life. But did not all religions promise a happy life in the future?

b. The great purity of the life displayed by the first Christians, in particular their love for and generosity to the poor. This assumes, and falsely, that the outstanding virtues of the early Christians were *naturally* acquired. As far as generosity is concerned, who honestly believes that in those early years the Christians were so wealthy that they could attract by their alms so many thousands of men, especially when one considers that the profession of Christianity exposed one to all sorts of difficulties and dangers?

c. The doctrine of the equality of all men in the sight of God, which attracted slaves—and they made up a large part of the population—by the hope of freedom which it held out to them. This doctrine was certainly most welcome and heartening for such poor persons, but at the same time we must realize that the slaves were for the most part men given to the most degrading immorality, an immorality which certainly did not find an ally in the moral teaching of Christianity. Although Christian teaching finds its logical conclusion in the abolition of slavery, the primitive Church did not promise freedom to slaves. At that time the abolition of slavery was not one of its aims; on the contrary, following the example of the Apostles,[14] the Church urged slaves to obey their masters, whether the latter were Christian or not. Most likely a few slaves obtained their freedom from Christian masters or from others through the good office of fellow Christians. But *what are these few among so many?*

d. The unification of many peoples under the one Roman rule. This union of peoples undoubtedly helped to spread knowledge of Christianity more quickly. In fact the Fathers often expressed the opinion that God had extended Roman domination so far and wide precisely in order to prepare a way for a swifter promulgation of the Gospel. But it is one thing to know the Christian religion and quite another to accept it. And from another point of view the far-flung power of the Roman empire was just as much a factor in effectively checking Christianity as it was in its swift expansion.

Of course one can readily grant that some natural causes aided in the spread of the Christian religion. But that these natural causes, even taken cumulatively, offer an adequate explanation for the wondrous spread of Christianity is simply untenable.

The rapid expansion of Christianity finds no explanation at all in a supposed syncretism which would have brought about an accommodation of the new religion to the current convictions and customs of the pagans, an adoption by the new religion of whatever vital and fruitful elements it found in these convictions and customs. This should be clear from what has already been said.[15] The whole history of Christianity cries out that no such syncretism ever existed.

2. Others claim that the argument based on the spread of Christianity is considerably weakened by the fact that other religions and other sects have enjoyed wide expansion: Buddhism, Mithraism, Mohammedanism, Protestantism. But the cases are not at all the same. The argument in favor of Christianity is based, not on the simple fact of expansion, but on the fact that *such a difficult and austere religion, hampered by so many obstacles, and with practically no natural advantages on its side, still attained such far-flung expansion.*

Buddhism proposes no mystery for belief; in fact, it has no firmly established theoretical doctrine. Popular Buddhism, which alone is widespread, is accommodated to all the existing superstitions of the people and incorporates the worship of national gods under the name of Devas. It proposes its moral doctrines, often quite pure in individual precepts—especially the negative ones—not as binding under the divine law, but simply as commendable from a human point of view. It has no desire to change social customs, forbids neither polygamy nor divorce. It was founded by the son of a prince (Siddhartha Sakyamuni, Gautama Buddha) and from its very inception was preached by members of the upper social classes.

It has not been subject to persecution; the tales sometimes told about persecutions leveled against Buddhism are quite untrue. On the contrary, it has always found in the secular arm a favorable propaganda machine. In spite of this, its expansion was relatively insignificant until the zealous efforts of King Asoka, who died in 232 B.C. (at least 150 and more probably 250 years after Buddha's death), extended its influence.[16]

The *worship of Mithra* saw a wide expansion throughout the western provinces of the Roman empire during the second and third centuries after Christ, as Cumont has pointed out quite well in his book, *Les mystères de Mythra* (1900). Mithraism, however, was not an exclusive cult, but adapted itself and became almost indistinguishable from the other religions then in vogue. It was also much like the cult of the Phrygian gods (Cybele, the great mother, and Attis) which the Roman authorities had officially allowed the people to practice.

Roman Mithraism, which was essentially the worship of the unvanquished Sun, found favorable support in the philosophy of the day which taught that the heavenly bodies had souls and were in fact divine, and strove to arrange all the gods in a sort of hierarchy under the head of one supreme deity. This was a very strong point of contact with Mithraism, which set the unvanquished Sun above all other gods. Politics favored it. The emperors, especially since the time of Heliogabalus, were considered emanations from the sun, indeed, "of the same nature as the sun." The cult of Mithra included that of the emperors and as a result was quite flattering to imperial absolutism, and emperors and military leaders did the most to spread Mithraism.[17] As soon as it encountered repressive measures, it died out.

The *religion of Mohammed* fostered lust and greed and was

spread largely by means of violence and war. As long as Mohammed tried mere persuasion he made little headway.[18]

Protestantism was nothing but a passing from a difficult religion
to one whose doctrine and moral practice were, from almost every
point of view, more lax. It grew strong, not by converting pagans,
but by welcoming apostate Catholics.[19] Its rapid spread was due in
large measure to greed and politics,[20] and after a half-century of
rapid expansion, popular excitement gradually subsided and its
advance slowed to a shuffling walk.

PROPOSITION 2. *The preservation of the Christian-Catholic religion* 123
throughout all ages, considering all the circumstances, must be
acclaimed a moral miracle.

I. The fact of the unbroken preservation of the Catholic Church
and of her religion is self-evident; the matter of special concern
here is the nature of that stability which has been a characteristic
of the Church throughout twenty centuries. It is one thing for an
institution hidden away in a corner of the world to lead a long,
but sterile existence. It is another matter for a religion, spread all
over the face of the globe, constantly engaged in controversy with
clever adversaries, part and parcel of the ever changing social scene,
to go on living an always active life and to continue to grow and
become stronger day by day. Since it is a well-known fact that
the Catholic Church is characterized by the latter and not the
former type of stability, that stability is assumed as the basis for
the following discussion.

II. The unbroken stability of the Catholic religion cannot be 124
explained on natural grounds. This conclusion flows from a consideration of the magnitude of the perils which have constantly
threatened it, and of the inadequacy of natural helps.

1. Extremely grave dangers have threatened to bring about the
ruin of the Catholic Church and of her religion throughout the
entire period of Church history.

a. One constant source of danger is the diversity of the peoples
which the Catholic Church gathers to her bosom. National partic-
ularism and the aversions felt by some peoples to others make
difficult their joining in one society, and even more difficult their
remaining together. The difficulty increases in proportion to the
number of nations involved and to their differences in character,
culture, and customs. These factors explain why all the great
empires which have included many different peoples were founded

(211)

only by armed might, and why they eventually came to naught. They explain, too, why all other religions and sects were more or less national in character. But from the time of its earliest expansion, the Catholic religion gathered into a real unity many widely separated peoples, and with the passing of the centuries the Church has continued to bring ever more and more within the fold. In view of such a great diversity of peoples united in her fold, she should have encountered, and history witnesses to the fact that she did encounter, many perilous obstacles. Kings and princes did more than their share to increase the natural peril. Sometimes they were themselves Catholics who time and again strove to extend their rule so that it would include also spiritual matters; sometimes they were non-Catholics who thought, or at least pretended, that "ultramontanism" was a threat to the welfare of the state. The danger was increased rather than diminished by the fact that those professing the Catholic religion in such a nation often formed a weak minority.

b. Another danger, or rather an endless series of dangers, comes from the bitter attacks and calamities which have always scourged the Catholic religion. On the heels of the cruel persecutions of the first centuries came Neo-Platonic philosophy, the mother of many heresies. Soon there followed the great heresies often sponsored by the Byzantine emperors: Arianism, Nestorianism, Monophysitism.

During the same period the barbarians, partly pagan and partly Arian, flooded Europe, overran the Roman Empire, and threatened the ruin of all that the Church had built. At the dawn of the Middle Ages a new threat came in the shape of Mohammedanism, one of the fiercest enemies the Church has ever seen. Even within the Church was the menace of Caesaropapism, which caused the great Greek Schism in the East and in the West the struggle for bishoprics and lay investiture.

Not long afterward came the sad Western Schism which helped pave the way for the Protestant Revolution of the sixteenth century. Protestantism was followed in subsequent centuries by Jansenism, Gallicanism, Josephinism, the French Revolution, rationalism, liberalism, and Modernism. The latter three were perhaps the fiercest enemies which the Church ever had to face. Add to these the internal difficulties, worst of all, the attacks on religion occasioned by the corrupt morals of the clergy. If all these facts are taken into careful and mature consideration, the statement of a contemporary non-Catholic becomes eminently justified:

(212)

"As a general result of historical investigation we can say that the Church has constantly been in a situation which forces human reason to forecast: 'It cån t last a fortnight longer " (Dr. R. Pierson, *Geschiedenis v.h. Roomsch-Katolicisme*, IV, 330).

However, that end, so ardently desired in many quarters and so often foretold, has not materialized after nineteen centuries and is far from doing so at present.[21] Certainly, the Catholic Church, oppressed by calamities, has often groaned deep within her heart and has wept at the loss of so many of her children, indeed of whole nations. But, purged in the fire of battle, she has always emerged from the front more vigorous than ever, has recouped her losses elsewhere with interest, whereas her adversaries perished altogether or lay wounded in the field.

2. Where are the arms, where are the weapons which the Cath- 125 olic religion has used to overcome so many enemies, to survive so many calamities with the flush of youth still fresh on her cheeks? It is quite true that the Church has never neglected the natural means of learning and persuasion. When she was in a position to use these honorable means, her adversaries used deceit, calumny, lies, corruption, subterfuge, and tricks of every kind, which are ordinarily most effective in fooling men. Secular princes frequently attacked the Church herself or sponsored her adversaries. And even when they sided with the Church, in many instances they restricted her liberty to a large extent, so that their protection, though advantageous from one aspect, was exceedingly harmful from another. Consequently, one can make the general statement that the Church's adversaries have almost always won over her by force of arms and natural means, while throughout it all the Church has remained unarmed, strong in patience alone. "This is a characteristic of the Church; to be victorious in defeat, to be understood when maligned, to hold fast when deserted." So wrote St. Hilary (*De Trinitate*, bk. 7, c. 4).

Conclusion. Just as the first expansion of the Catholic religion, 126 so is its perennial conservation an effect which can be in no way explained as due to visible and merely natural causes. Consequently, unless one is ready to admit an effect without a proportionate cause, the conclusion follows that the inviolate stability of the Church is due for the most part to the special help of God, who constantly and efficaciously moves men throughout the world to embrace the faith. The whole history of the Catholic religion shows how true were the words spoken by Gamaliel when Christianity was but a few years old:

So now I say to you, Keep away from these men and let them alone. For if this plan or work is of men, it will be overthrown; but if it is of God, you will not be able to overthrow it. Else perhaps you may find yourselves fighting against God (Acts 5:38–39).

127 *Scholion. Some difficulties answered.*

1. There are those who claim that the Catholic religion was preserved naturally through the principle of authority which has always been very strong within it. Certainly a proximate means of the Church's preservation is the principle of authority, the authority of a ruling body together with a corresponding obedience on the part of the faithful. For the government of pastors could not preserve religion, if the faithful did not subject themselves to that government. And it is precisely this obedience with which untold numbers of men of every age freely accept the burden of the faith and continue to carry it that cannot be explained without appeal to the special action of God.

2. Some object that other religions, also, have enjoyed a long existence. Examples are Buddhism, Mohammedanism, some Christian sects in the East. There is, however, a vital and complex difference. Those religions do not impose such difficult obligations, nor do they reveal the same unity, nor are they spread throughout so many widely differing nations, nor do they make new gains, nor are they caught up in the disputes of the learned,[22] nor are they attacked very frequently or very severely. Withal, they are torpid, almost like corpses which owe their preservation to the skill of the embalmer. The case of modern Judaism is not much different. The Jewish people, stubbornly adhering to the abrogated Law, scattered throughout the nations, but not absorbed by them, are preserved by a decree of Providence as a perpetual argument in favor of the Christian religion.[23] Although the Jews exert a great influence as a result of their intelligence, astuteness, and industry, Judaism, as a religion, exerts little influence.

Notes

1. P. Muck, *Das gröszte Wunder der Weltgeschichte,* 1905.
2. Excellent treatments of this matter are to be found in A. Harnack's *Die Mission und Ausbreitung des Christentums in den ersten drei Jahrhunderten,* 3rd ed. (1915), and in F. Spitta's *Jesus und die Heidenmission*

(1909). Apart from their treatment of this point, however, the books of Harnack and Spitta are definitely not recommended. See also:

M. Meinertz, "Jesus und die Heidenmission," NtAb (1908);

P. Heinisch, "Die Idee der Heidenbekehrung im Alten Testament," Bibl Zf, VIII, 1 and 2;

P. Batiffol, *L'Eglise naissante et le Catholicisme*, 2nd ed. (1922);

J. Riviere, "La propagation du Christianisme dans les trois premiers ` siecles," Coll. *Science et religion*, nos. 454–455;

P. Allard, *Dix leçons sur le martyre* (1906), pp. 10–83;

Der Kath. (1903), I, 240 (against Harnack), and 289 (against Loisy).

3. *Annal.*, bk. 15, ch. 44; "a huge crowd." See no. 75.

4. "These men [Peter and Paul] who had led holy lives were joined by a great multitude of the elect that suffered numerous indignities and tortures through jealousy and thus became illustrious examples among us" (*Epistle to the Corinthians*, 6. 1, ACW I, 12).

5. Romans 1:8: *Your faith is proclaimed all over the world;* see 10:18. Colossians 1:6: *The gospel truth which has reached you, even as it is in the whole world, both bearing fruit and growing; just as it does among you.* So also St. Clement of Rome writes of St. Paul: "He taught the right manner of life to the whole world" (*Epistle to the Corinthians*, 5. 7, ACW I, 12).

6. A. Harnack concludes his book, *Die Mission und Ausbreitung des Christentums*, with these words:

> Did the spread of the Christian religion take place with startling rapidity? Permit me to answer this question in the affirmative. The impression entertained by the Fathers of the fourth century, like Arnobius, Eusebius, and Augustine, that their faith had spread, generation after generation, with inconceivable swiftness, continues valid. *Seventy* years after the founding of the first Gentile-Christian community at Syrian Antioch, Pliny writes in the strongest terms of the spread of Christianity in distant Bithynia, and sees the continued existence of the remaining local worship already threatened in that province. *Seventy* years later, the Easter controversy reveals a confederation of churches stretching from Lyons to Edessa, with Rome as their capital. Another *seventy* years later the emperor Decian (*Ep. 55 s. Cypriani*, no. 9) declares that he would rather have to put up with a rival emperor at Rome than with a Christian bishop. And then it takes hardly seventy years more for the cross to be stitched upon the Roman military pennants (1st ed., 1902, p. 545).

7. P. Allard writes:

> In the cemetery where Callistus held sway [later, 218–222, he was Supreme Pontiff], the greatest families of Rome are represented. You can find there the burial stones of Caecilii, Cornelii, Aemilii, Bassi, Annii, Jallii and Pomponii. There you may run across tombs of people related to the imperial families. Just as there were Christian Flavians in the first century, there were Christian Antonines at the end of the second century and at the beginning of the third (*Histoire des persecutions pendant la première moitié du 3e siècle*, 1894, p. 191).

8. The difficulties which Christian teaching presented to the minds of the pagans can be more readily appreciated if the words of a modern unbeliever, who was brought up in Catholic surroundings, are examined. Sully-Prudhomme writes:

> Catholicism offends every human faculty. It offends the intellect with its mysteries, which are as baffling in the realm of ideas as miracles are in the

realm of facts. It offends the senses with the mortifications it imposes upon them and with the illusions by which it ensnares them in the matter of the Eucharist. It offends the heart by repressing all stirrings of passion and even inborn inclinations. It offends the will by the self-denial which it imposes in the practice of obedience and humility. Finally, it offends the conscience with its teaching on the consequences of original sin, which is wholly incompatible with the sentiment of personal responsibility (*La vraie religion selon Pascal* (1905), p. 154).

9. This is the origin of the accusation of "hatred for the human race" recorded by Tacitus. P. Allard states:

Even in the eyes of enlightened people, who held themselves above vulgar rumors, the care which the faithful took to avoid profane festivals, their hatred for the theater, their voluntary aloofness from public functions, which were all too often tainted with idolatry—all this gave grounds for a charge which was all the more formidable because of its vagueness. They saw Christians as a class apart, and those who did not charge them with secret murders or clandestine orgies, accused them at least of *hating the human race.—Le Christ et l'empire romain* (1897), p. 13.

10. Again Allard states:

The fortune of Rome seemed linked with its religion. The more sophisticated contemporaries of Augustus or Tiberius were no less imbued with this conviction than had been the rude inhabitants of the primitive city on the Palatine. They were perhaps not too concerned about the basis of this religion, about its absolute certitude or its historical origin. But the national gods were sacred to them because of political interests, and because of an overweening superstition from which even the most skeptical among them did not try to defend themselves. They believed that Roman power would be cursed the day its traditional religion crumbled. So ingrained in Roman paganism is this idea that it will reappear unaltered in its last proponents, contemporaries of St. Augustine and St. Ambrose. *Ibid.,* p. 4.

Consequently Tertullian stated that the people thought that "Christians were at the bottom of every public disaster, of every common misfortune If the Tiber rose to the walls, if the Nile did not inundate the fields, if heaven stood still or the earth moved, if famine came, or plague, immediately the cry went up, 'Throw the Christians to the lion!' So many Christians for one lion?" (*Apolog.,* bk. 40, c. 136).

In a similar strain St. Augustine recalls a "popular adage: 'We are suffering a drought; the Christians are to blame' " (*City of God,* bk. 2, ch. 3). Even Porphyrius, according to Eusebius, wrote: "And now let no one wonder if the city has been sorely tormented by this pestilence for so many years, since Aesculapius and the other gods have withdrawn from familiar association with men. For from the time people began to worship Jesus, no one has experienced the aid of the gods in the matter of the common, public weal" (*Praeparatio evangelica,* bk. 5, c. 1). And Porphyrius, we must recall, was an eminent philosopher of the third century—one who sought wisdom.

11. "In the pagan empire, every time the persecution had begun afresh, on either the official or the popular level, the Jews turned up in the vanguard, fanning the flames of anger or abetting the acts of violence" (Allard, *Julien l'apostate,* bk. 3, p. 187).

The synagogues, which Tertullian (*Scorpiac.,* c. 10) calls "well-springs of persecutions," spread false rumors not only among the Jews, but, through

(216)

their ubiquitous emissaries (St. Justin, *Dialogue with Trypho,* 17), even among the pagans. They claimed, for example, that Christ had seduced men through the use of magic (Origen, *Contra Celsum,* bk. 1, c. 28), that His crucifixion had been fully justified (St. Justin, *op. cit.,* 93), that His resurrection was a fable and that His corpse had been stolen (*ibid.,* 108), and that the accounts of His activities were the figments of His disciples' imaginations (Origen, *op. cit.,* bk. 2, c. 13). They added for good measure that the Christians killed and ate little boys during their meetings, then put out the lights and gave vent to their lust in the most shameful manner possible (St. Justin, *Apol.,* bk. 2, c. 12; Tertullian, *Apolog.,* bk. 7, c. 32, Origen, *op. cit.,* bk. 6, c. 27); and that they worshipped the genitalia of their priests (Minucius Felix, *Octav.,* 9).

Christians were further accused of being atheists (St. Justin, *Apol.,* bk. 1, c. 6), of adoring the sun (Tertullian, *Ad Nat.,* bk. 1, c. 13) or an ass's head (Tertullian, *Apolog.,* bk. 16, c. 79); etc. This last mentioned accusation has been immortalized in one of the famous *graffiti* of the Palatine. See Jack Finegan, *Light from the Ancient Past,* Princeton, 1947, p. 292, figure 124.

12. Even Paulsen writes: "Of all the events recorded in world history, none is so amazing as the conversion of the ancient world to Christianity. Never has there been a spiritual movement which was so very poor as Christianity in all those resources which, in the ordinary course of events, would be requisite for conquering the world" (*System der Ethik* (1889), p. 78).

13. *The Decline and Fall of the Roman Empire* (1777), ch. 15.

14. 1 Timothy 6:12; 1 Corinthians 7:20-22; Ephesians 6:5ff; St. Ignatius Martyr, *Ad Polycarpum,* 4. See F. X. Kiefl, *Die Theorien des modernen Sozialismus über den Ursprung des Christentums* (1915); ZkTh (1909), p. 625; J. von Walter (a non-Catholic) admits: "The New Testament, in spite of the fact that it considers slavery a condition unbecoming to Christian freedom, does not demand the abolition of slavery, but rather exhorts slaves to maintain their actual position" (*Die Sklaverei im N. T.* (1914), pp. 4ff).

15. See above, no. 74a. A. Harnack is an outstanding proponent of the thesis that the spread of Christianity finds its explanation in syncretism.

16. See Broglie, *Problèmes et conclusions de l'histoire des religions* (1913), p. 22, article by L. de la Valée Poussin; Joseph Dahlmann, *Buddha* (1898); O. Maas, *Der Buddhismus in alten und neuen Tagen* (1913); A. Roussel, *Le Boeddhisme primitif* (1912); Dr. E. Hardy, *Der Buddhismus nach älteren Pali-Werken,* 2nd ed. (1919); *Der Kath.* (1913), I, 165, 276, 415; II, 90, 217.

Buddhism brought little advantage to its adherents. E. von Hartmann states:

"This indifferentism drugged the nations converted to Buddhism like a daily dose of opium, induced a quietistic enervation, and through its contempt for science, art, and all material progress paralyzed all movement towards higher cultural standards. Thus it repressed the basically sound instincts of these peoples, eliminated them from the vital stream of history, kept them perforce in dreamy ignorance, and thereby planted the germ which infallibly brought about the dissolution of religious life itself" (*Das religiöse Bewusstsein der Menschheit,* p. 347, cited by Gutberlet, *Apologetica,* II, 2nd ed., 61).

17. Harnack states: "The emperor and the military supported it and

thereby endowed it with importance for wider circles" (*Die Mission und Ausbreitung des Christentums*, p. 536).

18. B. Carra de Vaux, *La doctrine de l'Islam* (1909); H. Lammens, *L'Islam: croyances et institutions* (1926); J. Huby, *op. cit.*, p. 541.

19. We may apply to Protestantism and, generally speaking, to any sect, the reprimand which Tertullian leveled against the heretics of his day:

They set themselves the task not of converting pagans, but of perverting our brethren. They consider it a greater glory to knock down those who are standing than to raise up those who are prostrate, for their edifice is not of their own building, but is founded on the destruction of the truth. They undermine ours to build theirs (*De praescriptione*, c. 42).

There is in fact no nation, or hardly any nation, even of those now divided by heresy or schism, which received its first knowledge of the Gospel from heretics or schismatics. See Wilmers, *De religione revelata*, no. 640.

20. For example, Brochmann, a pastor of the Reformed Church, writes: "Dr. Luther gave monasteries to the princes, wives to the priests, freedom to the common man,—and that helped matters considerably." Frederick the Great stated: "If you want to reduce the causes of the progress of the Reformation to simple principles, you will find that in Germany it was a matter of political interest, in England of love, and in France of novelty" (Quoted in Liebermann, I, 10th ed., 370).

21. In 1840 Macauley, a Protestant author, wrote a passage of surpassing beauty and power in his *Critical and Historical Essays*:

There is not, and there never was on this earth, a work of human policy so deserving of examination as the Roman Catholic Church. The history of that Church joins together the two great stages of human civilization. No other institution is left standing which carries the mind back to the times when the smoke of sacrifice rose from the Pantheon, and when camelopards and tigers bounded in the Flavian amphitheatre. The proudest royal houses are but of yesterday, when compared with the line of the Supreme Pontiffs. That line we trace back in an unbroken series, from the Pope who crowned Napoleon in the nineteenth century, to the Pope who crowned Pepin in the eighth; and far beyond the time of Pepin the august dynasty extends, till it is lost in the twilight of fable. The republic of Venice was modern, when compared with the Papacy; and the republic of Venice is gone, and the Papacy remains. The Papacy remains, not in decay, not a mere antique, but full of life and youthful vigour. The Catholic Church is sending forth to the farthest ends of the world missionaries as zealous as those who landed in Kent with Augustine, and still confronting hostile kings with the same spirit with which she confronted Attila. The number of her children is greater than in any former age. Her acquisitions in the new world have more than compensated her for what she has lost in the old. . . . Nor do we see any sign which indicates that the term of her long domination is approaching. She saw the establishment of all the governments and of all the ecclesiastical establishments that now exist in the world; and we feel no assurance that she is not destined to see the end of them all. She was great and respected before the Saxon had set foot on Britain, before the Frank had passed the Rhine, when Grecian eloquence still flourished in Antioch, when idols were still worshipped in the temple of Mecca. And she may still exist in undiminished vigour when some traveller from New Zealand shall, in the midst of a vast solitude, take his stand on a broken arch of London Bridge to sketch the ruins of St. Paul's.—We often hear it said that the world is becoming more and more enlightened, and that this enlightening must be favourable to Protestantism, and unfavourable to Catholicism. We wish that we could think so. But we see great reason to doubt whether this be a well-founded expectation. We see that during the last 250 years the human mind has been in the highest degree active, that it has made great advances. Yet we see that, during these 250 years, Protestantism has made no conquests worth speaking of. Nay, we believe that, as far as there has been a change, that change has, on the whole, been in favour of the Church of Rome. We cannot, therefore, feel confident that progress of knowledge will necessarily be fatal to a system which has, to say the least, stood its ground in spite of the immense progress made by the human race in knowledge since the days of Queen Elizabeth.

22. De Maistre states:

All the churches separated from the Holy See at the beginning of the 12th century can be compared to frozen corpses whose shapes are preserved by the cold. This cold is ignorance. But when the wind of knowledge, which is warm, comes to blow on these churches, that will happen which must happen according to the laws of nature: the ancient forms will disintegrate and there will be nothing left but dust (*Du Pape*, IV, 2).

23. St. Augustine wrote:

They are scattered throughout all nations, with no stability, no fixed habitation. If there are still Jews, it is that they may carry our books, books which serve to confound them. For when we want to prove that Christ was referred to in prophecies of old, we show those books to the pagans. And lest, resisting belief, they claim that we Christians composed them and created the prophets together with the Gospel which we preach, we convince them by pointing out that all those books in which Christ was foretold are in the possession of the Jews. We borrow books from one set of enemies to confound another set. The Jew carries the book which serves as a source of faith for the Christian. They have become our librarians, just like the slaves who frequently follow their masters and carry their books. The former grow weary from carrying; the latter grow strong from reading (*In Ps. 56*, no. 9).

Article III

THE DIVINE ORIGIN OF THE CHRISTIAN-CATHOLIC RELIGION IS PROVED BY ITS PERENNIAL FRUITFULNESS IN THE FIELD OF HOLINESS

PROPOSITION: The harvest of holiness produced by the Christian-Catholic religion must be acclaimed a moral miracle.

1. Christianity has brought forth an abundant harvest of holiness:
   a. on the intellectual plane;
   b. on the moral plane;
   c. on the social plane.
   d. This harvest has been constantly preserved and continued.
2. This harvest of holiness cannot be explained on merely natural grounds:
   a. Supernatural help is necessary for even a knowledge of religion.
   b. The moral reform effected by the Church is morally impossible for any merely human institution.

Article III

THE DIVINE ORIGIN OF THE CHRISTIAN-CATHOLIC RELIGION IS PROVED BY ITS PERENNIAL FRUITFULNESS IN THE FIELD OF HOLINESS

The Christian-Catholic religion has produced a harvest of 128 sanctity greater than merely natural means could ever produce, and hence this harvest must be in great part attributed to the direct influence of God on men s souls. By making the Catholic religion so wondrously holy God clearly puts His seal of approval on that religion. It is obvious that He could not approve a religion which falsely claimed a divine origin.

This fact is self-evident once it has been established that the Christian-Catholic religion truly produces such a harvest of holiness as is impossible apart from the very special help of God. Indeed, this marvelous harvest is in truth a miracle of the moral order.

PROPOSITION: *The harvest of holiness produced by the Christian-* 129 *Catholic religion must be recognized as a miracle of the moral order.*

I. Christianity has produced an abundant harvest of holiness.[1]

1. On the intellectual plane it has filled all the peoples whom it has reached with sound theoretical and practical doctrine concerning God and matters divine.[2] With the sole exception of the Jews, all peoples, before the Christian religion reached them, erred greatly in this matter. (See no. 25.)

2. On the moral plane, wherever Christianity took root, it brought about a truly great moral reform.

Writers, both Christian and pagan, bear eloquent testimony to this fact for the early ages of Christianity.[3]

For references to converted Jews see the Acts of the Apostles, 2:42–47; 4:32–35.

The following Christian writers tell us of the converted Gentiles:

St. Clement of Rome wrote thus to the Corinthians:

(221)

Indeed, was there ever a visitor in your midst that did not approve your excellent and steadfast faith? Or did not admire your discreet and thoughtful Christian piety? Or did not proclaim the magnificent character of your hospitality? . . . You certainly did everything without an eye to rank or station in life, and regulated your conduct by God's commandments (*First Epistle to the Corinthians*, 1:2–3, ACW, I, 9).

Aristides, in his apology to Antoninus Pius, says:

Christians have the commandments [of God] engraved upon their hearts and observe them in the expectant hope of the world to come. And so they do not commit adultery or fornication, or bear false witness, or embezzle what they hold in pledge, or covet the goods of others. They honor father and mother, love their neighbors and judge with equity. They appeal to those who injure them and try to win them as friends; they are eager to do good to their enemies. Their wives are as pure as virgins, and their daughters are modest. Their men keep themselves from any illicit union and from any manner of uncleanness. They observe the commands of their Christ with great care and live chaste and holy lives as the Lord their God commanded them (*Apologia*, 15).

St. Justin Martyr relates:

We who formerly used to delight in fornication now embrace chastity alone. We who formerly used to practice magical arts have consecrated ourselves to the good and unbegotten God. We who used to value above all else the acquisition of money and property now donate our possessions to a common fund and share it with anyone who may be in need. We who used to hate and destroy one another and would have no truck with people who were not of our own tribe because their customs differed from ours, now, since the coming of Christ, live with them and pray for our enemies. And we try every means of persuasion to soften those who persecute us out of malicious hate. . . . Indeed, many people of both sexes who were instructed in Christ's teaching as children look back at the age of sixty or seventy on a life of unsullied purity; and I claim to be able to show you such people in every race of mankind (*Apology*, bk. 1, chs. 14–15).

Athenagoras wrote:

But among us you will find uneducated persons, simple laboring men, and old women, who, even if they cannot express in words the advantages of our doctrine, by their deeds show forth the benefits arising from their persuasion of its truth. They do not compose fine speeches and commit them to memory, but let their actions speak for them. When struck they do not strike back; when robbed they do not go to court; they give to those that ask of them, and they love their neighbors as themselves (*Legatio pro Christianis*, 11).

Tertullian exclaims:

It is always with your [pagan] peoples that the prison is steaming, the mines are sighing, the wild beasts are fed. It is from you that those who run the gladiatorial shows always receive their herds of criminals to feed up for the occasion. You find no Christian there, unless it is precisely because he is a Christian (*Apologia*, bk. 44, ch. 148; see bk. 39, chs. 130–133).

Origen says that one should seriously consider:

to what acts of injustice and covetousness [Christians] were addicted before [their conversion] . . . how, from the time they accepted that doctrine they became more just, more serious and more steady, to such an extent that some of them, out of a desire for perfect chastity and a wish to worship God with greater purity, abstain even from those pleasures of love permitted them by law (*Contra Celsum*, bk. 1, ch. 26).

The same author also testifies:

The churches of God which are instructed by Christ compared with the assemblies of the districts in which they live are as beacons in the world. For who would not admit that the inferior members of the Church and those who suffer by comparison with the better, are vastly superior than those who belong to the popular assemblies? (*Ibid.*, bk. 3, ch. 29).

St. Denis of Alexandria tells of the great charity of those Christians, who during a plague attended the sick and buried the dead, "even though the survivors were continually following those who had gone before them. But with the heathen everything was quite different" (Quoted by Eusebius, HE, 7, ch. 22). The heathen fled from those who became sick, even from their dearest ones, and threw corpses out to lie unburied.

Eusebius, the early historian, writes:

> Persians no longer marry their own mothers once they have accepted the teaching of Christ; nor do Scythians feed any longer on human flesh. Other barbaric tribes have given up incestuous relations with their daughters and sisters. The men of other races have ceased to burn with mad lust for their fellow men and no longer indulge those other pleasures of the flesh which violate the law of nature (*Praeparatio Evangelii*, bk. 1, ch. 4).

There is, in addition, the testimony of pagans. Pliny the Younger testifies:

> But the [Christians] insisted that this was the full extent of their guilt or error—call it what you will—namely, that they were accustomed to assemble before dawn on a given day, and to sing together a hymn to Christ as to a god. They claimed that if they bound themselves by an oath, it was not with a view to committing some crime or other, but rather with a view to avoiding theft, robbery, adultery, disloyalty, or the refusal to hand back a deposit upon request (*Epistolae*, bk. 10, no. 97, *ad Trajanum*).

Galen, a pagan physician and philosopher:

> The majority of men cannot understand a speech involving a long logical argument. That is why they need examples and illustrations. We see an instance of this in our own day in these people who call themselves Christians. They have based their faith on parables. And yet they sometimes reach practical conclusions not unlike those reached by men who are skilled in philosophy. Their scorn for death, for instance, is well-known to all of us. Again, some sense of shame leads them to stay far away from the pleasures of love. For there are men and women among them who have abstained from intercourse throughout their whole lives. There are among them also men who have made such progress in the ruling and disciplining of their minds and in an assiduous striving for goodness that they yield not at all to men who are real philosophers (*De sententiis politiae platonicae*).[4]

Julian the Apostate wrote to Arsacius, a pagan priest:

Have we not noticed what has been principally responsible for the growth of the religion of the Christians? Is it not their kindness to strangers, their diligent care in burying their dead, and their feigned seriousness of manner? I am of the opinion that we too must adopt each of these policies. For while none of the Jews goes begging, and while the impious Galileans provide not only for their own poor but for ours as well, it would indeed be disgraceful if we were to let our own needy appear deprived of the help and assistance we can give them (In Sozomenus' *Historia Ecclesiastica*, bk. 5, ch. 16).

Such activity occurred not only during the first centuries of Christianity but marked its progress throughout all subsequent generations. Every time a nation was converted to the Christian-Catholic religion, a remarkable moral reform followed. This fact is clear from the history of individual Christian nations and from the history of missionary activity.

3. On the social plane: little by little the Christian religion used its influence to restore the family, urging the unity and indissolubility of marriage, the dignity of women,[5] the rights and duties of children. At first it alleviated the rigors of slavery and finally brought about its abolition; [6] it reformed civil society itself by promoting freedom, charity, and the rights of nations.[7]

4. These holy and wholesome effects which the Christian 130 religion caused everywhere among recently converted nations, it still continues to produce throughout the world.

Never has that religion ceased to impart religious truth to the nations within its fold. Never has it allowed religious doctrine, whether theoretical or practical, to be toned down or obscured. On the contrary, it has consistently attacked all error, no matter who fostered it, and has zealously kept it from infecting the followers of the truth. Every age has seen the Church urging countless men to an earnest and persevering search for virtue, to a truly noble life.[8] Never has it lacked men of heroic sanctity. Rather it has been always and everywhere conspicuous for the host of men and women who have followed the evangelical counsels to the point of dedicating themselves completely to the service of God and neighbor. In every age it has had its martyrs, at times in great numbers. It cannot be denied, however, that at times the morals of a nation and even of the Catholic clergy have become shamefully loose in one place or another. Yet, even in those instances there was no lack of wheat in the midst of the weeds; although religion was at a low ebb in one region, it was flourishing elsewhere; it frequently happened that nations which became depraved were restored by the Church to even greater holiness.

It would be a mistake to think that the above remarks bearing on Christianity's fruitfulness are applicable at least in general to all Christians, Catholics or not. Since there is scarcely any nation in existence which first heard of the Gospel from an heretical sect, the marvelous moral reform which has accompanied the advance of the Christian religion throughout the world is due to the Catholic Church alone. There is no heretical or schismatic sect whose origin was remarkable because of a notable moral improvement. In fact, the case was more frequently just the opposite. In the pseudo-Reformation the results caused Luther to say: "Men are now more vindictive, more greedy, more pitiless, more immoral and unrestrained, and much more evil than they were under the papacy" (*Postilla in Evangelium Dominicae 1ae Adventus*).[9] No sect has ever produced the vast number of outstandingly holy men, the untold throngs of martyrs that the Catholic Church has produced. It is therefore beyond doubt that the Catholic religion alone has brought to maturity the marvelously abundant harvest of holiness described above.[10]

131   **II. This harvest of holiness which is produced by the Catholic religion cannot be explained on merely natural grounds.**

1. If it is morally impossible for men to gain a fitting knowledge of religion by purely natural means, and if the Catholic religion has brought men such knowledge, clearly it has performed a task for which natural powers alone are inadequate.

2. No other religion, no philosophical system, no merely human institution has ever brought about a moral reform even remotely comparable in breadth, depth, or duration with the one effected by the Catholic Church, not only centuries ago but even in our own day. What human means have never accomplished must be labeled as morally impossible for them. No one who considers how difficult it is to get even one sinner to mend his ways will deny the moral impossibility of this type of reform.

It is certainly not unfitting to apply to the revolution which Christianity has effected in the realm of morality these words of the Psalmist: *By the Lord has this been done: it is wonderful in our eyes* (Psalm 117:23).

Notes

1. Christian customs from the Apostolic age up to the time of Hadrian are quite soberly and in general quite well described by the non-Catholic author, E. V. Dobschütz, *Die urchristlichen Gemeinde, Sittengeschichtliche Bilder*, 1902.

2. We mean a knowledge of natural religion.

3. The extent of moral corruption among the pagans before the rise of Christianity, especially in the Roman empire, is sufficiently well-known. See A. M. Weisz, *Apologie des Christenthums*, v. III, *Das Ende der alten Welt*.

4. This passage seems to be taken from the opusculum named in the text; see ZkTh (1899), p. 569. The testimony of Lucian, *In morte peregrini*, is found in Ottiger's *Theologia fundamentalis*, I, 862 and 874.

5. G. d'Azambuja, *Ce que le Christianisme a fait pour la femme*, in Coll. *Science et Religion*, n. 64.

6. Allard, P., *Les esclaves chrétiens depuis les premiers temps de l'Eglise*, 5th ed., 1912;

Steinman, A., *Die Sklavenfrage in der alten Kirche*, 1910;

Van Meerveldhoven, Paschasius, *Historisch-apologetische schets der slavernij*, 1913.

7. Read the following for fuller treatment of this matter:

Hettinger-Müller, *Apologie des Christentums*, IX, *Kirche und Bildung*, 5, 176–462;

Schanz, *Apologetik*, III, 3rd ed., no. 15;

Tanquerey, *De vera religione*, no. 155ff;

Van Oppenraay, *Apologie des Christendoms*.

Even V. Hellwald, who was quite hostile to anything Christian, could write: Disinterested parties, however, grant that in spite of this [in spite of its later degeneration in warmer climes], Christianity brought to maturity among the ancients views which are usually declared noble according to modern notions. Such, for example, were their views on abortion, infanticide, abandonment of babies, suicide. It finally brought about the suppression of gladiatorial combats, awakened a disgust for capital punishment and an extensive taste for charity which was altogether alien to classical antiquity. All in all, humaneness is an almost exclusive acquisition of the Christian era (*Kulturgeschichte*, 1875, p. 435, quoted by Schanz, *op. cit.*, p. 642).

8. Anna de Savornin Lohman states:

In the east and west Indies, in the Roman Catholic Rhineland, I have observed very closely the exemplary lives of Roman Catholics, missionaries and pastors, and the great assistance provided by nuns as teachers, nurses, etc. Not only I but men and women who in our country unthinkingly ridicule the Roman Catholic religion out of ignorance or fear—there, in the midst of laborers and despised Negroes, in the midst of the fear of death and of loneliness, I have heard others acknowledge with shame that Roman Catholic charity surpasses all others (*De Tijd*, 1902, Nov. 28, no. 16805; see 1907, March 6, no. 18097).

See J. Ferchat, "Apologie du Christianisme par la loi de partage des habitudes morales," in RPA, XIII, 675 ff.

9. Melanchthon and Erasmus speak in practically the same strain. Their

remarks are recorded in De Groot's *Summa apologetica*, 3rd ed., q. 7, art. 1, p. 223.

10. The above remarks suffice for the argument we have based on the superabundant harvest of holiness. But lest anyone think that this argument is nonetheless somewhat weakened by the fact that quite a few sectaries also lead truly Christian lives, we add these observations:

1. The societies which fell away from the Church kept many of the aids to holiness which the Catholic Church had given them. There is nothing strange in the fact that these aids still produce results, especially in those people who are not culpably in error.

2. We must not overlook the fact that sectaries, for whatever reason they may be separated from the Church, still continue to profit by the salutary influence of the Catholic Church, whether they like it or not, since they are constantly being motivated by the preaching and example of Catholics—if only to outdo the latter. The sects are doubly indebted to the Catholic religion. They owe it for what they took with them when they seceded and for the direct influence it has on them every day. And so even that stunted harvest of holiness found in the separated societies is to be attributed not to the sects themselves, but to the Catholic Church, whose influence extends even beyond its own limits. The same is true, in varying degrees, of modern rationalists; for they too, reared in a Christian society and in constant contact with Christians, still share generously in the riches of the Catholic religion. Who would set less value on the ability of a tree to bear fruit because its lopped-off branches are not completely sterile? See RSR, 1922, p. 1.

Article IV

THE MIRACULOUS STEADFASTNESS OF THE MARTYRS PROVES THE DIVINE ORIGIN OF THE CHRISTIAN-CATHOLIC RELIGION

PROPOSITION: Considering all the circumstances, the steadfastness of the Christian martyrs must be acclaimed a moral miracle.

1. The steadfastness of the martyrs is truly amazing.
    a. The Christian-Catholic religion has had innumerable martyrs.
    b. They withstood the most painful tortures, often prolonged, and often made more difficult to bear by the pleas and tears of relatives.
    c. All this they endured in a truly wonderful manner.
2. The steadfastness of the martyrs, such as we have described it, cannot be explained on merely natural grounds.

Conclusion: Unless we are ready to admit an effect without a proportionate cause, we must admit that the steadfastness of the martyrs is a moral miracle.

Scholion: Some objections answered:

1. Some have claimed that the martyrs suffered death from a desire for empty glory, from a natural hope of heavenly bliss, or from sheer fanaticism.
2. Others allege instances of rare fortitude occurring elsewhere.
3. Still others claim our argument involves a vicious circle.

Conclusion to the Chapter

Article IV

THE MIRACULOUS STEADFASTNESS OF THE MARTYRS PROVES THE DIVINE ORIGIN OF THE CHRISTIAN-CATHOLIC RELIGION

132   By martyrs (witnesses) are meant those who have testified to the truth of their religion by patiently suffering violent death.[1]

The argument of this article can be summarized thus: If God, by an extraordinary aid, sustained those who suffered torture and death for the truth of the Catholic religion, He thereby quite clearly acknowledged the truth and consequently the divine origin of that religion. It cannot be denied that God supported the martyrs with supernatural strength if their steadfastness was such that it cannot be explained on merely natural grounds. Such steadfastness is, indeed, another miracle of the moral order.[2]

133 PROPOSITION: *Considering all the circumstances, the steadfastness of the Christian martyrs must be acclaimed a moral miracle.*

I. The steadfastness of the martyrs is truly amazing.

Fortitude under torture is the more to be wondered at, the greater the number of those who are tortured, the more excruciating the tortures they endure, and the more nobly they bear them.[3]

1. The martyrs of the Christian-Catholic religion are so many as to be practically innumerable.

Under Nero a "huge crowd" suffered martyrdom; under Marcus Aurelius, there were "almost innumerable martyrs throughout the whole world" (Tacitus, *Annales*, bk. 15, c. 44; See Eusebius, HE, bk. 5, intro.). In the middle of the third century, St. Cyprian said that the Christian martyrs were past counting.[4] Concerning the persecution of Diocletian, Sulpicius Severus wrote that almost the whole world was drenched in the blood of the holy martyrs and that no war or series of wars had ever exhausted the world more than this war against the Christians.[5]

Martyrdom did not cease after the first three centuries, which are called the "age of martyrs." Here are a few examples by way of illustration.

During the fourth century many thousands of Christians perished in the Persian persecution under King Sapor II; [6] in the fifth century the fierce persecution conducted by the Vandals in Africa claimed a bitter toll.[7] In ensuing centuries very many of those who carried the Gospel to the barbarian tribes of Europe suffered death for Christ; scarcely any nation was converted to the faith without being baptized in the blood of martyrs. Then there were the untold numbers martyred by the Mohammedans, especially in Spain.[8] It is a notorious fact that many suffered martyrdom in France,[9] Germany, Holland, Sweden, and England [10] at the time of the Reformation.[11] During the seventeenth century a relentless and very bitter persecution raged in Japan.[12] At the time of the French Revolution in the eighteenth century many valiant men and women were condemned to death because they unhesitatingly refused to take the oath or to do anything else which was opposed to religion and to justice.[13] In our own day many have suffered a glorious martyrdom, natives [14] as well as missionaries: the Koreans, [15] Chinese,[16] and Annamites [17] in Asia; the people of Uganda [18] in Africa. And the world would stand aghast if it knew the full number of those who have suffered and are suffering diabolically inspired and devised tortures and death at the hands of God-hating Communists in so-called Iron Curtain countries.

Yes, in every age and in every part of the world the Catholic Church has had her martyrs. The roster includes men and women, boys and girls, feeble old men and women, noblemen and servants, soldiers, farmers, in a word, people of every nationality, age, temperament, and social position.[19]

2. *The martyrs endured the most painful tortures.*[20] Tortures **134** devised by fiendish cruelty were the order of the day. Modern tyrants are no less adept in the use of instruments of torture than were the ancients.[21] In 1886 thirty-one newly converted youths of Uganda were individually wrapped about with brushwood and laid face down on the earth. Then the wood was lighted near their feet.[22]

Tortures were often prolonged for days or inflicted again and again. Lactantius bears eloquent testimony to this:

> Their chief concern is to avoid killing their victims; they see to it that once tortured they be diligently cared for, so that their limbs will be fresh for new tortures, so that there will be plenty of fresh blood to spill anew (*Institutiones*, bk. 5, c. 11).

St. Jerome declared that a "cunning foe, in using punishments slow to kill, aimed at strangling souls rather than bodies. Cyprian, himself a victim, says those who wished to die were not allowed to be killed" (*Vita Pauli eremitae*, 2). Under the emperor Galerius slow fire was used so that death would not occur until "the flesh had been roasted for hours on end and the fire had penetrated to a mans bowels" (Lactantius, *De morte persecutoris*, 21). In the seventeenth century some martyrs in Japan were cut with saws in various parts of the body during a period of six days.[23]

Some martyrs had to contend with the pleas and the tears of relatives. On this point St. Augustine writes:

> The eyes of those who wept for them wrought more violence than the torture of their persecutors. How many children held on to their fathers to keep them from going to torture! How many wives threw themselves at the feet of their husbands, beseeching them not to leave them widows! How many children begged their parents not to die! (*In Psalmum* 47:13).

135   3. *The martyrs endured all this in a truly wonderful manner.* Not only did they steadfastly ignore the promises, the threats, and the tortures of tyrants, but they suffered cheerfully and without any indication of anger or vexation. In fact, most of them longed humbly for martyrdom.[24] Arraigned before judges, they gave answers marked by wisdom and prudence, and in the midst of injustice preserved their equanimity. They suffered not with unfeeling stoicism, nor with enthusiastic elation, but meekly and calmly, trusting in God alone rather than in their own strength, humbly begging the prayers of others, showering with love the tyrants themselves and the torturers employed by them.[25] In a word, they were models of the highest virtue held up for the admiration of men and angels.

136   **II. The steadfastness of the martyrs, such as we have described it, cannot be explained on merely natural grounds.**

Human nature cringes from suffering. No one will deny that steadfastness in the midst of most painful torture, torture endured to the point of death, is a supremely heroic act, especially if this steadfastness is accompanied by patience and meekness. Granted that this or that individual could reach such a height of fortitude by dint of exceptional natural endowments, it is at least doubtful that many would ever do so.

But in bearing witness to the truth of the Catholic religion, not just a few, but very many people of every age, temperament, and social position arrived at the highest peak of fortitude, with no human motive pushing them on; and this happened not once only, or in one corner of the world, but whenever and wherever tyrants raged against the Church.

Conclusion. Unless one is ready to grant an effect without a 137 proportionate cause, he must of necessity admit that Catholic martyrs suffered with inspired patience, supported by the special help of divine grace. In fact, the martyrs themselves admitted that they were sustained by God's grace.[26] All Christians have been deeply convinced of it, and many pagans who witnessed the martyrdoms felt what Lactantius has expressed in these words:

> When the people see men being torn to shreds by various kinds of tortures and yet maintaining an unruffled patience while their executioners grow weary, they come to the conclusion, as is really the case, that neither the unanimity of so many people nor the steadfastness of the dying is meaningless, and that patience itself could not rise above such great tortures without God's help (*Institutiones,* bk. 5, c. 13).

There is, in addition the famous dictum of Tertullian: "Torture us, torment us, condemn us, grind us to dust. The more you mow us down, the more we grow in number. The blood of the Christians is a seed" (*Apologia,* 50, no. 176).

Indeed, the blood of the martyrs was the seed of Christianity, because the pagans clearly perceived that such tortures could not be endured without the help of God and thus learned from the patience of the martyrs the divine origin of the Christian religion.[27]

Scholion. Some objections answered. 138

1. Some have sought to explain on natural grounds the martyrdom of Christians, claiming that the martyrs suffered death:

    a. from a desire for empty glory;

    b. from a natural hope of heavenly bliss;

    c. from sheer fanaticism.

a. The martyrs showed no desire for empty glory, but rather a great humility. Besides, they knew that they would be considered stupid and insane by many. A large number of the martyrs suffered in such circumstances as to be certain that their names would never be committed to posterity. And who can honestly believe that so many people, even those of the lower classes, children and servant girls, preferred an empty glory to life and security?

b. There is no denying the fact that the martyrs were buoyed up by hope of eternal happiness, but this was no merely natural hope. A realization of the goods of eternity so vivid, constant, and effective that one would endure such frightful tortures for them is unthinkable apart from some supernatural help.

c. The manner in which the martyrs suffered, with equanimity, restraint, meekness, humility, shows clearly that they were not beside themselves with wild fanaticism. Furthermore, who can honestly believe that this fever of fanaticism, appearing as it did in most diverse regions, always broke out whenever some tyrant raged against the Church, and continued to burn only as long as the tyrant's fury flamed?

139   2. Others try to escape the argument based on martyrdom by alleging instances of rare fortitude occurring elsewhere, as with soldiers or criminals, or in other religions. But there is no comparison.

a. A soldier is exhorted to fight; in fact, he is usually forced to do so, and then, motivated by anger or hate, exposes himself to danger rather than to certain death, or, at the most, to a sudden and glorious death. A martyr freely advances to meet long drawn-out and horrible tortures with a calm spirit and without any desire for vengeance goading him on. In a word, the heroism of battle is one thing; that of patience is quite another.

b. It is true that some criminals, for example, some anarchists of our own day, have faced death bravely and with a certain show of bravado. But they were facing a death which they could not escape, and, at least usually, a death inflicted speedily, without prolonged suffering. It is one thing to die despondent, blaspheming and cursing, and quite another to endure a prolonged martyrdom with meekness and humble patience.

c. In referring to other religions or sects one must first exclude those individuals who quite evidently met their death out of sheer fanaticism (like those in India who threw themselves to the ground to be crushed by the wheels of a cart carrying their idols; [28] and the Circumcellions [Donatists] who in Augustine's day used to jump off cliffs).[29] These are not martyrs, but suicides. Also to be excluded are those who died in war, even though in a so-called Holy War, or as a result of a just condemnation for crimes they had committed. Apart from cases like these, the number of those who really died freely to bear witness to the truth of a religion or sect other than the Catholic is so insignificant that the matter can be explained on natural grounds, especially if all the circumstances are taken into account. The remarks of the Fathers concerning Christian sects separated from the Church are universally applicable.

St. Irenaeus:

> In every place, the Church, out of the love it has for God, is always sending on to the Father a host of martyrs, while all others not only have nothing of this sort to point to among themselves but even claim that martyrdom of this kind is not necessary at all (*Adversus Haereses*, bk. 4, 33.9).

St. Cyprian:

> The foe of Christ persecutes and attacks only Christ's camp and Christ's soldiers; heretics he despises and passes by, once he has brought them low and made them his own (*Epistola 61 ad Lucium*, no. 3).[30]

3. Finally, the adversaries claim that the Catholic doctrine on 140 martyrdom involves a vicious circle. Apologists, so they say, prove the truth of the Catholic religion from the fact that it can claim so many martyrs. But if you ask Catholic theologians who are truly martyrs they will answer: only those who die for the true religion, for "It is not suffering, but motive that makes a true martyr." And so in the argument based on martyrdom they clearly presume what they are setting out to prove, namely, the truth of the Catholic religion.

This argument has the appearance of a vicious circle because the word "martyr" is taken in different senses, first in the ordinary sense, and then in the theological.

In the apologetic argument just used, the word is taken in the ordinary sense to indicate all those who patiently undergo a violent death for their religion, prescinding from the question of whether that religion is true or not. When the question of martyrs is transferred to the province of theologians and canonists, then the term is understood of those whom the Church has officially recognized as witnesses to Christ, worthy of the promises which He made to such men.[31] Obviously witnesses to Christ purely and simply are those who die for the religion of Christ, the true and pure religion. So it is true that suffering alone does not make a martyr in the theological sense, but the cause for which suffering is inflicted.[32]

CONCLUSION TO THIS CHAPTER

141   It has been seen that the Christian-Catholic religion is divinely approved by many miracles of both the physical and moral orders.

It is true that some of these prove directly only the truth of our religion, but even so they mediately or indirectly demonstrate its divine origin. How would Catholic doctrine, containing as it does so many mysteries beyond the power of human inventiveness, be true if it were not divinely revealed? Furthermore, the Church claims for its preaching not just any authority, but divine authority, and requires men to accept her doctrines as the word of God. The only conclusion is that God, by showering His favors on the Catholic religion and thus approving it, is at the same time testifying to its divine origin. With right, then, does the Vatican Council state:

> The Church considered completely on her own merits is a solid and ever present motive of credibility, and an irrefutable witness to her own divine mission. The reasons are her wonderful expansion, eminent holiness, inexhaustible fruitfulness in all good works, her truly catholic unity and her unshaken stability (DB 1794).[33]

Moreover, if the Catholic Church carries out a divine mission, she does so only because she is continuing the mission of Christ Himself. She has never claimed divine authority for her preaching on any other grounds than that she is preaching in Christ's name the doctrine which she received from Him. Consequently, though the arguments set forth in this chapter had as their immediate object the divine origin of the Catholic religion, they at the same time indirectly confirmed the divine mission of Christ Himself.

Notes

1. See *The Catholic Encyclopedia*, IX, 736 ff; *Der Kath.*, 1918, I, 205; E. Hocedez, "Le concept de martyre," in NRT, (1928), pp. 81, 198.

2. RPA, IV, 625; VII-VIII, 801, 33.

3. See P. Allard, *Dix leçons*, 1906; DAFC under the heading "Martyre."

4. *Epistola ad Fortunatum, De exhortatione martyrii*, 2; see RPA XXII, (1916), 160.

5. *Historia ecclesiastica*, bk. 2, c. 32. Towards the end of the seventeenth century Dodwell made the assertion that only a few martyrs were put to death in the early persecutions. He was refuted by Ruinart, *Acta martyrum Preface*, and Zaccaria, *Raccolta di dissertazioni*, p. 42. Some present-day writers contend that martyrs were not so numerous, at least before the middle

of the third century. For a refutation of this view, see Allard, *op. cit.*, p. 134; DAFC, III, 349. Some savants, like Mommsen, Harnack and Max Conrad, claim that numberless Christians were indeed put to death in the Roman Empire, but not because of their religion. This view is refuted in *Stimmen, LV* (1898), 1 and 122. See RPA, X, 298.

6. Sozomenus, *Historia ecclesiastica*, bk. 2, c. 14, mentions sixteen thousand martyrs known by name.

7. See Victor Vitensis, *Historia persecutionis vandalicae.*

8. See Leclercq, *Les martyrs,* .1905.

9. During the Council of Trent the Cardinal of Lorraine told how within a few months more than three thousand religious had suffered a cruel martyrdom in France because they wanted to remain under obedience to the Holy See, Pallavicini, *Histoire du Concile de Trente*, XXIV, 3, no. 7.

10. Read, for example, Spillmann, *Die Englischën Martyrer;* B. Camm, *Lives of the English Martyrs;* see the Decree (Feb. 12, 1915) of the Beatification or declaration of martyrdom of 257 Servants of God in Ireland in the sixteenth and seventeenth centuries, AAS (1915), p. 125.

11. See DAFC, *loc. cit.*, p. 393.

12. See *Kirchenlexikon*, under the heading "Japan."

13. Read, for example, the Decree of Beatification or declaration of martyrdom in ASS (1916), XL, 162; XLI, 398; and in AAS (1916), VIII, 67 and 228.

14. See Constantius Kempf, *Die Heiligkeit der Kirche im 19en Jahrhundert*, 4th ed. (1914), pp. 278–352.

15. *Etudes*, 185 (1925), 541.

16. L. von Hammerstein has produced a few very touching examples which were originally published in the periodical *Katholischen Missionen*, in his *Katholicismus und Protestantismus* (1894), pp. 406–429; see Le Blant, *Persecuteurs et martyrs*, p. 343.

17. Hilarius Walter, *Leben, Wirken und Leiden der 77 seligën Martyrer von Annam und China*, (1903).

18. See Msgr. Carlo Salotti, *I martiri dell' Uganda* (1921); *Etudes*, 164 (1920), 5.

19. See Allard, *Dix leçons*, ch. 5.

On July 7, 1867, Pius IX enrolled on the list of the Blessed the following martyrs: Antoine Coray, his wife, and their twelve year old son Jean; also Lucy Fleites, an octogenarian. *Ned. Kath. St.* (1900), no. 30; see the Decree of Beatification or declaration of martyrdom (Aug. 14, 1912) of twenty-two venerable Servants of God: Charles Luanga, Mathias Murumba and their companions, commonly referred to as the "Martyrs of Uganda," who were killed, we are told, out of hatred for the faith; AAS (1912), p. 567.

20. See DAFC, *loc. cit.*, p. 357.

21. Indeed, modern psychological torture had added a satanic intensity to the physical torment inflicted in ages past.

22. From a letter (Sept. 29, 1886) of Msgr. Livinhac, Vicar Apostolic at Lake Nyanza; *Handelingen der gelukzalige Neger-Martelaren van Oeganda* (Boxtel, 1921).

23. *Kirchenlexikon*, under the heading "Japan," VI, 1253.

24. This is why Julian the Apostate was clearly unwilling to "start war"

against the Christians, "for," as he said, "they will fly to martyrdom as bees to a beehive" (St. John Chrysostom, *Oratio in Juvent. et Maximin.*). Still, bishops used to insist that the faithful avoid their persecutors as much as was feasible. See RPA, VII, 881; *Etudes,* 150 (1917), 537.

25. St. Cyprian and St. Thomas More both gave money to their executioners; Allard, *op. cit.,* p. 284.

26. So St. Felicity, for instance. While in prison she gave birth to a child. One of the guards heard her moaning in labor and asked, "If you are in such pain now, what will you do when you are thrown to the beasts?" Her confident reply was, "What I suffer now I suffer alone, but then there will be another within me who will suffer for me, because I in my turn will be suffering for Him." *Passio SS. Perpetuae et Felicitatis,* 15.

27. Hurter, in his *Theologiae dogmaticae compendium,* v. I, 11th ed., no. 90, argues:

> There is still another way of using the heroism of the martyrs of the early centuries as an argument. Going to an excruciating death for the faith after what was often a long imprisonment, the martyrs clearly evince a *very staunch conviction* of the truth of the Christian faith. Now such a strong conviction in men of widely varying character, including even men of outstanding learning and genius, would not have existed unless they had known objectively strong arguments for the truth of Christianity. But those arguments, as far as the early Christians were concerned, were above all the frequent miracles and charisms of the first centuries. These martyrs had either seen these feats as eye-witnesses or had got first-hand reports of them. We must conclude that these facts must have been altogether certain and evident for them.

Minucius Felix, in his work *Octav.,* no. 37, alludes briefly to both arguments when he says to the pagans: "Do you not understand, poor wretches, that no one would want to suffer pain without reason or would be able to undergo torture without the help of God?"

28. In the same class as these we must put the poor widows of India who, not freely, but from practical necessity and despondency, used to throw themselves into the flaming funeral pyre of a deceased husband. See Ottiger, *Theologia fundamentalis,* I, 890.

29. See St. Augustine, *De haeresi,* no. 69.

30. Still there is nothing to prevent a material heretic from winning through with the help of a special grace. But this grace would be granted because he was subjected to torture not precisely for his heresy, but because he was suffering for his Christian faith. See DTC, I, c. 538ff. This might be said, for instance, of the Protestant martyrs who were put to death in 1885–86 in Uganda. The circumstances show that they rendered testimony not precisely to Protestantism, but to Christianity. And cases of this sort, from the very fact that they are exceptional, present no threat to the argument in favor of the Roman Church based on Catholic (universal) martyrdom.

31. See Matthew 10:32, 16:25.

32. Some propose as an argument for the truth of the Christian religion the very mysteriousness of the hate with which Christ's foes attack Him and His most holy religion in spite of the unique love which Christ elicited and deserved on His own merits. See, among others, Hurter, *op. cit.,* nos. 84 and 88.

33. Leo XIII wrote:

Anyone who uses honest and prudent judgment will experience no difficulty in seeing which is the true religion. For very many and clear arguments show to be uniquely true that religion which Jesus Christ Himself founded and entrusted to His Church to be safeguarded and propagated. Such arguments are the truth of the prophecies, the frequency of miracles, the extremely rapid growth of the faith throughout the very camp of its enemies, notwithstanding formidable obstacles, the testimony rendered by the martyrs, and other arguments of like calibre (*Immortale Dei,* Nov. 1, 1885).

We have said nothing specifically and *ex professo* in this chapter about the marvelous unity and universality of the Catholic Church, as we shall have to treat these matters in our discussion of the marks of the Church. Still, our remarks about the spread and preservation of the Catholic religion necessarily suppose and involve its "catholic unity."

CHAPTER IV

God Foretold Christ and His Work

Article I

THE EXISTENCE OF MESSIANIC PROPHECIES

PROPOSITION: Messianic prophecies existed among the Jews many centuries before Christ.

   1. The Jews attributed, but vaguely, a threefold function to the future Messias:

      a. political;

      b. religious;

      c. eschatological.

   2. Their expectation was based on the Books of the Old Testament.

   3. Rationalist objections to prophecies.

Scholion: Some remarks aimed at helping in the understanding of Messianic prophecies:

   1. They were made at different times, and a progressive development is discernible.

   2. Divine truth was not manifested to the prophets with completely sharp clarity.

   3. There is in the prophecies an evident lack of temporal perspective.

CHAPTER IV

God Foretold Christ and His Work *

Christ's divine mission and the divine origin of the Catholic 142
religion have been demonstrated from arguments based on the
divine facts surrounding Christ and His religion. It remains now
to complete the proof by showing that God had foretold and prepared for Christ and His work many centuries before Christ's actual
coming to earth. Who cannot see that the arguments thus far
advanced in favor of the Christian religion would be marvelously
corroborated if it could be shown that in Christ and in the Catholic
religion are fulfilled the ancient prophecies about a future divine
legate and his kingdom? [1]

It is but natural, then, that this chapter should treat of the
so-called Messianic prophecies. First the real existence of such
prophecies must be shown, prophecies which promised that a legate
would someday come from God to found a kingdom. Then, a brief
consideration of these prophecies will show that they find their
fulfillment in Christ and in the Church. [2]

Article I

THE EXISTENCE OF MESSIANIC PROPHECIES

PROPOSITION: *Messianic prophecies existed among the Jews many* 143
centuries before Christ's birth.

At the time of Christ the Jews expected an outstanding prophet
to be sent by God, a prophet whom they called the Messias or
Christ. All classes shared this expectation: the people, the lawyers,
the priests, the king. Nor was it the exclusive possession of the
Jews, as it was found also among the Samaritans. [3]

The Jews, though somewhat confusedly, attributed a threefold
function to the future Messias: political, religious, and eschatological.

* See special bibliography on p. 248.

a. The political function. As the son of David the Messias would restore the kingdom of David and bring foreign nations into subjection. b. The religious function. He would be, like David, at one and the same time king and prophet, indeed, the greatest of all the prophets. He would deliver his people from their sins and like Moses would perform great wonders, establish a new law and bring all nations to the worship of the true God. c. The eschatological function. He would live forever, and through his efforts the earthly kingdom would be transformed into a kingdom of eternal glory. The dead would be raised and the Messias would then judge all nations, reign with his saints, and cast his wicked enemies into the fires of hell.[4] How these three functions would work together and how they would be carried out was unknown. Though many considered first and foremost the idea of political grandeur, there were many sincere and pious souls who were quite mindful of the religious functions of the Messias and indeed considered these the most important.

One thing is certain, and all agree on this point—Christians, Jews, and rationalists—the Jews based their expectation of the Messias on their sacred books, the books of the Old Testament.[5]

This is not the place to discuss the time of the composition of these books. That task is best left to writers on Scripture. Certainly these books were in existence long before the birth of Christ, since the Alexandrian translation (the Septuagint), begun in the third century B.C., was completed about 130 B.C. According to the rationalists, the books which have relevance here were written from the fifth century B. C. onward.[6] At any rate, there is not the slightest doubt that for several centuries before Christ there existed in written form various statements which the Jews understood as applying to the future Messias. These statements are known as the *Messianic prophecies*.

143a Rationalist View of the Prophecies

Rationalists and Modernists, naturally, claim that those statements are not real prophecies inspired by God, but rather lucky guesses, premonitions, or mere wishes, completely natural inventions [7] of the 'prophets," corresponding to the natural genius of the Israelites and to the various circumstances in which that race found itself. Moreover, the rationalists insist, subsequent events often gave the lie to these predictions.

This contention of the rationalists does not square at all with the character of the prophets or of prophetic messianism. On the one hand, rationalists are all too prone to lump together the prophets of Israel and the soothsayers and diviners of other peoples, and on the other hand they extol them as men pre-eminent for religious and moral knowledge, men who instructed their people in pure monotheism. But there is an evident lack of consistency here. Pagan soothsayers, as all will agree, were not shining examples of virtue and they neither purged nor tried to purge their national religion of polytheism and idolatry. Hence, if the prophets of Israel did perform such outstanding services, they constitute an altogether singular phenomenon, for which there is no analogy to be found anywhere, and for which any merely natural explanation is completely inadequate. Nor does this explain how the prophets, who were men outstanding for moral and religious convictions, could so apodictically call their empty promises divine.[8]

If real prophecy is eliminated, it is impossible to explain how the prophets could conceive the notion of a Messianic rule involving the spread of their own religion throughout the whole world, and how the whole nation could accept such a notion and continuously foster it. No nation, even among the Semites, ever conceived such a hope, and such a grandiose prospect matched not at all the historical condition of the Jews, who were often beaten in battle, and, as far as culture and civilization went, were far inferior to many other nations. Note that this Messianic hope was not an ephemeral thing, but centuries-old, and so firmly rooted that, when prophecy ceased in the fifth century,[9] this hope did not wither and die, but persisted so much so that, though it had been before a calm expectancy, at the time of Christ it burned with feverish intensity. Some insist that popular feelings are sometimes agitated by a premonition of coming changes which can already be discerned. Granted. But a hazy premonition of things about to happen is one thing, and a centuries-old expectation quite another. Furthermore, in the case under consideration, the actual event corresponded perfectly with the ancient prophecies, but quite imperfectly with the premonitions of the later period. In fact, the Messias and His kingdom were quite at variance with the breathless expectations of the Jews of His time.

The best argument against the rationalist school is the actual presentation of the prophecies and their comparison with the history of Christ and His religion. Such a study will show:

a. that the books of the Old Testament contain predictions, many of them quite detailed, of many things depending on the free will of God and of man, and

b. that these predictions are fulfilled in Christ and the Church. Once these two facts are established, no one will be able to entertain a reasonable doubt as to the philosophical truth of the Messianic prophecies.

144 *Scholion. Some remarks to help understand the Messianic prophecies.*

So that the Messianic prophecies may be discussed without frequent interruptions and some attention may be given to the more serious difficulties advanced by the rationalists, it is wise to present here some general observations on prophecies. These observations are not purely arbitrary inventions, but deductions from the true notion of prophecy and the results of a study of the prophecies themselves.

1. The Messianic prophecies were made at different times, and in such a way that a progressive development is discernible. In the oldest books of the Old Testament there appear just a few dim sketches, shadowy and without precision, of the Messianic picture. As time went on, these sketches were gradually developed and perfected by various additions. Was it not most fitting for God to paint the picture of the Messias in this long-range and gradual fashion? Does not the fact, evident at least in retrospect, that many details, added by different authors at different times, dovetailed into one historically true picture show quite clearly that one and the same Spirit guided all the painters? Moreover, if God wished to paint the picture of the Messias in this manner, it follows that for a correct understanding of the picture all the prophecies must be studied together, so that one may shed light on another, that they may complement each other. It is clear, too, that the true, divine meaning of individual prophecies is not necessarily that which contemporaries may have understood from a glimpse of just a fragment, but that which is seen to harmonize with the other fragments now that the picture has been completed.[10]

Since the progressive and piecemeal development of the Messianic picture, in the sense just explained, cannot *a priori* be called impossible or improbable, and can be proved *a posteriori* to have taken place in reality, rationalists are unjustified in their demand that each prophecy be considered by itself and explained on the basis of the immediate context alone. This procedure enables them to obscure the meaning of many Messianic prophecies, but makes it impossible for them to explain the history of the Jewish people, in which the Messianic hope plays such an essential role. Furthermore, once they have rejected the Messianic meaning, they are often at a loss to replace it with another meaning which makes sense.[11]

2. Divine truth was not manifested to the prophets themselves 145 with complete clarity: more often than not it was clothed in figures, symbols, and types. And they preached these things to others just as they had seen or heard them. Consequently, Messianic prophecies are full of figures and pictures. Although it should have seemed antecedently probable, given the peculiar genius of the Oriental, that certain clear truths were expressed in a figurative way by the prophets, still it must be admitted that their readers were not always able, before the fulfillment of the prophecies, to discern the precise extent of the figure or what was the exact sense intended by God. It is furthermore probable that the prophets themselves did not always perceive the clear and full meaning of their own prophecies. "With respect to the principal agent [the Holy Spirit] the mind of the prophet is an imperfect instrument" (*S.Th.* II-II, q. 173, a. 4). Much less did the prophets and their contemporaries always understand the typical meaning hidden in the prophecies, or rather in the events prophesied. If that is the case, then the rationalists are guilty of rashness when they conclude that some prophecies were never fulfilled just because they were not fulfilled in their obvious sense, perhaps the only sense the ancients perceived. *The letter kills, but the spirit gives life.*[12]

3. In revealing the future to His prophets, God did not intend 146 to give a running account of coming events or to satisfy human curiosity, but to buoy up flagging hope or to banish fear. Consequently, He sometimes let the prophets see future events somewhat as we see stars in the sky. We see them, it is true, but we cannot tell which are close to us and which are far away. So it is with prophecies. Often there is no indication of the passage of time, and various events are grouped which have some causal or typical interrelation, but are widely separated in point of time. So it is that the Messianic kingdom is sometimes joined with one of its types as if it were to follow immediately. At other times, the whole Messianic kingdom is described as a compact unit, under one figure which includes all at once Christ's first coming, the progres-

sive development of the Messianic kingdom, and its final consummation. Some of these elements are even now not at all, or at most imperfectly, fulfilled. No wonder, then, that those who read the prophecies before their fulfillment often thought that events prophesied at the same time would be fulfilled at the same time. But it is wrong to conclude from these phenomena that the prophets really meant to indicate simultaneous fulfillment. On this point they have nothing to say.

The above are the more important causes of that obscurity which surrounds many prophecies before their fulfillment. That obscurity proves nothing as far as the truth of the prophecies is concerned, since at least after their fulfillment it becomes sufficiently clear that they were based on a true and sure knowledge of the future. They do, however, point to the wise providence of God, who so enlightens men that, if they have the proper dispositions, they can recognize the truth without being swept to it by a flood of evidence.[13]

Special Bibliography for Messianic Prophecies

Caillard, *Jésus-Christ et les prophéties messianiques*, 1905.

Cerfaux, L., et al., *L'Attente du Messie*, 1954.

De Broglie, *Les prophéties messianiques*.

De Broglie, *Les prophéties et les prophètes* (in *Compte-rendu du 3 Congrès scientifique international des Catholiques*, 1894, II, 137).

Hoberg, G., *Katechismus der messianischen Weissagungen*, 1915.

Le Hir, M., *Etudes bibliques*, 1869, pp. 54-84.

Reinke, *Messianischen Psalmen*.

Reinke, *Messianischen Weissagungen*.

Schulte, *Die messianischen Weissagungen*, 1908.

Touzard, J., *Comment utiliser l'argument prophétique*, 1911.

Wolff, M., *Messianische Weissagungen, aus dem massoretischen und Vulgata-Texte für akademische Übungen zusammengestellt*, 1911.

A Catholic Commentary on Holy Scripture, 1953, under the heading "Messianic Prophecy."

Notes

1. St. Augustine wrote:

For all things that you now see happening in the Church of God, and in the name of Christ throughout the whole world, were already foretold ages before. And even as we read them, so also do we see them; and thereby are we edified unto faith (*The First Catechetical Instruction,* ch. 27, no. 53, ACW, II, 84). See *City of God,* bks. 17–18.

2. We are here considering the Church not precisely as a society in the strict sense, with a fixed constitution, but as the kingdom of religious truth, as suggested by our Lord's words: *"Thou sayest it; I am a king. That is why I was born, and why I have come into the world, to bear witness to the truth. Everyone who is of the truth hears my voice"* (John 18:37).

3. See the passages quoted in no. 76. But the truth of the matter rests not on Christian sources alone, but also on Jewish testimony, such as the *Psalms of Solomon, IV Esdras, Henoch,* etc. Josephus tells us that nothing provoked the Jews to desert the Romans and to defend the city stubbornly more than their hope in the Messias who was to come at that time (see *The Wars of the Jews,* bk. 6, c. 5). Rumor of this expectation had reached the ears of the Gentiles too. Tacitus says:

Very many were convinced that the ancient books of the priests contained a prediction that at that very time the Orient would grow strong and that, beginning with Judea, they would gain control of affairs (*Hist.,* bk. 5, c. 13).

Suetonius testifies:

Throughout all the Orient there had become prevalent that old undying conviction that it had been predicted that at that time, beginning with Judea, they would gain control of affairs (*Vespas.,* 4).

Tacitus and Suetonius, it is true, applied the prophecies to Vespasian, who was commanding the army in Palestine when word reached him that he was emperor. But for all that they still witness to the existence of the ancient "conviction." See Doller, "Die Messiaserwartung im A.T.," BiZ, IV (1911), 6–7; M. Lagrange, *Le messianisme chez les juifs* (1909); DAFC, II, 1615; RPA, XII, (1911), 401; *Der Kath.* I, (1917), 16; *De Katholiek,* CLXII (1922), 141; Zkth, (1927), pp. 370, 473.

4. The idea of the Messias which the Jews had fashioned for themselves was incomplete and in great part false, especially for the reason that they ignored a whole group of prophecies, those, namely, dealing with the humility, passion, and death of the Messias and with the repudiation of Israel as a nation. If they had heeded these, they would not have so confidently interpreted the prophecies about the restoration of the kingdom of David in the literal sense of an earthly kingdom and political domination. See Volz, *Jüdische Eschatologie von Daniel bis Akiba* (1903); Joseph Keulers, *Die eschatologische Lehre des vierten Esrabuches* (1922).

5. See Doller, *op. cit.*

6. Except for the Book of Daniel, which they usually assign to the second century B.C., and label an apocalypse. But the reasons behind this opinion, even if they have found favor with some Catholics, do not seem to be strong enough to rule out the traditional thesis concerning the date and literary form of the book of Daniel. See, for example, *Der Kath.,* II (1906), 201, 206.

7. This is the opinion of those who reject *a priori* everything supernatural, whether miracles (physical and moral) or prophecies strictly so-called, which are miracles on the intellectual plane. They distort all the facts of history to make them fit this completely arbitrary norm.

8. This occasioned the answer of the Biblical Commission (June 28, 1908) to *Dubium I*:

Whether it may be taught that the prophecies which are read in the Book of Isaias, and here and there in the Scriptures, are not real prophecies, but either narratives composed subsequent to the event, or, if it must be acknowledged that something was foretold before the event, that the prophet foretold the same, not from a supernatural revelation of God who foreknows the future, but by conjecturing through a happy sagacity and acuteness of natural intelligence from things that had already happened.

Answer: In the negative.

Dubium II asked:

Whether the opinion which holds that Isaias and the other prophets uttered prophecies concerning only those things which were to take place immediately or after a short space of time, can be reconciled with the prophecies, particularly the Messianic and the eschatological, which were undoubtedly uttered by the same prophets about the remote future, as well as with the common opinion of the Fathers who unanimously assert that the prophets foretold also those things which should be fulfilled after many ages.

Answer: In the negative.

See ASS (1908), p. 613; translation in RSS (1946), pp. 111–112.

9. See 1 Mac. 9:27, 4:46; Josephus, *C. App.*, bk. 1, c. 8.

10. Note the response of the Biblical Commission to *Dubium III*, which asks:

Whether it may be admitted that the prophets not only as correctors of human wickedness and heralds of the divine Word for the good of their hearers, but also as foretellers of future events must always have addressed themselves to a present and contemporary and not to a future audience, so that they could be clearly understood by them, etc.

Answer: In the negative. See ASS (1908), p. 613, translation in RSS (1946), p. 112.

11. Thus Lagrange:

We should find reassuring the fact that those who reject their messianic character are very embarrassed when they try to supply another sense that will be satisfactory (in RBibl [1900], p. 474).

12. Prophecy is a word of God addressed to future generations and it need not be understood until after its fulfillment. It is a puzzle to which the actual event is to give the key. If God wanted the prophecy to be intelligible only after the event, the meaning grasped by contemporaries (of the Prophet) is only an apparent meaning, an inexact meaning, a meaning which God permitted to occur to men s minds, but the truth of which He did not affirm. The divine meaning is that which the events reveal and which those living at the time of the event are in a position to grasp. Prophecy is a long-range vision, and the event is glimpsed in a cloudy fashion, intermingled with other intermediate or even distant events. It is only when it draws near that its proper lineaments disengage themselves. Sometimes the same event appears under successive, different

aspects; it is only from close up that one can see how they harmonize. The non-realization of the Jewish meaning does not at all prove that prophecy is not from God (De Broglie, *Compte-rendu du 3 Congres scientifique international des Catholiques,* 1894, II, 137).

De Broglie's statement makes one think of some words spoken by St. Irenaeus many years before:

Before any prophecy is fulfilled it presents puzzles and obscurities to men. But when the time has come and the event prophesied has occurred, then prophecies have a clear and sure explanation (*Adversus Haereses,* bk. 4, c. 26, no. 1).

13. If the future had been revealed to us with as much precision and consistency in details as we require of a history of the past, human liberty in the face of this sharp light would be badly frightened. Either it would be constrained to bring about what had been predicted of it, or it would tend to resist it with might and main, in order to hold on to itself and to convince itself that it [liberty] is not just an empty dream. The argument which we draw from prophecies would be considerably weakened. For there would always be the lurking fear that their fulfillment was really the effect of wills determined to conform to them (Le Hir, *Etudes bibliques,* I, 82).

Article II

A SUMMARY EXPOSITION OF MESSIANIC PROPHECIES

I. *The Protoevangelium*

II. *Prophecies of the Messias' Genealogy*

III. *Prophecies of the Messias' Life:*
1. the events of His life;
2. His passion and death;
3. His exaltation.

IV. *Prophecies of the Messias' Offices:*
1. prophet and founder of a new and universal covenant;
2. priest;
3. king.

Corollary: Apparent mutual incompatibility of some prophecies made them quite obscure before their fulfillment.

V. *Prophecies About the Time of the Messias' Coming:*
1. The prophecy of Jacob;
2. Daniel 9:24–27:
   a. eschatological interpretation;
   b. exclusively historical interpretation;
   c. directly Messianic interpretation;
   d. combination interpretation: literally Maccabean, typically Messianic.
3. Aggeus 2:7-10.
4. Malachy 3:1.

VI. *Prophecies of the Messianic Kingdom:*
1. It will supplant the old, imperfect covenant.
2. It will begin in Jerusalem, but will become universal.
3. It will banish idolatry, and an unfailingly certain knowledge of things divine will flourish.
4. It will be outstanding for remission of sin, true holiness, peace, a lavish effusion of the Holy Spirit, and charisms.
5. It will have priests from all nations and a true, unbloody sacrifice which will be offered everywhere.
6. It will be assailed everywhere but will stand firm forever.

Conclusion to this Chapter
Conclusion to the Whole Treatise

(252)

A SUMMARY EXPOSITION OF MESSIANIC PROPHECIES

It is impossible to treat in summary fashion all the critical and exegetical questions complicating the matter of Messianic prophecies. Consequently this section presents a synthesis of only the more important prophecies, states their meaning as briefly as possible, and shows how they are fulfilled in Christ and in His religion. The argument is drawn not from individual prophecies, but from all taken together.

I. The Protoevangelium   147

Our first parents received the first ray of Messianic hope. After the serpent, with the woman's help, had caused Adam to fall, God passed judgment on the serpent with these words: *"I will put enmity between you and the woman, between your seed and her seed; he shall crush your head, and you shall lie in wait for his heel"* (Genesis 3:15). Here God promises that the woman will beget one who will be completely victorious over the devil and his allies, but not without being wounded himself in the fray. The prophecy does not state precisely whether this "seed of the woman" will be an individual or a collectivity, but since a crowd cannot have victory without a leader, there is at least an implicit promise of a leader and a liberator who will lead many men to victory over the devil. The expression "seed of the woman" is also very fitting for the Christ who would be born of a virgin.

II. Prophecies of the Messias' Genealogy   148

The early prophecies are marked by a gradual progress in precision. They start with the vague insinuation that the Messias will take his origin from human stock, and then indicate successively the exact branch of this stock: the nation, the tribe, the family.

In the protoevangelium it was stated that the liberator would take his origin from human stock: "seed of the woman."

1. In Noe's prophecy the branch of this stock is foreshadowed: *Then he said: "Blessed be the Lord, the God of Sem; let Chanaan be his slave. May God expand Japheth; let him dwell in the tents*

of Sem; let Chanaan be his slave" (Genesis 9:26–27). Both Sem and Japheth receive a blessing. Sem's blessing consists in the fact that Yahweh will be with him in a special way.[1] Japheth's blessing consists in a natural expansion and in the fact that he will dwell in the tent of Sem, will share in the benefits promised the Semites by virtue of God's covenant. Thus, the spiritual blessing proclaimed in the protoevangelium will begin with the Semites, but the descendants of Japheth will also profit notably from it. This is an indication, admittedly obscure, that the promised Redeemer will be a Semite.

2. In the promise made to Abraham, Isaac, and Jacob the nation from which the redeemer will come is specified. To Abraham was said: *"In your descendants all the nations of the earth shall be blessed, because you have obeyed me"* (Genesis 22:18). The same promise is made then to Isaac [2] and to Jacob.[3] It is also found in the famous prophecy of Balaam: *"I see him, though not now; I behold him, though not near: A star shall advance from Jacob, and a staff shall rise from Israel"* (Numbers 24:17).

3. The dying Jacob indicates the tribe from which the redeemer will come: *"Juda, your brothers shall praise you; . . . the sons of your father shall bow down to you. . . . The sceptre shall not depart from Juda, nor the staff from between his feet, until he comes to whom it belongs. To him shall be the obedience of nations"* (Genesis 49:8–10).

4. In the choice of David is shown the choice of the family which will beget the Messias. Nathan the prophet says to David in the name of God: *"I will raise up thy seed after thee, which shall proceed out of thy bowels . . . and I will establish his kingdom forever"* (2 Kings 7:12–13). *"Once, by my holiness, have I sworn; I will not be false to David. His posterity shall continue forever, and his throne shall be like the sun before me; like the moon, which remains forever—a faithful witness in the sky"* (Psalm 88:36–38). *And there shall come forth a shoot from the stock of Jesse, and a sapling shall sprout out of his root, and the spirit of Yahweh shall rest upon him* (Isaias 11:1–2). — *Behold the days come . . . and I will raise up to David a just branch . . . and this is the name that they shall call him: The Lord Our Just One* (Jeremias 23:5–6).

In regard to the fulfillment of these prophecies in Jesus of Nazareth there is the clear testimony of St. Paul: *For it is evident that Our Lord has sprung out of Juda* (Hebrews 7:14), and: *Remember that Jesus Christ rose from the dead and was descended from David* (2 Timothy 2:8).[4]

III. Prophecies of the Messias' Life   149

Many details were foretold concerning the Messias' life, passion, and exaltation.

1. Touching on the events of his life are the following:

He will have a forerunner: *Behold I send my angel, and he shall prepare the way before my face. And presently the Lord whom you seek, and the angel of the testament whom you desire shall come to his temple* (Malachias 3:1; see Isaias 40:3; Matthew 11:10).

He will be born in Bethlehem: *And thou, Bethlehem Ephrata, art a little one among the thousands of Juda: out of thee shall he come forth unto me that is to be the ruler in Israel: and his going forth is from the beginning, from the days of eternity* (Michaeas 5:2).[5]

He will be born of a virgin-mother: *Behold a virgin shall conceive, and bear a son, and his name shall be called Emmanuel* (Isaias 7:14).

He will be meek and merciful: *He shall not cry out nor shout, nor cause his voice to be heard in the streets; the bruised reed he shall not break, and the dim wick he shall not quench; he shall bring forth right in truth* (Isaias 42:2–3; see Matthew 12:19–20).

His light or preaching will shine chiefly on Galilee: *In the former time he afflicted the land of Zabulon and the land of Jordan, Galilee of the Gentiles; The people that walked in darkness behold a great light, and upon them that dwell in a land of gloom a light shines* (Isaias 9:1–2; see Matthew 4:14–16). The meaning is: the land of Zabulon and Nephthali, near Lake Genesareth, called Galilee of the Gentiles because of its many Gentile inhabitants, was held in contempt by the Jews, but at a later time it would be held in greatest honor because there the light of the Messias would shine more brightly.

He will perform miracles: *God's requital has come; he himself has come to save you. Then shall the eyes of the blind be opened, and the ears of the deaf be unstopped; then shall the lame leap like a hart, and the tongue of the dumb shall sing* (Isaias 35:4–6; see Matthew 11:5).

He will enter Jerusalem humbly, riding an ass: *O daughter of*

Jerusalem, behold thy king will come to thee, the just and the saviour. He is poor and riding upon an ass and upon a colt, the foal of an ass (Zacharias 9:9; see Matthew 1:2ff).

150   2. The following speak of the passion and death of the Messias:

He will be sold for thirty silver coins: *And they weighed for my wages thirty pieces of silver. And the Lord said to me: Cast it into the statuary, a handsome price, that I was prized at by them. And I took the thirty pieces of silver, and I cast them into the house of the Lord, to the statuary* (Zacharias 11:12–13; see Matthew 27:9).

He will be flogged and spat upon: *I have my back to the smiters, and my cheek to them that plucked my beard; I have not hidden my face from insult and spitting* (Isaias 50:6; see Matthew 26:27, 27:30).

He will be condemned to death like a criminal: *Like a lamb that is led to the slaughter, and like a ewe that is dumb before its shearers. . . . Because he shall have poured out his soul to death, and been numbered with the rebellious* (Isaias 53:7, 12). And: *Christ shall be slain* (Daniel 9:26).

His hands and feet will be pierced: *They have pierced my hands and my feet; I can count all my bones* (Psalm 21:17–18).

In his thirst he will be offered gall: *Rather they put gall in my food, and in my thirst they gave me vinegar to drink* (Psalm 68:22; see John 19:28).

He will be shamefully mocked: *All who see me scoff at me; they mock me with parted lips, they wag their heads: "He relied on the Lord; let him deliver him, let him rescue him, if he loves him"* (Psalm 21:8–9; see Matthew 27:39–43).

His clothes will be divided: *They divide my garments among them, and for my vesture they cast lots* (Psalm 21:19; see John 19:24).

He will be stabbed: *They shall look upon me, whom they have pierced* (Zacharias 12:10; see John 19:37).

3. The following refer to his exaltation:

The glory of his tomb: *He shall give the ungodly for his burial, and the rich for his death* (Isaias 53:9; see Matthew 27:57–60). In the Hebrew: *They assigned his grave among the wicked, but in his death he is with the rich man.*

Freedom from decomposition and victory over death: *My body, too, abides in confidence; because you will not abandon my soul to the nether world, nor will you suffer your faithful one to undergo corruption. You will show me the path to life, fulness of joys in your presence, the delights at your right hand forever* (Psalm 15:9–11; see Acts 2:31).

IV. Prophecies of the Messias' Functions 151

1. The future Messias is announced as an outstanding prophet, that is, as a legate sent by God to teach men: *A prophet like me will the Lord, your God, raise up for you from among your own kinsmen; to him you shall listen* (Deuteronomy 18:15).[6]

And I will make with you an eternal covenant, I will give you the sure blessings of David. Behold, I appointed him a witness to peoples, a chief and commander of nations (Isaias 55:3–4).

The spirit of the Lord [Yahweh] *is upon me, because Yahweh has anointed me: he has sent me to bear good tidings to the afflicted, to encourage the brokenhearted; to proclaim liberty to captives, to prisoners deliverance* (Isaias 61:1).

Behold, my servant . . . I have put my spirit upon him, he shall bring forth right to the nations; . . . and the isles wait for his law. . . . And [I will] appoint thee for the covenant of the people, for the light of the nations (Isaias 42:1, 6).

The texts cited show not only that the Messias will be an outstanding prophet but also that he will be the founder of a new and universal covenant.

Jeremias promises in unmistakable terms a new covenant: *Behold the days shall come, saith the Lord, and I will make a new covenant with the house of Israel and with the house of Juda: Not according to the covenant which I made with their fathers, in the day that I took them by the hand to bring them out of the land of Egypt. . . . But this shall be the covenant that I will make with the house of Israel after those days. . . . I will give my law deep in their bowels and I will write it in their hearts: and I will be their God, and they shall be my people* (Jeremias 31:31–33).

Isaias teaches the universality of this new covenant: *It were too little that thou shouldst be my servant to raise up the tribes of Jacob, and to bring back the preserved of Israel; and I will make thee the light of the nations, that my salvation may be to the end of the earth* (Isaias 49:6).

2. He is proclaimed as a priest. He will offer himself as a victim for the sins of mankind: *But it was our sufferings that he bore, our pains that he endured; . . . But he was wounded for our rebellions, he was bruised for our sins; upon him was the chastise-*

ment which made us whole, and by his stripes we were healed. . . . And Yahweh made to light upon him the iniquities of us all; he was afflicted, but he was resigned. . . . Though his own life be made a sin-offering, he shall see a seed that shall have length of days (Isaias 53:4–10).

Thus will he sanctify many nations by sprinkling them, spiritually, with his blood: *He shall sprinkle many nations* (Isaias 52:15). (This verse, however, is of very doubtful reading in the Hebrew. Kissane, for instance, prefers to translate; *So shall many nations be amazed at him.*)

It is further said of the Messias: *You are a priest forever, according to the order of Melchisedech* (Psalm 109:4). There is a promise, too, of the institution of a new unbloody sacrifice to be offered everywhere, given by Malachias (1:11).

152   **3. He is proclaimed as a king:** *I myself have set up my king on Sion, my holy mountain* (Psalm 2:6).

His rule is described as a rule of justice and of peace, which will bring a blessing to all nations: *He shall defend the afflicted among the people, save the children of the poor, and crush the oppressor. . . . Justice shall flower in his days, and profound peace, till the moon be no more. . . . In him shall all the tribes of the earth be blessed; all the nations shall proclaim his happiness* (Psalm 71:4, 7, 17). It is described as a perpetual kingdom: *May he endure as long as the sun, and like the moon through all generations . . . till the moon be no more* (Psalm 71:5, 7). It is described as a universal kingdom: *Ask of me and I will give you the nations for an inheritance and the ends of the earth for your possession. . . . May he rule from sea to sea, and from the River to the ends of the earth. . . . All kings shall pay him homage, all nations shall serve him* (Psalms 2:8; 71:8, 11).

153 **Corollary**

The Messias is proclaimed now as a most powerful king,[7] now as a humble and meek man, remarkable not for strength of arms or worldly power, but for spiritual endowments alone,[8] and again as subject to the most abject wretchedness.[9] How all these characteristics would be realized in one and the same person must have been very obscure before the fulfillment of the prophecies. But after their fulfillment it can be seen that even the prophets themselves proclaimed their mutual coherence at least to some extent. Isaias hints that the Messias will be born in a lowly spot,[10] will quietly and peacefully preach justice,[11] and will ascend his throne only by the path of suffering and death: *Though his own life be made a sin-offering, he shall see a seed that shall have length of days, and the purpose of Yahweh shall prosper in his hand. Because of his soul's sorrow he shall see it, through his suffering he shall be filled; a righteous one, my servant, shall make many righteous, and their iniquities he shall bear; therefore will I give him a portion with the mighty, and with the powerful shall he divide the spoil* (Isaias 53:10–12).

Zacharias, too, gives sufficiently clear indication that the Messias, humble and meek, will achieve domination not by force of arms, but will attain to a universal rule in a thoroughly peaceful manner: *Rejoice greatly, O daughter of Sion, shout for joy, O daughter of Jerusalem: Behold thy king will come to thee, the just and saviour. He is poor and riding upon an ass and upon a colt, the foal of an ass. And I will destroy the chariot out of Ephraim and the horse out of Jerusalem: and the bow for war will be broken. And he shall speak peace to the Gentiles: and his power shall be from sea to sea, and from the rivers even to the end of the earth* (Zacharias 9:9–10).

At the same time, these prophecies make it obvious that the notion of a Messias such as that conceived by the carnal among the Jews, in which the idea of political domination is pre-eminent, is not the notion revealed by an over-all study of the Old Testament. Although some prophecies may seem to favor this notion, others exclude it.

Fulfillment. There can be not the slightest doubt that Jesus of 154 Nazareth was a prophet, indeed the greatest of all teachers and the founder of a new order of reality.

He was also a priest, for He offered Himself as a sacrifice for His disciples and for the whole human race.[12] At the Last Supper He instituted the unbloody sacrifice which, on the basis of its visible elements, bread and wine, bears a great likeness to that of Melchisedech.[13] This sacrifice has been offered in the most remote regions of the earth throughout nineteen centuries.

Finally, Jesus of Nazareth was and is a king, not a temporal one, it is true, but a spiritual one.[14] He founded and unceasingly governs, invisibly by Himself, visibly through His representatives, the Catholic Church, the kingdom of justice and of peace, the universal and unfailing kingdom.

155 V. Prophecies About the Time of the Messias' Coming

Four prophecies are involved in this question of time.

1. The prophecy of Jacob. Jacob, on his deathbed, *summoned his sons and said: "Come together, I will tell you what shall befall you in days to come. . . . Juda, your brothers shall praise you; your hand shall be on the neck of your enemies; the sons of your father shall bow down to you. . . . The sceptre shall not depart from Juda, nor the staff from between his feet, until he comes to whom it belongs. To him shall be the obedience of nations"* (Genesis 49:1, 8, 10).[15]

In these words there is a clear statement on the part of Jacob that power, rule of some sort (symbolized by the word sceptre), will remain in the house of Juda.

Although there is a great deal of discussion about the word *Shiloh* (translated above as *to whom it belongs*, by Jerome *he who is to be sent*) and the literal meaning of the passage, the entire context indicates that it is a reference to the Messias. In fact, not only Christians, but also the Jews of old understood this passage to refer to the Messias, a rare, but illustrative, instance of almost universal agreement.[16]

The word *until* can be taken to mean that the (temporal) rule will be taken away from Juda when the Messias comes, or that the rule (in a general sense) will remain forever in Juda and even that through the good offices of the Messias it will one day be extended to include the Gentiles also. The latter interpretation seems preferable, particularly in light of later prophecies dealing with the permanent establishment of the throne of David.[17]

If *until* is taken in the first sense, to denote the definitive end of Juda's rule, then the prophecy positively specifies the time of the Messianic era, and is fulfilled in this way: when the first foreign king, Herod the Idumaean, was ruling the Jews, Jesus of Nazareth was born, and subsequent events proved quite clearly that He had been justly proclaimed the one to come, to whom *shall be the obedience of nations*. Hardly had the Gentiles begun to pay Him obeisance when, with the destruction of Jerusalem, the temporal rule was completely and irrevocably snatched from Juda. This was the more common interpretation held by older theologians and exegetes.

If *until* is taken in the second sense, as not excluding the continuance of Juda's rule, at least in some general way, then the prophecy helps to determine the time of the Messianic era only negatively and retrospectively. It permits the conclusion that the Messias was to come before Juda clearly and irrevocably lost any domination worthy of the name. Of course, if any member of the tribe of Juda won the obedience of the Gentiles, and the tribe itself at almost the same time lost all other kind of power definitely, one should have to conclude that the individual through whom the tribe of Juda had power over the Gentiles, and apart from whose realm the tribe had no ruling power, must have been the promised Messias. Moreover, from the time of the complete destruction of the Jewish state in 70 A.D., all earthly power of any kind was taken from Juda, whereas a short time before the destruction there had emerged from Juda s tribe Jesus of Nazareth, to whom the Gentiles became obedient.

How the sceptre remained in the tribe of Juda up to the time 156 *of Christ.*

From Numbers 1:26–27; 10:14, and Judges 1:1–2; 20:18, it is evident that Juda s tribe enjoyed special prominence even in the desert and during the period of the Judges. With David and Solomon it ruled gloriously over all the tribes. From Roboam to the Babylonian Captivity, it had the obedience of Benjamin and Levi and many others who had migrated from other tribes to that of Juda.[18] Moreover, Juda (together with Benjamin and others) almost equalled the other ten tribes in population and resources. At the time of the Babylonian Captivity, the rule was interrupted for a comparatively short time, an interruption which later prophecies pointed to as a punishment sent by God.[19] When the Captivity ended, Juda ruled so completely over all who returned that all Hebrews, regardless of their tribe of origin, called themselves Jews, *Judaei,* belonging to Juda.[20]

The remarks above are based on the opinion which we think is more probable. Some claim that the sceptre was taken away in fact at the time of the Babylonian Captivity and remained in Juda only as a matter of right. In reality, however, the actual taking away of the sceptre no more destroys the validity of this prophecy than it does the promise of an everlasting throne which had been made to David.[21]

2. The prophecy of Daniel. Daniel lived during the period 157 of the Babylonian Captivity. One day, while prayerfully contemplating the promise made by Jeremias that the people would be liberated after seventy years,[22] he was given information by the archangel Gabriel. He wrote:

Seventy weeks are shortened [23] upon thy people and upon thy holy city, that transgression may be finished and sin may have an end and iniquity may be abolished and everlasting justice may be brought and vision and prophecy may be fulfilled and the Saint of Saints [24] may be anointed.

Know thou therefore and take notice: that from the going forth of the word to build up Jerusalem again, unto Christ the prince, there shall be seven weeks and sixty-two weeks: and the street shall be built again, and the walls in straitness of times.

And after sixty-two weeks Christ shall be slain [25] and the people that shall deny him [26] shall not be his. And a people, with their leader that shall come, shall destroy the city and the sanctuary: and the end thereof shall be waste, and after the end of the war the appointed desolation.

And he shall confirm the covenant with many, in one week: and in the half of the week the victim and the sacrifice shall fail: [27] and there shall be in the temple the abomination of desolation. And the desolation shall continue even to the consummation and to the end (Daniel 9:24–27).

The only certain and firmly established factor of this prophecy (held as certain and firmly established by the Fathers and theologians) is that the benefits listed in verse 24 are Messianic benefits, and that the prophecy consequently has some Messianic meaning. Apart from this single point of general agreement, there is no unanimous interpretation of the literal meaning of the prophecy. In fact, hardly any other prophecy has been so variously interpreted.[28]

157a   All attempts at an explanation fall into three classes.[29]

a. The Eschatological Explanation.[30] According to this interpretation the "seventy weeks" symbolize the whole history of the theocracy, divided into three parts. The number "seven" symbolizes the time of the Messias' coming—the Messias who has all power in heaven and on earth. There follows a period between the first and second comings of the Messias (Lord), a time for the hidden plans of God, symbolized by the number "sixty-two." The final "one week" signifies the time of the Parousia with all its attendant circumstances:

    7 weeks = the coming of the Messias,
    62 weeks = the time between the first and second comings,
    1 week = the Parousia (second coming).

This interpretation, the result of a wild and arbitrary mysticism, is a gratuitous assumption and is quite commonly rejected.

b. The Exclusively Historical Explanation.[31] On the assumption that the Book of Daniel is not a prophetic, but an historical work written by an unknown author of the Maccabean period, this interpretation asserts that verse 24 truly is a promise of Messianic benefits which are to materialize after the seventy weeks,[32] but the remaining verses represent an apocalyptic presentation of the past history of the Israelites up to the time of Antiochus Epiphanes. This history is divided into three periods.

The first period extends roughly from 587 to 536 B.C. The point of departure is the "going forth of the word," the prophecy of Jeremias about the rebuilding of the Holy City (Daniel was reflecting on this prophecy).[33] The end of this period is taken as the first year of the reign of Cyrus, who gave orders for the rebuilding of the Temple of Jerusalem.[34]

The second period, "sixty-two weeks," during which "the street shall be built again, and the walls in straitness of times," begins with the year 536 and ends in 171 B.C., when "the Christ" or "anointed one," the high priest Onias III, was killed.[35]

The third is the period of one week, from 171 to 164 B.C. During this week the city and the sanctuary will be ravaged, victims and sacrifices will cease to be, and in the temple will appear the abomination of desolation, part of the tyranny of Antiochus Epiphanes. All of these events are narrated in the Books of the Macchabees.[36]

In short, this interpretation sees the author presenting past events in prophetic form:

"The going forth of the word" = the prophecy of Jeremias,
7 weeks = c. 587–536 (accession of Cyrus),
62 weeks = 536–171 (murder of Onias III).

This opinion is untenable. We cannot accept it even as a solidly probable hypothesis, even though it is ingeniously contrived and is by no means contrary to the teaching of the Church. In the first place, it lacks solid arguments, and in the second, it involves many difficulties. Its assumptions as to the date, author, and literary character of the Book of Daniel contradict the traditional view. It is less in harmony with the mind of the ecclesiastical magisterium; [37] indeed it seems to contradict Christ Himself, foretelling the *abomination of desolation, which was spoken of by Daniel the prophet* (Matthew 24:15) as something still in the offing, even in His day.

It offers no explanation for the fact that the second period of sixty-two weeks comprises not 434 years, but only 365 (from 536 to 171 B.C.).[38]

157b   c. Messianic Interpretation. The more common opinion, which respects the traditional view and is in our opinion the truer interpretation, holds that the "anointed leader" whose death is predicted is the Messias, and that the seventy shortened weeks last until the time of the Messias.

Assuming that this is the true interpretation, the Messias and his benefits will come within seventy weeks from the issuance of the edict to rebuild Jerusalem. This period is divided into three parts.

Within the first *seven weeks* the street and the walls will be restored. There will take place the complete material and moral restoration of Jerusalem "in straitness of times." [39]

After sixty-two weeks more (now a total of sixty-nine after the edict), there will be a leader for the people who will presently die a violent death. The destruction of the Temple and of the city is linked with the slaying of the Messias, and in that destruction can be seen a result of, and punishment for, the murder of the Anointed One. Still, the prophecy does not say that it will follow immediately or that it will take place within the limits of the seventy weeks.

In the one remaining week, the seventieth, *he shall confirm the covenant with many.* In other words, in that week the new covenant promised by God [40] will be established and irrevocably ratified. Moreover, *in the half of that week* there will be an end to victims and sacrifice—to the bloody and unbloody sacrifices of the Mosaic Law.

158   What are these seventy weeks? The Hebrew word *shābûaʻ* signifies a period embracing seven units. The Jews were familiar with periods in which the seven units were years; doubtless because of the law dealing with the sabbatical year.[41] The ordinary usage of the word among the Jews was strictly for seven days, but one could easily maintain that the term as used by Daniel refers, not to days, but to years.

Since a week of seven days is too short to satisfy the demands of the other terms of the prophecy, the obvious conclusion is that the angel meant to indicate groups of seven years. The seventy weeks, then, add up to 490 years. The angel probably expressed this span of time in terms of seventy weeks for the reason that

Daniel was reflecting on the seventy years of the captivity when the revelation was given. It was thus fitting that the great and true liberation which the Messias would effect within seventy groups of seven years should be linked with the liberation from the Babylonian Captivity which would come about after an interval of seventy years.

When do these "seventy weeks" begin?

They begin with *the going forth of the word to build up Jerusalem again.* These words seem to indicate very clearly a decree of some sort issued by a ruler to allow or to order the restoration of the city and its walls.

Although there exist many varying views on the matter, exegetes more commonly think the decree issued by Artaxerxes I Longimanus in the seventh year of his reign [42] or the one issued by him in the twentieth year of his reign [43] is the one referred to in Daniel's prophecy.

Modern scholars consider it practically certain that Artaxerxes ruled by himself from 465 B.C. onwards, and for some time before that (from 473?) he had shared the throne with his father. Those who say that the decree was issued in the seventh year usually count those years during which Artaxerxes reigned alone, and so express the view that the seventy weeks begin with the year 458 B.C. Those who believe the decree was issued in the twenty-first year feel that the years of joint rule should be taken into account, and in their opinion the seventy weeks begin with 453 B.C. But all have to admit that these numbers are not so definite as to exclude a possible margin of one or two years. Since the first year of Artaxerxes, just as the years of accession of other kings of this period, has to be determined by computing the number of years during which individual rulers were in power, an error of a few years is quite understandable.

Fulfillment. Since the exact year from which to start the reckoning of the seventy weeks is not known, the fulfillment of the prophecy cannot be mathematically verified.[44] Yet it is sufficiently clear that the prophecy of Daniel was fulfilled in Jesus of Nazareth. The different reckonings proposed, though varied in detail, all come to within a few years of 30 A.D.[45]

At this date, and during the general period preceding the overthrow of the city and Temple, no one else besides Jesus can be found to whom one might apply the prophecy. Jesus, publicly anointed by the Holy Spirit at the time of His baptism, preached for about three years. At the end of this period, on April 7, in the year 30 A.D. (783 A.U.C.),* He suffered a violent death to atone for the sins of men and to inaugurate the reign of justice. During the middle of the final week the Temple's veil was rent,[46] and the Mosaic cult, at least as far as it was the rightful and acceptable cult, passed out of existence. The same seventieth week, since it witnessed the institution and first spread of the Church, indeed established a new covenant for many. Finally, about forty years later *a people with their leader that shall come* ravaged the Temple and the city of Jerusalem, because it had not recognized its anointed leader, had *not known the time of its visitation.*[47]

The above interpretation may be represented thus:

> 7 weeks = rebuilding of Jerusalem;
> 62 weeks = from the rebuilding of Jerusalem to the
> coming of the Christ;
> 1 week = a. the life, work and death of Christ,
> b. the birth and first growth of the Church,
> c. the end of the Mosaic cult.

160 **3. The Prophecy of Aggeus.**[48] When the Jews who had returned from the Babylonian Captivity were plunged in grief at the lowliness of the Temple as restored by Zorobabel, Aggeus announced that the glory of the Temple of Jerusalem would be greater in the future than ever before, and that this would be due to the future Messias and to the peace which he would bring.

For thus saith the Lord of hosts: Yet one little while,[49] *and I will move the heaven and the earth and the sea and the dry land. And I will move all nations: and the desired of all nations*[50] *shall come: and I will fill this house with glory, saith the Lord of hosts. The silver is mine and the gold is mine, saith the Lord of hosts. Great shall be the glory of this last house more than of the first,*[51] *saith the Lord of hosts: and in this place I will give peace,*[52] *saith the Lord of hosts* (Aggeus 2:7–10).

Meaning. God, who in Old Testament times shook the earth with His miracles,[53] will soon move all nations to offer precious gifts in His House. To a certain extent this took place during the Maccabean period,[54] but it was perfectly realized only after the

---

* Ricciotti, G.: *The Life of Christ* (1947), p. 166. For the method of computation, and variant dates given by other scholars, cf. the same work, pp. 161–167.

Messias had come, when the converted nations offered themselves and their goods to God in His spiritual temple, the Church, of which the Temple in Jerusalem was a figure. The Temple itself will achieve its highest glory from the fact that in it God will give His peace, the Messias himself, the source of all the Messianic blessings.

The Messias was to come while the Temple was still standing.

4. **The Prophecy of Malachias.** What Aggeus had stated in 161 rather vague fashion Malachias stated quite clearly: The Messias will appear at the Temple in Jerusalem. *Behold I send my angel, and he shall prepare the way before my face. And presently* [55] *the Lord whom you seek, and the angel of the testament whom you desire shall come to his temple. Behold he cometh, saith the Lord of hosts* (Malachias 3:1).

Meaning. The ruler whom the Jews desired, and who was to establish a new covenant, can be none other than the promised Messias. The Messias, whose divinity is fairly clearly indicated in this passage,[56] will come to his Temple at Jerusalem, the only legitimate sanctuary of the true God before the Christian era. To enable the people to recognize the Messias, a divinely appointed forerunner is to appear, then the Messias himself is to appear, while the Temple at Jerusalem is still standing.

Fulfillment of the prophecies of Aggeus and Malachias. Jesus of Nazareth, the *mediator of a new covenant* (Hebrews 9:15), at whose birth the angels sang *on earth peace among men of good will* (Luke 2:14), to whom numberless people gave their allegiance, was heralded by John the Baptist and arrived while the Temple was still in its great glory. He entered this Temple frequently, and while there revealed Himself as the source of all grace and peace.[57] The elements of both prophecies fit Him admirably. Indeed, they fit Him alone, for no one else appeared in the Temple of Jerusalem to whom these prophecies might possibly apply.

Since later rabbis were of the opinion that the time foretold by the prophets for the coming of the Messias had long since passed, they forbade further attempts to reckon these dates. Hence Moses Maimonides wrote in the twelfth century:

The wise men, whose memory is blessed, forbade us to compute the date of the Messias' coming, because the people take scandal at the fact that the time has gone by and he has still not appeared. This is why the wise man said: "Let the swollen bones of those who compute periods of time be crushed to bits, for they scandalize the people." [58]

162 VI. Prophecies of the Messianic Kingdom

1. The Messianic Kingdom, as the perfect covenant, supplants the old, imperfect covenant between God and the Jewish nation. The beginning of the Messianic Kingdom necessitates the end of the old dispensation. Read Jeremias 31:31–33; Daniel 9:24–27; Malachias 1:10–11.

2. The kingdom of the Messias will begin in Jerusalem and will be proclaimed to the Gentiles. The coming of the latter will insure a steady growth and it will become a universal kingdom.

The law shall go forth out of Sion, and the word of the Lord out of Jerusalem (Micheas 4:2).

And I will set a sign among them; and I will send such as escape of them unto the nations, Tarshish, Put and Lud, Meshek and Rosh, Tubal and Greece, and the distant isles that have not heard my name nor seen my glory, and they shall declare my name among the nations. And they shall bring all your brethren from all nations as an offering to Yahweh (Isaias 66:19–20).

Enlarge [O Sion] the place of thy tent, and let them spread out the curtains of their dwelling; spare not, lengthen thy tent-ropes, make thy tent-pegs strong; For thou shalt break forth to the right and the left, and thy seed shall dispossess the nations (Isaias 54:2–3).

And it shall come to pass in the last days that the mountain of the house of the Lord shall be prepared in the top of mountains and high above the hills: and people shall flow to it. And many nations shall come in haste and say: Come let us go up to the mountain of the Lord and to the house of the God of Jacob: and he will teach us of his ways and we will walk in his paths. For the law shall go forth out of Sion, and the word of the Lord out of Jerusalem (Micheas 4:1–2).

163

3. The kingdom of the Messias will banish idolatry; the knowledge of things divine will flourish, and this knowledge will be unfailingly certain.

And it shall come to pass in that day, saith the Lord of hosts, that I will destroy the names of idols out of the earth, and they shall be remembered no more (Zacharias 13:2).

For the land shall be filled with the knowledge of Yahweh, as the waters cover the sea (Isaias, 11:9; see 54:13).

I will give my law in their bowels and I will write it in their heart: and I will be their God, and they shall be my people. And they shall teach no more every man his neighbor, and every man his brother, saying: Know the Lord. For all shall know me from the least of them even to the greatest, saith the Lord (Jeremias, 31:32–33).

As for Me, this is My covenant with them, said Yahweh: My spirit which is upon thee, and My words which I have put in thy mouth, shall not depart from thy mouth, nor from the mouth of thy seed nor from the mouth of thy seed's seed forever, said Yahweh (Isaias, 59:21).

4. The kingdom of the Messias will be outstanding for remission 164 of sin, true justice or holiness, and peace, a lavish outpouring of the Holy Spirit, and spiritual gifts.

In that day there shall be a fountain open to the house of David and to the inhabitants of Jerusalem: for the washing of the sinner and of the unclean woman (Zacharias 13:1).

Justice shall flower in his days, and profound peace (Psalm 71:7).

And it shall come to pass after this, that I will pour out my spirit upon all flesh: and your sons and your daughters shall prophesy: your old men shall dream dreams, and your young men shall see visions (Joel 2:28; see Zacharias 12:10).

5. The kingdom of the Messias will have priests chosen from every nation, and a true unbloody sacrifice which will be offered everywhere.

And of these also [the Gentiles] will I take as priests and levites, said Yahweh (Isaias 66:21).

For from the rising of the sun even to the going down, my name is great among the Gentiles: and in every place there is sacrifice and there is offered to my name a clean oblation. For my name is great among the Gentiles, saith the Lord of hosts (Malachias 1:11).[59]

6. The kingdom of the Messias will be assailed wherever it 165 exists, but, thanks to God's protection, will never be vanquished and will stand firm forever.

Why do the nations rage, and the peoples utter folly? The kings of the earth rise up, and the princes conspire together against the Lord and against his anointed: "Let us break their fetters and cast their bonds from us!" He who is throned in heaven laughs; the Lord derides them (Psalm 2:1–4).

And it shall come to pass in that day that I will make Jerusalem a burdensome stone to all people. All that shall lift it up shall be rent and torn: and all the kingdoms of the earth shall be gathered together against her (Zacharias 12:3).

No weapon that is fashioned against thee shall avail, and every tongue that will contend with thee in judgment thou shalt confute. This is the heritage of the servants of Yahweh, and this is their reward from Me, said Yahweh (Isaias 54:17).[60]

But in the days of those kingdoms the God of heaven will set up a kingdom that shall never be destroyed: and his kingdom shall not be delivered up to another people . . . and itself shall stand forever (Daniel 2:44; see 7:13–14).

Note: The magnificent prophecies of Messianic *peace* should be interpreted, to some extent at least, in a spiritual sense as referring to internal peace of heart, or as referring to that perfect peace which the grace of the Messias would bestow were everyone to accept it wholeheartedly. The prophecies which speak of the *universality* of the Messianic kingdom do not necessitate an absolute universality, only a relative. The prophets sometimes painted the Messianic picture in general terms, not distinguishing the temporal and spiritual elements to too great an extent.

166   *Fulfillment.* An examination of the Catholic Church and the religion she professes, in the light of the ancient prophecies, forcefully brings out that she and she alone verifies all the elements of the Messianic kingdom described by the prophets.

1. The Catholic religion has always claimed to be the perfect religion, the fulfillment of the old dispensation. It came into existence precisely at the time when the observance of the Old Law ceased. When the Church began to grow, the city and Temple of Jerusalem were completely and irrevocably destroyed.

2. The Catholic religion originated in Jerusalem, then reached even the most distant nations by the work of zealous missioners. The conversion of these nations assured, and still assures, its steady growth. It became and has remained a universal kingdom, a religion extending throughout the whole world.

3. Wherever the Catholic religion has become deeply rooted, idolatry has been destroyed and the knowledge and practice of a revealed worship has flourished. Throughout many centuries the Catholic Church has treasured and kept safe the true knowledge

of the Lord for her numberless children, and the Church promises to safeguard this knowledge forever, claiming infallibility in matters divine.

4. The Catholic religion teaches that all men can receive true forgiveness of sin and the abiding presence of the Holy Spirit. It constantly produces a remarkable harvest of holiness, and has never experienced a complete lack of miracles and special spiritual gifts. Truly, the Catholic religion is the kingdom of peace. It brings to man peace with God and with himself; it brings *the peace of God which surpasses all understanding* (Philippians 4:7), the peace of Christ which the world cannot give. Love is the bond of union within this kingdom, uniting all under one shepherd, making all men brothers. If wars occur among nations and peoples, it means only that those nations and peoples have refused the Catholic religion, or have given it only lip service.

5. The Catholic religion has a visible priesthood, restricted not to one family or to one nation, but including men of all nations. It has an unbloody, spotless sacrifice offered everywhere from sunrise to sunset.

6. As long as the Catholic religion has been in existence, it has been attacked by men using both material and spiritual weapons. Yet after nineteen centuries they have not been able to conquer it, a fact which emboldens one to predict that it will never be vanquished, come what may, but will stand firm forever. Note how strikingly these words of the prophet Isaias are realized in the Catholic Church: *Every tongue that resisteth thee in judgment thou shalt condemn* (Isaias 54:17). From the beginning till now the Catholic Church has condemned any and all who proclaim as divine any religious teaching contrary to that received by her from Christ.

* * *

Just as the Catholic Church perfectly fulfills the prophecies of 167 the Messianic kingdom, so there exists besides her no society possessing all the characteristics noted above.

Non-Christian societies may be dismissed. Since it is clear from the arguments given that Christ is the true Messias, a religion which has no link with Christ could not possibly be the kingdom of the Messias. Nor would it require much labor to show that the characteristics of the Messianic kingdom are not realized in any of the non-Christian religions.

Christians separated from the Catholic Church are the Oriental sects and the Protestant churches. Neither the Oriental sects nor the Protestant churches enjoy that *universality* which the prophets pointed to as a prime characteristic of the Messianic kingdom. In addition, the Protestant churches have no sacrifice. Nor can it be said of any Christian society other than the Catholic Church that it has been the object of constant attack and that it has condemned every tongue speaking in opposition to it. The conclusion is evident.

168   CONCLUSION TO THIS CHAPTER

From the remarks made in the article concerning the Messianic prophecies and their fulfillment, one fact stands out above all others—the Old Testament predictions about the Messias and his kingdom are true, divinely inspired prophecies. Who would seriously dare to maintain that so many details predicted of the coming Messias, predicted in different ages and by different persons, were only hazardous guesses that accidentally turned out to be true!

If the philosophical truth of the prophecies is admitted, then their fulfillment in Christ and in the Catholic Church demonstrates beyond shadow of doubt the following conclusions:

1. Jesus of Nazareth was the true Messias, the special divine legate whom *God who . . . spoke in times past to the fathers by the prophets* (Hebrews 1:1), promised to the human race.

2. The Catholic Church is truly the kingdom of the Messias, the kingdom to which all nations are invited, and in which the knowledge of the Lord is unswervingly and faithfully preserved.

169   CONCLUSION TO THE ENTIRE TREATISE

It has been shown by various arguments that the Catholic religion is the religion divinely revealed in and by Christ.

Internal arguments served as persuasions for the divine origin of this religion. Such arguments were based on the wondrous excellence of this religion whereby it surpasses anything that man could discover of himself.

External arguments demonstrate the divine origin of this religion. Such arguments are based on divine signs which point out immediately Jesus Christ as the author of this religion; or directly recommend that religion, the Catholic religion, which has flourished for over nineteen centuries; or show that Christ and His work, the Catholic religion, had been promised long before by God Himself and prepared by Him.

The arguments prove irresistibly the credibility of the Catholic religion in such a way that they are enough to give any man who considers them with earnestness and sincerity, real moral certitude about the fact of revelation and the divine origin of the Catholic Church. This certitude is moral because it is based on human testimony. Still, it is real certitude in the strictest sense of the term, positively excluding any possibility of prudent doubt. The reason why one cannot have metaphysical or physical certitude about the matter in question is quite simple. Since this is a fact of history, the only type of certitude possible is moral.[61]

Two conclusions follow from this demonstration:

1. Every religious teaching is false to the extent that it contradicts the Catholic religion. Since this is true of all religions other than the Catholic, then the Catholic religion is the only true and legitimate one.

2. Every man who becomes aware of the divine truth of the Catholic religion has a strict obligation to embrace that religion and to be loyal to it. Christ Himself said quite clearly that His religion must be accepted by all under penalty of damnation: *"All power in heaven and on earth has been given to me. Go, therefore, and make disciples of all nations . . . teaching them to observe all that I have commanded you"* (Matthew 28:18–20). *"He who believes and is baptized shall be saved, but he who does not believe shall be condemned"* (Mark 16:16).

Notes

1. Later, in the same sense: *"I am . . . the God of Abraham, the God of Isaac, the God of Jacob"* (Exodus 3:6), and *"Blessed be the Lord, the God of Israel"* (Luke 1.68).

2. See Genesis 26:4.

3. See Genesis 28:14.

4. See Luke 1:31–33; Feldmann, "Die Weissagungen über den Gottesknecht im Buche Jesaias," Bibl Zf, II (1908), 10.

5. Bethlehem Ephrata (see Genesis 35:19), to distinguish it from the other city of the same name in the tribe of Zabulon (Josue 19:15–16), was too small to have a chiliarch put in charge of it.

6. In view of the context the passage is apparently to be understood not of the Messias alone, but of the whole series of prophets whom God was to send after Moses. The Messias would of course be included in this series. That the prophecy was applied to the Messias at the time of Christ is clear

from John 1:45, 5:45–47, 6:14, but especially from Acts 3:22 and 7:37. In the light of these passages, at least we Christians are sure that the term "prophet" in Deuteronomy 18:15 includes also, and indeed chiefly, Christ. See A. Clamer, *La Sainte Bible*, II (Paris, 1946), 633 ff.

7. See, for example, Psalm 109 and Isaias 9:6–7.

8. Isaias 11:1–5, 42:1–4, 61:1–3; Zacharias 9:9–10.

9. Psalm 21; Isaias 52:14; 53.

10. Isaias 7:15, 53:2.

11. Isaias 42:2–3, 61:1.

12. "*And for them I sanctify myself, that they also may be sanctified in truth*" (John 17:19). "*I lay down my life for my sheep*" (John 10:15). *For there is one God, and one Mediator between God and men, himself man, Christ Jesus, who gave himself a ransom for all* (1 Timothy 2:5–6).

13. Luke 22:19–20; see Genesis 14:18.

14. Jesus answered, "*My kingdom is not of this world*" . . . *Pilate therefore said to him, "Thou art then a king?" Jesus answered, "Thou sayest it; I am a king*" (John 18:36–37).

15. See Kevin Smyth, "The Prophecy Concerning Juda: Gen. 49:8–12," CBQ, VII (1945), 290–305; A. Clamer, *La Sainte Bible*, I (Paris, 1953), 498–499.

16. For this passage see Lagrange in RBibl (1898), p. 525; Zapletal, *Alttestamentliches* (1903), p. 26; Burg in *Pastor Bonus*, XXVI, 257.

The interpretation of many rationalists: "until he comes to Silo [the city]" (See Josue 18:1), is at variance with all the versions and older commentators, and is voided by the following phrase "And he will be the expectation of the nations."

17. See 2 Kings 7:12–16; Psalm 88:29–38; 1 Paralipomenon 28:4.

18. See 2 Paralipomenon 11:13–17.

19. See 2 Kings 7:12–16; Psalm 88:28–38.

20. "It was Zorobabel of the tribe of Juda and of the royal line who led them back from captivity. Those who belonged to this tribe came back in droves and filled the whole country. The ten scattered tribes vanished among the Gentiles, except for those who, united under the name of Juda and under its standard, re-entered the land of their fathers" (Bossuet, *Discours sur l'histoire universelle*, II, 8).

21. See, for example, Pesch, *Praelectiones dogmaticae*, I, no. 225; Hoberg, *Die Genesis;* Schuster-Selbst, *Handbuch der biblischen Geschichte*, v. I.

22. See Daniel 9:2; Jeremias 25:11–12, 29:10.

23. *Shortened*, that is, fixed, determined.

24. *Saint of saints*, that is; the Messias Himself, anointed with the divinity at the time of the Incarnation and publicly proclaimed as such on the occasion of His baptism (Matthew 3:16). But since the Hebrew text has abstract terms here, *holiness of holiness*, many see in the expression not the person of the Messias, but the spiritual Holy Place which He built, the Church, anointed as it was with the Holy Spirit on Pentecost (Acts 2), or the actual Temple of Jerusalem, according to the interpretation of Dennefeld and others. See *La Sainte Bible*, VII (Paris, 1946), 690; Saydon, CCHS, p. 507.

25. *Shall be slain*. The Hebrew word indicates a violent death, of the sort inflicted for serious crimes.

26. In place of all the following words, *and the people that deny him*

shall not be his, the Hebrew has simply *and not to him.* Knabenbauer thinks the meaning is that the Messias' death will harm not Him, but the people and the city, as the following verses indicate. Others, like Dennefeld, translate *apart from any guilt of his.* Others offer still other renderings.

27. In Hebrew: *sacrifice and oblation-cake,* that is, bloody and unbloody sacrifices.

28. See Meignan, *Les derniers prophetes,* pp. 101, 103. By the end of the Middle Ages there were over twenty-two different interpretations of this prophecy, and at the present time there are more than one hundred. See Dennefeld, *op. cit.,* p. 688.

29. See Dr. Edmund Bayer, "Danielstudien, "ATAb (1912), no. 3, pp. 5, 74ff.

30. See Wolf, *Die 70 Wochen Daniels.* Kamphausen gives a synopsis of Wolf's thesis in ThLz (1899), p. 321. Among the older writers, Apollinaris of Laodicea and Hesychius seem to have followed this opinion.

31. This interpretation seems to be suggested by the Alexandrian Version of Daniel. Among the older writers, Julius Hilarionus, Harduin, and Calmet defend it. It is practically the common opinion among modern Protestants, whereas on the Catholic side Lagrange supports it (RBibl, 1904, p. 449). Lagrange met opposition from Hontheim in *Der Kath.* (1906), no. 2 p. 260, but finds support in Bayer, *op. cit.,* pp. 78ff.

We have taken our exposition of this passage chiefly from Bayer, who expressly avows that his opinion is only a hypothesis. Modern Catholic opinion seems to be a leaning towards a combination of the Maccabean and strictly Messianic interpretations. As Saydon says:

> Both interpretations have a side open to attack. The Messianic interpretation, which has always enjoyed the greatest favor in Catholic exegesis, seems to overlook the undeniable allusions of the prophecy to the Maccabean age and its relation to the general plan of the visions, while, on the other hand, the Maccabean interpretation ignores the fundamental fact that Daniel's interest, though centered on the age of Antiochus, extends far beyond the limits of that age, and that the restoration described by him, especially in 24, by far exceeds the rededication of the temple in 165 B.C. The combination of the two systems will give a more satisfactory interpretation (CCHS, 508 b).

The prophecy, then, will refer directly and literally to the Maccabean period, and indirectly, typically, to the Messianic. Fr. Dyson of the Pontifical Biblical Institute favors this view, as do Dennefeld, Gottsberger, and others. Indeed, it is a very attractive suggestion.

32. In answer to the objection that the Messianic benefits are foretold as coming before the end of the seventy weeks, Bayer replies that prophecies, without indicating any interval of time, often link different events which have some causal or typical connection, but are very widely separated in time. A good example of this is Christ's prediction of the Parousia; see above, no. 146.

33. Jeremias 30:18 (according to others 25:11 or 29:10); see 2 Paralipomenon 36:20–23. Note that, according to Bayer, "Daniel" borrowed from 1 and 2 Paralipomenon and from 1 and 2 Esdras.

34. See 2 Paralipomenon 36:22. It was the ancient custom to anoint the leader or king, and so it is Cyrus (according to this interpretation) who is referred to in the phrase *unto the anointed prince.*

35. Read 2 Maccabees 4 and Daniel 11:22.

36. See Daniel 9:26; 1 Macchabees 1:30–41; see also 1 Macchabees 1:12–14; 2 Macchabees 4:7ff and 1 Macchabees 1:57–62.

37. The Archbishop of Siena asked the Consistorial Congregation what the errors were for which a book of Holzhey's had been condemned. The Congregation answered on October 22, 1912, that "it lessens considerably, not to say denies completely, the Messianic character of the prophecy of the seventy weeks." See *Ned. K. St.* (1913), p. 41.

38. Bayer himself admits:

It must then be assumed here, if one wants to maintain the strictly historical interpretation, that Daniel did not know the extent of this span of time and hence committed a chronological error (*op. cit.*, pp. 86–87).

39. Others, however, are of the opinion that no fixed event corresponds to the end of the first seven weeks. As a matter of fact, the prophecy does not clearly state what will eventualize after the seven weeks.

40. See Jeremias 31:31.

41. Leviticus 25:8; see Gen. 29:18, 28.

42. 1 Esdras 7; 9:9. Note, however, that many recent authors agree with Van Hoonacker in placing Esdras' mission after that of Nehemias. But if this be true, then the decree of 1 Esdras 7 is not to be attributed to Artaxerxes Longimanus, but to Artaxerxes II Mnemon and is to be dated 398 B.C.

43. 2 Esdras 2:1–8. In this decree alone does one find explicit permission to rebuild the walls.

44. Besides, neither the year of Christ's birth nor that in which He started His public life has been definitely established. It is true that the Christian Era begins with 754 A.U.C.., but almost all agree that our Lord's circumcision took place not in 754 A.U.C., but some years before, some time between 748 and 752 A.U.C. For recent attempts to establish a precise chronology, see F. Borgongini Duca, *Le LXX settimane di Daniele et le date messianiche* (Padova, 1951); a summary of this work has appeared in English as *Messianic Chronology in Daniel* (New York, 1952); Damianus Lazzarato, *Chronologia Christi* (Neapoli, 1952); the latter discusses Borgongini Duca's work in *De ex Danielico 'nuncio Christi annis* (Neapoli, 1953).

45. Various reckonings are found in exegetical works and in lives of Christ.

46. See Matthew 27:51.

47. See Luke 19:41–44.

48. A. Van Hoonacker, *Les douze petits prophetes* (1908), p. 563.

49. The meaning is a short time later, after a little while, that is, with respect to time already elapsed.

50. In place of the words, *and the desired of all nations shall come,* the Hebrew has: "And there will come the desire (desirable, precious things) of all the nations." The LXX version agrees. So while St. Jerome's version indicates directly the coming of the Messias, the Hebrew text signifies directly the conversion of the Gentiles, offering themselves and their possessions to God—and this supposes the coming of the Messias Himself.

51. The Hebrew text, with which the LXX agrees, has: "The latest glory of this house will be greater than the early (glory)." And so the contrast is not precisely between the temple of Zorobabel and that of Solomon. It is a question rather of the latest glory of the temple of Jerusalem, which, even though materially renovated under Zorobabel and again under Herod the

Idumean, is considered practically one and the same sanctuary from the time of Solomon up to its final destruction. Thus disappears the question as to how the temple which our Lord entered could be the same as that of Zorobabel notwithstanding the renovation by Herod (John 2:20).

52. Peace consists in the totality of all the benefits which the Messias will bring. This is why Isaias calls the Messias the "Prince of Peace," and Micheas designates Him by the epithet, "Peace."

53. Exodus 19:16; Deuteronomy 5:23; Psalm 67:8–9; see Hebrews 12:26.

54. See 2 Maccabees 3:2, 5:16.

55. *Presently,* that is, immediately, or, according to the Hebrew text, unexpectedly. For many will not hear his forerunner and so will not be prepared.

56. For *a.* he is called *hā'adōn* (lord), a word predicated frequently, though not exclusively, of God; b. he comes to his temple, and God alone is Lord of the temple; *c.* preparing the way before the face of the Lord to come and preparing the way before the Lord of Hosts are considered as one and the same thing.

57. See John 7:37–39.

58. Iggereth hatteman, 125, 4, cited by Sepp, *Leben Jesu,* IV, 282.

59. The word *minḥâ* (offering) usually indicates an unbloody sacrifice. But this is by no means its exclusive signification, and to insist upon it is both unnecessary and unwarranted, especially since it is used throughout this very prophecy in the sense of sacrifice in general.

60. The meaning is: every instrument of war, that is, every weapon used against you, will prove harmless, and every tongue speaking in opposition to you will be condemned by you. Therefore the Messianic kingdom will be vanquished by neither material nor spiritual weapons.

61. See DB 1790.

Appendix 1

REVEALED RELIGION BEFORE CHRIST

1. Both primitive and Mosaic revelations had God as their author.
2. They were both preparations for and distant beginnings of the Christian religion.
3. Primitive religion contained, after a fashion, the very substance of the Christian religion.
4. The Mosaic Law, for the Hebrew people only, was given as a further development of primitive religion.
5. It was abrogated with the establishment of the Christian dispensation, not by formal revocation, but by being sublimated and perfected by Christ.

Appendix I

REVEALED RELIGION BEFORE CHRIST

I. Both the primitive and the Mosaic revelations had God as 170
their author. Both Christ and His Apostles recognized them as
divine. Christ and the Apostles considered the books of the Old
Testament divinely inspired and used them as such. These books
make it quite clear that God revealed some truths to Adam and
Eve and gave the Hebrew people a law through His representative,
Moses.

II. Both the primitive and the Mosaic revelations were prep- 171
arations for and distant beginnings of the Christian religion.
The Messianic prophecies prove this for both revelations. Those
prophecies contained, from the very beginning of the human race,
a promise of the great Liberator, the Christ, to whom all men of
antiquity must look for spiritual benefits. That promise, to be sure,
was expressed rather vaguely at first, but was given clearer meaning by later revelations. That the Mosaic revelation was a preparation for Christ is clear from the words of St. Paul: *For Christ is the
consummation of the Law unto justice for everyone who believes*
(Romans 10:4). And again: *But before the faith came we were
kept imprisoned under the Law, shut up for the faith that was to
be revealed. Therefore the Law has been our tutor unto Christ*
(Galatians 3:23-24).

Indeed Christ Himself declared: *"Do not think that I have
come to destroy the Law or the Prophets. I have not come to
destroy, but to fulfill"* (Matthew 5:17). *"Do not think that I shall
accuse you to the Father. There is one who accuses you, Moses, in
whom you hope. For if you believed Moses you would believe me
also"* (John 5:45-46).

III. Primitive revelation contained, after a fashion, the sub- 172
stance of the Christian religion. The ancient revelation began
by placing before our First Parents as an object of belief those two
basically fundamental truths which contain, ontologically, not
logically, all other articles of our religion, and form, therefore, the
essential core of the Christian religion. These truths are the existence of the one God who is the final end and who provides for

(281)

mankind in the supernatural order.[1] The third chapter of Genesis and the eleventh chapter of the Epistle to the Hebrews prove the statement just made.

Since the substance of our religion was revealed at the very beginning of the world, it may be said that man has always had substantially the same revealed religion. Thus, the Christian religion can be traced back to Adam and Eve. Of course, with them it existed in a very imperfect form.

173   **IV. The Mosaic Law, for the Hebrew people only, was given as a further development of primitive religion.** The Mosaic Law was given to the nation of Israel alone. Why, cannot be said, except that that nation was chosen by God. *"For you are a people sacred to the Lord, your God; he has chosen you from all the nations on the face of the earth to be a people peculiarly his own'* (Deuteronomy 7:6). As such, the Israelites were to perpetuate belief in the Messias to come and "to enjoy a privilege of holiness because of Christ, who was to come from them" (*S.Th.*, Ia-IIae, q. 98, a. 5). It was not God's will that the Law be promulgated among other nations, and, like the Gospel, be accepted by all.*

The Mosaic Law contained three types of precepts; moral, ceremonial, and judicial: "moral, which were really demands of natural law; ceremonial, which were detailed regulations for divine worship; judicial, which were determinations of the justice men were to observe in their dealings with one another" (*S.Th.*, Ia-IIae, q. 99, a. 4).

The ceremonial and judicial precepts affected foreign peoples in no way. The moral precepts did bind them materially, but not formally (*i.e.*, not because they were part of Mosaic legislation, but because of their inclusion in the natural law). See what St. Paul has to say on this matter in his Epistle to the Romans 2:12–15.

The sanctions of the Mosaic Law were limited to the temporal order. This was quite in harmony with the imperfection of the Law itself and the people to whom it was given.[2] It finds further explanation in the fact that the promises and threats of the Mosaic Law generally concerned, not individual persons, but the nation of Israel as such. Nonetheless, men living under the Law did not lack

---

* Foreigners could be reckoned as Jews by submitting to circumcision and thus becoming *"as natives of the land"* (Exodus 12:48); or, without being circumcised, by worshipping Yahweh and by keeping certain precepts of the Law. The former were known as proselytes of justice or of the covenant; the latter were called proselytes of the gate. Those who are called in Acts *phoboumenoi theon* (fearing God) seem to be practically the same as *proselytes of the gate.*

faith and the hope of receiving spiritual benefits, but these were promised, not by the Law, but by primitive religion. See the Epistle to the Hebrews 11:6; 13–16.

V. The Mosaic Law was abrogated with the establishment 174 **of the Christian.** St. Paul proves that the binding force of the Law was taken away by Christianity: *But before the faith came we were kept imprisoned under the Law, shut up for the faith that was to be revealed. Therefore the Law has been our tutor unto Christ, . . . But now that faith has come, we are no longer under a tutor. . . . There is neither Jew nor Greek* (Galatians 3:23–28).

The entire Law was abrogated and consequently its moral principles bind Christians, not because they are part of Mosaic legislation, but because they are contained in the natural law and in the Law of Christ.[3]

Once the Law had ceased to bind, the sanctions which it had formulated also lost their force. Consequently, the promises added to the fourth precept of the Decalogue must now, in the light of the Gospel, be understood in a spiritual sense.[4]

The Mosaic Law was abrogated, however, not as the result of any formal revocation, but simply because the purpose for which it had been given, and the state of affairs it envisioned, no longer obtained. It stands to reason that with the coming of what which the Law had been designed to foreshadow and prepare, the shadow and the preparation had no more reason for existence. Christ Himself said: *"I have not come to destroy, but to fulfill"* (Matthew 5:17). Christ fulfilled the Law of Moses and the Prophets by bringing their work to completion and perfection. He perfected the moral precepts by giving a more perfect explanation of God's will; He perfected the ceremonial precepts by substituting for the shadows and types the truth, the sacrifice and sacraments of the New Law; He perfected the judicial precepts by establishing the Catholic Church, of which the former people of God had been a figure. Hence the Old Law was abrogated, not by being ruled null and void, but by being perfected. That is why no formal revocation of the Law can be found in the New Testament, but simply the declaration of the Apostles that it no longer has any binding force.[5]

Notes

1. See St. Thomas, *S.Th.*, II-II, q. 1, a. 7; q. 2, a. 7.
2. See Hebrews 7:19; Romans 3:20; St. Thomas, *loc. cit.*, q. 99, a. 6.
3. This is at least the much more common view; see *Catechismus Romanus*, 3.4, no. 4. However, some authors think that only the ceremonial

and judicial precepts were abrogated, but that the moral precepts were even formally (as precepts of the Law) confirmed by Christ. See Vasquez, In *S.Th.*, I-II, disp. 180, c. 3.

4. Wilmers replies as follows to an objection based on Ephesians 6:2–3: The Apostle recalls the happy life in the land of Canaan, which was of old promised as a special reward of respect for parents in order to show how pleasing to God this respect is. But you may not conclude from this the same promise holds good in the New Testament. The truth of the matter is that life or happiness as promised in each Testament must be interpreted in the light of the conditions peculiar to each Testament. To the temporal happiness or earthly life as promised in the Old Testament corresponds the spiritual happiness or spiritual life as promised in the New (*De religione revelata*, p. 481). See St. Thomas, *S.Th.*, II-II, q. 122, a. 5, ad 4; Van Kasteren, *Van den Sinai*, p. 58.

5. See, for instance, Acts 15, Colossians 2:16, 17; Galatians 3:24; Hebrews 7:12, 18; 8:13; see A. Th. Harmann, *Die enge Verbindung des Alten Testaments mit dem Neuen* (1831); also RPA 28 (1919), 382; K. Benz, "Die Stellung Jesu zum alttestamentlichen Gesetz," *Bibl. Studien*, XIX (1914), 1.

Appendix II

CHRIST'S TEACHING ON THE PAROUSIA

---

1. Rationalists and Modernists insist that Christ believed that His second coming (parousia) and the end of the world were both imminent. Since He was sorely mistaken on this point, He was neither a true prophet nor a divine emissary. They base their objections on:

   a. our Lord's own words;

   b. the attitude of the Apostles and first Christians.

2. Investigation and refutation of these arguments.

CHRIST'S TEACHING ON THE PAROUSIA

Rationalist exegetes and Modernists unanimously claim that 175 Christ often and clearly foretold as quite imminent both His parousia (*i.e.,* His coming in glory to judge the world) and the end of the world. Since He was sadly mistaken in this matter, He could not have been a true prophet or an emissary of God.

Their objections are based on two arguments. The first, which will be taken up in detail, concludes that Christ s words, as recorded by the Evangelists, show that He believed the parousia and the end of the world were both near at hand. The second claims that statements made by the authors of the books in the New Testament prove that the Apostles and Christians of the first generation believed the day of judgment close at hand.[1]

1. The first argument, as noted, is based on the words of Christ Himself. Five principal statements, or discourses, of our Lord are advanced by the rationalists and Modernists as showing His belief in an imminent parousia.

a. In the twenty-fourth chapter of Matthew s Gospel Christ says to His disciples: *"Do you see all these things* [the buildings of the temple]*? Amen I say to you, there will not be left here one stone upon another that will not be thrown down"* (v. 2). His disciples then asked Him: *"Tell us, when are these things to happen, and what will be the sign of thy coming and of the end of the world?"* (v. 3). Christ then set about to answer this double question in one and the same discourse (vs. 5–33). From this fact the critics conclude that Christ taught that the destruction of the Temple and Jerusalem would coincide with the end of the world.

b. After the discourse on the end of the world, Christ said: *"Amen I say to you, this generation will not pass away till all these things have been accomplished"* (Matthew 24:34). Do not these words indicate that Christ believed the end of the world would come within a few years? Such is the conclusion of the rationalists and Modernists.

---

* See the special bibliography on p. 299.

c. When He sent His newly-chosen disciples to preach the Gospel *to the lost sheep of the house of Israel* (Matthew 10:6), Christ added: *"Amen I say to you, you will not have gone through the towns of Israel before the Son of Man comes"* (Matthew 10:23).

d. Christ taught His disciples that He would come to judge each individual on the basis of his works. He claimed that He was to come one day with angels and in the glory of the Father to act as judge, and He added: *"Amen I say to you, there are some of those standing here who will not taste death, till they have seen the Son of Man coming in his kingdom"* (Matthew 16:28).

e. On trial before the high priest Christ said: *"I say to you, hereafter you shall see the Son of Man sitting at the right hand of the Power and coming upon the clouds of heaven"* (Matthew 26:64).

The five passages quoted above are those usually quoted by the critics to support their contention. However, it is well also to study the parallel passages in the other Synoptics.

176   It is easy to see the serious consequences of the rationalist and Modernist contention. If their interpretation of our Lord's words is correct, then Christ was certainly neither divine nor a messenger of God. But since there are so many solid arguments for Christ's divine mission, arguments whose force not one of our adversaries has been able to weaken, it is very unreasonable to attribute an error of such magnitude to Christ, unless definite and conclusive proof can be given. Such proof has not been advanced, as shall be clear from the following considerations.

This is not an attempt to deny that the first Christians, particularly those who were Jewish converts, expected the Lord's parousia to come quickly. The Jews, though, pictured to themselves a Messias who would judge his own people and the Gentiles, then inaugurate a reign of endless happiness. Consequently one must be careful to determine whether the expectation held by many early Christians had its source in the preaching of Christ and His Apostles, or in an age-old Jewish conviction now clouding Christian doctrine.

177   1. Certainly Christ often and emphatically foretold that He would one day come in glory to act as judge. But Christ clearly signified that His coming would not be that expected by the Jews, a coming in which He would lead the people of Israel to victory and crush the Gentiles. His coming was to affect the spiritual world, not the temporal. When He came in glory, He would judge all

men on the basis of their works. Just as He purified the idea of the Messias and the Messianic kingdom, so He purged from the idea of judgment the materialistic and nationalistic elements added by the Jews. For illustrations of this read the Gospel of St. Matthew, 7:22–23, 10:32–33, 13:36–50, 16:24–27, and chapter 25. Read St. Luke's Gospel, 13:23–26.

Christ admitted frankly that no one knew the time of this judgment and the end of the world: *"But of that day or hour no one knows, neither the angels in heaven, nor the Son, but the Father only"* (Mark 13:32).[2] *"It is not for you to know the times or dates which the Father has fixed by his own authority"* (Acts 1:7). Since the judge will come without warning, He emphatically warned the Apostles and all to be alert lest they be caught unprepared: *"Take heed, watch and pray, for you do not know when the time is. . . . And what I say to you, I say to all, 'Watch'"* (Mark 13:33–37). This warning, based on the uncertainty of the day of judgment, is valid whether the end of the world is imminent or not; for since the last day of the world will find each man in the same condition in which his own last day found him, even supposing a delayed parousia, these words applied most aptly and still apply to all men: *"Watch, for you do not know when the time is."*

Since this is the case, there was no need for Christ to assail directly and explicitly the false notion of an imminent end of the world. Neither can one reasonably expect of Him a refutation of this sort, since He was wont to ignore errors which posed no threat to religion and good moral conduct.

Indirectly, however, our Lord did rule out the aforementioned 178 opinion, especially by the prophecies of His earthly kingdom. He clearly foretold that the Gospel would be preached to all the nations of the entire world before His second coming. *"The gospel must first be preached to all nations"* (Mark 13:10). *"And this gospel of the kingdom shall be preached in the whole world, for a witness to all nations; and then will come the end"* (Matthew 24:14. See 26:13, 28:19–20; Luke 24:47; Acts 1:8). The words themselves, their subject matter, and the Messianic prophecies are clearly not quoted as referring to a merely relative universality of the kingdom.

It is evident that preaching of this sort could not possibly be carried out within little more than a generation or, for that matter, within any short span of time. Further indications of a long delay are the various accidents and perils which Christ says will be the lot of His disciples,[3] and especially the manner in which the kingdom of Heaven will develop. Christ compared His kingdom to a grain of mustard seed, to yeast hidden in flour: *"Thus is the kingdom of God, as though a man should cast seed into the earth, then sleep and rise, night and day, and the seed should sprout and grow without his knowing it. For of itself the earth bears the crop, first the blade, then the ear, then the full grain in the ear'* (Mårk 4:26–28).

Christ clearly noted that the end of the world would neither coincide with the destruction of Jerusalem, nor follow on its heels. After He had foretold the destruction of Jerusalem He added: *"And they will be . . . led away as captives to all the nations. And Jerusalem will be trodden down by the Gentiles, until the times of the nations be fulfilled"* (Luke 21:24).

These considerations show us that Christ was by no means convinced that the end of the world was close at hand.

179   2. What of the words of our Lord cited by the rationalists and Modernists? In explaining the teaching of any author, correct method requires that a real contradiction among his assertions should not be admitted so long as there lies at hand another probable solution. Surely this rule is to be applied to the teaching of Christ, whose divine mission stands established by so many compelling arguments. An explanation which brings the objectionable passages into harmony with the doctrine already set forth is far from being impossible.

a. The first statement was taken from the twenty-fourth chapter of Matthew's Gospel. From our Lord's words there (24:4ff) the critics concluded that He taught that the destruction of the Temple and Jerusalem would coincide with the end of the world. The whole difficulty' disappears if the *literary form* of the discourse is considered. That form is prophetic, not historical. It is a prophecy in which two events (the destruction of the city and the end of the world) are linked together figuratively without regard for chronology. Christ had been asked a double question. In His answer He prescinds from the question of time and considers those elements which both events will have in common. As a result, in describing the type, He inserts elements which apply to the antitype.[4]

180   b. The second text brought forward by the critics is this: *"Amen I say to you, this generation will not pass away till all these things have been accomplished"* (Matthew 24:34). This text (and the parallel texts in the other Synoptics) follows the eschatological

discourse, wherein is combined a treatment of the destruction of the city and of the end of the world. All admit that the treatment is of such nature that it is hard to decide which of its elements apply to the former disaster, which to the latter, and which to both. Some believe that our Lord deliberately gave His hearers a picture without perspective, wishing to conceal from them the exact time sequence, much as the Old Testament prophets were wont to do. Others, especially recent authors, think that here are found gathered together into one discourse several statements about things to come made by our Lord on various occasions, so that the confusion and vagueness are due, not to Christ's manner of speaking, but to editorial tradition.[5]

According to Billot this case presents a prophecy with a twofold aspect. Consequently, it can be said to be fulfilled in a twofold manner: primarily in itself (real fulfillment), and secondarily in the event anticipating it, in its image or figure (figurative fulfillment). The secondary fulfillment, indeed, does not immediately strike the senses, since it is not literal and material, but it is yet based on truth. The figure as such already contains in some manner the thing prefigured, and gives it an anticipated existence, especially when the type and the antitype had been previously combined in the same prophecy. In cases of this kind, the perfect fulfillment of the one cannot even be thought of apart from the complete fulfillment of the other.[6] According to this theory, everything which concerns the last day in the prophecy under consideration was fulfilled to a certain extent in the destruction of the city of Jerusalem, and consequently before "this generation" had passed away. The prophecy contains two aspects. One was fulfilled literally and completely shortly afterwards. The other is said to be fulfilled in a figurative manner only, but still in a way sufficient to justify the use of the phrase *until all these things.*

Moreover, if everything is weighed carefully, and if the word "generation" is taken in the obvious sense of Christ's contemporaries, this statement can apply not to the final judgment considered in itself, but only to the destruction of the city. After the destruction, as is known from the words and prediction of Christ Himself, there was to begin an era during which the Jews would be scattered abroad and Jerusalem would be trodden underfoot by the Gentiles *until the times of the nations be fulfilled* (Luke 21:24). How could Christ, foreseeing the "times of the nations" following the destruction of Jerusalem, have said that the generation of His contemporaries would survive until the end of the world? The context seems to indicate that this position is correct. After the words *"this generation will not pass away till all these things have been accomplished"* there follows: *"But of that day and hour no one knows, not even the angels of heaven, but the Father only"* (Matthew 24:36). From this one can deduce that the words "all these things" look to the nearer event, the destruction of the city, which will take place during the lifetime of this generation, in contrast to that day, still far away and altogether uncertain and hidden, the day of the Lord's coming.*

181   c. The third text adduced is this: *"You will not have gone through the towns of Israel before the Son of Man comes"* (Matthew 10:23). Although these words were recorded by St. Matthew on the occasion of the temporary mission of the Apostles to the Jews, they do not refer, at least not exclusively, to that trial mission, but to the Apostles' definitive mission to the whole world. The context makes this clear. Were the Apostles, during that short trial mission, handed over to councils, scourged in synagogues, hailed before governors and kings? Was it at that time that a brother handed his brother over to death, and a father his son? (See Matthew 10:17–21.) Matthew gathered together in this passage admonitions and predictions which our Lord made to His followers on various occasions, and the other Evangelists record them in other passages. If this is kept in mind, the meaning of the text is: the Apostles will not finish the cities where the Israelites dwell; they will not complete the conversion of Israel before the last day arrives. In this way Christ suggested rather vaguely what

---

* The foregoing explanation of this difficult passage, while satisfactory and still quite popular among commentators, is perhaps unnecessary. It is an attempt to unravel the apparent fusion of temporal and eschatological elements in our Lord's discourse. Recently, however, A. Feuillet published in *Revue Biblique* a series of brilliant articles in which he demonstrated that the fusion is only apparent. Actually, our Lord confines His remarks to the one event, the destruction of Jerusalem. The apocalyptic style in which He couches those remarks has misled commentators in the direction of the eschatological and has complicated their exegesis. Feuillet's view eliminates much of the complication, much of the confusion. His explanation is natural, unstrained, consistent and convincing. There is question of *a parousia*, yes, but not of *the* Parousia; of the victorious Christ's temporal judgment of Jerusalem, but not of His eschatological judgment of mankind. This very attractive solution throws refreshing light not only on the so-called Eschatological Discourse, but also on many other statements of our Lord which have hitherto furnished grist for rationalistic mills. An extended application of Feuillet's system may be seen in *CCHS*, 715b ff.

St. Paul later wrote quite clearly: *For I would not, brethren, have you ignorant of this mystery . . . that a partial blindness only has befallen Israel, until the full number of Gentiles should enter* (Romans 11:25).

d. The fourth text is: *"Amen I say to you, there are some of* 182 *those standing here who will not taste death, till they have seen the Son of Man coming in his kingdom"* (Matthew 16:28 and parallel passages in the Synoptics).

The meaning of these words seems to be: the Son of Man will one day come to judge the whole world. Do not wonder that I say this of Myself: there are some of those who are standing here who will not die before they have seen a manifestation of My royal power so dazzling that they will have no further doubts about My power as a judge.

There is some dispute which manifestation Christ had in mind. Some explain it as referring to the Transfiguration, which all the Synoptics go on immediately to describe, and which was in fact a sort of anticipated parousia. But the Transfiguration took place six days later, and the words *"there are some"* seem to imply a longer interval. Others think that it refers to our Lord's Ascension, when the Son of Man came into His kingdom,[7] or to the pouring forth of the Holy Spirit with the ensuing miracles, by means of which the kingdom of Christ was manifested in glory. Still, many refer the words to the destruction of Jerusalem, which was a frightful judgment leveled by Christ, now reigning in heaven, against a sinful nation, and at the same time, a sort of confirmation of the Messianic kingdom which He had previously established. Only a few of Christ's hearers were to survive until this manifestation of divine power: *"There are some"*

e. The fifth objection is based on the following passages: *Here-* 183 *after you shall see the Son of Man sitting at the right hand of the Power and coming upon the clouds of heaven* (Matthew 26:64); *And you shall see the Son of Man sitting at the right hand of the Power and coming with the clouds of heaven* (Mark 14:62); *But henceforth, the Son of Man will be seated on the right hand of the power of God* (Luke 22:69). After comparing these parallel passages, it seems more likely that the words of our Lord before the high priest do not refer to the parousia. To see the Son of Man sitting at the right hand of God and coming with the clouds of heaven are metaphorical expressions taken from the Old Testament,[8] the meaning of which is to see or to have visible proof that the Son of Man has taken possession of His kingdom. Christ then, said in effect: You have said it yourself; I am the true Messias, in a lowly state at present. But before long you will know (through My resurrection and ascension, the descent of the Holy Spirit, the miracles of the Apostles, etc.) that I have received My kingdom from the hands of God, that through My efforts the kingdom of God promised by the prophets has been inaugurated.

184   3. The above remarks about the preconceived notions and the imperfect knowledge of chronology among the first Christians may have prepared a clear path to a fuller solution of various difficulties.

It is evident, from what has already been said, that the opponents bring forward many sayings of Christ which seem to be eschatological, but which in fact have nothing to do with the parousia. The source for the eschatological flavor of those sayings can be discovered. An examination of parallel passages shows that the Evangelists, in general, did not always record our Lord's statements in His exact words, but in their own words or words taken from the oral catechesis or written sources. May not the apparent eschatological meaning apparently given by some statements because of their wording or context be explained partly from the fact that the day of each man's death is for him equivalent to the day of the general judgment, the parousia,[9] and partly from the faulty understanding of the men who edited the material used by the Evangelists? If those editors were not certain of what precise events our Lord's predictions referred to, may one not suspect that this lack of clear understanding on their part exerted some influence on the way in which they arranged our Lord's statements?

Furthermore, every Christian knows for certain that the remarks of our Lord in the Gospels referred to by the adversaries do not actually say: "The end of the world is near." Yet, at first glance they do seem to have this meaning. What is the source of this impression? It may be:

a. Christ Himself. In this case one must suppose with Maldonatus that Christ purposely spoke in a confused and vague way "lest anyone should learn the time of the end of the world," or, more probably, lest anyone should learn how far away the parousia was.

b. The Evangelists. If this is true, another question remains unanswered, namely, why did they choose to be so obscure?

c. Editorial tradition, to which we must perhaps assign the situation and arrangement of the different statements of our Lord as they stand in the Gospels.

d. Our own understanding. Certainly prophetic style is always somewhat obscure,[10] and the texts of the Old Testament are not so clear as they were to the first Christians, especially those converted from Judaism, nor do present hearers have the advantage of the explanations and oral instructions which the Apostles gave them.[11]

4. The objections drawn from the writings of the Apostles, 185 especially those of St. Paul, may be answered as follows: [12]

a. Texts expressly concerned with the parousia. Numerous texts of this nature are found in the writings of the Apostles. Of particular interest are the words of St. Paul in his First Epistle to the Thessalonians 5:1-6, the Second Epistle to the Thessalonians 2:1-9, and the Second Epistle of Peter 3:8-14.

In these instances the Apostles clearly teach that the time of the parousia has *not* been revealed, that the judgment will take place without warning at a date unknown to us: *the day of the Lord is to come as a thief in the night* (1 Thessalonians 5:2; see 2 Peter 3:10; Acts 1:7-8).

The Apostles, following Christ, teach that no one knows the date of the parousia, and so with Christ they urge watchfulness: *Therefore, let us not sleep . . . but let us be wakeful and sober* (1 Thessalonians 5:6).[13]

Again, the Apostles were not of the opinion that the parousia was near at hand. For they knew that their ministry was to continue *even to the consummation of the world* (Matthew 28:20), whenever that should be, and consequently they took care to select not only co-workers but also successors. They knew, too, that the Gospel was to be preached to the whole world; [14] they knew, finally, that various signs had to be verified before the Lord would come: *We beseech you . . . not to be . . . terrified . . . as though the day of the Lord were near at hand. Let no one deceive you in any way, for . . . unless the apostasy comes first . . .* (2 Thessalonians 2:1ff).

As a matter of fact, the Apostles very often intimate that the parousia is quite distant: *Do not be ignorant of this one thing, that one day with the Lord is as a thousand years, and a thousand years as one day. The Lord does not delay in his promises, but for your sake is long-suffering* (2 Peter 3:8-9).

b. In addition, many other texts are pointed out by our adver- 186 saries in which the Apostles speak or seem to speak of the parousia, not expressly, but in passing. Judging from these passages it would seem quite clear, according to the rationalists, that the Apostles believed that the day of judgment was soon to dawn.

However, note the words 'seem to speak," for in very many instances they do not consider even in passing the parousia, but are concerned with the particular judgment or the final period of the world's existence.[15] When the Apostles urge watchfulness, harmony, patience, when they exhort their readers to cast off the works of darkness and to put on the weapons of light, when they ask their readers to live perfect lives because *the night is far advanced; the day is at hand* (Romans 13:12), *The Lord is near* (Philippians 4:5), etc., they refer not so much to the nearness of the Lord's coming at the end of the world, as to the imminence of the particular judgment of individual men.[16] This is evident first of all from the fact that the Apostles, when speaking of the general judgment, always refer to the brilliance and majesty of the Judge coming to judgment.[17] It is also evident from those passages in which the Apostles urge watchfulness, but at the same time state quite clearly and explicitly that they are doing so because the Lord's coming is near at hand for individual men by reason of life's shortness.[18] That the Apostles were not even thinking of the end of the world and its destruction can be deduced from the fact that they repeatedly speak not of the ruin, but of the universal restoration of the world through the Gospel and the grace of Jesus Christ.[19]

Yet, other texts are pointed to in which the Apostles seem to speak of the parousia as close at hand, as when they say that they are living *in the last days* (Acts 2:17), that *it is the last hour* (1 John 2:18), that *the final age of the world has come* (1 Corinthians 10:11), and then go on to enumerate the signs appearing at that awful time.[20]

But in the light of the manner of expression peculiar to Sacred Scripture,[21] such phrases are to be taken as referring to the final period of the world's existence, stretching from the day of the Messias to the second coming of the Lord to judge the world. The Apostles used terms not unlike those employed by the Old Testament prophets, who used the same words to announce that the Messianic era was coming.[22]

In addition to the passages quoted, there remain some texts in the Apostolic writings, especially in Paul's Epistles, in which the question of the parousia is actually considered, though just in passing. Indeed, it must be admitted that in the texts the nearness of the day of the Lord seems to be implied to some extent,[23] but they need not necessarily be taken as referring to that nearness.

Is it not reasonable to explain difficult passages in the light of clearer ones? Moreover, had this been the general teaching of Christ, the Apostles would naturally have taught that the end of the world was imminent. Otherwise they would have been contradicting themselves and Christ.[24] But an explanation harmonizing the difficult passages with the doctrine set forth above is not impossible, as the following remarks will show.

c. Rationalists find a special objection in the words of St. Paul 187 in his First Epistle to the Thessalonians: *For this we say to you in the word of the Lord, that we who live, (hemeis hoi zôntes) who survive until the coming of the Lord, (hoi perileipomenoi 'eis̄ ten parousian tôu Kyriou) shall not precede those who have fallen asleep* (1 Thessalonians 4:15; see verses 12–13 and 15–17).

Does it not follow from these words, say the opponents, that St. Paul thought he would still be alive when our Lord came to judge the world? And, holding such an opinion, was he not clearly in error?

In the light of the explanation given above, the opinion of the rationalists is *a priori* extremely improbable, since in this case the Apostle would have been contradicting himself. In his other Epistles,[25] and, to be sure, in this Epistle,[26] he frankly admits his ignorance of the date of the parousia. We have no right to admit this contradiction as long as a harmonious and reasonable explanation is still possible. And indeed, even though this passage is variously explained, an explanation which excludes any real contradiction is definitely possible.

It should be remarked at the outset that St. Paul's view here is very limited. He is not considering the general question of the parousia. He is concerned not with all men, but only with Christians, and not even with all Christians, but only with the just. Furthermore, his remarks are called forth by a very special difficulty in one particular church, that of Thessalonica. And the point of the difficulty in this instance is not precisely either the fact or the time of the parousia, but merely the rather strange concern of his correspondents over the question of precedence—will the dead be at a disadvantage in comparison to the living when the Lord comes in glory? His answer prescinds from the time element, which does not enter the picture. And it is quite significant that in all his other letters he hardly even alludes to the matter of the parousia. If it were of such vital importance, of such immediate concern, how explain this silence? Indeed, there are many clear indications, and not just in his later Epistles, that St. Paul did not expect to survive until the Lord should come in glory. Much of the difficulty arises from a failure to study this text, and others also, in the light of the general context of Pauline teaching and even in the immediate context of the letter itself.

The more common opinion, advanced long ago by the Fathers,[27] holds that the Apostle was using a rhetorical figure known as *enallage,* or switch of person, which would amount to this: "We who are alive, that is, *whoever* shall be alive, whether it be some of us or some of those who will come after us, whose personality I take upon myself that I may speak of them in my own name." [28]

Billot [29] has developed this explanation more fully and clearly, deducing from the contrast with *those asleep in the Lord* (v. 15), that *we who live* are those living in the Lord, those who still remain for the coming of the Lord. And as the pronoun "we" in ordinary conversation often is used to designate a class of people in which we wish to include ourselves, so St. Paul, writing to living Christians, by using the phrase *we who live,* meant: ours, that is, those who are on our side, the faithful, those living in the Lord, who are still on earth when the Lord appears. This finds corroboration in the appositional phrase *who survive,* for this verb suggests a "very small remainder," and so Paul seems to suggest that the day of the parousia is still a long way off, since the number of the faithful who will be alive on that day will be quite insignificant compared with the number of those dying in Christ.

Furthermore, to insist that St. Paul, by using the expression *we who live,* indicated that he expected to be still on earth for the parousia, would be to attribute to him the absurd expectation that all of his readers would likewise survive. For they, too, would be included in the *we who.* One can use the same argument as that advanced by the rationalists and prove that St. Paul expected not to be alive for the parousia. In First Corinthians he writes: *Now God has raised up the Lord and will also raise us up by his power* (6:14).

Some feel that in view of the two participles in Greek (*zôntes, perileipomenoi*) the sense of the phrase is conditional, namely, "if he and his contemporaries should still be living." [30]

Others [31] think that St. Paul is expressing an opinion held by the Thessalonians, and that he is using an *argumentum ad hominem.* According to this opinion, a double error had crept into the thinking of the Thessalonians; first, that those who had died would be at a disadvantage compared with the living at the time of the parousia, and second that the parousia was very imminent. They would have expressed their first error as follows: "we who live, who survive until the coming of the Lord, shall precede those who have fallen asleep." With these same words St. Paul refutes this first error by saying that *we who live . . . shall not precede those who have fallen asleep.*

Others [32] think that the Apostle designates by the words *until the coming ('eis̄ ten parousian)* the goal to which those who are yet alive are destined, aside from the question as to whether those now living (himself among them) would reach that goal or not; [33] this we cannot know, since the date of the parousia is unknown to all.

Whatever the explanation may be, one thing is clear, and that is that the words do not indicate that the parousia was so near that St. Paul hoped to be present to witness the glorious second coming of the Lord.

Special Bibliography for Appendix II

Billot, Louis Cardinal: *La parousie* (1920).

Schenz, A.: *Der Zeitpunkt der Wiederkunft Jesu nach den Synoptikern* (1922).

Weiss, K.: "Exegetisches zur Irrtumslosigkeit und Eschatologie Jesu Christi," NtAb (1906), 4ff.

The following publications also contain articles of importance for this subject:

CCHS 670a ff; 715a ff;

Etudes (1917–1918);

RBibl XII (1915), 393; LV (1948), 481–502; LVI (1949), 61–92; 340–364; LVII (1950), 43–62; 180–211;

RPA XI (1911), 176; 27 (1918), 801; 28 (1919), 5, 161;

ThGl (121), pp. 257, 321; (1922), p. 1.

Notes

1. See Romans 13:11; 1 Corinthians 7:29–31; 10:11; 1 Thessalonians 4:15–17; Hebrews 10:37; 1 Peter 4:5–7; James 5:8–9; 1 John 2:18; etc.

2. It is clear from the fact that the Son is contrasted to the Father that the statement is to be understood of the Son insofar as He is a man. In any respect, it makes no difference in the present discussion whether Christ as man was at that time really ignorant about the date of the judgment or whether He really did know it, but with a knowledge which He could not divulge, for some reason or other.

3. See Matthew 24:4–14; 10:16ff; Mark 13:5–13; Luke 21:8–19.

4. See Knabenbauer, *In Matthaeum*, II, 353; Le Hir, "Les prophetes d'Israel," in *Etudes bibliques*, v. 1 (1869), p. 81; Billot, *La parousie*, pp. 15ff. Note that St. Luke clearly indicates the chronological sequence. Verses 10–23 have to do with the ruin of the temple and the city; verse 24 with the time between the end of the city and that of the world; and verses 25–31 with the parousia. Billot, *op. cit.*, pp. 72ff, is excellent for this passage.

5. Batiffol states: "We prefer to think that editorial tradition created the confusion by gathering into one single discourse all the statements of Jesus concerning the future." (*L'enseignement de Jesus*, p. 257). Be careful not to confuse the "editorial tradition" with the Evangelists themselves. For the Evangelists, according to a critical hypothesis which is at least probable, often made use of source material in which the primitive tradition had gathered together different sermons or remarks of Christ. The result would be that the sequence of grouping our Lord's statements such as we find it in the Gospels today is not always the work of the Evangelists themselves.

6. This method is characteristic of all the prophets. See, for instance, Isaias 7:13–16, 9:6; Malachias 4:5; Matthew 11:14, 17:12; Psalm 7:1. See also Billot, *op. cit.*, pp. 61ff; Le Hir, *op. cit.*, pp. 67ff.

7. See Daniel 7:13–14.

8. Psalm 109:1—*Sit at my right hand till I make* (see Matthew 22:43); Daniel 7:13–14—*I beheld therefore in the vision of the night, and lo, one like the son of man came with the clouds of heaven, and he came even to the Ancient of days: and they presented him before him. And he gave him power, and glory, and kingdom.*

Lagrange states:

The Sanhedrin was by no means made up of apocalyptics, and when Jesus made reference in its presence to the symbol of the Son of Man, all those who interpreted Daniel according to the spirit of his text would have understood it as referring simply to the establishment of the kingdom of God, not to a dazzling vision after the fashion of a catastrophe (RBibl, (1904), p. 508).

9. Why then does Christ say to all [Mark 13:37] what applies only to those who will then be living, if it is not because it does not apply to all in the manner I have explained? For that day [of the Lord's coming] will come for each one when the day comes for him to pass away in the condition in which he is to be judged on that day (St. Augustine, *Epistola 199 ad Hesych.*, no. 3).

See St. Leo the Great, *Sermo 19*, no. 3.

10. See above nos. 144ff.

11. See 1 Thessalonians 5:1; 2 Thessalonians 2:5.

12. See Billot, *op. cit.*, pp. 192ff; F. Tillmann, *Die Wiederkunft Christi nach den Paulinischen Briefen* (1909); *Ned. K. St.* (1915), p. 241; ZkTh (1916); p. 167; RBibl (1915), p. 393; *Civiltà* (1918–1920); RAp, 33 (1921), 226, 307.

13. See no. 177. Worthy of note is the response of June 18, 1915, of the Biblical Commission to *Dubium II:*

Whether, keeping before one's eyes the genuine idea of the Apostolic Office and of St. Paul's undoubted fidelity to the teaching of the Master; likewise, the Catholic dogma regarding the inspiration and inerrancy of the Scriptures, whereby all that the sacred writer asserts, enunciates, suggests, must be held to be asserted, enunciated, suggested by the Holy Ghost; also, weighing the text of the Apostle's Epistles, considered in themselves, which are before all in harmony with the speech of the Lord Himself, it is meet to affirm that the Apostle Paul in his writings certainly said nothing which is not in harmony with that ignorance of the time of the Parousia which Christ Himself claimed to be men's portion.

Answer: In the affirmative—See AAS (1915), p. 357, translation in RSS, p. 128.

14. See no. 178. When St. Paul remarks here and there that the Gospel has been preached to the whole world, etc. (Colossians, 1:6, 23; Romans 1:8), he must be understood as meaning relative universality; see Billot, *op. cit.*, pp. 94ff.

15. In these explanations we are following the opinion of Billot, although others have different explanations. We are omitting objections taken from the Apocalypse, because in his opinion there is no question there of the parousia (except for ch. 20), and consequently it occasions no difficulty.

16. See above, no. 177.

17. See 2 Thessalonians 1:7, 10, 2:8; 1 Timothy 6:15; Titus 2:13; 1 Corinthians 1:7; Colossians 3:4; 1 Peter 4:13ff; Apocalypse 20.

18. See 1 Thessalonians 4:11; 2 Thessalonians 3:12; 1 Timothy 2:1; James 4:13–16; 1 Corinthians 7:25–35; 1 Peter 4; 2 Peter 1:13–15.

19. See Romans 13:1–7; Ephesians 5:1–9; 1 Peter 2:13–23; 3:1–7; Colossians 3:18–25; James 2:1–17, 5:1–6; 1 John 3:11–24, etc.

20. See Acts 2:16–21 (along with Joel 2:28–32); 1 John 2:18–19.

21. See Isaias 2:2; Jeremias 48:47, 49:39. This sort of interpretation turns up in rabbinic exegesis too, and in the writings of the Fathers, such as St. Augustine. See his *De genesi contra Manichaeos*, bk. 1, ch. 23; *In Joan. Evang.*, bk. 9, no. 6, etc.

It must be said that no definite chronological information can be gathered from expressions like "it is the last hour" or other similar expressions which we read in Scripture. For expressions of this sort are used to signify not some short hour of time, but rather the final condition of the world, which is, as it were, in the last era. It is like the term "old age," which indicates the final age of a man, but does not signify precisely any definite length of time (St. Thomas, *Suppl.*, q. 88, a. 3, ad 3).

22. See no. 162, 2.

23. For example, 1 Thessalonians 4:12–17; 1 Corinthians 15:51–52; 2 Corinthians 5:3.

24. That the Apostles as hagiographers taught error in religious matters (or any other matters) is excluded by the Catholic principle of the inspiration and consequent inerrancy of Sacred Scripture. Nor "is it permitted to the Catholic exegete to assert that the Apostles, although under the inspiration of the Holy Ghost, teach no error, nevertheless express their own human views, into which error or deception can enter," according to the response of the Biblical Commission to *Dubium I*. See AAS (1915), translation in RSS, p. 127.

Holzmeister, in ZkTh (1916), p. 170, makes a distinction and thinks that St. Paul did not expect the parousia as certainly imminent, but that he considered it possible, even probable. Indeed, according to the teaching of Christ, the time of the parousia was unknown, and so it is always possible that it is at hand. This possibility developed into probability and finally into hope as the result of indications then present and prevelant. In this case St. Paul did not form an erroneous opinion, but only a judgment of probability.

Although this view does not seem to conflict with the response of the Biblical Commission, still we cannot take a favorable view of it. Do not Christ and the Apostles imply that the end of the world is not imminent (see nos. 178 and 185)? Furthermore, it is hard to imagine that St. Paul, in preaching Christ's doctrine of the parousia, played the philosopher, making a distinction between an "opinion" and a "judgment of probability," and that his hearers and first readers understood this distinction.

25. See 2 Corinthians 1:8–9, 4:11–12, 16, 5:2, 8–9; 1 Thessalonians 2:1–9.

26. See no. 185.

27. St. John Chrysostom, *In Ep. 1 ad Thess. 4, Hom. 8, no. 2; In I Cor. Hom. 42, no. 2;* St. Augustine, *The City of God,* bk. 20, c. 20; St. Thomas, *In omnes divi Pauli epistolas commentarium,* Leonine Edition (1858).

The Biblical Commission weighs this patristic opinion and answers thus to *Dubium III:*

> Whether, attention being paid to the Greek phrase, *hemeis hoi ˉzontes, hoi perileipomenoi,* also the explanation of the Fathers being weighed, especially that of St. John Chrysostom, who was highly versed both in his country's language and in the Pauline Epistles, it is lawful to reject as far-fetched and destitute of solid foundation, the interpretation traditional in the Catholic schools—also retained by the reformers of the sixteenth century themselves—which explains the words of St. Paul without in any wise implying the affirmation of a Parousia so imminent that the Apostle added himself and his readers to those of the faithful who should survive to meet Christ. Answer: In the negative (See AAS (1915), p. 357, translation in RSS, p. 128).

28. Thus Cornelius a Lapide on this passage.

29. Billot's *La parousie,* pp. 253–262.

30. Holzmeister, ZkTh (1917), pp. 167–182.

31. Cornely, *Introductio specialis in Novum Testamentum,* 2nd ed., pp. 413ff; F. Prat, *The Theology of St. Paul,* volume II.

32. P. Konstantin Rosch, TuG˙ (1911), p. 492, and *Munster Pastoralblatt* (1918), p. 18; see Tillmann, *op. cit.,* p. 55.

33. The preposition *eis* rarely signifies time, but quite often purpose; see Mark 6:8; Luke 9:13, 5:4; Matthew 8:34; 25:1, John 12:13; 1 Corinthians 16:1; Ephesians 3:2; Jude 6.

We speak in the same manner: "When a colonel reports, 'Of the assault troops assigned there are still a thousand men left for the coming battle,' he affirms only that these thousand can be taken into account for the coming battle, not that they are actually used therein." See TuG (1918), p. 449.

Scriptural Index

Genesis
3:15 — 253
9:26–27 — 254
22:18 — 254
29:18, 28 — 276, n. 41
41 — 89
49:1, 8, 10 — 260
49:8–10 — 254
49:8–12 — 274, n. 15

Exodus
7:8–12 — 99
8:16–19 — 99
12:48 — 282
19:16 — 266

Leviticus
25:8 — 276, n. 41

Numbers
1:26–27 — 261
10:14 — 261
11:25–26 — 99
22–24 — 96
24:17 — 254

Deuteronomy
5:23 — 267
7:6 — 282
13:1–3 — 99
18:15 — 257

Josue
18:1 — 274, n. 16

Judges
1:1–2 — 261
20:18 — 261

2 Kings
7:12–13 — 254
7:12–16 — 260, 261

1 Paralipomenon
28:4 — 260

2 Paralipomenon
11:13–17 — 261
36:20–23 — 262
36:22 — 262

1 Esdras
7; 9:9 — 264, n. 42

2 Esdras
2:1–8 — 276, n.43
6:12ff — 101

Psalms
2:1–4 — 270
2:6–8 — 258
7:1 — 300
15:9–11 — 257
15:10 — 175
21:8–9, 17–18, 19 — 256
67:8–9 — 266
68:22 — 256
71:4, 5 — 258
71:7 — 258, 269
71:8, 11, 17 — 258
88:29–38 — 260, 261
88:36–38 — 254
109:1 — 293, n. 8
109:4 — 258
117:23 — 226

Isaias
2:2 — 296, n. 21
7:13–16 — 300
7:14 — 255
9:1–2 — 255
9:6 — 300
11:1–2 — 254
11:9 — 113, 269

Isaias
35:4–6 — 255
38 — 101
40:3 — 255
42:1, 6 — 257
42:2–3 — 255
49:6 — 257
50:6 — 256
52:15 — 258
53:4–10 — 258
53:7, 9, 17 — 256
53:10–12 — 259
54:2–3 — 268
54:13 — 269
54:17 — 270, 271
55:3–4 — 257
59:21 — 269
61:1 — 257
66:19–20 — 268
66:21 — 269

Jeremias
23:5–6 — 254
25:11 — 262
25:11–12 — 261
29:10 — 261, 262
30:18 — 262
31:31 — 264
31:31–33 — 257, 268
31:32–33 — 269
48:47 — 296, n. 21
49:39 — 296, n. 21

Daniel
2:44 — 270
4 — 89
5 — 88, 89
7:13–14 — 270, 293, n. 7
9:2 — 261
9:24–27 — 252, 262, 268

Daniel			**Matthew**		**Matthew**	
9:26	256, 263		2:4	131	17:12	300
11:22	262		3:16	274, n. 24	17:19	199, n. 23
			4:14–16	255	17:26	151
Joel			5–7	143, n. 1	19:3–31	125, n. 12
2:28	269		5:2	255	20:18–19	148
2:28–32	296, n. 20		5:17		21	125, n. 12
				125, n. 12, 281, 283	21:2ff	149
Jonas			5:25	144, n. 2	21:12, 19	144, n. 2
3:4	101		5:39	143, n. 2	21:33ff	132
			6:31	143, n. 2	22:43	300, n. 8
Micheas			7:22–23	289	23:8–9	144, n. 2
4:2	268		7:29	125, n. 12, 134	23:37, 39	113
4:1–2	268		8:34	302	24:2, 3, 5–33	287
5:2	255		9:6	83	24:4–14	300, n. 3
			10:6	288	24:14	289
Aggeus			10:17–21	292	24:15	263
2:7–10	252, 266		10:23	288, 292	24:24	99
			10:32	235, n. 11	24:30	144, n. 3
Zacharias			10:32–33	289	24:34	287, 290
9:9	256		10:40	133	24:36	292
9:9–10	259		11:3	131	25	289
11:12–13	256		11:4–6	132	25:1	302
12:3	270		11:5	255	26:13	289
12:10	256, 269		11:14	300	26:21, 25	149
13:1	269		11:27	133	26:27	256
13.2	268		11:29	141	26:34, 69–74	149
			11:30	142	26:63–64	132
Malachias			12:19–20	255	26:63–66	168, n. 8
1:10–11	268		12:22–37	168	26:64	288, 293
1:11	258, 269		12:34	144, n. 2	26:68	99
3:1	252, 255, 267		12:38–40	167–168	27:4, 19, 24	144, n. 6
4:5	300		12:41	132	27:5ff	162
			12:41–42	168	27:9, 30, 39–43	256
1 Machabees			13:13	168, n. 6	27:51	266, n. 46
1:12–14	263		13:16–17	132	27:57–60	256
1:30–41	263		13:36–50	289	27:62–64	167
1:57–62	263		13:57	132	27:63	169, n. 11
4:46	250, n. 9		13:58	161	27:64	174, n. 24
9:27	250, n. 9		14:14ff	155	28:2–4	187, n. 48
			15:28	161	28:6	172, n. 16
2 Machabees			16:5–6	172, n. 17	28:7	180
3:2	266		16:15–16	132	28:9	173, n. 18
4	263		16:21	166	28:9–10	180
5:16	266		16:24–27	289	28:11–15	172, 176
			16:25	235, n. 31	28:12	173, n. 18
Matthew			16:28	288, 293	28:15	174
1:2ff	256		17:5	162, 163	28:16	173, n. 18, 180
1:22	100		17:9	166	28:17	177, n. 36, 180

Matthew

28:18–20	134, 144, n. 3, 273
28:19–20	289
28:20	183

Mark

2:1ff	83
3:21	143, n. 2
4:26–28	290
6:5	161, 199, n. 23
6:8	302
8:32	167
8:33	146, n. 15
9:12	180
9:32–33	146, n. 15
10:32–34	148
11:2–3	149
11:13, 15	144, n. 2
12:1ff	132
13:2	150
13:5–13	300, n. 3
13:10	289
13:22	99
13:32	289
13:33–37	289
14:27–28	166–167
14:30	149
14:62	293
15:16	273
15:44–45	170
16:1–8	171
16:6	172, n. 16
16:7	180
16:8	186, n. 42
16:9	173, n. 18
16:9–16	186, n. 42
16:12–13, 14	173, n. 18
16:14	161
16:15–16	144, n. 3
16:16	134
16:18	180

Luke

2:8	162
2:14	267
2:25–26	131
2:49	146

Luke

2:51	145, n. 11
4:16–21	132
4:40	155
5:4	302
5:17ff	83
7:11ff	157
8:49ff	157
9:13	302
10:16, 22	133
10:41	146, n. 15
11:15–18	159
11:16	168, n. 5
13:23–26	289
14:26	143, n. 2
16:22	174, n. 27
17:6	199, n. 23
18:32–33	148
18:34	177, n. 36
19:41–44	266, n. 47
19:43–44	150, 152
19:45	144, n. 2
20:9ff	132
20:20–40	141
21:8–19	300, n. 3
21:24	149, 151, 290, 291
21:43	150
22:10–12, 13	149
22:69	293
23:27–30	146, n. 15
24:5–6	172, n. 16, 17
24:9	172, n. 17
24:11	177
24:13–33	173, n. 18
24:19–24	177, n. 33
24:25–27	132, 136, n. 8
24:29	149
24:34	173, n. 18
24:36–43	173, n. 18, 178, n. 38
24:36–44	177, n. 34
24:39–44	173, n. 19
24:47	289
24:50–51	173, n. 18

John

1:19–36, 41, 45	131

John

2:13–17	144, n. 2
2:14–22	167
2:20	277, n. 51
3:2	160
4:18	151
4:25	131
4:26	132
4:34	145, n. 9
4:46ff	157
4:47ff	161
5:19, 22ff	144, n. 3
5:36	151, 160
5:45–46	281
6	162
6:14	131
7:16, 28–29	133
7:31	131
7:37–39	267, n. 57
7:46	134
8:29, 46	141
8:42	133
8:50	145, n. 10
8:52ff	132
9:1ff	155
9:5ff	162
9:6, 35	161
10:17–18	168, n. 7
10:24	131
10:24–38	160
10:25–26	132
10:30	144, n. 3
11	155
11:11–15	151
11:25	162
11:41–43	160
11:49–52	96
11:51	88
12:13	302
12:44–50	133
13:19	152
13:20	133
14:6	144, n. 3
14:30	141
15:5	144, n. 3
16:30	152
18:37	133
19:7	168, n. 8
19:24, 28, 37	256

John

19:30, 33–34	169
19:36	100
19:39ff	169, n. 9
20	177, n. 35
20:2, 15	172, n. 15, 177
20:6–7	174, n. 23
20:11–17, 19–23	173, n. 18
20:21	133
20:24–29	173, nn. 18, 19
20:25–27	170, n. 12
21:1–23	173, n. 18

Acts

1:3	173
1:4–5, 8	149
1:7–8	289, 295
1:9ff	173, n. 18
1:22	166, n. 1
2	274, n. 24
2:1ff	149
2:16–21	296, n. 20
2:22–36	166, n. 1
2:24–31, 27	175
2:29	174, n. 27
2:31	174, n. 29, 257
241	176, n. 30, 203
2:42–47	221
3:6	198, n. 4
3:14	144, n. 7
3:15–16	166, n. 1
4:1–22	174, n. 25
4:4	203
4:10–33	166, n. 1
4:32–35	221
5:1–11	96
5:14	203
5:15	198, n. 4
5:38–39	214
6:7	176, n. 30
6:8	198, n. 5
8:4	203
8:6–13	198, n. 5
9:3	187, n. 47
9:40	198, n. 4
10:10ff	88

Acts

10:38	141
10:40–42	182
14:7	198, n. 4
15	284, n. 5
16:16	100
17:18, 31, 32	186, n. 43
19:12	198, n. 4
20:10	198, n. 4
21:19–20	203

Romans

1:8	215, n. 5
2:12–15	282
3:20	283, n. 2
6:4	174, n. 28
6:9	181
10:4	281
10:18	215, n. 5
11:25	293
13:1–7	296, n. 19
13:11	299
13:12	296

1 Corinthians

1:7	296, n. 17
1:23	186, n. 45, 207
1:26	205
6:14	298
7:7	118
7:20–22	217, n. 14
7:25–35	296, n. 18
7:29–31	299
9:1	187, n. 47
10:11	296, 299
11:4–5	99
12ff	192
15	175
15:3	173, 174, 179
15:3–4	175
15:3–7	179
15:3–8	171, 178
15:5	173, n. 18, 180
15:6–7	173, n. 18
15:8	187, n. 47
15:11, 12–16	179
15:14	166
15:35–44	179

1 Corinthians

15:44, 50	179, n. 39
15:51–52	296, n. 23
16:1	302

2 Corinthians

1:8–9	297, n. 25
3:17	179, n. 39
4:11–12, 16	297, n. 25
5:2, 8–9	297, n. 25
5:3	296, n. 23
5:21	144, n. 7
12:12	83

Galatians

3:23–24	281
3:23–28	283
3:24	284, n. 5

Ephesians

3:2	302
5:1–9	296, n. 19
6:2–3	284, n. 4
6:5	217, n. 14

Philippians

2:8	141
4:5	296
4:7	271

Colossians

1:6	215, n. 5
2:12	174, n. 28
2:16, 17	284, n. 5
3:4	296, n. 17
3:18–25	296, n. 19

1 Thessalonians

1:5	294, n. 11
2:1–9	297, n. 25
4:12–17	296, 297, n. 23
4:15–17	299
5:1–6	295

2 Thessalonians

1:7, 10	296, n. 17
2:1ff	295
2:5	294, n. 11

2 Thessalonians

2:8	296, n. 17
3:12	296, n. 18

1 Timothy

2:1	296, n. 18
6:12	217, n. 14
6:15	296, n. 17

2 Timothy

2:8	255

Titus

2:13	296, n. 17
3:10–12	198, n. 2

Hebrews

1:1	272
7:12, 18	284, n. 5
7:14	254
7:19	283, n. 2

Hebrews

8:13	284, n. 5
9:15	267
10:37	299
11:6, 13–16	283
12:26	277, n. 53

James

2:1–17	296, n. 19
4:13–16	296, n. 18
5:1–6	296, n. 19
5:8–9	299

1 Peter

1:18–19	144, n. 7
2:13–23	296, n. 19
2:22	144, n. 7
3:1–7	296, n. 19
4	296, n. 18
4:5–7	299
4:13ff	296, n. 17

2 Peter

1:13–15	296, n. 18
3:8–16	295

1 John

2:1	144, n. 7
2:18	299
2:18–19	296, n. 20
3:5	144, n. 7
3:11–24	296, n. 19

2 John

1:9–10	198, n. 2

Jude

1:6	302

Apocalypse

1:11	203
20	296, n. 17

Index of Authors

A Lapide, 302
Abelard, xxxiii, lvi, lvii
Achelis, 6
Adrian of Rotterdam, xxxix
Aegidius Romanus, xxxviii
Aeneas of Gaza, 193
Albert the Great, St., xxii, xxxv
Alcuin, xxxi
Alexander of Hales, xxxv, lvi
Alfano, 199
Allard, 135, 206, 215, 216, 227, 237, 238
Allo, 125
Alvarez, xl
Ambrose, St., xxix
Amitrano, 199
Ammianus Marcellinus, 150
Anderson, 42
Andreas, xxxvii
Anselm, St., xxiii, xxviii, xxxi ff, lvi
Antoine, xli
Apollinaris of Laodicea, 275
Aristides, 221
Aristotle, xxxiv
Arnobius of Sicca, 158, 206
Arts, xliv
Athanasius, St., xxix
Athenagoras, 222
Attwater, lii
Atzberger, xliii
Aubert, 55, 102
Augustine, St., xxii, xxiii, xxviii ff, lvi, 5, 56, 73, 87, 89, 120, 123, 162, 172, 192, 196, 197, 216, 219, 232, 238, 300 ff

Baader, xli
Bachelet, 101
Baierl, 12
Bainvel, lviii, 2
Baius, 102
Balfour, 21

Banez, xl
Bardenhewer, 163
Bartmann, xlv
Basil, St. xxix
Batiffol, 125, 135, 136, 163, 197, 215, 300
Bauer, B., 129
Bauer, G., xliii
Baur, 199
Baustert, 198
Bautain, 55, 98
Bavinck, 96
Bayer, 275, 276
Becanus, xl
Becker, liv
Bellamy, 123
Bellarmine, St. Robert, xxxix
Benedict XIV, 97, 99
Bensdorp, xliv
Benz, 284
Bernheim, 81
Berti, xli
Bertrin, 198
Beysens, lviii, 21, 55, 98
Biel, xxxvii
Billot, xlii, 124, 164, 291, 298, 300ff
Billuart, xli
Bittremieux, 47
Blondel, 101, 102
Boissarie, 198
Bonaventure, St., xxxv, xxxvi, lvi
Bonetty, 55
Borchert, 30
Bord, xliii
Borgongini-Duca, 276, n. 44
Bosco, xl
Bossuet, 274
Bougard, xliii, 144
Boulenger, xliv
Breal, 30
Bricout, 198
Briefs, 134

Brochmann, 218
Bros, 98
Brüll, xliv
Brunet, li, lvi
Bruneteau, 21, 97
Brunsmann, xliii
Buchberger, lviii
Burg, 274
Burke, lii
Burkitt, 135
Buzy, 164

Caerularius, 193
Caillard, 248
Caird, 6
Cajetan, xxxviii, 42
Calmet, 275
Camm, 237
Cano, xl
Capreolus, xxxviii
Carro de Vaux, 218
Casanova, xliii
Castelein, 198
Cathrein, 7, 124
Cavenne, 199
Cayre, ix, xxx,' lv, lvi
Cellini, 177, n. 31
Celsus, 181
Cerfaux, 248
Chable, 164
Charcot, 98
Chesterton, ix, 70–71, 84, 103
Child, ix, 20
Chryssipus, 99
Cicero, 5, 15, 91, 99, 100
Clamer, 123
Clement of Alexandria, xxix, 205
Clement of Rome, St., 203, 221
Colet, xxxviii
Comte, 30
Congar, l, li, liii, lv
Connell, ix, xxv
Conrad, 237
Contenson, xl
Conway, x, 19
Cooper, 31
Cornely, 302
Corrigan, 19
Cotter, xliii

Cottiaux, lvi
Cros, 198
Cumont, 210
Cyprian, St., 100, 230, 231, 235, 238
Cyril of Alexandria, St., 157
Cyril of Jerusalem, St., 197, n. 1

Dahlmann, 210, n. 16, 217
D'Ales, A., xliii, 102
Daniel-Rops, 134
Dausch, 163
D'Azambuja, 227
De Broglie, 2, 217, 248, 251, n. 12
De Brosses, 30
Dechamps, Card., xliii
Dechamps, Dr. A., 199
De Geoffre, xliii
De Ghellinck, xi, xxxi, xxxiv, lv, lvi, lvii
De Grandmaison, 98, 103, 125, 134
De Groot, xliii, lvii, 92, 101, 228
De Journel, Rouet, xi
De Lapparent, 19
De Lugo, xl
De Maistre, 219
Deneffe, 125
Denis, 101
Denis of Alexandria, St., 223
Denis the Areopagite, 206
Dennefeld, 274, 275
Dentler, 174, n. 25
Denziger, xli
Denziger-Bannwart-Umberg, xi
De Ripalda, xl
De Rohellec, 42
De Rubeis, xli
De Saint-Projet, xliii
De Smedt, 98
D'Herbigny, lii, 198
Dieckmann, 2, 170, n. 15
Diekamp, xxx, xlv, li, lv ff
Dieringer, 198, 199
Dionysius the Carthusian, xxxviii
Disteldorf, 170, n. 15
Dobschütz, 227
Dodwell, 236
Doller, 244, n. 5
Donlan, lii
Dorsch, xliii, 2

Dory, xlv
Douglas, 158
Drews, 135, 172
Duns Scotus, xxxvi, xxxvii, liii
Duperron, xxxix
Durkeim, 30
Durst, lviii
Dwight, 19
Dyson, 275

Eck, xxxix
Egger, xlii, 55
Einig, xlv
Ennius, 91
Erasmus, xxxviii, 227
Eschmann, li
Esser, G., xliv
Estius, xl
Eugene IV, xxxvi
Eusebius, 135, 156, 224, 230
Eyre, 31

Feeder, xliii
Felder, 136, 163, 144
Feldman, 273
Felten, 135
Fenton, lii
Ferchat, 227
Ferland, xlvi, li, liv, 42
Feuillet, 292
Fichte, 6
Fillion, 134, 163
Finegan, 217
Fonck, 159
Fonsegrive, 102
Fouard, 134
Fournier, 2, 35, 46
Francis of Vittoria, xl
Francis Sylvester of Ferrara, xxxviii
Franon, 21
Frassen, xli
Frazer, 27, 30
Frederick the Great, 218
Freud, 30
Friedrich, 136
Funk, 135
Furrer, 158, 159

Gagnebet, liii

Galen, 224
Galerius, 232
Galvani, 19
Gardeil, li, 101
Garrigou-Lagrange, lii, lvii, 2, 35, 42, 46, 47, 97, 99, 102, 103, 118, 164
Gaufridius, 194
Gelasius I, xxix
Gemelli, 198
Gener, xli, lv
Gibbon, 208
Gilson, lvii
Goethe, 124
Gondal, 2
Gonet, xl
Gossard, 46
Gotti, xli
Gottsberger, 275
Graber, 134
Grabmann, l, lv, lvii
Granderath, 55, 152
Gregory the Great, St., lv, 162, 196
Gregory of Nyssa, St., xxix
Gregory of Valencia, xl
Gretser, xxxix
Gspann, 124
Guardini, 134
Guibert, 97
Guitmond, xxxi
Gunter, 199
Gunther, xli
Gutberlet, xlii, xliii, 98, 101, 135

Haeckel, 30
Harduin, 275
Hardy, 217
Harmann, 284
Harnack, 74, 124, 125, 135, 136, 163, 171, 178, 181, 214, 215, 217, 237
Hase, 158, 167, n. 2, 168
Haskins, li, lvi
Heenan, 134
Hegel, 6, 124
Heigl, 125
Heiner, 24
Heinisch, 215
Heinrich, xlii, 145
Hennemann, 146
Hermes, xli, lviii

(311)

Herrmann, xlv, 2, 6
Herve, xlv
Hesychius, 275
Hettinger, F., xliii, 135, 144, 152
Hettinger-Müller, 227
Hilary, St., xxix, 213
Hincmar of Rheims, xxxi
Hoberg, 248, 274
Hoffmann, A., xlvi
Hoffman, M. H., 80
Holtzclau, xli
Holtzmann, 143, 159, 163, 170
Holzhey, 276
Holzmeister, 301, 302
Hontheim, xlv, 275
Horace, 53
Hove, 103
Howitt, ix
Huby, 164, 218
Hüffer, 198
Hugh of St. Victor, xxxiii
Hugon, xlv
Huguney, xlv
Hume, 76
Hurter, xlii, l, 135, 198, 238
Huxley, T., 7

Ignatius of Antioch, St., 197, 198, 203, 217
Irenaeus, St., 192, 198, 204, 235, 251, n. 12
Isenkrahe, 199
Isidore of Seville, St., lv

Jacobi, 6
Jacquier-Bourchany, 163, 170, n. 15
Janssens, xlv
Jerome, St., 231, 260, 276
John Chrysostom, St., 238, 302
John Damascene, St., xxviii, xxx, xxxi
John XXII, xxxv
John of St. Thomas, xl
John the Scot, xxxi, xxxii, lvi
Josephus, 127, 130, 135, 150, 152, 156, 250, n. 9
Jouffroy, 123
Journet, lii
Jovino, 168, n. 4
Juenin, xli'

Julian the Apostate, 255, 237
Julius Hilarionus, 275
Jung, 134
Justin, St., 156, 163, 198, 204, 217, 221
Justinian I, 193

Kamphausen, 275
Kant, 6, 7, 19, 95
Katschthaler, xlv
Kempf, 237
Kettenmeyer, 98
Keulers, 134, 244, n. 14
Kilber, xli
Kissane, vi, ix, 258
Klee, xli
Kleutgen, xli, lv
Klug, xlv
Knabenbauer, 153, 275, 300
Kneib, xliv, 143
Kneller, 19, 97, 135
Knox, 103
Koch, xliv
Koppers, x, 2, 30, 31
Kreling, lii
Kuhn, 30

Laberthonniere, 101'
Laboulaye, 124
Lactantius, 5, 205, 232, 233
Ladeuze, 170, n. 15, 186, n. 41–42
Laennec, 19
Lagrange, 19, 125, 250, n. 11, 274, 275, 300
Lammens, 218
Landgraf, li
Lanfranc, xxxi
Lang, 28
Langhorst, lviii
Laquer, 135
Lattey, 103
Lazzarato, 276
LeBachelet, lvii
LeBec, 170, n. 14, 199
LeBlant, 237
LeCamus, 177, n. 31
Lebreton, liv, 134
Leclercq, 237
LeHir, 248, 251, n. 13, 300

Leo the Great, St., xxix
Leo XIII, 14, 17, 53, 239
Lepin, 136
Lercher, xlii
Leroy, 31
LeRoy, 47, 170
L'esetre, 99
Lessius, xl
Lewis, 103
Liebermann, xli, 163, 218
Lightfoot, 168, n. 4
Linacre, 19
Linck, 135
Lingens, 124
Livinhac, 237
Lohman, A., 227
Lohmann, H., 170, n. 15
Loisy, 170, 171, 174
Lombard, Peter, xxx, xxxiv, xxxv, xxxvii, xl, lvi
Lottin, li
Lottini, xlii
Louwerens, 99
Lowie, 2, 31
Lubbock, 30
Lucian, 227
Luther, 30, 226

Maas, 217
Macauley, 218
Madgett, x, 2, 80
Maisonneuve, lviii
Maldonatus, 294
Manchen-Helfen, 31
Mandonnet, lvii
Mangenot, 186, n. 41
Mannens, xlii, 46
Manson, 103
Manzoni, xlii
Marcellinus, 193
Marchand, 198
Marcus Aurelius, 230
Marett, 30
Maritain, xix, 42
Martin, li, lvii
Marx, 21
Mattiussi, 97
Mausbach, xliv
Maximinus Daza, 205

Mayer, xlii
Mayron, xxxvii
Mazzella, xlii, 101
McLinnan, 30
Meffert, 134
Meignan, 275
Meinertz, 215
Melanchthon, 227
Mendel, 19
Menge, 124
Mersch, lii
Messenger, ix, 2, 4, 7, 27, 29, 31, 103
Meyenber, 134
Meyer, 170
Michel, 103
Michelitsch, xliv
Migne, xi
Minges, xlii
Minucius Felix, 100, 238
Miller, 134
Mohan, 7, 21
Molina, xl
Mommsen, 237
Morawski, xlv
More, St. Thomas, 238
Morin, xli
Moses Maimonides, 267
Muck, 214
Muller, 14, 19, 30
Muser, 170, n. 15
Muth, 123

Neguerulea, xliv
Neubauer, xli
Newman, 103
Newton, 95
Nicholas of Cusa, xxxviii
Nicholas of Lyra, xxxviii
Nicholau, lii, 2, 46, 102
Nietzsche, 21
Noggler, xlv
Nostitz-Rieneck, 85

Odenwald, 98
Oldra, 134
Olle-Laprune, 102
Oppenraay, xlv
Origen, xxix, 157, 186, n. 41, 46, 217, 223

Otten, xlv
Ottiger, xliv, liv, 2, 55, 101, 123, 159, 167, n. 3, 227, 238

Pacian, St., 197
Pallavicini, 237
Palmer, lii
Palmieri, xlii
Papias, 163
Paquet, xlv
Pare, li, lvi '
Parente, xlvi, lii, liii, 2
Paschasius Radbert, xxxi
Pasteur, 19
Paulinus, 192
Paulsen, 6, 18, 97, 217
Paulus, 129, 158, 168
Pegues, 47'
Penido, 42
Perier, 97 '
Perrone, xli
Pesch, xliii, li, 99, 101, 274
Peschel, 14
Petavius, xl
Peter of Alliaco, xxxvii
Peter of Aquila, xxxvii
Peter Canisius, St., xxxix
Peter of Ledesma, xl
Peter of Poitiers, xxxiv
Peter of Rotterdam, xxxix
Pfleiderer, 6, 140
Phelan, 42
Philip Sidetes, 163
Phillips, 98, 102, 103
Pierson, A., 145
Pierson, R., 213
Pighius of Campia, xxxix
Pinard de Boullaye, 31
Piolanti, xlvi
Pirngrüber, 125, n. 16
Pius V, St., 102
Pius IX, 24
Pius X, St., xxvii, l, lv, 102
Pius XII, ix, xxvii, 19
Platel, xli
Plato, 53
Pliny, 127, 131, 135, 204, 224
Plumpe, lii
Pohl, 2

Pohlet, xlv
Polycarp, 197, 198
Porphyrius, 216
Poulipiquet, 102, 103, 95, 96
Prat, 30, 134, 170, n. 14, 177, n. 31, 179, n. 39, 302
Preuschen, 163
Procopius of Caesarea, 193
Pusey, 19

Quadratus, 156
Quasten, lii, lv, 163

Rabeau, lii
Rademacher, xlvi
Ratram, xxxi
Raybould, x
Reginald of Piperno, xxxvi
Reim, 170
Reimarus, 129
Reinach, 7, 30
Reinhold, xliv, 101
Reinke, 248
Renan, 74, 97, 98, 125, 139, 144, 158, 169, n. 10, 173, n. 20, 177, n. 32
Renouvier, 97
Reville, 170, 174, n. 25
Ricciotti, 129, 134, 136, 170, n. 14, 177, n. 31, 266
Richard of St. Victor, 182
Ridderbos, 30
Ritschl, 6
Riviere, 215 '
Robert of Melun, xxxiii, lvi, lvii
Robert Pulleyn, xxxiii
Robertson Smith, 30
Rohr, 125
Roland, xxxiv
Rolfes, xlv
Rosch, 302'
Rose, 170, n. 15, 178, n. 37
Ross, x, 2, 30
Roure, 19
Rousseau, 21, 146
Roussel, 217
Royer, 199
Ruinart, 236

Sabatier, 19

Salaverri, lii, 2, 46, 102
Salotti, 237
Salvador, 168
Sanda, xlvi
Sanderens, xliii
Sanders, 134
Sawicki, xlv, 124
Saydon, 274, 275
Schanz, xliv, lviii, 6, 14, 101, 135, 227
Scheeben, ix, xliii, xlvi, li ff
Schiffini, 2
Schill, xliv
Schleiermacher, 6
Schmid, 152
Schmidt, 2, 27, 28, 30, 31, 107, 123
Schopenhauer, 6, 46
Schulte, 248
Schultes, lii
Schuster-Selbst, 274
Schwartz, 30
Schweitzer, 129, 170
Secchi, 19
Sepp, 277
Serol, 19
Serquieff (Jean de Cronstadt), 99
Sheppard, 7
Sheedy, lvi
Sichirollo, 102
Silva, 199
Silvius, xl
Simpson, ix, 20, 21
Sixtus V, lv
Sloet, xlv
Smising, xl
Smit, 159
Smith, lii
Smyth, 274
Socrates, 150
Sortais, 103
Soto, xl
Souben, 124
Sozomenus, 237
Specht, xliii
Spencer, 6, 30
Spillman, 237
Spinoza, 124
Spitta, 214
Staerck, 99
Stalin, 21

Stapleton, xxxix
Staudenmaier, xli
Steffes, lviii
Steinman, 227
Stensen, 19
Stokl, xliv, 124
Straubinger, xliv, li
Strauss, 7, 47, 97, 129
Stummer, xliv
Suarez, xl, 100
Suermondt, lvii
Suetonius, 127, 131, 135, 136
Sully-Prudhomme, 215
Sulpicius Severus, 230
Szydelski, xliv

Tacitus, 127, 130, 135, 150, 203, 216, 230
Tanquerey, xliii, li, liv, 118, 227
Tapper, xxxix
Taylor, 30
Tepe, xliii
Tertullian, 156, 163, 174, n. 23, 198, 204, 216ff, 223, 233
Tessen-Weisierski, 103
Thackeray, 135, 152
Thils, xix
Thomas Aquinas, St., v, xi, xix, xx, xxiv, xxvi, xxx, xxxiv ff, xl, li, liii, lv, lvi, 6, 7, 13, 14, 16, 20, 35, 41, 45, 47, 56, 64ff, 73, 96, 97, 98, 99, 100, 101, 102, 113, 118, 247, 282ff, 301, 302
Thomas of Charmes, xli
Thomassin, xli
Thompson, 134
Thone, 47
Thurston, 98
Tillmann, 300, 302
Tobac, 179, n. 39
Toledo, xl
Tolstoi, 6
Tonquedec, 97, 98, 102, 103
Tosi, 24
Tournely, xli
Touzard, 99, 248
Tremblay, li, lvi
Tricot, 135
Tromp, S., xliii, 135

Tursellini, 194
Tux, xliv, 163
Twistleton, 198

Vacant-Mangenot, xlvi
Valla, xxxviii
Vandervelt, 98
Van Hoonacker, 276
Van Hoestenberghe, 199
Van Kasteren, 170, n. 14, 284
Van Laak, xxiv, lii ff, 2, 46, 47
Van Leeuwen, lviii
Van Meerveldhoven, 227
Van Noort, v, vi, liv, 101, 125
Van Oppenraay, 227
Van Walenburg, xxxix
Varro, 53
Vasquez, xl, 284
Verhaar, vi
Victor Vitensis, 193, 237
Vesalius, 19
Vigil, 24
Vollert, ix, xlvi, lii, liii
Volz, 244, n. 4
Von Hammerstein, 237
Von Hartmann, 6, 124, 217
Von Hellwald, 227
Von Walter, 217
Vosen, xliv

Walter, 237
Watterott, 163

Weber, xliv
Wegscheider, 97, 100
Weiss, B., 158
Weisz, A., xliv
Weisz, J., 143
Wellhausen, 136
Wendt, 167, n. 2
Werner, li
Whitehead, x, 7, 95
William of Auxerre, xxxiv
William of Ockham, xxxvii
Wilmers, W., xliv, xlv, 135, 164, 167,
    n. 2, 198, 218, 284
Windle, 2, 19
Wisz, 227
Witasse, xli
Wohleb, 135
Wolf, 275
Wolff, 248
Wrede, 136
Wundt, 6, 18
Wylie, 144

Yelle, 2, 35, 46

Zaccaria, 236
Zaccherini, xliii, 2
Zacchi, 103
Zapelena, xliii
Zapletal, 274
Zigliari, xliv
Zizzamia, 134

General Index

A

Abelard, his spur to scholastic theology, xxxiii; use of term "theology," lvi, n. 36; alleged rationalism, lvii, n. 38

Aggeus, prophecy of Christ's coming, 266

Agnosticism, notion of, 11, n.

Allard, Paul, on Christianity's penetration of all classes of society, 215, n. 7; Christians accused of hatred of human race, 216, n. 9; Roman view of religious worship and welfare of state, 216, n. 10; on Jewish abetting of persecutions, 216, n. 11

Analogical knowledge, imperfection of, 142; brief bibliography on, 142, n.

Anarchists, different behavior from martyrs in face of death, 234

Animism, 27; 30, n. 6

Anselm, St., father of scholastic theology, xxxii

Apologetics of Immanence, notion, 91; critique of, 93ff

Apostles, their incredulity regarding Resurrection, 177; their attitude towards Parousia, 295ff

Apparitions of risen Christ, 172–3; discrepancies in Gospel accounts, 185, n. 31

Aristides, on moral life of Christians, 222

Arnobius, on Christ's miracles, 158; on the conversion of the better educated to Christianity, 205

Athenagoras, on moral life of Christians, 222–3

Augustine, St., on usefulness of miracles, 73; on symbolic meaning of Christ's miracles, 162; on the title "Catholic" Church, 197, n. 1; on the preservation of Judaism, 219, n. 23; on anguish caused martyrs by relatives, 232

B

Balfour, compares irreligious men to parasites, 21, n. 14

Batiffol, on the reason for obscurity in eschatological passages, 300, n. 5

Bautain, proposition subscribed to by, 98, n. 25

Bayer, on the prophecy of the Seventy Weeks, 276, n. 38

Benedict XIV, on miracles in false religions, 99, n. 38

Beauty of Catholic doctrine, 114ff

Bernard, St., his miracles, 193

Bernheim, on limits of psychotherapy in curing disease, 81; see Faith-healing

Biblical Commission, on Isaias and his prophecies, 250, n. 8; on the Parousia, 300, n. 13; 301, n. 24

Bibliographies, special, on theology, l-lii; on lives of Christ, 134; on apologetics and comparative religion, 2; on miracles, 102–3; on Messianic prophecy, 248; on Parousia, 299

Billot, explanation of Eschatological Discourse, 291

Blondel, see Apologetics of Immanence

Bodily actions, their place in religious worship, 16

Body of Christ, not stolen from tomb, 173

Bossuet, on Juda's ruling power after the Babylonian captivity, 274, n. 20

Bougaud, on Christ's holiness, 144, n. 8

Brockmann, on the reasons for the spread of Protestantism, 218, n. 20

Buddhism, popular B. not atheistic, 14, n.; natural explanation for its expansion, 209, 214; unhealthy effects on adherents, 217, n. 16

C

"Catholic," why heretics could never steal the name; St. Pacian on meaning of, 197, n. 1

Catholic doctrine, not unworthy of God, 112; sublimity of, 112ff; superhuman character of, 118; not result of evolution from Judaism, 120; not a product of Syncretism, 121

Catholicism, its miraculous expansion, 203; penetration of all classes of society, 205; its miraculous preservation, 211; its wonderful fruitfulness in field of holiness, 221; outstanding for its martyrs, 230ff; foretold by the prophets, 268ff. See also under Church

Celsus, on Christ's miracles, 157; on the limited appearances of the risen Christ, 181

Ceremonies, usefulness for religion, 16

Charcot, on faith-healing, 98, n. 32; see faith-healing

Chesterton, on rationalist dogma against miracles, 70–71; on fake miracles, 84

Child, Gordon, equates religion and magic, 20, n. 7

Christ, an historical person, 129; His own testimony about Himself, 131–4; not a lunatic or ecstatic, 138; not a charlatan, 139; His perfect holiness, 141ff; His prophecies, 148ff; His revealing of things hidden, 151; historical truth of His miracles, 155ff; their philosophical truth, 157ff; their relevant truth, 159; their symbolic meaning, 162; His predictions of the Resurrection, 166; He really died, 168; He really came back to life, 170ff; He and His work foretold by the prophets, 253ff; He had no mistaken notion

of the end of the world, 287

Christian Era, beginning of, 276, n. 44

Church, the Catholic, name, 191; its continuation of Christ's mission, 182; constant rejection of heretics, 191; approved by physical miracles, 191; its spread in apostolic times, 203; in post-apostolic times, 203; its marvelous stability, 211ff; see also under Catholicism

Cicero, on pagan oracles, 99–100, n. 44

Clement of Alexandria, St., on the spread of Christianity, 205

Clement of Rome, St., on St. Paul as a teacher of the whole world, 215, n. 5; on the high moral tone of Christian lives, 221–2

Comparative religion, confusion caused by mixing scientific and philosophic problems, 3–4

"Credo ut intelligam," meaning of axiom, liv, n. 10

Criteria of revelation, notion, 59; division of, 59; schema of, 61; compared for relative value, 63; Vatican Council and, 64

Cronstadt, John of, miraculous healings, 99, n. 38

Cyprian, St., enemies of Christ do not attack heretics, 235

Cyril of Jerusalem, St., on title "Catholic" Church, 197, n. 1

D

Daniel, prophecy of the Seventy Weeks, 261

Death of Christ, a proven fact, 168; foretold by the prophets, 256

De Broglie, on nature of prophecy, 250, n. 12

De Maistre, on continued preservation of schismatic eastern churches, 219, n. 22

Denis of Alexandria, St., on moral life of the Christians, 223

Dentler, on theft of Christ's body, 185, n. 25

Dodwell, on small number of the martyrs, 236, n. 5

Dogmatic theology, *see* Theology

E

Economy, patristic division of theology, liii, n. 4

End of the world, *see* Parousia

Eusebius, on moral life of Christians, 224

Evangelists, their account of the apparitions of the risen Christ, 185, n. 31

Evolution, as basis for morality, 21, n. 13

Evolution of Christianity, from Judaism, 120–21

Evolutionary theory of religion, 25ff

Existence of Christ, denied by Bruno Bauer, 129, n.

F

Faith, differs from theology, xxii; bound up with theology, xxii; sometimes required of sick before cure by Christ, 161

Faith-healing, 80–81; *see* Hypnotism, Psychotherapy

Fanatics, martyrs not to be considered such, 234

Felicity, St., on Christ suffering in His martyrs, 238, n. 26

Fetishism, notion, 26; not a religion, 27, n.

Feuillet, on Eschatological Discourse, 292, n.

Fideists, exaggerate need of revelation, 55, n. 1

Fig tree, cursing of, 144 and 144, n. 2

Fonsegrive, preference for internal criteria, 102, n. 54

Francis Xavier, St., his miracles, 194

Frazer, Sir J., *see* Fetishism

Frederick the Great, on reasons for the spread of Protestantism, 218, n. 20

Fundamental theology, *see* Theology

Furrer, natural explanation of Christ's miracles, 158, n.

G

Galen, on moral life of the Christians, 224

Gaufridius, on St. Bernard's miracles, 194

Gervase and Protase, their miraculous relics, 192

Gilson, defense of Abelard on the score of rationalism, lvii, n. 38

"God speaks," not to be taken anthropomorphically, 35, n.

Goethe, sublimity of gospel morality, 124, n. 6

Gregory the Great, St., on the symbolic meaning of Christ's miracles, 162; on why there were more miracles in early days of Church, 196

Gutberlet, description of analogical knowledge, 42, n.

H

Happiness, characteristic of Catholicism, 116

Harnack, miracles always doubtful, 74; admits Christ claimed to be Messias, 136, n. 8; on Christ's resurrection, 171; on the spread of Christianity, 215, n. 6; on the spread of Mithraism, 217, n. 17

Hatred for Christ, as an argument for Catholicism, 238, n. 32

Heinrich, on Christ's holiness, 145, n. 12 and 13

Heretic, material, dying for religion of Christ, 238, n. 30

History of theology, patristic era, xxviii-xxx; pre-scholastic era, xxxi; scholastic era, xxxii ff; modern era, xxxix ff; brief list of post-Vatican theological authors, xlii ff

Holiness, of Catholic doctrine, 113–4; no double standard of in Catholicism, 118, n.; abundant harvest of in Catholic religion, 221; no natural explanation for this harvest, 226; holiness among heretics and schismatics, 226

Holiness of Christ, 140ff; objections to, 142–3 and 144, n. 2

(319)

Holtzmann, miracles part and parcel of Gospel story, 163, n. 6; natural explanation for miracles, 159, n.; on the theft of Christ's body, 170

Humani Generis, on value of scholastic theology, xxvii

Hume, argument against miracles, 76

Huxley, T., definition of religion, 7

Hypnotism, 80–81

I

Ignatius Martyr, St., his use of title "Catholic" Church, 197, n. 1; on spread of Church, 203

Immanence, *see* Apologetics of

Immanentism, notion, 11, n.

Impossibility, physical and moral, 49–50; of proving miracles, 74–76

Indifference in religious matters, absolute, 13ff; relative, 23ff

Irenaeus, St., on Apostles' detestation of heresy, 198, n. 2; on the spread of Christianity, 204; on miracles in the Church, 192; on martyrs as the exclusive possession of the Church, 235; on obscureness of prophecy, 251, n. 12

J

Jacob, prophecy of Juda's rule, 254; 260

Josephus, testimony about Christ, 130; dispute over its authenticity, 135, n. 3; on fall of Jerusalem, 150; on Messianic hope as factor in Jewish revolt against Rome, 249, n. 3

Jouffroy, sublimity of Catholic doctrine even in catechism, 123, n. 5

Julian the Apostate, on Christ's miracles, 157; on Christian practice of virtue, 225; on eagerness of Christians for martyrdom, 237, n. 24

Justin, St., on Christ's miracles, 156; on spread of Christianity, 204; on moral lives of Christians, 222

K

Kant, his definition of religion, 7, n. 2;

on uselessness of religion in strict sense, 19, n. 3

Kingdom of the Messias, as foretold by the prophets, 268ff

Knowledge, analogical, 42, n.; prophetic, 87–9

Koppers, W., nobility of religion of primitives, 29–30

L

Laberthonniere, *seè* Apologetics of Immanence

Laboulaye, sublimity of Christ's doctrine, 124, n. 9

Lactantius, on spread of Christianity, 205; on long drawn-out martyrdom, 231; on martyrs' superhuman endurance, 233

Lagrange, M-J., on novelty of Christ's doctrine, 125, n. 14; on Messianic prophecies, 250, n. 11; on Matt. 26:64, 300, n. 8

Le Hir, on obscureness of prophecy, 251, n. 13

Leo XIII, on obligation to practice religion, 14; on obligation of public worship, 17; on the true religion and its proofs, 239, n. 33

Le Roy, E., objection to mysteries, 41, n. 12 and 47, n. 12; on theft of Christ's body, 170

Lightfoot, on the phrase: "three days and three nights," 183, n. 4

Loisy, on the Resurrection, 171

Lourdes, its miracles, 194

Luther, on the unhappy results of the Reformation, 226

M

Macauley, on the astounding permanence of the Catholic religion, 218, n. 21

Maimonides, Jews forbidden to calculate date of Messias' coming, 267

Malachias, prophecy of Christ's coming, 267

Martyr, definition, 230; great number of martyrs, 230; their frightful tortures, 231; admirable way they bore them, 232; endurance not capable of natural explanation, 232; objections to this argument, 233; they were not fanatics, 234

Maximinus Daza, on spread of Christianity, 205

Mediate revelation, possibility of, 43–45; suitability, 45–46

Messianic prophecies, see Prophecies, Messianic

Messias, Jewish expectation of, 131–2; the sort expected by Christ's contemporaries, 244; Messianic hope based on Old Testament, 244; known also to non-Jews, 243

Messias' functions, in prophetic books, 257; in opinion of Christ's contemporaries, 243

Meyer, on apparitions of risen Christ, 170

Minucius Felix, on argument drawn from steadfastness of martyrs, 238, n. 27

Miracles, notion, 64; definition, 65; and instrumental causality, 65–66; division of, 66; relative miracles, 67; absolute miracles, 67; purpose of, 68; possibility of, 69ff; fittingness of, 73; recognizability of, 74ff; probative force of, 83–84; moral miracles, 85–86; objections against, 71–73; 74; 76; 78–80; 84; marks of approval of true religion, 191; why relatively rare now, 196

Miracles of Christ, historical truth of, 155; inseparable from whole Gospel story, 155; philosophical truth of, 157; relevant truth of, 159; objections, 161; symbolic meaning, 162

Miracles of God the Father, in favor of Christ, 162

Mithraism, its spread naturally explicable, 210

Modernists, notion of religion, 11–12; all religions of equal value, 23; on prophecy, 244; on the Parousia, 287

Mohammedanism, spread by natural means, 210; 214

Morality, its foundation is religion, 17; Rousseau on morality without God, 21, n. 13; evolution as a basis for, state as norm of, 21, n. 13

Moral Theology, notion of, xxiii; place in theology, xxiv; dependence on dogmatic theology, xxiv

Mosaic Law, divine, 281; a preparation for Christ, 281; given to Jews only, 282; made up of moral, ceremonial, and judicial precepts, 282; backed up by temporal sanctions, 282; abrogated not by revocation, but by fulfillment, 283

Motives of credibility, notion, 59; see Criteria of revelation

Muller, Max, no people found without religion, 14, n.

Mysteries, notion, 36; first and second class, 37; possibility of, 39; objections to, 40–42; usefulness of, 43

Mysteries, pagan, not basis for doctrine of Resurrection, 181

N

Natural laws, in what sense immutable, 71–72

Natural religion, notion of, 9; and need for revelation, 49ff; difficulty of knowing natural religion, 51, n.; philosophers inadequate teachers of, 53

Naturalists, notion, 34, n.; on revelation, 34

Nietzsche, "Superman morality," 21, n. 13

Nostitz-Rieneck, description of moral miracles, 85, n.

O

Object of theology, see Theology

Objections to: revelation, 39; mysteries, 40–42; miracles, 71–73; 74; 76; 78–80; 84; prophecies, 89

Obligation, to practice religion, 13; of external religion, 15–16; of public worship, 17

Oracles, pagan, 87; Cicero's opinion of, 99, n. 44

Origen, on moral life of Christians, 223

Origin of Christianity, not explainable by evolution from Judaism, 120–1; nor by syncretism, 121–3

P

Parousia, Christ's attitude, 288ff; solution of difficulties, 290ff; Feuillet on Eschatological Discourse, 292, n.; Apostles' attitude, 295ff

Passion of Christ, in prophetic books, 256

Patristic Era, see Theology

Paulsen, on origin of religion, 18, n. 2; on miracles, 97, n. 22; on spread of Christianity, 217, n. 12

Paulus, G., natural explanation of Christ's miracles, 158, n.

Peschel, no people found without religion, 14, n.

Pfleiderer, on Christ's messianic consciousness, 139–40, n.

Philosophers, failure to reach correct knowledge of natural religion, 53

Pierson, A., on Christ's holiness, 145; on perils besetting Church, 213

Pilate, surprise at Christ's death, 184, n. 13; his "Acts," 156

Pius XII, on value of scholastic theology, xxvii; on value of science to religion, 19–20, n. 7

Pliny the Younger, on spread of Christianity, 204; on moral life of Christians, 224

Porphyrius, on the gods' withdrawing their favors because of worship of Christ, 216, n. 10

Positive theology, relationship to speculative, xxv

Poverty, the kind praised by Church, 117

Pre-scholastic Era, see Theology

Primitive religion – divinely revealed, 281; preparation for and beginning of Christian religion, 281

Progress, and Catholicism, 116

Progressive religious evolution, rejection of theory of, 25–30

Prophecies of Christ, about Himself, 148; about His disciples, 148; about fall of Jerusalem, 149; their philosophical truth, 151; relevance to His mission, 151

Prophecies, messianic, philosophical truth of, 244–6; how to understand them rightly, 246; summary exposition of, 253ff; the Protoevangelium, 253; predictions of the Messias' genealogy, 253; of His life, 255; of His functions, 257; of the time of His coming, 260; of His kingdom, 268; of His majesty and lowliness, apparently irreconcilable, 258

Prophecy, notion, 86; definition, 87; theological exposition of, 87–89; corporeal, imaginary, intellectual, 87–89; recognizability of, 89; possibility of, 89

Prophets, different from pagan seers, 245

Protestantism, spread due to natural causes, 211

Protestants, orthodox, on criteria of revelation, 96, n. 7

Protoevangelium, 253

Psychotherapy, see Faith-healing and Hypnotism

Q

Quadratus, on Christ's miracles, 156

R

Rationalists, notion, 34, n.; on revelation, 34; on Gen. 49:10, 274, n. 16; on the Parousia, 287; on mysteries, 112

Reim, on apparitions of risen Christ, 170

Religion, notion of, 1; definition of, 5; variety of, 2; queer definitions of, 6, n. 2; subjective and objective, 5–6; natural and supernatural, 9; objective foundation for, 11; origin of according to Modernists, 11; obligation to practice, 13; foundation of morality, 17; true and false, 23; unity of the true religion, 23ff; religion and science, 19–20, n. 7

Renan, on Christ's miracles, 74; 98, n. 32; 158, n.; Christ no mere perfecter of Judaism, 125, n. 14; on Christ's messianic complex, 139, n.; on the expulsion of devils, 158, n.; on the certainty of Christ's death, 184, n. 10; on the Resurrection, 185, n. 20; 186, n. 32

Renouvier, C., on possibility of miracles, 97, n. 20

Resurrection, best proof of Christ's claims, 166; foretold, 166, as sign of His divine mission, 167; proof of, 172; attested not by just His friends, 181; not borrowed from pagan mystery religions, 181

Revelation, notion, 34; divisions of, 35–36; schema of criteria of, 61; possibility of, 34ff; necessity of, 49ff; recognizability of, 59ff; primitive, Mosaic, and Christian, 107–8; 279ff

Reville, on Jews' theft of Christ's body, 170

Richard of St. Victor, on adequacy of criteria of revelation, 182

Ridderbos, on primitive monotheism, 30

Rousseau, morality without God ridiculous, 21, n. 13; complaint against mediate revelation, 47, n. 16; on holiness of Christ, 146, n. 13

S

Sabatier, A., on religiousness of non-churchgoers, 19, n. 7

Schamanism, see Evolutionary theory of religion

Schmidt, W., defense of primitive monotheism, 28–9; on opposition between religion and animism or totemism, 27, n.

Scholastic theology, see Theology

Schopenhauer, on revelation, 46, n. 1

Schweitzer, on apparitions of risen Christ, 170

Science, no obstacle to religion, 19, n. 7; famous Catholic men of, 19, n. 7; Pius XII's tribute to, 19–20, n. 7;

changeability of according to Whitehead, 95, n. 3

Simpson, G. G., evolution as basis for morality, 21, n. 13

Soldier, quite different from martyr in facing death, 234

Spread of Christianity, in apostolic times, 203; up to IV century, 203; throughout all classes of society, 205; obstacles in its path, 206; natural means inadequate, 207; a moral miracle, 208; objections to this argument, 208

Stability of Catholic religion, 211; obstacles thereto, 211; no sufficient natural reason for, 213; objections, 214

Sublimity of Catholic doctrine, 111ff

Suetonius, on Christ and Christians, 135, n. 5; on pagan expectation of Jewish Messias, 249, n. 3

Sully-Prudhomme, on the offensiveness of Catholicism, 215, n. 8

Sybilline Books, 100, n. 44; see Oracles, pagan

Symbolism of Christ's miracles, 162

Syncretism, cannot explain origin of Christianity, 120–3

T

Tacitus, on Christ, 130; on the ruin of Jerusalem, 150; on pagan expectations of Jewish Messias, 249, n. 3

Talmud, on Christ's miracles, 156; on not reckoning the date of the Messianic era, 267

Tertullian, on Christ's miracles, 156; his mockery of alleged theft of Christ's body, 185, n. 23; on the spread of Christianity, 204; on calumnies against Christians, 216, n. 10; on heretics not converting pagans but perverting Catholics, 218, n. 19; on blood of martyrs as seed of Christians, 233

Theology, notion and definition, xxvii-xxviii; material and formal object of, xix-xx; difference between dogmatic and fundamental, xx-xxii; difference between theology and faith, xxii; divisions of theology, xxiii ff; schematic presentation of entire field of theology, xxiv-xxv; positive and speculative, xxv-xxvii; brief history of, xxviii ff; modern authors of, xli ff

Thils, G., new definition of secondary object of theology, xix **

Thomas, St., on theological method, xxvi; on nature of miracles, 64; on division of miracles, 66; on fittingness of miracles, 73; on prophecy, 88-9

Toledoth Jesu, on Christ's miracles, 156

Tomb, the empty, 173

Totemism, notion of, 27; not a religion, 27, n.

Traditionalists, *see* Fideists

Tursellini, Orazio, on miracles of St. Francis Xavier, 194

Typassa (Tefessed), scene of famous miracle, 192

U

Uganda, its 32 young martyrs, 231

Unity, of true religion, 23ff. *See* indifference in religious matters

Universality of religion, 14-15

V

Vatican Council, on revelation: possibility of, 38-39; necessity of, 49, 51-2; criteria of, 64; on miracles as proof of revelation, 69

Victor of Vita, on the miracle of Tefessed (Typassa), 193

Von Hartmann, Christian morality selfish, 124, n. 7; on unhappy effects of Buddhism, 217, n. 16

Von Hellwald, on Christianity's wholesome influence on ancient world, 227, n. 7

W

Weeks, Seventy, Daniel's prophecy of, 261

Weiss, B., natural explanation of Christ's miracles, 158, n.

Whitehead, definition of religion, 7, n. 2; on changeability of science, 95, n. 3

Worship, notion, 1; definition, 1; internal and external, 5; public, 7

Wundt, on nature of religion, 18-19, n. 2